SHAKESPEARE'S HOLINSHED

SHAKESPEARE'S

HOLINSHED

An Edition of
HOLINSHED'S CHRONICLES
(1587)
Source of Shakespeare's
History Plays, *King Lear*,
Cymbeline, and *Macbeth*

Selected, Edited, and Annotated by
RICHARD HOSLEY

1968

G. P. PUTNAM'S SONS
NEW YORK

The illustration on the title page is reproduced by permission of The Huntington Library, San Marino, California.

Library of Congress Catalog

Card Number: 66-20280

PRINTED IN THE UNITED STATES OF AMERICA

For Diana

Dramatic poetry is like history made visible, and is an image of past actions as if they were present.

—SIR FRANCIS BACON

Preface

Two sets of references are incorporated in the text of this edition, both enclosed in square brackets and printed in boldface type. The one set of references is to Holinshed, specifically to the pages of the 1587 edition of the *Chronicles* (for example, [**222**]). This kind of reference occurs only at the head of a paragraph, in each case at the head of that new paragraph which is the first to be quoted from the page in question of the 1587 edition. The other set of references is to Shakespeare, specifically to the act-, scene-, and line-numbers of the edition of 1936 by G. L. Kittredge (for example, [**2.2.222**]), these being generally the same as the numbers of the Globe edition. This kind of reference never occurs at the head of a paragraph. Hence, since act- and scene-numbers are not repeated in a reference to the same scene as that of the immediately preceding reference, a single-number reference occurring within or at the end of a paragraph will be not to a page in Holinshed but to a line of Shakespeare in the last-cited act and scene.

The title-page illustration, showing Macbeth, Banquo, and the Weird Sisters, is reproduced from a woodcut in the 1577 edition of the *Chronicles,* Vol. 1, *History of Scotland,* p. 243.

It is a pleasure to record my indebtedness to the Humanities Council of Princeton University for the grant of a fellowship making possible the work on which this book is based. I am indebted also to the University of Arizona for bearing the cost of various expenses connected with the work. I am grateful for numerous courtesies to the staffs of the University of Arizona Library and the Princeton University Library, and to the authorities of the Henry E. Huntington Library for permission to reproduce a woodcut from the Huntington copy of the 1577 edition of Holinshed's *Chronicles.* For helpful advice of various kinds I must thank Professor Gerald Eades Bentley of Princeton University and Professor Irving Ribner of the University of Delaware. Mrs. Cathryn Nelson gave valuable assistance with the proofs and the bibliography. The map of England and Western France was drawn by my friend Robert Swaim, A.I.A.

R.H.

Tucson, Arizona
January, 1968

Contents

Introduction

Holinshed tells a good story. His qualities in this respect are naturally overshadowed by Shakespeare's achievement, but they need not therefore be lost sight of. That they occasionally have been lost sight of may be due in part to the somewhat forbidding aspect of the *Chronicles* in the original editions of 1577 and 1587—forbidding, that is, to the reader not accustomed to handling a fourteen-pound folio, to reading a black-letter text tightly packed into long, dense double columns, and to coping with the frequently curious spelling and punctuation of the period. In modern editions of Holinshed—such as W. G. Boswell-Stone's of 1896, the Everyman's Library edition of 1927, or Geoffrey Bullough's selections in his *Narrative and Dramatic Sources of Shakespeare* (1960–2)—the ponderosity, gothic print, and double columns are eliminated, but the distracting costume of archaic spelling and punctuation remains. Another difficulty in the way of the general reader's seeing Holinshed plain is that editors of Holinshed have tended (perhaps understandably) to serve Shakespeare at the expense of Holinshed. Boswell-Stone set the pattern in arranging his selections in the chronological order of Shakespeare's plays, and Allardyce and Josephine Nicoll followed suit in the Everyman edition. There is one considerable advantage to this method. Knowing the order of events in Shakespeare, one can quickly locate a given passage or a given scene and compare it with Holinshed's version. Thus, one can see at a glance what Shakespeare did with a specific part of his source material, as when (in the speech on the Salic Law by the Archbishop of Canterbury in *Henry V*) he versifies large swatches of Holinshed's prose or as when (in the deposition scene of *Richard II*) he alters, develops, and amplifies an episode already treated in considerable detail by Holinshed.

This method of presenting Holinshed, however, has two disadvantages. One results in a disservice to Holinshed. Since Shakespeare, in blithe disregard of historical "fact," relocates and telescopes the events of his sources, one cannot, if Holinshed is arranged in Shakespeare's chronological order, read through the historian's account of a given sequence of events in the order in which those events were designed to be comprehended and within the historical contexts appropriate to them. (Compare the exiled Queen Margaret's arrival in France in 1462, Warwick the Kingmaker's embassy to the French court to negotiate a marriage for Edward IV in 1464, and the reconciliation between Queen Margaret and the disaffected Warwick in 1470; these temporally discrete events, each with its own historical context, are fused by Shakespeare into the single scene 3.3 of *3 Henry VI.*) In short, one cannot "read" Holinshed. The other disadvantage results in a disservice to Shakespeare. Again because of the dramatist's characteristic rearrangement of the events of his sources, one cannot, if Holinshed is arranged in Shakespeare's chronological order, see what, in general, Shakespeare made of Holinshed in devising the structure of a given play. (Any of the plays will serve as a case in point.) One sees the trees clearly enough (particular speeches or particular scenes in relation to their sources in Holinshed), but one cannot see the forest (the whole play in relation to its source in Holinshed).

In the present edition, therefore, not only have I modernized spelling and punctuation, but I have also (following the example of Geoffrey Bullough) attempted to serve both Holinshed and Shakespeare by presenting my selections in Holinshed's chronological order. Thus Holinshed can be appreciated for his own sake, as an historian, and not simply as a quarry from which Shakespeare drew various useful materials. Happily, the straightforward presentation of Holinshed also serves Shakespeare by making possible an understanding of the playwright's larger design in rearranging the elements of his source. The method of presentation forcibly reminds us that the dramatic and narrative modes of storytelling make different demands on the raw materials of story, that a play is an artifact which, in order to achieve its optimum effect as drama, insists on a particular ordering of events. Moreover, the reader who is interested in a particular speech or scene in Shakespeare can, by leafing through the appropriate pages of this book, easily locate the corresponding passage in Holinshed by means of the Shakespeare references with which the text is peppered.[1]

Holinshed is an agreeable stylist. To be sure, his predilection for long,

[1]Two further points may be made about the selections of the present edition. Pertinent passages of general interest not used by Shakespeare are occasionally given, as for example Holinshed's account of the murder of Thomas of Woodstock. And passages used by Shakespeare which are of a more limited interest and not connected with Holinshed's narrative (that is, the narrative reprinted in the present edition) are occasionally omitted, as for example Holinshed's account of the laws and golden crown of Cymbeline's ancestor King Mulmutius (*cf. Cymbeline,* 3.1.55–62).

balanced sentences is perhaps not fully congenial to modern taste, and he sometimes reveals a distressingly unbelted attitude in matters grammatical: he is (like Shakespeare) not embarrassed by what we would call a dangling modifier, he frequently omits the subject of a main clause when it has been expressed in a preceding subordinate clause, and he likes to repeat his subject after an interrupting subordinate clause of any length. Moreover, Holinshed has his clichés, a mildly annoying example being the oft-repeated and seemingly inevitable statement that so-and-so has been "advertised" of such-and-such an event. But, having grown accustomed to these aspects of Holinshed's style, one can perceive others which give a pleasant and satisfying quality to his writing. His metaphors are simple, yet effective. Fire is a strong favorite, becoming through iteration a symbol of civil war: "Somewhat before this season fell a great division in the realm of England which of a sparkle was like to grow to a great flame." Richard Duke of York, in preparing to claim the crown, fastens his "chain" between those "two strong pillars," the Earls of Warwick and Salisbury. And later, at Wakefield, York is "environed on every side like fish in a net" by Queen Margaret's forces. Holinshed cannot resist a jingle: Glendower's "divination" is played off against "deviation," and at Conway the Archbishop of Canterbury (a Bolingbroke supporter pointedly omitted by Shakespeare) comforts Richard II "not as a prelate but as a Pilate." (Shakespeare used the allusion—but not the jingle—in a slightly different context.) Holinshed alliterates frequently, in a manner characteristically Elizabethan: "the painful penance of their pleasant pastime" sounds like the title of a miscellany. The phrase is also, as often, invested with irony, since Holinshed is discussing the execution of conspirators of whom he disapproves. He likes balanced antitheses in the euphuistic manner, writing this of Henry V's soldiers during their retreat toward Calais: ". . . daily it rained and nightly it freezed; of fuel there was great scarcity, of fluxes plenty; money enough, but wares for their relief to bestow it on had they none." Sometimes, as in the following account of Henry VI, he combines two or three such tricks of style to produce a fine sentence: "Thus far touching the tragical state of this land under the rent regiment of King Henry, who (beside the bare title of royalty and naked name of king) had little appertaining to the port of a prince." And he can invest an historical insight with a sense of foreboding all the more effective for its alliteration, quiet tone, and simple image: "After the death of that noble prince the Duke of Bedford, the bright sun in France toward Englishmen began to be cloudy and daily to darken."

Two aspects of Holinshed's style it has been inadvisable to illustrate fully or impossible to illustrate at all in this edition. One is his occasional quotation of sententious passages from Latin authors; an example is given in the selections relating to *King John.* The other consists of the marginal glosses of the original editions (especially the more copious ones of 1587). Some of these seem to have caught Shakespeare's eye, for their wording is reflected in that of the plays, and some of them are interesting or amusing in their own right, as when the 1587 glosser's Tudor indignation moves him to interject "O singular dissimulation of King Richard" at the point where Richard Crookback agrees to accept the crown, but only out of love for his deceased brother Edward IV.

So far I have been speaking of Holinshed as though he were one person. He *was* one person, of course, though we know precious little about the Raphael Holinshed (or Hollingshead) who was born in Cheshire about 1498, is reported by Anthony à Wood to have been a "minister of God's word," and died about 1580. (From the *Chronicles* we may infer that Holinshed was a strict moralist, a firm believer in God's providence, and a bit of a misogynist; his notorious anti-Catholicism is only apparent, for it originates largely in the edition of 1587.) But in a sense Holinshed was not an individual person but a group of persons; the name designates a whole syndicate of writers, for the historical Holinshed was assisted in preparing the first edition of the *Chronicles* (1577) by Richard Stanyhurst, Edmund Campion, and William Harrison (who wrote the fascinating *Description of England* of Vol. 1), and the greatly expanded second edition (1587), which appeared some seven years after Holinshed's death, is chiefly the work of Abraham Fleming, in collaboration with John Hooker, Francis Thynne, and John Stow. (This second edition, since it was used by Shakespeare,[2] forms the basis of the present edition.) One continues, for the sake of convenience, to speak of the single author Holinshed, but the reader is warned that the usage is inexact and potentially misleading.

In addition to being the work of several writers, Holinshed's *Chronicles* is derived from numerous sources. Earlier writers mentioned and made use of in the selections given in this book include Edward Hall, Sir Thomas More, Robert Fabyan, John Bale, Polydore Vergil, Ranulf Higden, Thomas Walsingham, John Whethamstede, the author

[2]An example of evidence for Shakespeare's use of the second edition of Holinshed (see Boswell-Stone, p. x) is the word *pickthanks* (*1 Henry IV*, 3.2.25), which occurs in the edition of 1587 but not in that of 1577.

of *Anglorum Proelia,* the "author of the Book of Barnwell Abbey," Jean Froissart, Jean du Tillet, Enguerrand de Monstrelet, Strabo, and Cornelius Tacitus. And there are others who are made use of but not mentioned. Holinshed's range is wide. Moreover, though Holinshed sometimes accepts whoppers (his fascination with astronomical portents may be described as fatal), his eye is, upon occasion, extremely judicious. Frequently he criticizes his sources, balancing one account against another, as when he suggests that some writers have exaggerated the smallness of English casualties at the Battle of Agincourt. And he sometimes poses (if he does not always answer) difficult and interesting questions, as when, in shrewdly suggesting that King John's unpleasant reputation may have been due in part to his aggressions against the Church (from whose ranks most of the early chroniclers naturally were drawn), he points out that John nevertheless founded an abbey.

Holinshed is without question the most important of Shakespeare's sources, since he provided the basic material for no fewer than thirteen plays: the ten plays dealing with English history and three others, *King Lear, Cymbeline,* and *Macbeth.* But Holinshed is not the single source of any of Shakespeare's plays, as a glance through the compilation of Shakespeare's sources by Geoffrey Bullough will show. The point is perhaps especially noteworthy in the case of the history plays, since what is there in question is not the obvious amalgamation of different stories (for example, of Holinshed with a Boccaccio novella as in *Cymbeline* or of Holinshed with a story drawn from Sidney's *Arcadia* as in *King Lear*) but the rather subtler amalgamation of different versions of the same story (of Holinshed with another chronicle). First and always, one must remember Edward Hall's *Union of the Two Noble and Illustrious Families of Lancaster and York* (1548), and one must also consider, from time to time, other of the sixteenth-century chronicles, those, for example, of Robert Fabyan, Polydore Vergil, Richard Grafton, and John Stow. And behind the sixteenth-century chronicles, most of which Shakespeare knew in addition to Holinshed, stand the fifteenth-century chronicles, most of which he did not know: the *Chronicle* of John Hardyng, Higden's *Polychronicon,* the continuation of the *Brut,* the continuation of the *Croyland Chronicle,* the life of Henry V by the "Translator of Livius," the *History of the Arrival of Edward IV,* Mancini's account of the usurpation of Richard III, and others. For Shakespeare, Holinshed is unquestionably the greatest and most inclusive source of English history. Hall is a good runner-up; but Hall does not treat the earlier period of King John, and in any case Holinshed, as a source for Shakespeare, has the advantage over Hall of reproducing thousands upon thousands of words of the earlier chronicler almost verbatim.

★ ★ ★

It is rightly customary to see a special unity in Shakespeare's eight plays dealing with the unbroken sweep of English history from 1398 to 1485: *Richard II; 1* and *2 Henry IV; Henry V; 1, 2,* and *3 Henry VI;* and *Richard III*. Thus, we have initially a "division" in the House of Plantagenet, then a "contention" betwixt the Houses of York and Lancaster, and ultimately a "union" of the contending families in the House of Tudor. But if we include *King John* and *Henry VIII* in the pattern, we can perceive, despite a large gap between 1216 and 1398 and a considerable one between 1485 and 1520, a larger if somewhat looser unity, for John, in his conflict with the papacy, was understood by Tudor writers to be a prefiguration of Henry. (Compare Bale's *King John,* in which the spirit of Henry VIII speaks a kind of extended epilogue.) Thus, with *Henry VIII* we return full circle to *King John*. Moreover, the two "gaps" in the cycle of Shakespeare's plays from *King John* to *Henry VIII* are (to a degree) filled in by non-Shakespearian plays—the earlier by Peele's *Edward I* (admittedly a poor example of a history play), Marlowe's *Edward II,* and the anonymous *Edward III, Jack Straw,* and *Woodstock;* the later (corresponding to the reign of Henry VII) by Ford's *Perkin Warbeck*. In addition, Shakespeare's treatment of the reign of Edward IV is "amplified" by Heywood's *1* and *2 Edward IV* (Heywood helped himself to materials on Jane Shore and Edward's French war which Shakespeare passed over), and his treatments of the reigns of Henry IV and Henry VIII are amplified by several "biographical plays" presenting the "fall" of a historical person of consequence other than a prince: Drayton's *Sir John Oldcastle,* Munday's *Sir Thomas More,* and the anonymous *Thomas Lord Cromwell*. All told, there are extant more than two dozen Elizabethan plays (including Shakespeare's) which deal with all but one (Henry III) of the fourteen rulers of England from John in 1199 to Henry VIII in 1509. These rulers and the corresponding plays are listed in an appendix giving the main outlines of English history during the period in question.

The plays discussed in the last paragraph deal with what may be called the "matter of England." Such plays constitute the largest and most interesting class of Elizabethan history plays, but by no means the only one. Other plays deal with the "matter of Rome"—for example, Lodge's *Wounds of Civil War,* Chapman's *Caesar and Pompey,* May's *Cleopatra,* Jonson's *Sejanus* and *Catiline,* and Shakespeare's *Julius Caesar, Antony and Cleopatra,* and *Coriolanus.* Others deal with the "matter of Britain"—for example, Sackville and Norton's *Gorboduc,* Hughes' *Misfortunes of Arthur,* the anonymous *Locrine,* and Shakespeare's *King Lear* and *Cymbeline.* Still others deal with historical materials too various for classification—for example, Preston's *Cambyses,* Peele's *Battle of Alcazar,* the anonymous *Alarum for London,* Chapman's *1* and *2 Charles Duke of Byron,* Barnes' *Devil's Charter,* Marlowe's *Massacre at Paris,* the same writer's *1* and *2 Tamburlaine,* Fletcher and Massinger's *Sir John van Olden Barnavelt,* and Shakespeare's *Macbeth.* To be sure, many of these plays are "historical tragedies" rather than true "history plays," but some, such as *Gorboduc, Julius Caesar, Sejanus,* and *Coriolanus,* are indeed true history plays, for although they do not deal with the "matter of England," they are, like such "true" examples as *King John, Edward II, Woodstock,* and *Richard II,* concerned with presenting vital political questions in the form of a dramatic fiction based on history. The word "vital" is designed to direct attention to the peculiar aptness for the times of the political questions treated in Elizabethan history plays. We must keep in mind, for example, that in 1595 Queen Elizabeth understood Richard II as an "image" of herself, that in 1601 a performance of *Richard II* was commissioned in an attempt to arouse sentiment favorable to Essex's Rebellion, that Jonson's *Catiline* of 1611 is a "mirror" of the Gunpowder Plot of 1605, and that in 1649, after a series of civil wars as bitter and hardfought as any of Rome or of fifteenth-century England, a captive king was tried and executed for treason. It could (and did) happen here.

In a number of respects our understanding of Shakespeare's English history plays has suffered a sea-change during the past thirty years or more. For one thing, we are today much better informed about the plays in relation both to literary tradition and to Renaissance history and historiography because of the publication of such works as J. Dover Wilson's *Fortunes of Falstaff* (1944), E. M. W. Tillyard's *Shakespeare's History Plays* (1946), and Lily B. Campbell's *Shakespeare's "Histories"* (1947). For another, there has been a most welcome renaissance of production, beginning with the linked productions of *1* and *2 Henry IV* by the Old Vic in the 1940's (Falstaff was played by Sir Ralph Richardson; Hotspur and Shallow by Sir Laurence Olivier), continuing with productions of the Henry VI plays by the Birmingham Rep and the Old Vic in the 1950's, and culminating in a production of the eight-play Lancaster-York cycle by the Old Vic early in the 1960's. American and Canadian academic and festival theaters have also made many contributions. The early plays have benefited especially by this renaissance. *2* and *3 Henry VI* turn out to be good plays in the theater, and there is even something to be said on behalf of *1 Henry VI*. *King John* is a remarkably strong play in performance. Yet such plays were rarely produced before the Second World War.

Another important change is that we now understand the so-called bad quartos to be memorial reconstructions of the corresponding Shakespeare texts rather than "sources" or "early drafts" of those texts. (On this complex question the interested reader may consult W. W. Greg's *Shakespeare First Folio,* 1955, where references to specialized studies may be found.) There is a bad quarto of *Henry V,* and bad quartos of *2* and *3 Henry VI,* as was established in the 1920's, masquerade under the beguiling titles of *The Contention Betwixt the Two Famous Houses of York and Lancaster* and *The True Tragedy of Richard Duke of York*. Moreover, *The True Tragedy of Richard III* appears to be, though not a bad quarto of *Richard III,* either a bad quarto of a supposed lost play on Richard or a text somehow derivative from such a lost play or from Shakespeare's play itself (or from both). Furthermore, *The Troublesome Reign of King John,* far from being, as is perhaps still generally thought, a source of Shakespeare's *King John,* is actually derivative from Shakespeare's play. This proposition, originally formulated by Peter Alexander, was first elaborated by the Arden editor E. A. J. Honigmann in 1954 and has recently been supported with great persuasiveness by the Signet editor William Matchett. The proposition makes a considerable difference in our general understanding of Shakespeare's sources (not to mention his particular use of Holinshed in writing *King John*); it also forces us to revise our notions about the chronology of Shakespeare's early plays, since we must now date *King John* in or before 1591 (the date of publication of *The Troublesome Reign*) instead of, as we had been doing, around 1596.

Finally, a better understanding of the bad quartos in their relation to the corresponding Shakespeare texts has led to a better understanding of the authorship of Shakespeare's early history plays. The general drift of twentieth-century scholarship toward accepting the integrity of most of Shakespeare's plays includes the Henry VI plays, once a happy-hunting-ground for the "disintegrators" of Shakespeare. Leo Kirschbaum's article (1952) on the integrity of *1 Henry VI* is a milestone on this road, and relief from the burden of supposing *The Contention* and *Richard Duke of York* to be the work of anonymous hack writers revised by Shakespeare has enabled us to see what might well have been plain enough before: that *2* and *3 Henry VI* are not only good plays but also Shakespeare's original creations and unassisted work. Concerning the authorship of the late play *Henry VIII,* doubt remains. Since modern critics have argued effectively for Shakespeare's sole authorship and for his collaboration with Fletcher, the general reader may take his choice of the two theories.

King Lear

[**12**][1] Lear the son of Bladud was admitted ruler over the Britons in the year of the world 3105, at what time Joas reigned in Judah. This Lear was a prince of right noble demeanor, governing his land and subjects in great wealth. He made the town of Caerleir, now called Leicester, which standeth upon the river of Soar. It is written that he had by his wife three daughters, without other issue; whose names were Goneril, Regan, and Cordelia, which daughters he greatly loved; but specially Cordelia the youngest far above the two elder. When this Lear therefore was come to great years and began to wax unwieldy through age, he thought to understand the affections of his daughters toward him, and prefer her whom he best loved to the succession over the kingdom. Whereupon he first asked Goneril, the eldest, how well she loved him; who, calling her gods to record, protested that she loved him more than her own life, which by right and reason should be most dear unto her. With which answer the father being well pleased, turned to the second and demanded of her how well she loved him; who answered, confirming her sayings with great oaths, that she loved him more than tongue could express and far above all other creatures of the world.

[**13**] Then called he his youngest daughter Cordelia before him and asked of her what account she made of him, unto whom she made this answer as followeth: "Knowing the great love and fatherly zeal that you have always borne toward me (for the which I may not answer you otherwise than I think and as my conscience leadeth me), I protest unto you that I have loved you ever and will continually (while I live) love you as my natural father. And if you would more understand of the love that I bear you, ascertain[2] yourself that so much as you have, so much you are worth, and so much I love you and no more." The father, being nothing content with this answer,

[1]Vol. 1, *History of England*.
[2]Assure.

married his two eldest daughters, the one unto Henninus the Duke of Cornwall and the other unto Maglanus the Duke of Albany; betwixt whom he willed and ordained that his land should be divided after his death, and the one half thereof immediately should be assigned to them in hand; but for the third daughter, Cordelia, he reserved nothing.

Nevertheless it fortuned that one of the princes of Gallia (which now is called France), whose name was Aganippus, hearing of the beauty, womanhood, and good conditions of the said Cordelia, desired to have her in marriage and sent over to her father requiring that he might have her to wife; to whom answer was made that he might have his daughter, but as for any dower he could have none, for all was promised and assured to her other sisters already. Aganippus, notwithstanding this answer of denial to receive anything by way of dower with Cordelia, took her to wife, only moved thereto (I say) for respect of her person and amiable virtues. This Aganippus was one of the twelve kings that ruled Gallia in those days, as in the British history it is recorded. But to proceed.

After that Lear was fallen into age, the two Dukes that had married his two eldest daughters, thinking it long ere the government of the land did come to their hands, arose against him in armor and reft from him the governance of the land upon conditions to be continued for term of life; by the which he was put to his portion, that is, to live after a rate assigned to him for the maintenance of his estate, which in process of time was diminished as well by Maglanus as by Henninus. But the greatest grief that Lear took was to see the unkindness[3] of his daughters, which seemed to think that all was too much which their father had, the same being never so little; insomuch that, going from the one to the other, he was brought to that misery that scarcely they would allow him one servant to wait upon him.

In the end, such was the unkindness or (as I may say) the unnaturalness which he found in his two daughters, notwithstanding their fair and pleasant words uttered in time past, that being constrained of necessity, he fled the land and sailed into Gallia, there to seek some comfort of his youngest daughter Cordelia whom before time he hated. The Lady Cordelia, hearing that he was arrived in poor estate, she first sent to him privily a certain sum of money to apparel himself withal and to retain a certain number of servants that

[3]Unnaturalness.

might attend upon him in honorable wise, as appertained to the estate which he had borne; and then, so accompanied, she appointed him to come to the court; which he did, and was so joyfully, honorably, and lovingly received, both by his son-in-law Aganippus and also by his daughter Cordelia, that his heart was greatly comforted, for he was no less honored than if he had been king of the whole country himself.

Now when he had informed his son-in-law and his daughter in what sort he had been used by his other daughters, Aganippus caused a mighty army to be put in areadiness, and likewise a great navy of ships to be rigged, to pass over into Britain with Lear, his father-in-law, to see him again restored to his kingdom. It was accorded that Cordelia should also go with him to take possession of the land, the which he promised to leave unto her, as the rightful inheritor after his decease, notwithstanding any former grant made to her sisters or to their husbands in any manner of wise.

Hereupon, when this army and navy of ships were ready, Lear and his daughter Cordelia with her husband took the sea and, arriving in Britain, fought with their enemies and discomfited them in battle, in the which Maglanus and Henninus were slain; and then was Lear restored to his kingdom, which he ruled after this by the space of two years; and then died, forty years after he first began to reign. His body was buried at Leicester, in a vault under the channel of the river of Soar, beneath the town. . . .

Cordelia, the youngest daughter of Lear, was admitted Queen and supreme Governess of Britain in the year of the world 3155, before the building of Rome 54, Uzia then reigning in Judah and Jeroboam over Israel. This Cordelia, after her father's decease, ruled the land of Britain right worthily during the space of five years, in which meantime her husband died; and then, about the end of those five years, her two nephews Margan and Cunedag, sons to her aforesaid sisters, disdaining to be under the government of a woman, levied war against her and destroyed a great part of the land; and finally took her prisoner and laid her fast in ward,[4] wherewith she took such grief, being a woman of a manly courage and despairing to recover liberty, there she slew herself, when she had reigned (as before is mentioned) the term of five years.

[4]Prison.

Cymbeline

[32][1] "Kymbeline" or "Cymbeline," the son of Theomantius, was of the Britons made king after the decease of his father in the year of the world 3944, after the building of Rome 728, and before the birth of our Saviour 33. This man (as some write) was brought up at Rome and there made knight by Augustus Caesar, under whom he served in the wars, and was in such favor with him that he was at liberty to pay his tribute or not. Little other mention is made of his doings, except that during his reign the Saviour of the world, our Lord Jesus Christ the only son of God, was borne of a virgin about the twenty-third year of the reign of this Cymbeline. . . . Touching the continuance of the years of Cymbeline's reign, some writers do vary, but the best approved affirm that he reigned thirty-five years and then died, and was buried at London, leaving behind him two sons Guiderius and Arviragus.

But here is to be noted that, although our histories do affirm that as well this Cymbeline as also his father Theomantius lived in quiet with the Romans, and continually to them paid the tributes which the Britons had covenanted with Julius Caesar to pay, yet we find in the Roman writers that after Julius Caesar's death, when Augustus had taken upon him the rule of the empire, the Britons refused to pay that tribute. Whereat, as Cornelius Tacitus reporteth, Augustus (being otherwise occupied) was contented to wink. Howbeit, through earnest calling upon to recover his right by such as were desirous to see the uttermost of the British kingdom, at length, to wit in the tenth year after the death of Julius Caesar, which was about the thirteenth year of the said Theomantius, Augustus made provision to pass with an army over into Britain, and was come forward upon his journey into Gallia Celtica or, as we may say, into these hither parts of France.

[1]Vol. 1, *History of England.*

But here receiving advertisements that the Pannonians, which inhabited the country now called Hungary, and the Dalmatians, whom now we call Slavonians, had rebelled, he thought it best first to subdue those rebels near home rather than to seek new countries and leave such in hazard whereof he had present possession. And so, turning his power against the Pannonians and Dalmatians, he left off for a time the wars of Britain. . . . But whether this controversy, which appeareth to fall forth betwixt the Britons and Augustus, was occasioned by Cymbeline or some other prince of the Britons, I have not to avouch. For that by our writers it is reported that Cymbeline, being brought up in Rome and knighted in the court of Augustus, ever showed himself a friend to the Romans, and chiefly was loath to break with them because[2] the youth of the Briton nation should not be deprived of the benefit to be trained and brought up among the Romans; whereby they might learn both to behave themselves like civil[3] men and to attain to the knowledge of feats of war.

[**33**] But whether for this respect or for that it pleased the almighty God so to dispose the minds of men at that present, not only the Britons but in manner all other nations were contented to be obedient to the Roman Empire. That this was true in the Britons, it is evident enough by Strabo's words, which are in effect as followeth. At this present (saith he) certain princes of Britain, procuring by ambassadors and dutiful demeanors the amity of the Emperor Augustus, have offered in the Capitol unto the gods presents or gifts, and have ordained the whole isle in a manner to be appertinent, proper, and familiar to the Romans. They are burdened with sore customs which they pay for wares, either to be sent forth into Gallia or brought from thence, which are commonly ivory vessels, shears, ouches[4] or earrings, and other conceits[5] made of amber and glasses, and suchlike manner of merchandise. So that now there is no need of any army or garrison of men-of-war to keep the isle, for there needeth not past one legion of footmen, or some wing of horsemen, to gather up and receive the tribute. . . .

Guiderius, the first son of Cymbeline (of whom Harrison saith nothing), began his reign in the seventeenth year after the incarnation

[2]So that.
[3]Educated.
[4]Brooches.
[5]Fancy articles.

of Christ. This Guiderius being a man of stout courage,[6] gave occasion of breach of peace betwixt the Britons and Romans, denying to pay them tribute and procuring the people to new insurrections which by one mean or other made open rebellion, as Gyldas saith.

★ ★ ★

[154][7] From thence the army of the Danes passed through Angus unto the river of Tay, all the people of the countries by which they marched fleeing afore them. King Kenneth [of Scotland] at the same time lay at Stirling, where, hearing of these grievous news, he determined forthwith to raise his people and to go against his enemies. . . .

[155] The Danes, being backed with the mountain, were constrained to leave the same and with all speed to come forward upon their enemies, that by joining, they might avoid the danger of the Scottishmen's arrows and darts. By this means therefore they came to hand strokes, in manner before the sign was given on either part to the battle. The fight was cruel on both sides; and nothing hindered the Scots so much as going about to cut off the heads of the Danes, ever as they might overcome them. Which manner being noted of the Danes, and perceiving that there was no hope of life but in victory, they rushed forth with such violence upon their adversaries that first the right and then after the left wing of the Scots was constrained to retire and flee back, the middleward[8] stoutly yet keeping their ground; but the same stood in such danger, being now left naked on the sides, that the victory must needs have remained with the Danes had not a renewer of the battle come in time by the appointment (as is to be thought) of almighty God.

For as it chanced, there was in the next field at the same time an husbandman, with two of his sons busy about his work, named Hay; a man strong and stiff in making and shape of body but endued with a valiant courage[9] [**5.3.15**]. This Hay, beholding the King with the most part of the nobles fighting with great valiancy in the middleward, now destitute of the wings and in great danger to be oppressed by the great violence of his enemies, caught a ploughbeam in his hand and,

[6]Brave spirit.
[7]Vol. 2, *History of Scotland*.
[8]Main body of soldiers.
[9]Spirit.

with the same exhorting his sons to do the like, hasted toward the battle, there to die rather amongst other in defense of his country than to remain alive after the discomfiture, in miserable thralldom and bondage, of the cruel and most unmerciful enemies. There was near to the place of the battle a long lane fenced on the sides with ditches and walls made of turf, through the which the Scots which fled were beaten down by the enemies on heaps.

Here Hay with his sons supposing they might best stay the flight, placed themselves overthwart the lane, beat them back whom they met fleeing, and spared neither friend nor foe; but down they went, all such as came within their reach, wherewith divers hardy personages cried unto their fellows to return back unto the battle, for there was a new power of Scottishmen come to their succors by whose aid the victory might be easily obtained of their most cruel adversaries the Danes. Therefore might they choose whether they would be slain of their own fellows coming to their aid, or to return again to fight with the enemies. The Danes, being here stayed in the lane by the great valiancy of the father and the sons, thought verily there had been some great succors of Scots come to the aid of their King and, thereupon, ceasing from further pursuit, fled back in great disorder unto the other of their fellows fighting with the middleward of the Scots.

The Scots also that before was chased, being encouraged herewith, pursued the Danes unto the place of the battle right fiercely. Whereupon Kenneth, perceiving his people to be thus recomforted, and his enemies partly abashed,[10] called upon his men to remember their duties; and now, sith their adversaries' hearts began (as they might perceive) to faint, he willed them to follow upon them manfully, which if they did he assured them that the victory undoubtedly should be theirs. The Scots, encouraged with the King's words, laid about them so earnestly that in the end the Danes were constrained to forsake the field, and the Scots, eagerly pursuing in the chase, made great slaughter of them as they fled. This victory turned highly to the praise of the Scottish nobility, the which, fighting in the middleward, bore still the brunt of the battle, continuing manfully therein even to the end. But Hay, who in such wise (as is before mentioned) stayed them that fled, causing them to return again to the field, deserved immortal fame and commendation, for by his means chiefly was the

[10]Put to confusion.

victory achieved. And therefore, on the morrow after, when the spoil of the field and of the enemies' camp (which they had left void) should be divided, the chiefest part was bestowed on him and his two sons, by consent of all the multitude; the residue being divided amongst the soldiers and men-of-war, according to the ancient custom used amongst this nation.

Macbeth

[149][1] . . . In the meantime the King [Duff] fell into a languishing disease, not so grievous as strange, that none of his physicians could perceive what to make of it.

. . . He had also a temperate desire and appetite to his meat and drink, but yet could he not sleep in the nighttime by any provocations that could be devised, but still fell into exceeding sweats which by no means might be restrained **[1.3]**.

. . . But about that present time there was a murmuring amongst the people how the King was vexed with no natural sickness but by sorcery and magical art, practiced by a sort[2] of witches dwelling in a town of Morayland called Forres.

. . . So were they taught by evil spirits and hired to work the feat by the nobles of Morayland. The standers-by, that heard such an abominable tale told by these witches, straightways broke the image and caused the witches (according as they had well deserved) to be burned to death.

[150] It was said that the King, at the very same time that these things were adoing within the castle of Forres, was delivered of his languor and slept that night without any sweat breaking forth upon him at all, and the next day, being restored to his strength, was able to do any manner of thing that lay in man to do, as though he had not been sick before anything at all. But howsoever it came to pass, truth it is that, when he was restored to his perfect health, he gathered a power of men and, with thc same, went into Morayland against the rebels there; and chasing them from thence, he pursued them into Ross, and from Ross into Caithness, where, apprehending them, he brought them back unto Forres and there caused them to be hanged up on gallows and gibbets.

Amongst them there were also certain young gentlemen, right

[1]Vol. 2, *History of Scotland.*
[2]Group.

beautiful and goodly personages, being near of kin unto Donwald, captain of the castle, and had been persuaded to be partakers with the other rebels, more through the fraudulent counsel of divers wicked persons than of their own accord; whereupon the foresaid Donwald, lamenting their case, made earnest labor and suit to the King to have begged their pardon; but having a plain denial, he conceived such an inward malice toward the King (though he showed it not outwardly at the first) that the same continued still boiling in his stomach[3] and ceased not till, through setting on of his wife and in revenge of such unthankfulness, he found means to murder the King within the foresaid castle of Forres where he used to sojourn. For the King, being in that country, was accustomed to lie most commonly within the same castle, having a special trust in Donwald as a man whom he never suspected.

But Donwald, not forgetting the reproach which his lineage[4] had sustained by the execution of those his kinsmen whom the King for a spectacle to the people had caused to be hanged, could not but show manifest tokens of great grief at home amongst his family, which his wife perceiving, ceased not to travail with him till she understood what the cause was of his displeasure. Which at length when she had learned by his own relation, she, as one that bore no less malice in her heart toward the King for the like cause on her behalf than her husband did for his friends', counseled him (sith the King oftentimes used to lodge in his house without any guard about him other than the garrison of the castle, which was wholly at his commandment) to make him away and showed him the means whereby he might soonest accomplish it [**1.7**].

Donwald, thus being the more kindled in wrath by the words of his wife, determined to follow her advice in the execution of so heinous an act. Whereupon, devising with himself for a while which way he might best accomplish his cursed intent, [he] at length got opportunity and sped his purpose as followeth. It chanced that the King, upon the day before he purposed to depart forth of the castle, was long in his oratory at his prayers and there continued till it was late in the night. At the last, coming forth, he called such afore him as had faithfully served him in pursuit and apprehension of the rebels, and giving them hearty thanks, he bestowed sundry honorable gifts

[3]Mind.
[4]Family.

amongst them, of the which number Donwald was one, as he that had been ever accounted a most faithful servant to the King.

At length, having talked with them a long time, he got him into his privy chamber, only with two of his chamberlains who, having brought him to bed, came forth again and then fell to banqueting with Donwald and his wife, who had prepared divers delicate dishes and sundry sorts of drinks for their rare[5] supper or collation; whereat they sat up so long, till they had charged their stomachs with such full gorges that their heads were no sooner got to the pillow, but asleep they were so fast that a man might have removed the chamber over them sooner than to have awaked them out of their drunken sleep [**1.7**].

Then Donwald, though he abhorred the act greatly in heart, yet through instigation of his wife he called four of his servants unto him (whom he had made privy to his wicked intent before and framed to his purpose with large gifts); and now declaring unto them after what sort they should work the feat, they gladly obeyed his instructions, and speedily going about the murder, they entered the chamber (in which the King lay) a little before cock's crow; where they secretly cut his throat as he lay sleeping, without any bustling at all [**2.2**]. And immediately, by a postern gate, they carried forth the dead body into the fields, and, throwing it upon an horse there provided ready for that purpose, they conveyed it unto a place about two miles distant from the castle, where they stayed and got certain laborers to help them to turn the course of a little river running through the fields there; and digging a deep hole in the channel, they buried the body in the same, ramming it up with stones and gravel so closely that, setting the water in the right course again, no man could perceive that anything had been newly digged there. This they did by order appointed them by Donwald (as is reported), for that the body should not be found and, by bleeding when Donwald should be present, declare him to be guilty of the murder. For such an opinion men have that the dead corpse of any man, being slain, will bleed abundantly if the murderer be present. But for what consideration soever they buried him there, they had no sooner finished the work but that they slew them whose help they used herein, and straightways thereupon fled into Orkney.

Donwald, about the time that the murder was in doing, got him

[5]Late.

amongst them that kept the watch and so continued in company with them all the residue of the night. But in the morning, when the noise was raised in the King's chamber how the King was slain, his body conveyed away, and the bed all berayed[6] with blood, he with the watch ran thither as though he had known nothing of the matter and, breaking into the chamber and finding cakes[a] of blood in the bed and on the floor about the sides of it, he forthwith slew the chamberlains as guilty of that heinous murder [**2.3**]; and then, like a madman running to and fro, he ransacked every corner within the castle, as though it had been to have seen if he might have found either the body or any of the murderers hid in any privy place; but at length, coming to the postern gate and finding it open, he burdened the chamberlains whom he had slain with all the fault, they having the keys of the gates committed to their keeping all the night, and therefore it could not be otherwise (said he) but that they were of counsel in the committing of that most detestable murder.

[**151**] Finally, such was his overearnest diligence in the severe inquisition and trial of the offenders herein that some of the lords began to mislike the matter and to smell forth shrewd tokens that he should not be altogether clear himself. But forsomuch as they were in that country where he had the whole rule, what by reason of his friends and authority together, they doubted[7] to utter what they thought till time and place should better serve thereunto; and hereupon got them away, every man to his home. For the space of six months together after this heinous murder thus committed, there appeared no sun by day nor moon by night in any part of the realm; but still was the sky covered with continual clouds, and sometimes such outrageous winds arose [**2.3**], with lightnings and tempests, that the people were in great fear of present destruction.

[**152**] . . . Monstrous sights also that were seen within the Scottish kingdom that year were these: horses in Lothian, being of singular beauty and swiftness, did eat their own flesh and would in no wise taste any other meat[8] [**2.4**]. In Angus there was a gentlewoman brought forth a child without eyes, nose, hand, or foot. There was a sparrowhawk also strangled by an owl. Neither was it any less wonder that the sun, as before is said, was continually covered with

[6]Defiled.
[a]Clots.
[7]Feared.
[8]Food.

clouds for six months' space. But all men understood that the abominable murder of King Duff was the cause hereof, which being revenged by the death of the authors (in manner as before is said), Cullen was crowned as lawful successor to the same Duff at Scone, with all due honor and solemnity, in the year of our Lord 972, after that Duff had ruled the Scottish kingdom about the space of four years.

★ ★ ★

[**156**] . . . At what time the blind love he [King Kenneth] bore to his own issue caused him to procure a detestable fact[9] in making away one of his nearest kinsmen. This was Malcolm the son of King Duff, created in the beginning of Kenneth's reign Prince of Cumberland, by reason whereof he ought to have succeeded in rule of the kingdom after Kenneth's death. Whereat the same Kenneth grieving not a little, for that thereby his sons should be kept from enjoying the crown, found means to poison him. But though the physicians understanding by such evident signs as appeared in his body that he was poisoned indeed, yet such was the opinion which men had of the King's honor and integrity that no suspicion at all was conceived that it should be his deed.

[**158**] . . . Thus might he seem happy to all men, having the love both of his lords and commons; but yet to himself he seemed most unhappy, as he that could not but still live in continual fear lest his wicked practice[10] concerning the death of Malcolm Duff should come to light and knowledge of the world. For so cometh it to pass that such as are pricked in conscience for any secret offense committed have ever an unquiet mind. And (as the fame goeth) it chanced that a voice was heard [**2.2**] as he was in bed in the nighttime to take his rest, uttering unto him these or the like words in effect: "Think not, Kenneth, that the wicked slaughter of Malcolm Duff, by thee contrived, is kept secret from the knowledge of the eternal God; thou art he that didst conspire the innocent's death, enterprising by traitorous means to do that to thy neighbor which thou wouldst have revenged by cruel punishment in any of thy subjects, if it had been offered to thyself. It shall therefore come to pass that both thou thyself and thy issue, through the just vengeance of almighty God, shall suffer worthy punishment, to the infamy of thy

[9]Crime.
[10]Plot.

house and family for evermore. For even at this present are there in hand secret practices to dispatch both thee and thy issue out of the way, that other may enjoy this kingdom which thou dost endeavor to assure unto thine issue."

The King, with this voice being stricken into great dread and terror, passed that night without any sleep coming in his eyes.

★ ★ ★

[**168**] After Malcolm, succeeded his nephew[b] Duncan, the son of his daughter Beatrice. For Malcolm had two daughters. The one, which was this Beatrice, being given in marriage unto one Abbanath Crinen, a man of great nobility and Thane of the Isles and west parts of Scotland, bore of that marriage the foresaid Duncan. The other, called Doada, was married unto Sinel the Thane of Glamis, by whom she had issue one Macbeth, a valiant gentleman and one that, if he had not been somewhat cruel of nature, might have been thought most worthy the government of a realm. On the other part, Duncan was so soft and gentle of nature that the people wished the inclinations and manners of these two cousins to have been so tempered[11] and interchangeably bestowed betwixt them that, where the one had too much of clemency and the other of cruelty, the mean virtue betwixt these two extremities might have reigned by indifferent partition[12] in them both; so should Duncan have proved a worthy king and Macbeth an excellent captain. The beginning of Duncan's reign was very quiet and peaceable, without any notable trouble; but after it was perceived how negligent he was in punishing offenders, many misruled[13] persons took occasion thereof to trouble the peace and quiet state of the commonwealth by seditious commotions which first had their beginnings in this wise.

Banquo, the Thane of Lochaber, of whom the House of the Stuarts is descended, the which by order of lineage hath now for a long time enjoyed the crown of Scotland even till these our days, as he gathered the finances due to the King and further punished somewhat sharply such as were notorious offenders, being assailed by a number of rebels inhabiting in that country and spoiled of the money and all

[b]Grandson.
[11]Blended.
[12]Impartial division.
[13]Unruly.

other things, had much ado to get away with life after he had received sundry grievous wounds amongst them. Yet escaping their hands, after he was somewhat recovered of his hurts and was able to ride, he repaired to the court, where, making his complaint to the King in most earnest wise, he purchased[14] at length that the offenders were sent for by a sergeant-at-arms, to appear to make answer unto such matters as should be laid to their charge; but they, augmenting their mischievous act with a more wicked deed, after they had misused the messenger with sundry kinds of reproaches, they finally slew him also.

Then, doubting not but for such contemptuous demeanor against the King's regal authority they should be invaded with all the power the King could make, Macdowald, one of great estimation among them, making first a confederacy with his nearest friends and kinsmen, took upon him to be chief captain of all such rebels as would stand against the King in maintenance of their grievous offenses lately committed against him [**1.2**]. Many slanderous words also and railing taunts this Macdowald uttered against his prince, calling him a fainthearted milksop more meet to govern a sort of idle monks in some cloister than to have the rule of such valiant and hearty men-of-war as the Scots were. He used also such subtle persuasions and forged allurements that in a small time he had gotten together a mighty power of men; for out of the Western Isles there came unto him a great multitude of people offering themselves to assist him in that rebellious quarrel; and out of Ireland in hope of the spoil came no small number of kerns[15] and gallowglasses,[16] offering gladly to serve under him, whither[17] it should please him to lead them.

[**169**] Macdowald, thus having a mighty puissance about him, encountered with such of the King's people as were sent against him into Lochaber and, discomfiting them, by mere[18] force took their captain Malcolm and, after the end of the battle, smote off his head. This overthrow, being notified to the King, did put him in wonderful fear by reason of his small skill in warlike affairs. Calling therefore his nobles to a council, he asked of them their best advice for the subduing of Macdowald and other the rebels. Here in sundry heads

[14]Arranged.
[15]Light-armed Irish footsoldiers.
[16]Mounted Irish soldiers armed with poleaxes.
[17]Wherever.
[18]Sheer.

(as ever it happeneth) were sundry opinions, which they uttered according to every man his skill. At length Macbeth, speaking much against the King's softness and overmuch slackness in punishing offenders (whereby they had such time to assemble together), he promised notwithstanding, if the charge were committed unto him and unto Banquo, so to order the matter that the rebels should be shortly vanquished and quite put down, and that not so much as one of them should be found to make resistance within the country.

And even so it came to pass: for being sent forth with a new power, at his entering into Lochaber the fame of his coming put the enemies in such fear that a great number of them stole secretly away from their captain Macdowald, who nevertheless, enforced thereto, gave battle unto Macbeth with the residue which remained with him. But being overcome and fleeing for refuge into a castle (within the which his wife and children were enclosed), at length, when he saw how he could neither defend the hold any longer against his enemies nor yet upon surrender be suffered to depart with life saved, he first slew his wife and children and lastly himself, lest if he had yielded simply he should have been executed in most cruel wise for an example to other. Macbeth, entering into the castle by the gates, as then set open, found the carcass of Macdowald lying dead there amongst the residue of the slain bodies; which when he beheld, remitting no piece of his cruel nature with that pitiful sight, he caused the head to be cut off and set upon a pole's end, and so sent it as a present to the King, who as then lay at Bertha[c] [**1.2**]. The headless trunk he commanded to be hung up upon an high pair[19] of gallows.

. . . Thus was justice and law restored again to the old accustomed course by the diligent means of Macbeth. Immediately whereupon word came that Sueno King of Norway was arrived in Fife with a puissant army, to subdue the whole realm of Scotland.

[**170**] . . . The Scots, having won so notable a victory, after they had gathered and divided the spoil of the field, caused solemn processions to be made in all places of the realm, and thanks to be given to almighty God, that had sent them so fair a day over their enemies. But whilst the people were thus at their processions, word was brought that a new fleet of Danes was arrived at Kinghorn, sent thither by Canute King of England in revenge of his brother Sueno's overthrow. To resist these enemies, which were already landed and

[c]Perth.
[19]Set.

busy in spoiling the country, Macbeth and Banquo were sent with the King's authority; who, having with them a convenient power, encountered the enemies, slew part of them, and chased the other to their ships. They that escaped and got once to their ships obtained of Macbeth, for a great sum of gold, that such of their friends as were slain at this last bickering might be buried in Saint Colme's Inch.[d]

. . . Shortly after happened a strange and uncouth[20] wonder, which afterward was the cause of much trouble in the realm of Scotland, as ye shall after hear [**1.3**]. It fortuned, as Macbeth and Banquo journeyed toward Forres, where the King then lay, they went sporting by the way together without other company save only themselves, passing through the woods and fields, when suddenly, in the midst of a laund,[21] there met them three women in strange and wild apparel, resembling creatures of elder[22] world; whom when they attentively beheld, wondering much at the sight, the first of them spoke and said, "All hail, Macbeth, Thane of Glamis!" (for he had lately entered into that dignity and office by the death of his father Sinel). The second of them said, "Hail, Macbeth, Thane of Cawdor!" But the third said, "All hail, Macbeth, that hereafter shalt be King of Scotland!"

Then Banquo. "What manner of women," saith he, "are you, that seem so little favorable unto me, whereas to my fellow here, besides high offices, ye assign also the kingdom, appointing forth nothing for me at all?" "Yes," saith the first of them, "we promise greater benefits unto thee than unto him, for he shall reign indeed, but with an unlucky end; neither shall he leave any issue behind him to succeed in his place, where contrarily thou indeed shalt not reign at all, but of thee those shall be born which shall govern the Scottish kingdom by long order of continual descent." Herewith the foresaid women vanished immediately out of their sight. This was reputed at the first but some vain fantastical illusion by Macbeth and Banquo, insomuch that Banquo would call Macbeth, in jest, King of Scotland, and Macbeth again would call him, in sport likewise, the father of many kings. But afterward the common opinion was that these women were either the Weird[23] Sisters, that is (as ye would say), the goddesses of des-

[d]Saint Columba's Isle (Inchcolm, in the Firth of Forth).
[20]Unusual.
[21]Glade.
[22]Ancient.
[23]Able to control fate.

tiny, or else some nymphs or fairies[24] endued with knowledge of prophecy by their necromantical science, because everything came to pass as they had spoken. For shortly after, the Thane of Cawdor being condemned at Forres of treason against the King committed, his lands, livings, and offices were given of the King's liberality to Macbeth [**1.2**].

[**171**] The same night after, at supper, Banquo jested with him and said: "Now Macbeth, thou hast obtained those things which the two former sisters prophesied; there remaineth only for thee to purchase that which the third said should come to pass." Whereupon Macbeth, revolving the thing in his mind, began even then to devise how he might attain to the kingdom; but yet he thought with himself that he must tarry a time which should advance him thereto by the divine providence, as it had come to pass in his former preferment. But shortly after it chanced that King Duncan, having two sons by his wife (which was the daughter of Siward Earl of Northumberland), he made the elder of them (called Malcolm) Prince of Cumberland, as it were thereby to appoint him his successor in the kingdom immediately after his decease [**1.4**]. Macbeth, sore troubled herewith, for that he saw by this means his hope sore hindered (where, by the old laws of the realm, the ordinance was that, if he that should succeed were not of able age to take the charge upon himself, he that was next[e] of blood unto him should be admitted), he began to take counsel how he might usurp the kingdom by force, having a just quarrel[25] so to do (as he took the matter), for that Duncan did what in him lay to defraud him of all manner of title and claim which he might, in time to come, pretend[26] unto the crown.

The words of the three Weird Sisters also (of whom before ye have heard) greatly encouraged him hereunto; but specially his wife lay sore upon him[27] to attempt the thing, as she that was very ambitious, burning in unquenchable desire to bear the name of a queen [**1.5**]. At length, therefore, communicating his purposed intent with his trusty friends, amongst whom Banquo was the chiefest, upon confidence of their promised aid he slew the King at Inverness or (as some say) at Bothgowanan, in the sixth year of his reign [**2.2**]. Then,

[24]Beings possessing supernatural power.
[e]Nearest.
[25]Cause.
[26]Claim.
[27]Pressed him hard.

having a company about him of such as he had made privy to his enterprise, he caused himself to be proclaimed King and forthwith went unto Scone, where (by common consent) he received the investure of the kingdom according to the accustomed manner [**2.4**]. The body of Duncan was first conveyed unto Elgin and there buried in kingly wise; but afterward it was removed and conveyed unto Colmekill, and there laid in a sepulture amongst his predecessors, in the year after the birth of our Saviour 1046.

Malcolm Cammore and Donald Bane, the sons of King Duncan, for fear of their lives (which they might well know that Macbeth would seek to bring to end for his more sure confirmation in the estate), fled into Cumberland, where Malcolm remained till time that Saint Edward the son of Ethelred recovered the dominion of England from the Danish power; the which Edward received Malcolm by way of most friendly entertainment; but Donald passed over into Ireland where he was tenderly cherished by the King of that land [**2.3**]. Macbeth, after the departure thus of Duncan's sons, used great liberality toward the nobles of the realm, thereby to win their favor; and, when he saw that no man went about to trouble him, he set his whole intention to maintain justice, and to punish all enormities and abuses which had chanced through the feeble and slothful administration of Duncan. . . . Macbeth, showing himself thus a most diligent punisher of all injuries and wrongs attempted by any disordered[28] persons within his realm, was accounted the sure defense and buckler of innocent people; and hereto he also applied his whole endeavor, to cause young men to exercise themselves in virtuous manners, and men of the Church to attend their divine service according to their vocations.

. . . To be brief, such were the worthy doings and princely acts of this Macbeth in the administration of the realm that if he had attained thereunto by rightful means and continued in uprightness of justice, as he began, till the end of his reign, he might well have been numbered amongst the most noble princes that anywhere had reigned. He made many wholesome laws and statutes for the public weal of his subjects. . . .

[**172**] These and the like commendable laws Macbeth caused to be put as then in use, governing the realm for the space of ten years in equal justice. But this was but a counterfeit zeal of equity showed by him, partly against his natural inclination, to purchase thereby the

[28]Unruly.

favor of the people. Shortly after, he began to show what he was, instead of equity practicing cruelty. For the prick of conscience (as it chanceth ever in tyrants and such as attain to any estate by unrighteous means) caused him ever to fear lest he should be served of the same cup as he had ministered to his predecessor. The words also of the three Weird Sisters would not out of his mind, which as they promised him the kingdom, so likewise did they promise it at the same time unto the posterity of Banquo [**3.1**]. He willed therefore the same Banquo, with his son named Fleance, to come to a supper that he had prepared for them; which was indeed, as he had devised, present death at the hands of certain murderers whom he hired to execute that deed, appointing them to meet with the same Banquo and his son without the palace, as they returned to their lodgings, and there to slay them, so that he would not have his house slandered but that in time to come he might clear himself if anything were laid to his charge upon any suspicion that might arise [**3.3**].

It chanced by the benefit of the dark night that, though the father were slain, yet the son, by the help of almighty God reserving him to better fortune, escaped that danger; and afterward, having some inkling (by the admonition of some friends which he had in the court) how his life was sought no less than his father's, who was slain not by chance-medley[f] (as by the handling of the matter Macbeth would have had it to appear) but even upon a prepensed[29] device, whereupon to avoid further peril he fled into Wales. But here I think it shall not much make against my purpose if (according to the order which I find observed in the Scottish history) I shall in few words rehearse the original line of those kings which have descended from the foresaid Banquo, that they which have enjoyed the kingdom by so long continuance of descent, from one to another and that even unto these our days, may be known from whence they had their first beginning.

[**174**] . . . But to return unto Macbeth in continuing the history, and to begin where I left, ye shall understand that after the contrived slaughter of Banquo, nothing prospered with the foresaid Macbeth; for in manner every man began to doubt[30] his own life and durst uneath[31] appear in the King's presence; and even as there were many

[f]Accidental homicide.
[29]Premeditated.
[30]Fear for.
[31]Hardly.

that stood in fear of him, so likewise stood he in fear of many, in such sort that he began to make those away by one surmised[32] cavillation or other whom he thought most able to work him any displeasure.

At length he found such sweetness by putting his nobles thus to death that his earnest thirst after blood in this behalf might in no wise be satisfied; for ye must consider he won double profit (as he thought) hereby, for first they were rid out of the way whom he feared, and then again his coffers were enriched by their goods which were forfeited to his use, whereby he might better maintain a guard of armed men about him to defend his person from injury of them whom he had in any suspicion. Further, to the end he might the more cruelly oppress his subjects with all tyrantlike wrongs, he builded a strong castle on the top of an high hill called Dunsinane, situate in Gowrie ten miles from Perth, on such a proud height that, standing there aloft, a man might behold well near all the countries of Angus, Fife, Stormont, and Earndale, as it were lying underneath him. This castle, then, being founded on the top of that high hill, put the realm to great charges before it was finished, for all the stuff necessary to the building could not be brought up without much toil and business. But Macbeth, being once determined to have the work go forward, caused the thanes of each shire within the realm to come and help toward that building, each man his course about.

At the last, when the turn fell unto Macduff Thane of Fife to build his part, he sent workmen with all needful provision and commanded them to show such diligence in every behalf that no occasion might be given for the King to find fault with him in that he came not himself, as other had done, which he refused to do for doubt[33] lest the King, bearing him (as he partly understood) no great good will, would lay violent hands upon him as he had done upon divers other. Shortly after, Macbeth coming to behold how the work went forward and, because he found not Macduff there, he was sore offended and said: "I perceive this man will never obey my commandments till he be ridden with a snaffle; but I shall provide well enough for him." Neither could he afterward abide to look upon the said Macduff, either for that he thought his puissance overgreat, either else for that he had learned of certain wizards in whose words he put great confidence (for that the prophecy had happened so right which the three fairies or Weird Sisters had

[32]Falsely alleged.
[33]Fear.

declared unto him) how that he ought to take heed of Macduff, who in time to come should seek to destroy him.

And surely hereupon had he put Macduff to death but that a certain witch whom he had in great trust had told that he should never be slain with man borne of any woman, nor vanquished till the wood of Birnam came to the castle of Dunsinane [**4.1**]. By this prophecy Macbeth put all fear out of his heart, supposing he might do what he would, without any fear to be punished for the same; for by the one prophecy he believed it was impossible for any man to vanquish him, and by the other impossible to slay him. This vain hope caused him to do many outrageous things, to the grievous oppression of his subjects. At length Macduff, to avoid peril of life, purposed with himself to pass into England to procure Malcolm Cammore to claim the crown of Scotland [**3.6**]. But this was not so secretly devised by Macduff but that Macbeth had knowledge given him thereof, for kings (as is said) have sharp sight like unto Lynx[g] and long ears like unto Midas. For Macbeth had in every nobleman's house one sly fellow or other in fee with him, to reveal all that was said or done within the same, by which sleight he oppressed the most part of the nobles of his realm.

Immediately, then, being advertised whereabout Macduff went, he came hastily with a great power into Fife and forthwith besieged the castle where Macduff dwelled, trusting to have found him therein. They that kept the house without any resistance opened the gates and suffered him to enter, mistrusting none evil. But nevertheless Macbeth most cruelly caused the wife and children of Macduff, with all other whom he found in that castle, to be slain [**4.2**]. Also, he confiscated the goods of Macduff, proclaimed him traitor, and confined[34] him out of all the parts of his realm; but Macduff was already escaped out of danger and gotten into England unto Malcolm Cammore, to try what purchase he might make by means of his support to revenge the slaughter so cruelly executed on his wife, his children, and other friends. At his coming unto Malcolm he declared into what great misery the estate of Scotland was brought by the detestable cruelties exercised by the tyrant Macbeth, having committed many horrible slaughters and murders, both as well of the nobles as commons; for the which he was hated right mortally of all his liege people, desiring nothing more than

[g]Lynceus the Argonaut.
[34]Banished.

to be delivered of that intolerable and most heavy yoke of thralldom which they sustained at such a caitiff's[35] hands [**4.3**].

Malcolm, hearing Macduff's words, which he uttered in very lamentable sort, for mere compassion and very ruth[36] that pierced his sorrowful heart, bewailing the miserable state of his country, he fetched a deep sigh; which Macduff perceiving, began to fall most earnestly in hand with him to enterprise the delivering of the Scottish people out of the hands of so cruel and bloody a tyrant as Macbeth by too many plain experiments[37] did show himself to be; which was an easy matter for him to bring to pass, considering not only the good title he had but also the earnest desire of the people to have some occasion ministered whereby they might be revenged of those notable injuries which they daily sustained by the outrageous cruelty of Macbeth's misgovernance. Though Malcolm was very sorrowful for the oppression of his countrymen the Scots, in manner as Macduff had declared, yet doubting[38] whether he were come as one that meant unfeignedly as he spoke or else as sent from Macbeth to betray him, he thought to have some further trial; and thereupon dissembling his mind at the first, he answered as followeth.

[**175**] "I am truly very sorry for the misery chanced to my country of Scotland, but though I have never so great affection to relieve the same, yet by reason of certain incurable vices which reign in me I am nothing meet thereto. First, such immoderate lust and voluptuous sensuality (the abominable fountain of all vices) followeth me that, if I were made King of Scots, I should seek to deflower your maids and matrons in such wise that mine intemperancy should be more importable[39] unto you than the bloody tyranny of Macbeth now is." Hereunto Macduff answered: "This surely is a very evil fault, for many noble princes and kings have lost both lives and kingdoms for the same; nevertheless there are women enough in Scotland, and therefore follow my counsel. Make thyself King, and I shall convey the matter so wisely that thou shalt be so satisfied at thy pleasure in such secret wise that no man shall be aware thereof."

Then said Malcolm: "I am also the most avaricious creature on the

[35]Villain's.
[36]Pity.
[37]Proofs.
[38]Mistrusting.
[39]Unendurable.

earth, so that if I were King, I should seek so many ways to get lands and goods that I would slay the most part of all the nobles of Scotland by surmised accusations, to the end I might enjoy their lands, goods, and possessions. . . . Therefore," saith Malcolm, "suffer me to remain where I am, lest if I attain to the regiment[40] of your realm, mine unquenchable avarice may prove such that ye would think the displeasures which now grieve you should seem easy in respect of the unmeasurable outrage which might ensue through my coming amongst you."

Macduff to this made answer how it was a far worse fault than the other. "For avarice is the root of all mischief, and for that crime the most part of our kings have been slain and brought to their final end. Yet notwithstanding, follow my counsel and take upon thee the crown. There is gold and riches enough in Scotland to satisfy thy greedy desire." Then said Malcolm again: "I am, furthermore, inclined to dissimulation, telling of leasings,[41] and all other kinds of deceit, so that I naturally rejoice in nothing so much as to betray and deceive such as put any trust or confidence in my words. Then, sith there is nothing that more becometh a prince than constancy, verity, truth, and justice, with the other laudable fellowship of those fair and noble virtues which are comprehended only in soothfastness,[42] and that lying utterly overthroweth the same, you see how unable I am to govern any province or region; and therefore, sith you have remedies to cloak and hide all the rest of my other vices, I pray you find shift to cloak this vice amongst the residue."

Then said Macduff: "This yet is the worst of all, and there I leave thee and therefore say: 'O ye unhappy and miserable Scottishmen, which are thus scourged with so many and sundry calamities, each one above other! Ye have one cursed and wicked tyrant that now reigneth over you without any right or title, oppressing you with his most bloody cruelty. This other, that hath the right to the crown, is so replete with the inconstant behavior and manifest vices of Englishmen that he is nothing worthy to enjoy it; for by his own confession he is not only avaricious and given to insatiable lust but so false a traitor withal[h] that no trust is to be had unto any word he speaketh. Adieu, Scotland, for now I account myself a banished man forever, without comfort or con-

[40]Rule.
[41]Lies.
[42]Truthfulness.
[h]Besides.

solation.' " And with those words the brackish tears trickled down his cheeks very abundantly.

At the last, when he was ready to depart, Malcolm took him by the sleeve and said: "Be of good comfort, Macduff, for I have none of these vices before remembered[43] but have jested with thee in this manner only to prove[44] thy mind; for divers times heretofore hath Macbeth sought by this manner of means to bring me into his hands, but the more slow I have showed myself to condescend to thy motion and request, the more diligence shall I use in accomplishing the same." Incontinently[45] hereupon they embraced each other, and, promising to be faithful the one to the other, they fell in consultation how they might best provide for all their business, to bring the same to good effect. Soon after, Macduff, repairing to the borders of Scotland, addressed his letters with secret dispatch unto the nobles of the realm, declaring how Malcolm was confederate with him to come hastily into Scotland to claim the crown; and therefore he required them, sith he was right inheritor thereto, to assist him with their powers to recover the same out of the hands of the wrongful usurper [**5.2**].

In the meantime, Malcolm purchased such favor at King Edward's hands that old Siward, Earl of Northumberland, was appointed with ten thousand men to go with him into Scotland, to support him in this enterprise for recovery of his right. After these news were spread abroad in Scotland, the nobles drew into two several factions, the one taking part with Macbeth and the other with Malcolm. Hereupon ensued oftentimes sundry bickerings and divers light skirmishes; for those that were of Malcolm's side would not jeopard to join with their enemies in a pitched field[46] till his coming out of England to their support. But after that Macbeth perceived his enemies' power to increase, by such aid as came to them forth of England with his adversary Malcolm, he recoiled back into Fife, there purposing to abide in camp fortified, at the castle of Dunsinane, and to fight with his enemies if they meant to pursue him [**5.3**]. Howbeit, some of his friends advised him that it should be best for him either to make some agreement with Malcolm or else to flee with all speed into the Isles; and to take his treasure with him, to the end he might wage[47] sundry great princes

[43]Mentioned.
[44]Test.
[45]Immediately.
[46]Battle.
[47]Engage.

of the realm to take his part, and retain strangers[48] in whom he might better trust than in his own subjects, which stole daily from him. But he had such confidence in his prophecies that he believed he should never be vanquished till Birnam Wood were brought to Dunsinane, nor yet to be slain with any man that should be or was borne of any woman.

[**176**] Malcolm, following hastily after Macbeth, came the night before the battle unto Birnam Wood; and when his army had rested awhile there to refresh them, he commanded every man to get a bough of some tree or other of that wood in his hand, as big as he might bear, and to march forth therewith in such wise that on the next morrow they might come closely and without sight in this manner within view of his enemies [**5.4**]. On the morrow, when Macbeth beheld them coming in this sort, he first marveled what the matter meant, but in the end remembered himself that the prophecy which he had heard long before that time, of the coming of Birnam Wood to Dunsinane Castle, was likely to be now fulfilled [**5.5**]. Nevertheless, he brought his men in order of battle and exhorted them to do valiantly. Howbeit, his enemies had scarcely cast from them their boughs, when Macbeth, perceiving their numbers, betook him straight to flight; whom Macduff pursued with great hatred even till he came unto Lunfannaine, where Macbeth, perceiving that Macduff was hard at his back, leapt beside his horse, saying: "Thou traitor, what meaneth it that thou shouldst thus in vain follow me that am not appointed to be slain by any creature that is borne of a woman? Come on, therefore, and receive thy reward which thou hast deserved for thy pains!" And therewithal he lifted up his sword, thinking to have slain him [**5.8**].

But Macduff, quickly avoiding[49] from his horse ere he came at him, answered (with his naked sword in his hand), saying: "It is true, Macbeth, and now shall thine insatiable cruelty have an end, for I am even he that thy wizards have told thee of, who was never borne of my mother but ripped out of her womb." Therewithal he stepped unto him and slew him in the place. Then, cutting his head from his shoulders, he set it upon a pole and brought it unto Malcolm. This was the end of Macbeth, after he had reigned seventeen years over the Scottishmen. In the beginning of his reign he accomplished many worthy acts, very profitable to the commonwealth (as ye have heard); but afterward, by illusion of the devil, he defamed the same with most terrible cruelty.

[48]Foreigners.
[49]Dismounting.

He was slain in the year of the Incarnation 1057, and in the sixteenth year of King Edward's reign over the Englishmen.

Malcolm Cammore thus recovering the realm (as ye have heard) by support of King Edward, in the sixteenth year of the same Edward's reign, he was crowned at Scone the twenty-fifth day of April in the year of our Lord 1057. Immediately after his coronation he called a parliament at Forfar, in the which he rewarded them with lands and livings that had assisted him against Macbeth, advancing them to fees and offices as he saw cause, and commanded that specially those that bore the surname of any offices or lands should have and enjoy the same. He created many earls, lords, barons, and knights. Many of them that before were thanes were at this time made earls, as Fife, Menteith, Atholl, Lennox, Murrey, Caithness, Ross, and Angus. These were the first earls that have been heard of amongst the Scottishmen (as their histories do make mention) [**5.8**]. Many new surnames were taken up at this time amongst them, as Cawdor, . . . Seyton, . . . with many other that had possessions given them which gave names to the owners for the time. Others got their surnames by offices, as Steward, Durward,[50] and Bannerman. Also the proper names of many valiant captains were turned into general surnames, as Kennedy, Graham, Hay, with divers other too long here to rehearse. So that it came to pass then, as it hath done many times since, that new surnames have worn the old out of use. . . .

[**180**] This Donald Bane, who (as before is mentioned) fled into the Isles to eschew the tyrannical malice of Macbeth, after he once heard that his brother King Malcolm was dead, returned into Scotland by support of the King of Norway, unto whom he covenanted to give the dominion of all the Isles if by his means and furtherance he might obtain the crown of Scotland. Hereupon landing with an army in the realm, he found small resistance and so with little ado received the crown. For many of the people, abhorring the riotous manners and superfluous gormandizing brought in among them by the Englishmen, were willing enough to receive this Donald for their King, trusting (because he had been brought up in the Isles, with the old customs and manners of their ancient nation, without taste of the English lickerous delicates)[51] they should by his severe order in government recover again the former temperance of their old progenitors [**5.3**].

[50]Doorward, gatekeeper.
[51]Wanton pleasures.

★ ★ ★

[**192**][52] About the thirteenth year [1054] of King Edward [the Confessor] his reign (as some write), or rather about the nineteenth or twentieth year, as should appear by the Scottish writers, Siward the noble Earl of Northumberland, with a great power of horsemen, went into Scotland and, in battle, put to flight Macbeth, that had usurped the crown of Scotland; and, that done, placed Malcolm surnamed Cammore, the son of Duncan sometime[53] King of Scotland, in the government of that realm; who afterward slew the said Macbeth and then reigned in quiet [**5.4**]. . . .

It is recorded also that, in the foresaid battle in which Earl Siward vanquished the Scots, one of Siward's sons chanced to be slain [**5.7**]; whereof, although the father had good cause to be sorrowful, yet when he heard that he died of a wound which he had received in fighting stoutly, in the forepart of his body, and that with his face toward the enemy, he greatly rejoiced thereat, to hear that he died so manfully [**5.8**].

[**195**] . . . As hath been thought, he [King Edward] was inspired with the gift of prophecy, and also to have had the gift of healing infirmities and diseases [**4.3**]. He used to help those that were vexed with the disease commonly called the King's Evil,[54] and left that virtue as it were a portion of inheritance unto his successors the kings of this realm.

[52]Vol. 1, *History of England.*
[53]Formerly.
[54]Scrofula.

King John

[**122**][1] Now to return [1190] unto the King [Richard the First], who in this meantime was very busy to provide all things necessary to set forward on his journey [to the Holy Land]. His ships which lay in the mouth of the river of Seine being ready to put off, he took order in many points concerning the state of the commonwealth on that side; and chiefly he called to mind that it should be a thing necessary for him to name who should succeed him in the kingdom of England if his chance should not be to return again from so long and dangerous a journey. He therefore named (as some suppose) his nephew Arthur, the son of his brother Geoffrey Duke of Brittany, to be his successor in the kingdom [**1.1.9**], a young man of a likely proof and princely towardness but not ordained by God to succeed over this kingdom. . . .

[**137**] In the meanwhile the French King [Philip the Second], being advertised that King Richard was detained as prisoner [in Austria], rejoiced not a little thereat, and with all speed by secret messages did send for his brother Earl John, who was ready to come at his call [1193]. And being come, he exhorted him not to suffer so convenient an occasion to pass, but to take the government of the realm of England now into his hands, promising him all such aid as he could of him reasonably require, with other like talk still tending to the provocation of the Earl to forsake his allegiance unto his brother. And to say the truth, Earl John was easily persuaded so to do.

[**146**] . . . Then was a motion made for peace betwixt the two Kings [Richard and Philip], being now wearied with long wars [1195]; whereof when Earl John was advertised, who (as it should seem by some writers), having tarried with the French King till this present, began now to doubt[2] lest if any agreement were made he might haply be betrayed of the French King by covenants that should pass betwixt them. He determined therefore with himself to commit his whole safety to his natural brother and to no man else, perceiving that the French King

[1]Vol. 3, *History of England.*
[2]Fear.

made not so great account of him after the loss of his castles in England as he had done before. . . .

[**147**] But by some writers it should appear that Earl John, immediately upon conclusion of the first truce, came from the French King and submitted himself to his brother, and, by mediation of the Queen their mother [Eleanor of Aquitaine], was pardoned, received again into favor, and served ever after against the French King very dutifully, seeking by new-achieved enterprises brought about (to the contentation of his brother) to make a recompense for his former misdemeanor, reputing it mere madness to make means to further mischief. . . .

[**150**] About this time also [1196], as [Constance] the Countess of Brittany, the mother of Duke Arthur, came into Normandy to have spoken with King Richard, Ranulph Earl of Chester her husband, meeting her at Pontorson, took her as prisoner and shut her up within his castle at Saint James de Beumeron. And when her son Arthur could not find means to deliver her out of captivity, he joined with the King of France and made great havoc in the lands of his uncle King Richard; whereupon the King gathered a mighty army and, invading Brittany with great force, cruelly wasted and destroyed the country. . . .

[**155**] In this meantime King Richard, being now at rest from troubles of war, studied busily to provide money, meaning to make a new voyage into the Holy Land. . . .

After this, he determined to chastise certain persons in Poitou which, during the wars betwixt him and the French King, had aided the Frenchmen against him; whereupon with an army he passed forth toward them [1199]. But by the way he was informed that one Widomar, a viscount [of Limoges] in the country of Brittany,[a] had found great treasure; and therefore, pretending[3] a right thereto by virtue of his prerogative, he sent for the Viscount, who, smelling out the matter and supposing the King would not be indifferent[4] in parting[5] the treasure, fled into Limousin, where, although the people were tributaries to the King of England, yet they took part with the French King.

There is a town in that country called Châlus Cheverel into which the said Viscount retired for safeguard of himself, and then gave the townsmen a great portion of treasure to the end they should defend him and his quarrel[6] for the rest. King Richard, still following him, as one

[a]The Limousin.
[3]Claiming.
[4]Impartial.
[5]Dividing.
[6]Cause.

that could not avoid his fatal ordinance, hasted into the confines of Limousin, fully determining either to win the town by force, if the inhabitants should make resistance, or, at leastwise, to get into his hands the prey[7] which he so earnestly pursued. At his first approach he gave many fierce assaults to the town, but they within, having thoroughly provided aforehand for to defend a siege, so resisted his attempts that within three days after his coming he ceased to assail the town, meaning to undermine the walls; which otherwise he perceived would very hardly be gotten, considering the stoutness[8] of them within and, withal,[9] the natural strength and situation of the place itself.

Hereupon, therefore, on the twenty-sixth of March [1199], whiles he, together with Captain Mercadier, went about unadvisedly to view the town (the better to consider the place which way he might convey the course of his mine), they came so far within danger that the King was stricken in the left arm or (as some write) in the shoulder, where it joined to the neck, with a quarrel[10] envenomed (as is to be supposed by the sequel). Being thus wounded, he got to his horse and rode home again to his lodging, where he caused the wound to be searched and bound up, and, as a man nothing dismayed therewith, continued his siege with such force and assurance that within twelve days after the mishap the town was yielded unto him, although very little treasure (to make any great account of) was at that time found therein.

In this mean season the King had committed the cure of his wound to one of Mercadier his surgeons, who, taking in hand to pluck out the quarrel, drew forth only the shaft at the first and left the iron still within; and afterward, going about most unskillfully to get forth the head of the said quarrel, he used such incisions and so mangled the King's arm, ere he could cut it, that he himself despaired of all help and longer life, affirming flatly to such as stood about him that he could not long continue by reason of his butcherly handling. To be short, feeling himself to wax weaker and weaker, preparing his mind to death which he perceived now to be at hand, he ordained his testament or rather reformed and added sundry things unto the same which he before had made at the time of his going forth toward the Holy Land.

[**156**] Unto his brother John he assigned the crown of England and

[7]Booty.
[8]Bravery.
[9]Besides.
[10]Crossbow arrow.

all other his lands and dominions [**2.1.192**], causing the nobles there present to swear fealty unto him. . . .

At length King Richard, by force of sickness (increased with anguish of his incurable wound), departed this life on the Tuesday before Palm Sunday, being the ninth[b] of April and the eleventh day after he was hurt, in the year after the birth of our Saviour 1199, in the forty-fourth year of his age and after he had reigned nine years, nine months, and odd days. He left no[11] issue behind him. He was tall of stature and well proportioned, fair and comely of face, so as in his countenance appeared much favor and gravity, of hair bright auburn, as it were betwixt red and yellow, with long arms and nimble in all his joints; his thighs and legs were of due proportion and answerable to the other parts of his body.

As he was comely of personage, so was he of stomach[12] more courageous and fierce, so that not without cause he obtained the surname of Coeur-de-lion, that is to say the Lion's-heart. Moreover, he was courteous to his soldiers, and toward his friends and strangers[13] that resorted unto him very liberal; but to his enemies hard and not to be entreated, desirous of battle, an enemy to rest and quietness, very eloquent of speech and wise, but ready to enter into jeopardies, and that without fear or forecast in time of greatest perils. . . .

[**157**] John, the youngest son of Henry the Second, was proclaimed King of England, beginning his reign the sixth day of April in the year of our Lord 1199, the first of Philip Emperor of Rome, and the twentieth of Philip King of France, King William as yet living in government over the Scots. This man, so soon as his brother Richard was deceased, sent Hubert Archbishop of Canterbury and William Marshall Earl of Striguil (otherwise called Chepstow) into England, both to proclaim him king and also to see his peace kept, together with Geoffrey Fitzpeter Lord Chief Justice and divers other barons of the realm, whilst he himself went to Chinon, where his brother's treasure lay; which was forthwith delivered unto him by Robert de Turnham, and therewithal the castles of Chinon and Saumur and divers other places which were in the custody of the foresaid Robert. But Thomas de Furness, nephew to the said Robert de Turnham, delivered the city and castle of Angiers

[b]Sixth.
[11]*I.e.,* no legitimate.
[12]Disposition.
[13]Foreigners.

unto Arthur Duke of Brittany. For by general consent of the nobles and peers of the countries of Anjou, Maine, and Touraine, Arthur was received as the liege and sovereign lord of the same countries [**1.1.11**].

For even at this present, and so soon as it was known that King Richard was deceased, divers cities and towns on that side of the sea,[14] belonging to the said Richard whilst he lived, fell at odds among themselves, some of them endeavoring to prefer King John, other laboring rather to be under the governance of Arthur Duke of Brittany, considering that he seemed by most right to be their chief lord, forsomuch as he was son to Geoffrey elder brother to John. And thus began the broil in those quarters whereof in process of time ensued great inconvenience[15] and finally the death of the said Arthur, as shall be showed hereafter.

Now whilst King John was thus occupied in recovering his brother's treasure and travailing with his subjects to reduce them to his obedience, Queen Eleanor his mother, by the help of Hubert Archbishop of Canterbury and other of the noblemen and barons of the land, travailed as diligently to procure the English people to receive their oath of allegiance to be true to King John.

[**158**] . . . And all this was done chiefly by the working of the King's mother, whom the nobility much honored and loved. For she, being bent to prefer her son John, left no stone unturned to establish him in the throne, comparing oftentimes the difference of government between a king that is a man and a king that is but a child. For as John was thirty-two years old, so Arthur Duke of Brittany was but a babe to speak of.[16] In the end, winning all the nobility wholly unto her will and seeing the coast to be clear on every side without any doubt[17] of tempestuous weather likely to arise, she signified the whole matter unto King John, who forthwith framed all his endeavors to the accomplishment of his business.

Surely Queen Eleanor the King's mother was sore against her nephew Arthur, rather moved thereto by envy conceived against his mother than upon any just occasion given in the behalf of the child, for that she saw, if he were King, how his mother Constance would look to bear most rule within the realm of England till her son should come to lawful age to govern of himself [**32, 2.1.123**]. So hard it is to bring women to agree

[14]The English Channel.
[15]Misfortune.
[16]Aged eleven at the time of Richard's death.
[17]Fear.

in one mind, their natures commonly being so contrary, their words so variable, and their deeds so indiscreet. . . .

When this doing of the Queen was signified unto the said Constance, she, doubting the surety of her son, committed him to the trust of the French King, who, receiving him into his tuition,[18] promised to defend him from all his enemies and forthwith furnished the holds[19] in Brittany with French soldiers. . . .

After this, King John, entering into Anjou, held his Easter at Beaufort (which feast fell that year the eighteenth day of April); and from thence he went straight unto Rouen, where, on the Sunday next after Easter, being Saint Mark's Day, he was girded with the sword of the duchy of Normandy, in the high church there, by the hands of Walter Archbishop of Rouen; and so, being invested Duke of Normandy, received the oath, according to the custom, that he should defend the Church and maintain the liberties thereof, see justice ministered, good laws put in execution, and naughty[20] laws and orders abolished. In the meantime his mother Queen Eleanor, together with Captain Mercadier, entered into Anjou and wasted the same because they of that country had received Arthur for their sovereign lord and Governor. And amongst other towns and fortresses they took the city of Angiers, slew many of the citizens, and committed the rest to prison [**2.1**].

This enterprise being thus luckily achieved, the residue of the people in those parties were put in such fear that, of their own accord, they turned to their wonted obedience, seeming as though they would continue still therein. The French King, all this while conceiving another exploit in his head more commodious[21] [**573**] unto him than as yet to attempt war against the Englishmen upon so light an occasion, dissembled the matter for a time, as though he would know nothing of all that was done, till the King should be otherwise occupied in England about his coronation.

In the mean season King John, having set some stay in his business on the further side of the sea, he left his mother still in Guienne to defend that country against the enemies and, taking the sea, came over himself into England, landing at Shoreham the twenty-fifth day of May [1199]. On the next day, being Ascension Eve, he came to London, there to receive the crown. . . .

[18]Guardianship.
[19]Forts.
[20]Evil.
[21]Profitable.

[**160**] Whilst these things were adoing in England, Philip King of France, having levied an army, broke into Normandy and took the city of Évreux, the town of Arques, and divers other places from the English. And passing from thence into Maine, he recovered that country, lately before through fear alienated. In another part, an army of Bretons with great diligence won the towns of Gournay, Boteavant, and Gensolin, and, following the victory, took the city of Angiers, which King John had won from Duke Arthur in the last year passed. These things being signified to King John, he thought to make provision for the recovery of his losses there with all speed possible. . . .

About the same time, King Philip made Arthur Duke of Brittany knight, and received of him his homage for Anjou, Poitiers, Maine, Touraine, and Brittany. Also, somewhat before the time that the truce should expire, to wit on the morrow after the feast of the Assumption of our Lady and also the day next following, the two Kings talked by commissioners in a place betwixt the towns of Boteavant and Le Goulet. Within three days after, they came together personally and commoned[22] at full of the variance depending between them. But the French King showed himself stiff and hard in this treaty, demanding the whole country of Veulquessin to be restored unto him as that which had been granted by Geoffrey Earl of Anjou, the father of King Henry the Second, unto Louis le Gros to have his aid then against King Stephen. Moreover, he demanded that Poitiers, Anjou, Maine, and Touraine should be delivered and wholly resigned unto Arthur Duke of Brittany [**152**].

But these and divers other requests which he made, King John would not in any wise grant[23] unto, and so they departed without conclusion of any agreement. Therefore divers earls and barons of France which before that time had served King Richard repaired unto King John and took an oath to assist him and not to agree with the French King without his consent, and he likewise swore unto them not to make peace with the French King except they were therein comprised.

. . . The same year [1199], Philip, bastard son to King Richard, to whom his father had given the castle and honor[24] of Cognac, killed the Viscount of Limoges [**3.2.3**] in revenge of his father's death, who was slain, as ye have heard, in besieging the castle of Châlus Cheverel. . . .

[**161**] King John also came over from Normandy into England and there levied a subsidy, taking of every ploughland three shillings. In the

[22]Conferred.
[23]Consent.
[24]Lordship.

Lent following [1200] he went to York in hope to have met the King of Scots there, but he came not; and so King John returned back and sailed again into Normandy because the variance still depended between him and the King of France. Finally, upon the Ascension Day in this second year of his reign [1200], they came eftsoons[25] to a communication betwixt the towns of Vernon and L'Isle d'Andely, where finally they concluded an agreement, with a marriage to be had betwixt Louis, the son of King Philip, and the Lady Blanch, daughter to Alfonso King of Castile, the eighth of that name, and niece to King John by his sister Eleanor [**2.1.423**].

In consideration whereof, King John, besides the sum of thirty thousand marks in silver as in respect of dowry assigned to his said niece, resigned his title to the city of Évreux and also unto all those towns which the French King had by war taken from him [**486, 527**], the city of Angiers only excepted, which city he received again by covenants of the same agreement. The French King restored also to King John, as Ralph Niger writeth, the city of Tours and all the castles and fortresses which he had taken within Touraine, and, moreover, received of King John his homage for all the lands, fees, and tenements which at any time his brother King Richard or his father King Henry had holden of him the said King Louis or any his predecessors, the quitclaims[26] and marriages always excepted. The King of England likewise did homage unto the French King for Brittany and again, as after you shall hear, received homage for the same country and for the county of Richmond of his nephew Arthur [**552**]. He also gave the earldom of Gloucester unto the Earl of Évreux, as it were by way of exchange for that he resigned to the French King all right, title, and claim that might be pretended to the county of Évreux.

By this conclusion of marriage betwixt the said Louis and Blanch, the right of King John went away which he lawfully before pretended unto the city of Évreux and unto those towns in the confines of Berry, Château Roux or Raoul, Cressy, and Issoudun, and likewise unto the country of Vexin or Veulquessin which is a part of the territory of Gisors, the right of all which lands, towns, and countries was released to the King of France by King John, who supposed that by his affinity and resignation of his right to those places the peace now made would have continued forever. And in consideration thereof, he procured fur-

[25]Again.
[26]Releases.

thermore that the foresaid Blanch should be conveyed into France to her husband with all speed. That done, he returned into England.

[**162**] . . . About the same time [1200], King John and Philip King of France met together near the town of Vernon, where Arthur Duke of Brittany, as vassal to his uncle King John, did his homage unto him for the duchy of Brittany and those other places which he held of him on this side and beyond the river of Loire; and afterward, still mistrusting his uncle's courtesy, he returned back again with the French King and would not commit himself to his said uncle, who, as he supposed, did bear him little good will. . . .

[**163**] Ye have heard how King John had conceived no small displeasure against the Monks of the White Order[27] for that they would not part with any money [**1.1.48**], excusing themselves that they might not do it without consent of a general chapter[28] of their order. Whereupon the King had caused them divers ways to be molested, but chiefly in restraining them of liberty to have any horses or other cattle going to pasture within his forests. . . .

About the month of December [1200] there were seen in the province of York five moons, one in the east, the second in the west, the third in the north, the fourth in the south, and the fifth as it were set in the midst of the other, having many stars about it [**4.2.182**]; and went five or six times encompassing the other as it were the space of one hour and shortly after vanished away. . . .

[**164**] Queen Eleanor, that was Regent in those parties, being put in great fear with the news of this sudden stir, got her into Mirebeau, a strong town situate in the country of Anjou, and forthwith dispatched a messenger with letters unto King John requiring him of[29] speedy succor in this her present danger [1202]. In the meantime Arthur, following the victory, shortly after followed her and won Mirebeau, where he took his grandmother [**3.2.6**] within the same, whom he yet entreated[30] very honorably and with great reverence, as some have reported. But other write (far more truly) that she was not taken but escaped into a tower within the which she was straitly[31] besieged. Thither came also to aid Arthur all the nobles and men-of-arms in Poitou, and namely[32] the fore-

[27]Cistercians.
[28]Assembly.
[29]*I.e.,* of him.
[30]Treated.
[31]Closely.
[32]Particularly.

said Earl of March, according to appointment betwixt them, so that by this means Arthur had a great army together in the field.

King John, in the meantime, having received his mother's letters and understanding thereby in what danger she stood, was marvelously troubled with the strangeness of the news and, with many bitter words, accused the French King as an untrue prince and a fraudulent league-breaker, and in all possible haste speeded him forth, continuing his journey for the most part both day and night to come to the succor of his people. To be brief, he used such diligence that he was upon his enemies' necks ere they could understand anything of his coming or guess what the matter meant when they saw such a company of soldiers as he brought with him to approach so near the city [**2.1.79**]. For so negligent were they that, having once won the town, they ranged abroad over the country hither and thither at their liberty without any care. So that now, being put in a sudden fear as prevented[33] by the hasty coming of the enemies upon them, and wanting leisure to take advice what was best to be done, and having not time in manner to get any armor on their backs, they were in a marvelous trouble, not knowing whether it were best for them to fight or to flee, to yield or to resist.

This their fear being apparent to the Englishmen (by their disorder showed in running up and down from place to place with great noise and turmoil), they set upon them with great violence and, compassing them round about, they either took or slew them in a manner at their pleasure. And having thus put them all to flight, they pursued the chase toward the town of Mirebeau, into which the enemies made very great haste to enter; but such speed was used by the English soldiers at that present that they entered and won the said town before their enemies could come near to get into it. Great slaughter was made within Mirebeau itself, and Arthur, with the residue of the army that escaped with life from the first bickering, was taken [**3.2.5**]; who, being hereupon committed to prison, first at Falaise and after within the city of Rouen, lived not long after, as you shall hear. The other of the prisoners were also committed unto safe keeping, some into castles within Normandy and some were sent into England. . . .

[**165**] The French King, at the same time lying in siege before Arques, immediately upon the news of this overthrow raised from thence and returned homeward, destroying all that came in his way till he was entered into his own country. It is said that King John caused his

[33]Confronted.

nephew Arthur to be brought before him at Falaise and there went about to persuade him all that he could to forsake his friendship and alliance with the French King and to lean and stick to him, being his natural uncle [**2.1.156, 3.3.2**]. But Arthur, like one that wanted good counsel and abounding too much in his own willful opinion, made a presumptuous answer, not only denying so to do but also commanding King John to restore unto him the realm of England, with all those other lands and possessions which King Richard had in his hand at the hour of his death. For sith the same appertained to him by right of inheritance, he assured him, except restitution were made the sooner, he should not long continue quiet [**2.1.165**]. King John, being sore moved with such words thus uttered by his nephew, appointed, as before is said, that he should be straitly kept in prison, as first in Falaise and after at Rouen within the new castle there. Thus, by means of this good success the countries of Poitou, Touraine, and Anjou were recovered.

Shortly after, King John, coming over into England, caused himself to be crowned again [**4.2.1**] at Canterbury by the hands of Hubert the Archbishop there on the fourteenth day of April [1202], and then went back again into Normandy, where immediately upon his arrival a rumor was spread through all France of the death of his nephew Arthur. True it is that great suit was made to have Arthur set at liberty, as well by the French King as by William de Riches a valiant baron of Poitou and divers other noblemen of the Bretons, who, when they could not prevail in their suit, they banded themselves together and, joining in confederacy with Robert Earl of Alençon, the Viscount Beaumont, William de Fulgiers, and other, they began to levy sharp wars against King John in divers places insomuch, as it was thought, that so long as Arthur lived there would be no quiet in those parts [**3.4.131**]. Whereupon it was reported that King John, through persuasion of his counselors, appointed certain persons to go unto Falaise, where Arthur was kept in prison under the charge of Hubert de Burgh, and there to put out the young gentleman's eyes.

But through such resistance as he made against one of the tormentors[34] that came to execute the King's commandment (for the other rather forsook their prince and country than they would consent to obey the King's authority herein [**4.1.6, 86**]) and such lamentable words as he uttered, Hubert de Burgh did preserve him from that injury, not doubting but rather to have thanks than displeasure at the King's

[34]Executioners.

hands for delivering him of such infamy as would have redounded unto his highness if the young gentleman had been so cruelly dealt withal. For he considered that King John had resolved upon this point only in his heat and fury (which moveth men to undertake many an inconvenient[35] enterprise unbeseeming the person of a common man, much more reproachful to a prince, all men in that mood being mere[36] foolish and furious and prone to accomplish the perverse conceits of their ill-possessed hearts . . .); and that afterward, upon better advisement, he would both repent himself so to have commanded and give them small thank that should see it put in execution [**4.2.205**]. Howbeit, to satisfy his mind for the time and to stay the rage of the Bretons, he caused it to be bruited abroad through the country that the King's commandment was fulfilled and that Arthur also through sorrow and grief was departed out of this life [**4.1.128**]. For the space of fifteen days this rumor incessantly ran through both the realms of England and France [**4.2.187**], and there was ringing for him through towns and villages as it had been for his funerals. It was also bruited that his body was buried in the monastery of Saint Andrew's of the Cîteaux order.

But when the Bretons were nothing pacified but rather kindled more vehemently to work all the mischief they could devise in revenge of their sovereign's death, there was no remedy but to signify abroad again that Arthur was as yet living and in health [**251**]. Now when the King heard the truth of all this matter, he was nothing displeased for that his commandment was not executed, sith there were divers of his captains which uttered in plain words that he should not find knights to keep his castles if he dealt so cruelly with his nephew. For if it chanced any of them to be taken by the King of France or other their adversaries, they should be sure to taste of the like cup. But now touching the manner in very deed of the end of this Arthur, writers make sundry reports. Nevertheless, certain it is that, in the year next ensuing [1203], he was removed from Falaise unto the castle or tower of Rouen out of the which there was not any that would confess that ever he saw him go alive. Some have written that as he assayed to have escaped out of prison and proving[37] to climb over the walls of the castle, he fell into the river of Seine and so was drowned [**4.3.1**]. Other write that through very grief and languor he pined away and died of natural sickness. But some affirm that King John secretly caused him to be murdered and made away, so

[35]Morally unsuitable.
[36]Entirely.
[37]Attempting.

as it is not thoroughly agreed upon in what sort he finished his days; but verily King John was had in great suspicion, whether worthily or not the Lord knoweth.

[**167**] . . . Thus Normandy, which King Rollo had purchased[38] and gotten three hundred and sixteen years before that present time, was then recovered by the Frenchmen, to the great reproach and dishonor of the English, in this year 1204. About this time Queen Eleanor the mother of King John departed this life [**4.2.120**], consumed rather through sorrow and anguish of mind than of any other natural infirmity. . . .

[**169**] The thirteenth of July [1205] Hubert Archbishop of Canterbury departed this life at Tenham, the King not being greatly sorry for his death (as some have written) because he gathered some suspicion that he bore too much good will toward the French King. . . .

After his decease the monks of Canterbury, without knowledge of the King, chose one Reginald the subprior of their house to be their archbishop; who secretly went to Rome to obtain his confirmation of the Pope. Which thing bred much mischief and great discord betwixt Pope Innocent [the Third] and King John, since the Pope would not confirm the election (because he saw some piece of secret practice) till he might understand and be certified by report of sufficient witness (for that he wanted the letters commendatory from the King) that the same election was lawful and orderly made. Of this delay also the monks being speedily advertised, and to the end they might now recover the King's favor whom they had very sore offended in not making him privy to the first election, they made request unto him that by his nomination it might be lawful for them to choose another archbishop.

The King gladly hereunto assented, requiring them to grant their voices unto John Grey the Bishop of Norwich, being both his chaplain and president of his Council. The monks, to gratify the King, obeyed his request; and so, electing the same Bishop of Norwich, they sent their procurators to Rome in the year following [1206] to signify the same unto the Pope and to require him to confirm this their second election, as unmindful of their first and clearly annihilating[39] the same to all intents and purposes. . . .

[**170**] King John also in this meanwhile, moved with the increase of these his new associates and also with desire to revenge so many injuries and losses sustained at the French King's hands, preparing an army of

[38]Acquired by conquest.
[39]Nullifying.

men and a navy of ships, took the sea with them and landed at Rochelle the ninth of July [1206], where he was received with great joy and gladness of the people; and no small number of gentlemen and others that inhabited thereabout repaired unto him, offering to aid him to the uttermost of their powers. He therefore, with assured hope of good speed,[40] departed from thence and won the town of Montauban, with a great part of all the country thereabouts. Finally he entered into Anjou and, coming to the city of Angiers, appointed certain bands of his footmen and all his light horsemen to compass the town about, whilst he with the residue of the footmen and all the men-of-arms did go to assault the gates. Which enterprise with fire and sword he so manfully executed that, the gates being in a moment broken open, the city was entered and delivered to the soldiers for a prey. So that of the citizens some were taken, some killed, and the walls of the city beaten flat to the ground [**2.1.399**]. . . .

In this meanwhile the strife depended still in the court of Rome betwixt the two elected Archbishops of Canterbury, Reginald and John. But after the Pope was fully informed of the manner of their elections, he disannulled them both and procured by his papal authority the monks of Canterbury, of whom many were then come to Rome about that matter, to choose one Stephen Langton [**3.1.143**] the Cardinal of Saint Chrysogonus, an Englishman born and of good estimation and learning in the court of Rome, to be their Archbishop [1207].

[**171**] . . . The monks, doubting to offend the Pope, consented all of them to gratify him, except Elias de Brantfield, who refused. And so the foresaid Stephen Langton, being elected of them, was confirmed of the Pope, who signified by letters the whole state thereof to King John, commending the said Stephen as Archbishop unto him.

The King, sore offended in his mind that the Bishop of Norwich was thus put beside that dignity to the which he had advanced him, caused forthwith all the goods of the monks of Canterbury to be confiscate to his use and after banished them the realm, as well I mean those at home as those that were at Rome, and herewith wrote his letters unto the Pope, giving him to understand for answer that he would never consent that Stephen, which had been brought up and always conversant with his enemies the Frenchmen, should now enjoy the rule of the bishopric and diocese of Canterbury. Moreover, he declared in the same letters that he marveled not a little what the Pope meant in that he did not

[40]Success.

consider how necessary the friendship of the King of England was to the see of Rome sith there came more gains to the Roman Church out of that kingdom than out of any other realm on this side the mountains.[41] He added hereto that for the liberties of his crown he would stand to the death if the matter so required. And as for the election of the Bishop of Norwich unto the see of Canterbury, sith it was profitable to him and to his realm, he meant not to release it. . . .

Also, upon the first of October [1207] Henry, the son of King John begotten of his wife Queen Isabel, was born at Winchester; who after succeeded his father in the kingdom. But now again to our purpose. The Pope, perceiving that King John continued still in his former mind, which he called obstinacy, sent over his bulls into England directed to William Bishop of London, to Eustace Bishop of Ely, and to Mauger Bishop of Worcester, commanding them that, unless King John would suffer peaceably the Archbishop of Canterbury to occupy his see and his monks their abbey, they should put both him and his land under the sentence of interdiction, denouncing him and his land plainly accursed [1208]. . . .

[**172**] These Bishops, with other to them associate, made instant request and suit to the King for the observing of the Pope's commandment, and to eschew the censures of the Church; but that was in vain, for the King in a great rage swore that if either they or any other presumed to put his land under interdiction, he would incontinently[42] thereupon send all the prelates within the realm out of the same unto the Pope and seize all their goods unto his own use. And further he added that what Romans soever he found within the precinct of any his dominions, he would put out their eyes and slit their noses, and so send them packing to Rome that by such marks they might be known from all other nations of the world. And herewith he commanded the bishops to pack out of his sight if they loved their own health and preservation.

Hereupon the said Bishops departed and, according to the Pope's commission to them sent, upon the eve of the Annunciation of our Lady, denounced both the King and the realm of England accursed; and, furthermore, caused the doors of churches to be closed up and all other places where divine service was accustomed to be used, first at London and after in all other places where they came. . . .

The King, taking this matter in very great displeasure, seized upon all their temporalties and converted the same to his use, and persecuted

[41] The Alps.
[42] Immediately.

such other of the prelacy as he knew to favor their doings, banishing them the realm and seizing their goods also into his hands. . . .

The King also, doubting lest the Pope should proceed further and absolve all his subjects of their allegiance which they ought to him and that his lords would haply revolt and forsake him in this his trouble, took hostages of them whom he most suspected. . . .

[**173**] There lived in those days [1209] a divine named Alexander Cementarius, surnamed Theologus, who by his preaching incensed the King greatly unto all cruelty (as the monks and friars say) against his subjects, affirming that the general scourge wherewith the people were afflicted chanced not through the Prince's fault but for the wickedness of his people, for the King was but the rod of the Lord's wrath, and to this end a prince was ordained that he might rule the people with a rod of iron and break them as an earthen vessel, to chain the mighty in fetters and the noblemen in iron manacles [**155**]. He did see (as it should seem) the evil-disposed humors[43] of the people concerning their dutiful obedience which they ought to have borne to their natural prince King John; and therefore, as a doctrine most necessary in that dangerous time, he taught the people how they were by God's laws bound in duty to obey their lawful prince, and not through any wicked persuasion of busy heads and lewd[44] discoursers to be carried away to forget their loyal allegiance, and so to fall into the damnable sink of rebellion.

[**174**] He went about also to prove, with likely arguments, that it appertained not to the Pope to have to do concerning the temporal possessions of any kings or other potentates touching the rule and government of their subjects [**153**], sith no power was granted to Peter (the special and chief of the apostles of the Lord) but only touching the Church and matters appertaining thereunto. By such doctrine, of him set forth, he won in such wise the King's favor that he obtained many great preferments at the King's hands and was Abbot of Saint Austin's in Canterbury.

. . . In the same year also [1211], the Pope sent two legates into England, the one named Pandulph a lawyer and the other Durant a Templar, who coming unto King John exhorted him with many terrible words to leave his stubborn disobedience to the Church and to reform his misdoings [**137**]. The King for his part quietly heard them and, bringing them to Northampton, being not far distant from the place where he met them upon his return forth of Wales, had much confer-

[43]Whims.
[44]Wicked.

ence with them; but at length, when they perceived that they could not have their purpose, neither for restitution of the goods belonging to priests which he had seized upon, neither of those that appertained to certain other persons which the King had gotten also into his hands by means of the controversy betwixt him and the Pope, the legates departed, leaving him accursed and the land interdicted, as they found it at their coming [**172**].

[**175**] Touching the manner of this interdiction there have been divers opinions. Some have said that the land was interdicted thoroughly and the churches and houses of religion closed up, that nowhere was any divine service used. But it was not so strait,[45] for there were divers places occupied with divine service all that time, by certain privileges purchased either then or before. Children were also christened, and men houseled[46] and anoiled,[47] through all the land, except such as were in the bill of excommunication by name expressed. . . .

In the meantime Pope Innocent, after the return of his legates out of England, perceiving that King John would not be ordered by him, determined, with the consent of his cardinals and other counselors and also at the instant[48] suit of the English bishops and other prelates being there with him, to deprive King John of his kingly state; and so [1212] first absolved all his subjects and vassals of their oaths of allegiance made unto the same King, and after deprived him by solemn protestation of his kingly administration and dignity, and lastly signified that his deprivation unto the French King and other Christian princes, admonishing them to pursue King John, being thus deprived, forsaken, and condemned, as a common enemy to God and His church [**191**]. He ordained furthermore that whosoever employed goods or other aid to vanquish and overcome that disobedient prince should remain in assured peace of the Church as well as those which went to visit the sepulcher of our Lord, not only in their goods and persons, but also in suffrages[49] for saving of their souls.

But yet, that it might appear to all men that nothing could be more joyful unto his Holiness than to have King John to repent his trespasses committed and to ask forgiveness for the same, he appointed Pandulph, which lately before was returned to Rome with a great number of Eng-

[45] Severe.
[46] Given the sacrament.
[47] Given extreme unction.
[48] Urgent.
[49] Intercessory prayers.

lish exiles, to go into France, together with Stephen the Archbishop of Canterbury and the other English bishops, giving him in commandment that, repairing unto the French King, he should communicate with him all that which he had appointed to be done against King John, and to exhort the French King to make war upon him as a person for his wickedness excommunicated [**117**]. . . .

[**176**] Ye shall understand the French King, being requested by Pandulph the Pope's legate to take the war in hand against King John, was easily persuaded thereto of an inward hatred that he bore unto our King, and thereupon with all diligence made his provision of men, ships, munition, and victual in purpose to pass over into England [**4.2.110**]; and now was his navy ready rigged at the mouth of Seine, and he in greatest forwardness to take his journey. When[50] Pandulph, upon good considerations, thought first to go eftsoons,[51] or at the least wise to send into England before the French army should land there, and to assay once again if he might induce the King to show himself reformable unto the Pope's pleasure. King John, having knowledge of the French King's purpose and ordinance, assembled his people [**5.1.73**] and lodged with them alongst by the coast toward France, that he might resist his enemies and keep them off from landing. . . .

But as he lay thus ready near to the coast to withstand and beat back his enemies, there arrived at Dover two Templars, who, coming before the King, declared unto him that they were sent from Pandulph the Pope's legate, who for his profit coveted to talk with him, for he had, as they affirmed, means to propone[52] whereby he might be reconciled both to God and His church although he were adjudged in the court of Rome to have forfeited all the right which he had to his kingdom.

[**177**] The King, understanding the meaning of the messengers, sent them back again to bring over the legate, who incontinently came over to Dover; of whose arrival when the King was advertised, he went thither and received him with all due honor and reverence [1213]. Now after they had talked together a little and courteously saluted each other as the course of humanity required, the legate, as it is reported, uttered these words following. . . .

"I do not think that you are ignorant how Pope Innocent, to do that which to his duty appertaineth, hath both absolved your subjects of that oath which they made unto you at the beginning, and also taken

[50] At which time.
[51] Again.
[52] Propose.

from you the governance of England according to your deserts, and finally given commandment unto certain princes of Christendom to expel you out of this kingdom and to place another in your room, so worthily to punish you for your disobedience and contempt of religion; and that Philip King of France, with the first being ready to accomplish the Pope's commandment, hath an army in areadiness and, with his navy newly decked, rigged, and furnished in all points, lieth at the mouth of the river of Seine looking for a prosperous wind, that, as soon as it cometh about, he may sail therewith hither into England, trusting, as he saith, with the help of your own people, which neither name you nor will take you for their king, to spoil you of your kingdom with small ado and to conquer it at his pleasure, for he hath, as he sticketh not to protest openly to the world, a charter made by all the chiefest lords of England touching their fealty and obedience assured to him. Therefore, sith God for your just desert is wroth with you and that you are as evil spoken of by all men as they that come against you be well reported, I would advise you, whilst that there is a place for grace and favor, rather to obey the Pope's just demands (to whose word other Christian princes are ready to give ear) than by striving in vain to cast away yourself and all others that take your part or are bent to defend your quarrel or cause."

These words being thus spoken by the legate, King John, as then utterly despairing in his matters when he saw himself constrained to obey, was in a great perplexity of mind and, as one full of thought,[53] looked about him with a frowning countenance, weighing with himself what counsel were best for him to follow. At length, oppressed with the burden of the imminent danger and ruin, against his will and very loath so to have done, he promised upon his oath to stand to the Pope's order and decree. Wherefore shortly after, in like manner as Pope Innocent had commanded, he took the crown from his own head and delivered the same to Pandulph the legate [**1**], neither he nor his heirs at any time thereafter to receive the same but at the Pope's hands [**3**]. Upon this he promised to receive Stephen the Archbishop of Canterbury into his favor, with all other the bishops and banished men, making unto them sufficient amends for all injuries to them done and so to pardon them that they should not run into any danger for that they had rebelled against him.

Then Pandulph, keeping the crown with him for the space of five days

[53]Anxiety.

in token of possession thereof, at length, as the Pope's vicar, gave it him again [**2**]. . . .

[**180**] There was in this season [1212] an hermit whose name was Peter [of Pomfret], dwelling about York, a man in great reputation with the common people because that, either inspired with some spirit of prophecy as the people believed or else having some notable skill in art magic, he was accustomed to tell what should follow after. And forsomuch as oftentimes his sayings proved true, great credit was given to him as to a very prophet, which was no good consequence that therefore his predictions comprised undoubted events. Nay, rather, sith in this pseudoprophet or false foreteller of afterclaps, these necessary concurrents[54] . . . were wanting . . . , necessarily it followeth that he was not as he was taken but rather a deluder of the people and an instrument of Satan raised up for the enlargement of his kingdom, as the sequel of this discourse importeth. This Peter, about the first of January last past, had told the King that at the feast of the Ascension it should come to pass that he should be cast out of his kingdom [**4.2.147**]. And whether to the intent that his words should be the better believed or whether upon too much trust of his own cunning, he offered himself to suffer death for it if his prophecy proved not true. Hereupon being committed to prison within the castle of Corfe, when the day by him prefixed came without any other notable damage unto King John, he was by the King's commandment drawn from the said castle unto the town of Wareham and there hanged together with his son [**157**].

The people much blamed King John for this extreme dealing because that the hermit was supposed to be a man of great virtue and his son nothing guilty of the offense committed by his father, if any were, against the King. Moreover, some thought that he had much wrong to die because the matter fell out even as he had prophesied, for the day before the Ascension Day King John had resigned the superiority of his kingdom, as they took the matter, unto the Pope and had done to him homage, so that he was no absolute king, indeed as authors affirm [**5.1.25**]. One cause, and that not the least, which moved King John the sooner to agree with the Pope rose through the words of the said hermit; that did put such a fear of some great mishap in his heart, which should grow through the disloyalty of his people, that it made him yield the sooner.

[**181**] . . . About the feast of Saint Michael [1213], came Nicholas the

[54]Concurring circumstances.

Cardinal of Tusculum into England, sent from the Pope, to take away the interdiction. . . .

[**183**] The nobles, supposing that longer delay therein was not to be suffered, assembled themselves together [**4.3.11**] at the abbey of Bury (under color[55] of going thither to do their devotions to the body of Saint Edmund, which lay there enshrined), where they uttered their complaint of the King's tyrannical manners [1213].

. . . And therefore, being thus assembled in the choir of the church of Saint Edmund, they received a solemn oath upon the altar there that, if the King would not grant[56] to the same liberties with others which he of his own accord had promised to confirm to them, they would from thenceforth make war upon him till they had obtained their purpose and enforced him to grant not only to all these their petitions but also yield to the confirmation of them under his seal, forever to remain most steadfast and inviolable [**5.2.6**]. . . .

[**184**] The King, when he saw what they demanded (which in effect was a new order in things touching the whole state of the commonwealth), swore in a great fury that he would never condescend unto those petitions. Whereof when the barons had knowledge, they got them straight into armor, making their assembly at Stanford in the Easter week [1215], whither they had drawn unto them almost the whole nobility and gathered an exceeding great army. For the commons flocked unto them from every part, because the King was generally hated of the more part of his subjects. . . .

[**185**] Howbeit, the lords, having no confidence in his promise, came with their army within three miles of Windsor and there pitched down their tents in a meadow[57] betwixt Staines and Windsor, whither King John also came the fifteenth day of June [1215] and showed such friendly countenance toward every one of them that they were put in good hope he meant no deceit. Being thus met, they fell in consultation about an agreement to be had. . . .

Finally, when the King, measuring his own strength with the barons, perceived that he was not able to resist them, he consented to subscribe and seal to such articles concerning the liberties demanded, in form for the most part as is contained in the two charters Magna Carta and Carta de Foresta, beginning *Johannes Dei gratia,* etc. And he did not only grant unto them their petitions touching the foresaid liberties but also,

[55]Pretense.
[56]Assent.
[57]Runnymede.

to win him further credit, was contented that they should choose out certain grave and honorable personages which should have authority and power to see those things performed which he then granted unto them. . . .

[**186**] But the King, disquieted not a little for that he was thus driven to yield so far unto the barons, notwithstanding as much as was possible he kept his purpose secret, devised by what means he might disappoint all that had been done, and promised, on his part, at this assembly, betwixt him and the lords a pacification (as ye have heard). Wherefore the next day, very late in the evening, he secretly departed to Southampton, and so over into the Isle of Wight, where he took advice with his Council what remedy he might find to quiet the minds of his lords and barons and to bring them unto his purpose. At length, after much debating of the matter, it was concluded by the advice of the greater part that the King should require the Pope's aid therein. . . .

[**190**] Indeed, about the same time Pope Innocent, who before at the instant suit of King John had excommunicated the barons in general, did now [1216] excommunicate them by name and in particular. . . .

The barons of the realm, being thus afflicted with so many mischiefs all at one time, as both by the sharp and cruel wars which the King made against them on the one side and by the enmity of the Pope on the other side, they knew not which way to turn them nor how to seek for relief. . . . Therefore, considering that they were in such extremity of despair, they resolved with themselves to seek for aid at the enemies' hands [**5.2.20**]; and thereupon Saer Earl of Winchester and Robert Fitzwalter, with letters under their seals, were sent unto Louis the son of Philip the French King, offering him the crown of England and sufficient pledges for performance of the same and other covenants to be agreed betwixt them, requiring him with all speed to come unto their succor. This Louis had married, as before is said, Blanch daughter to Alfonso King of Castile, niece to King John by his sister Eleanor.

Now King Philip the father of this Louis, being glad to have such an occasion to invade the realm of England, which he never loved, promised willingly that his son should come unto the aid of the said barons with all convenient speed; but first he received four and twenty hostages which he placed at Campagne for further assurance of the covenants accorded;[58] and herewith he prepared an army and divers ships to transport his son and his army over into England.

[58]Agreed upon.

[191] . . . The Pope, desirous to help King John all that he might because he was now his vassal, sent his legate Gualo into France to dissuade King Philip from taking any enterprise in hand against the King of England [**73**]. But King Philip, though he was content to hear what the legate could say, yet by no means would be turned from the execution of his purpose, alleging that King John was not the lawful King of England, having first usurped and taken it away from his nephew Arthur the lawful inheritor; and that now, sithence[59] as an enemy to his own royal dignity he had given the right of his kingdom away to the Pope, which he could not do without consent of his nobles, and therefore through his own fault he was worthily deprived of all his kingly honor. "For the kingdom of England," saith he, "never belonged to the patrimony of Saint Peter nor at any time shall [**3.1.153**]. For admit that he were rightful king, yet neither he nor any other prince may give away his kingdom without the assent of his barons, which are bound to defend the same and the prerogative royal to the uttermost of their powers. Furthermore," saith he, "if the Pope do mean to maintain this error he shall give a parlous[60] example to all kingdoms of the world." Herewithal the nobles of France then present protested also, with one voice, that in defense of this article they would stand to the death, which is that no king or prince at his will and pleasure might give away his kingdom or make it tributary to any other potentate whereby the nobles should become thrall or subject to a foreign governor. These things were done at Lyons in the quindene[61] after Easter.

Louis, on the morrow following being the twenty-sixth of April [1216], by his father's procurement came into the Council chamber and, with frowning look, beheld the legate; where by his procurator he defended the cause that moved him to take upon him this journey into England [**5.2.78**], disproving not only the right which King John had to the crown but also alleging his own interest not only by his new election of the barons but also in the title of his wife, whose mother the Queen of Castile remained only alive of all the brethren and sisters of Henry the Second late King of England (as before ye have heard). . . .

Louis therefore, forthwith embarking himself with his people and all necessary provisions for such a journey, took the sea and arrived at a place called Stonar in the Isle of Thanet upon the twenty-first day of May, and shortly after came to Sandwich and there landed with all

[59]Since.
[60]Shocking.
[61]Fifteen-day period.

his people where he also encamped upon the shore by the space of three days. In which meantime there came unto him a great number of those lords and gentlemen which had sent for him, and there every-one, apart and by himself, swore fealty and homage unto him as if he had been their true and natural prince.

King John, about the same time that Louis thus arrived, came to Dover, meaning to fight with his adversaries by the way as they should come forward toward London. But yet, upon other advisement taken, he changed his purpose because he put some doubt in the Flemings and other strangers of whom the most part of his army consisted, because he knew that they hated the Frenchmen no more than they did the English. Therefore, furnishing the castle of Dover with men, munition, and victuals, he left it in the keeping of Hubert de Burgh, a man of notable prowess and valiancy, and returned himself unto Canterbury and from thence took the highway toward Winchester. Louis, being advertised that King John was retired out of Kent, passed through the country without any encounter and won all the castles and holds as he went; but Dover he could not win [**5.1.31**].

At his coming to Rochester he laid siege to the castle there and won it, causing all the strangers that were found within it to be hanged. This done, he came to London and there received the homage of those lords and gentlemen which had not yet done their homage to him at Sandwich [**32**]. On the other part he took an oath to maintain and perform the old laws and customs of the realm and to restore to every man his rightful heritage and lands, requiring the barons furthermore to continue faithful toward him, assuring them to bring things so to pass that the realm of England should recover the former dignity and they their ancient liberties. Moreover, he used them so courteously, gave them so fair words, and made such large promises that they believed him with all their hearts. . . .

The rumor of this pretended outward courtesy, being once spread through the realm, caused great numbers of people to come flocking to him, among whom were divers of those which before had taken part with King John, as William Earl Warren, William Earl of Arun-del, William Earl of Salisbury, William Marshall the younger, and divers other, supposing verily that the French King's son should now obtain the kingdom. . . .

[**192**] But this availed them not, neither took his excuse any such effect as he did hope it should, for those ambassadors that King John had sent thither replied against their assertions, so that there was hard

hold[62] about it in that court, albeit that the Pope would decree nothing till he heard further from his legate Gualo, who, the same time, being advertised of the proceedings of Louis in his journey, with all diligence hasted over into England and, passing through the middle of his adversaries, came unto King John, then sojourning at Gloucester, of whom he was most joyfully received, for in him King John reposed all his hope of victory [**5.2.69**]. This legate, immediately after his coming, did excommunicate Louis by name, with all his fautors[63] and complices, but specially Simon de Langton, with bell, book, and candle, as the manner was. . . .

In like manner, all the fortresses, towns, and castles in the south parts of the realm were subdued unto the obeisance of Louis (the castles of Dover and Windsor only excepted). . . . About which time letters came also unto Louis from his procurators whom he had sent to the Pope, by the tenor whereof he was advertised that, notwithstanding all that they could do or say, the Pope meant to excommunicate him and did but only stay till he had received some advertisement from his legate Gualo.

The chiefest points, as we find, that were laid by Louis his procurators against King John were these: that, by the murder committed in the person of his nephew Arthur he had been condemned in the parliament chamber before the French King by the peers of France; and that, being summoned to appear, he had obstinately refused so to do and therefore had by good right forfeited not only his lands within the precinct of France but also the realm of England, which was now due unto the said Louis (as they alleged) in right of the Lady Blanch his wife, daughter to Eleanor Queen of Spain. But the Pope refelled[64] all such allegations as they produced for proof hereof, and seemed to defend King John's cause very pithily, but namely in that he was under the protection of him as supreme lord of England, again for that he had taken upon him the cross (as before ye have heard). . . .

[**193**] About the same time [1216], or rather in the year last past as some hold, it fortuned that the Viscount of Melun, a Frenchman, fell sick at London; and perceiving that death was at hand, he called unto him certain of the English barons which remained in the city upon safeguard thereof and to them made this protestation [**5.4.10**]. "I lament," saith he, "your destruction and desolation at hand because

[62]Strong contention.
[63]Supporters.
[64]Refuted.

ye are ignorant of the perils hanging over your heads. For this understand: that Louis and with him sixteen earls and barons of France have secretly sworn, if it shall fortune him to conquer this realm of England and to be crowned King, that he will kill, banish, and confine all those of the English nobility which now do serve under him and persecute their own king as traitors and rebels; and, furthermore, will dispossess all their lineage of such inheritances as they now hold in England. And because,"[65] saith he, "you shall not have doubt hereof, I which lie here at the point of death do now affirm unto you and take it[66] on the peril of my soul that I am one of those sixteen that have sworn to perform this thing; wherefore I advise you to provide for your own safeties and your realm's (which you now destroy) and keep this thing secret which I have uttered unto you." After this speech was uttered he straightways died [**59**].

When these words of the Lord of Melun were opened unto the barons they were, and not without cause, in great doubt of themselves, for they saw how Louis had already placed and set Frenchmen in most of such castles and towns as he had gotten, the right whereof indeed belonged to them. And again it grieved them much to understand how, besides the hatred of their Prince, they were every Sunday and holiday openly accursed in every church, so that many of them inwardly relented and could have been contented to have returned to King John if they had thought that they should thankfully have been received [**52**]. . . .

[**194**] Thus, the country being wasted on each hand, the King hasted forward till he came to Wellstream Sands, where, passing the Washes, he lost a great part of his army with horses and carriages [**5.6.39**], so that it was judged to be a punishment appointed by God that the spoil which had been gotten and taken out of churches, abbeys, and other religious houses should perish and be lost by such means together with the spoilers. Yet the King himself and a few other escaped the violence of the waters by following a good guide. But, as some have written, he took such grief for the loss sustained at this passage that, immediately thereupon, he fell into an ague [**5.3.3**], the force and heat whereof, together with his immoderate feeding on raw peaches and drinking of new cider, so increased his sickness that he was not able to ride but was fain[67] to be carried in a litter [**16**] presently made of twigs, with a couch of

[65]So that.
[66]*I.e.,* an oath.
[67]Obliged.

straw under him, without any bed[68] or pillow, thinking to have gone to Lincoln; but the disease still so raged and grew upon him that he was enforced to stay one night at the castle of Laford and, on the next day, with great pain caused himself to be carried unto Newark, where, in the castle, through anguish of mind rather than through force of sickness, he departed this life the night before the nineteenth day of October [1216], in the year of his age fifty and one and after he had reigned seventeen years, six months, and seven and twenty days [**5.7.65**].

There be which have written that, after he had lost his army, he came to the abbey of Swineshead in Lincolnshire and, there understanding the cheapness and plenty of corn,[69] showed himself greatly displeased therewith, as he that, for the hatred which he bore to the English people that had so traitorously revolted from him unto his adversary Louis, wished all misery to light upon them; and, thereupon, said in his anger that he would cause all kind of grain to be at a far higher price ere many days should pass. Whereupon a monk that heard him speak such words, being moved with zeal for the oppression of his country, gave the King poison in a cup of ale whereof he first took the assay,[70] to cause the King not to suspect the matter; and so they both died in manner at one time [**5.6.30**]. . . .

The men-of-war that served under his ensigns, being for the more part hired soldiers and strangers, came together and, marching forth with his body, each man with his armor on his back, in warlike order conveyed it unto Worcester [**5.7.99**], where he was pompously buried in the cathedral church before the high altar, not for that he had so appointed, as some write, but because it was thought to be a place of most surety for the lords and other of his friends there to assemble and to take order in their business now after his decease. And because he was somewhat fat and corpulent, his bowels were taken out of his body and buried at Croxton Abbey, a house of monks of the order called Praemonstratenses in Staffordshire, the Abbot of which house was his physician. . . .

[**195**] Here therefore we see the issue of domestical or homebred broils, the fruits of variance, the gain that riseth of dissension, whereas no greater nor safer fortification can betide a land than when the inhabitants are all alikeminded [**112**]. By concord many an hard

[68]Stuffed sack.
[69]Grain.
[70]Performed the tasting.

enterprise (in common sense thought impossible) is achieved, many weak things become so defended that without manifold force they cannot be dissolved. From division and mutinies do issue (as out of the Trojan Horse) ruins of royalties and decays of commonalties. The sinews [**88**] of a realm is supposed of some to be substance and wealth; of other some, policy and power; of other some, convenient defenses both by water and land; but a most excellent description of a well-fortified country is that of Plautus, set down in most pithy words and grave sentences, no less worthy to be written than read and considered. The description is this:

Si incolae bene sunt morati, pulchre munitum arbitror.
perfidia et peculatus ex urbe et avaritia si exulant,
quarta invidia, quinta ambitio, sexta obtrectatio,
septimum periurium, octava indiligentia,
nona iniuria, decimum, quod pessimum adgressust, scelus:
haec unde aberunt, ea urbs moenita muro sat erit simplici;
ubi ea aderunt, centumplex murus rebus servandis parumst. . . .[71]

[**196**] He [King John] was comely of stature but of look and countenance displeasant and angry, somewhat cruel of nature, as by the writers of his time he is noted, and not so hardy as doubtful[72] in time of peril and danger. But this seemeth to be an envious report uttered by those that were given to speak no good of him whom they inwardly hated. Howbeit, some give this witness of him, as the author of the Book of Barnwell Abbey and other, that he was a great and mighty prince but yet not very fortunate, much like to Marius the noble Roman, tasting of fortune both ways, bountiful and liberal unto strangers but of his own people, for their daily treasons practiced toward him, a great oppressor, so that he trusted more to foreigners than to them, and therefore in the end he was of them utterly forsaken.

Verily, whosoever shall consider the course of the history written of this Prince, he shall find that he hath been little beholden to the

[71]"If the inhabitants are people of good character, I think that's the finest sort of fortification. If treachery, graft, and greed are exiled from the city; and, fourthly, envy; fifth, political corruption; sixth, gossip; seventh, perjury; eighth, laziness; ninth, fraud; and tenth and worst of all, crime—a city which lacks these faults will be well fortified with a single wall; but where they are present a hundredfold wall will not suffice to save the state" (*Persa,* 4.4, tr. Murphy).

[72]Full of fear.

writers of that time in which he lived, for scarcely can they afford him a good word except when the truth enforceth them to come out with it, as it were against their wills. The occasion whereof, as some think, was for that he was no great friend to the clergy. And yet undoubtedly his deeds show he had a zeal to religion, as it was then accounted, for he founded the abbey of Beaulieu in the New Forest, as it were in recompense of certain parish churches which, to enlarge the same forest, he caused to be thrown down and ruinated.

. . . Certainly it should seem the man had a princely heart in him and wanted nothing but faithful subjects to have assisted him in revenging such wrongs as were done and offered by the French King and others.

Moreover, the pride and pretended[73] authority of the clergy he could not well abide, when they went about to wrest out of his hands the prerogative of his princely rule and government. True it is that, to maintain his wars which he was forced to take in hand as well in France as elsewhere, he was constrained to make all the shift he could devise to recover[74] money; and because he pinched their purses, they conceived no small hatred against him, which when he perceived and wanted peradventure discretion to pass it over, he discovered[75] now and then in his rage his immoderate displeasure, as one not able to bridle his affections, a thing very hard in a stout stomach;[76] and thereby missed now and then to compass that which otherwise he might very well have brought to pass. . . .

[**197**] Henry the third of that name, the eldest son of King John, a child of the age of nine years, began his reign over the realm of England the nineteenth day of October in the year of our Lord 1216, in the seventh year of the Emperor Frederick the Second, and in the thirty-sixth year of the reign of Philip the second King of France.

Immediately after the death of his father King John, William Marshall Earl of Pembroke, general of his father's army, brought this young prince with his brother and sisters unto Gloucester and there called a council of all such lords as had taken part with King John. Anon, after it was once openly known that the sons and daughters of the late deceased Prince were brought into a place of safety, a great number of the lords and chief barons of the realm hasted thither, I

[73]Alleged.
[74]Obtain.
[75]Revealed.
[76]Fierce disposition.

mean not only such as had holden with King John but also divers other which, upon certain knowledge had of his death, were newly revolted from Louis, in purpose to aid young King Henry, to whom of right the crown did appertain. . . .

When the barons had heard this Earl's words, after some silence and conference had, they allowed[77] of his sayings and immediately, with one consent, proclaimed the young gentleman King of England [**101**]; whom the Bishops of Winchester and Bath did crown and anoint with all due solemnities at Gloucester upon the day of the feast of the apostles Simon and Jude, in presence of the legate.

[**201**] . . . But, while these things were adoing, the Earl of Pembroke and other the lords that took part with King Henry, having advertisement that a new supply of men was ready to come and aid Louis, they appointed Philip de Albany and John Marshall to associate with them the power of the Cinque Ports[78] and to watch for the coming of the adversaries, that they might keep them from landing; who, on Saint Bartholomew's Day [1217], set forth from Calais in purpose to arrive in the Thames and so to come up the river to London. Howbeit, Hubert de Burgh, captain of the castle of Dover, together with the said Philip de Albany and John Marshall, with other such power as they could get together of the Cinque Ports, having not yet above the number of forty ships great and small, upon the discovering of the French fleet, which consisted of eighty great ships besides other lesser vessels well appointed and trimmed, made forth to the sea; and, first coasting aloof from them till they had got the wind on their backs, came finally with their main force to assail the Frenchmen and, with help of their crossbows and archers, at the first joining made great slaughter of their enemies; and, so grappling together, in the end the Englishmen bore themselves so manfully that they vanquished the whole French fleet and obtained a famous victory [**5.3.11**].

. . . But Louis, after he understood of this mischance happening to his people that came to his aid, began not a little to despair of all other succor to come unto him at any time hereafter; wherefore he inclined the sooner unto peace, so that at length he took such offers of agreement as were put unto him and received furthermore a sum of money for the release of such hostages as he had in his hands,

[77]Approved.
[78]Incorporated English ports along the Dover Strait.

together with the title of the kingdom of England and the possession of all such castles and holds as he held within the realm [**5.7.84**]. . . .

This peace was concluded on the eleventh day of September [1217], not far from Staines, hard by the river of Thames, where Louis himself, the legate Gualo, and divers of the spiritualty, with the Earl of Pembroke Lord Governor of the realm and others, did meet and talk about this accord. Now when all things were ordered and finished agreeable to the articles and covenants of the peace so far as the time present required, the lords of the realm, when Louis should depart homeward, attended him to Dover in honorable wise as appertained and there took leave of him; and so he departed out of the realm about the feast of Saint Michael [1217].

Richard II

[**415**] Richard, the second of that name and son to Prince Edward called the Black Prince (the son of King Edward the Third), a child of the age of eleven years, began to reign over the realm of England the two and twentieth day of June in the year of the world 5344, of our Lord 1377, after the Conquest 310, about the two and thirtieth year of the Emperor Charles the Fourth, and in the fourteenth year of Charles the fifth King of France, and about the seventh year of the reign of Robert the second King of Scotland. He was named Richard of Bordeaux because he was born at Bordeaux in Gascony whilst his father ruled there.

[**429**] . . . In the meantime other incidents fell within the realm in the fourth year [1381] of King Richard, sore to the disquieting of the same. . . . The commons of the realm, sore repining not only for the poll groats that were demanded of them by reason of the grant made in parliament (as ye have heard) but also (as some write) for that they were sore oppressed (as they took the matter) by their landlords that demanded of them their ancient customs and services, set on by some devilish instinct and persuasion of their own beastly intentions, as men not content with the state whereunto they were called, rose in divers parts of this realm and assembled together in companies, purposing to enforce the Prince to make them free and to release them of all servitude whereby they stood as bondmen to their lords and superiors [**2H6 4.2**]. . . .

[**430**] This talk liked well the ears of the common uplandish[1] people, and by the less conveying the more they purposed to burn and destroy all records [**4.7.16**], evidences, courtrolls, and other monuments,[2] that the remembrance of ancient matters being removed out of mind, their landlords might not have whereby to challenge any right at their hands.

[1]Rural.
[2]Records.

[**431**] . . . They fell in talk with the Londoners of many lewd[3] devices, as of the apprehending of traitors and specially concerning such misliking as they had of [John of Gaunt] the Duke of Lancaster, whom they hated above all other persons. And hereupon agreeing in one mind, after divers other of their outrageous doings, they ran the same day to the said Duke's house of the Savoy [**1**], to the which, in beauty and stateliness of building, with all manner of princely furniture, there was not any other in the realm comparable; which, in despite of the Duke, whom they called traitor, they set on fire and by all ways and means endeavored utterly to destroy it.

. . . Now after that these wicked people had thus destroyed the Duke of Lancaster's house and done what they could devise to his reproach, they went to the Temple and burnt the men-of-law's lodgings, with their books, writings, and all that they might lay hand upon [**2**].

[**432**] . . . For, whereas divers forms of charters had been drawn according to the effect of the agreement with the Essexmen, and none of them might please this lordly rebel [Wat Tyler], at length the King sent to him one of his knights, called Sir John Newton, to request him to come to him that they might talk of the articles which he stood upon to have inserted in the charter, of the which one was to have had a commission to put to death all lawyers [**4.2.83**], escheators,[4] and other which by any office had anything to do with the law; for his meaning was that, having made all those away that understood the laws, all things should then be ordered according to the will and disposition of the common people. It was reported indeed that he should say with great pride the day before these things chanced, putting his hands to his lips, that within four days all the laws of England should come forth of his mouth [**4.7.7**].

[**436**] . . . To recite what was done in every part of the realm in time of those hellish troubles, it is not possible; but this is to be considered, that the rage of the commons was universally such as it might seem they had generally conspired together to do what mischief they could devise. As among sundry other, what wickedness was it to compell teachers of children in grammar schools [**37**] to swear never to instruct any in their art? Again, could they have a more mischievous meaning than to burn and destroy all old and ancient monuments [**16**] and to murder and dispatch out of the way all such as were able to commit to memory either any new or old records? For it was dan-

[3]Wicked.
[4]Legal officers.

gerous among them to be known for one that was learned, and more dangerous if any men were found with a penner[5] and inkhorn [**4.2.117**] at his side; for such seldom or never escaped from them with life. . . .

[**454**] About the beginning of March in this tenth year [1387], Richard Earl of Arundel, being appointed Lord Admiral, and Thomas Mowbray Earl of Nottingham, the Earl of Devonshire, and the Bishop of Norwich (as Froissart saith) went to the sea with a warlike power of men-of-arms and archers, so well trimmed and appointed as was possible. For the Lord Admiral, understanding that the Duke of Gloucester and many other noblemen would see the muster of his men, used all diligence and spared for no costs to have the most choicest and pickedst fellows that might be gotten; not following the evil example of others in times past which received tag and rag to fill up their numbers whom they hired for small wages and reserved the residue to their purses [**1H4 4.2, 2H4 3.2**]. And when to the advancement of the realm's commodity[6] they should have encountered the enemies, they shifted off all occasions thereto and only prolonged time, without achieving any enterprise available, to the end they might receive the whole wages and keep themselves from danger, which they should hardly have avoided when they had not about them such able men as were like to match the enemies. . . .

[**487**] In this twentieth year of his reign [1397], King Richard, receiving the sums of money for the which the strong town of Brest was engaged to him, by evil counsel (as many thought) delivered it unto the Duke of Brittany, by reason whereof no small spark of displeasure arose betwixt the King and [Thomas of Woodstock] the Duke of Gloucester; which kindled up such a flame (as it was easy to do, finding matter enough to feed upon in both their breasts) that finally it could no longer be kept down nor by any means quenched. . . .

Thus, as they fell into reasoning of this matter, the Duke said to the King: "Sir, your grace ought to put your body in pain to win a stronghold or town by feats of war ere you take upon you to sell or deliver any town or stronghold gotten with great adventure[7] by the manhood and policy[8] of your noble progenitors [**R2 2.1.252**]. To this the King, with changed countenance, answered and said, "Uncle, how say you that?" And the Duke boldly, without fear, recited the same

[5]Pencase.
[6]Welfare.
[7]Risk.
[8]Diplomacy.

again, not changing one word in any better sort. Whereupon the King, being more chafed, replied: "Sir, think you that I am a merchant or a very fool, to sell my land? By Saint John Baptist, no! . . ."

[**488**] The Earl of Saint-Pol, at his last coming into England to receive King Richard's oath for observing the truce, had conference with the King of divers matters. The King, by way of complaint, showed[a] unto him how stiff the Duke of Gloucester was in hindering all such matters as he would have go forward, not only seeking to have the peace broken betwixt the realms of England and France but also procuring trouble at home by stirring the people to rebellion. The Earl of Saint-Pol, hearing of this stout demeanor of the Duke, told the King that it should be best to provide in time against such mischiefs as might ensue thereof, and that it was not to be suffered that a subject should behave himself in such sort toward his prince. The King, marking his words, thought that he gave him good and faithful counsel, and thereupon determined to suppress both the Duke and other of his complices; and took more diligent regard to the sayings and doings of the Duke than before he had done. And as it cometh to pass that those which suspect any evil do ever deem the worst, so he took everything in evil part, insomuch that he complained of the Duke unto his brethren the Dukes of Lancaster and York in that he should stand against him in all things and seek his destruction, the death of his councillors, and overthrow of his realm.

The two Dukes of Lancaster and York, to deliver the King's mind of suspicion, made answer that they were not ignorant how their brother of Gloucester, as a man sometime rash in words, would speak oftentimes more than he could or would bring to effect, and the same proceeded of a faithful heart which he bore toward the King; for that it grieved him to understand that the confines of the English dominions should in any wise be diminished. Therefore his grace ought not to regard his words, sith he should take no hurt thereby. These persuasions quieted the King for a time, till he was informed of the practice which the Duke of Gloucester had contrived (as the fame went amongst divers persons) to imprison the King. For then the Dukes of Lancaster and York, first reproving the Duke of Gloucester for his too liberal talking . . . and perceiving that he set nothing by their words, were in doubt lest, if they should remain in the court still, he would, upon a presumptuous mind, in trust to be borne out by them,

[a]Explained.

attempt some outrageous enterprise. Wherefore they thought best to depart for a time into their countries, that by their absence he might the sooner learn to stay himself for doubt of further displeasure. But it came to pass that their departing from the court was the casting away of the Duke of Gloucester. For after that they were gone, there ceased not such as bore him evil will to procure the King to dispatch him out of the way.

The Duke, indeed, sore stomached the matter that his counsel might not be followed in all things, and specially for that he saw (as he took it) that the King was misled by some persons that were about him otherwise than stood with his honor; for reformation whereof he conferred with the Abbot of Saint Albans and the Prior of Westminster. . . . The Duke hereupon disclosed unto them all the secrets of his mind, and by their devices presently contrived an assembly of divers great lords of the realm at Arundel Castle that day fortnight, at what time he himself appointed to be there with the Earls of Derby, Arundel, Marshal, and Warwick; also the Archbishop of Canterbury, the Abbot of Saint Albans, the Prior of Westminster, with divers others.

These estates[9] being come to Arundel Castle at the day appointed, . . . they withdrew into a chamber and fell in counsel together where in the end they light upon this point: to take King Richard, the Dukes of Lancaster and York, and commit them to prison, and all the other lords of the King's Council they determined should be drawn and hanged. Such was their purpose, which they meant to have accomplished in August following. But [Thomas Mowbray] the Earl Marshal, that was Lord Deputy of Calais and had married the Earl of Arundel's daughter, discovered[10] all their counsel to the King, and the very day in which they should begin their enterprise. . . .

The King hereupon went to London. . . . After that the King began to approach the Duke's house at Pleshey in Essex, where he then lay, he commanded his brother the Earl of Huntingdon to ride afore, to know if the Duke [of Gloucester] were at home and, if he were, then to tell him that the King was coming at hand to speak with him.

[**489**] . . . The Earl of Huntingdon and divers other followed the Duke into the hall, and there stayed for him till he had put on his raiment. And within a while they came forth again all together into the base court, where the King was delighting with the Duchess in

[9]Lords.
[10]Revealed.

pleasant talk, whom he willed now to return to her lodging again for he might stay no longer; and so took his horse again, and the Duke likewise. But shortly after that the King and all his company were gone forth of the gate of the base court, he commanded the Earl Marshal to apprehend the Duke, which incontinently[11] was done according to the King's appointment.

Here we find some variance in writers. For, as by an old French pamphlet (which I have seen) it should appear, the King commanded first that this Duke should be conveyed unto the Tower [of London], where he meant to common[12] with him and not in any other place; but, nevertheless, the King shortly after appointed that he should be sent to Calais, as in the same pamphlet is also contained. Other write that, immediately upon his apprehension, the Earl Marshal conveyed him unto the Thames, and there being set aboard in a ship prepared of purpose, he was brought to Calais, where he was at length dispatched out of life, either strangled or smothered with pillows (as some do write). . . . Whereupon the King sent unto Thomas Mowbray, Earl Marshal and of Nottingham, to make the Duke secretly away [**1.1.133, 1.2.48**].

The Earl prolonged time for the executing of the King's commandment though the King would have had it done with all expedition; whereby the King conceived no small displeasure and swore that it should cost the Earl his life if he quickly obeyed not his commandment. The Earl, thus as it seemed in manner enforced, called out the Duke at midnight, as if he should have taken ship to pass over into England; and there, in the lodging called the Prince's Inn, he caused his servants to cast featherbeds upon him and so smother him to death; or otherwise to strangle him with towels (as some write). This was the end of that nobleman, fierce of nature, hasty, willful, and given more to war than to peace; and in this greatly to be discommended that he was ever repining against the King in all things, whatsoever he wished to have forward. . . . His body was afterward with all funeral pomp conveyed into England and buried at his own manor of Pleshey, within the church there in a sepulcher which he in his lifetime had caused to be made and there erected. . . .

In the meantime, whiles things were thus in broil, before the beginning of the parliament, divers other, beside them of whom we have spoken, were apprehended and put in sundry prisons. The parliament

[11]Immediately.
[12]Confer.

was summoned to begin at Westminster the seventeenth of September [1397], and writs thereupon directed to every of the lords to appear and to bring with them a sufficient number of armed men and archers in their best array; for it was not known how the Dukes of Lancaster and York would take the death of their brother, nor how other peers of the realm would take the apprehension and imprisonment of their kinsmen, the Earls of Arundel and Warwick, and of the other prisoners. Surely the two Dukes, when they heard that their brother was so suddenly made away, they wist[13] not what to say to the matter and began both to be sorrowful for his death and doubtful of their own states; for sith they saw how the King, abused by the counsel of evil men, abstained not from such an heinous act, they thought he would afterward attempt greater misorders from time to time. Therefore they assembled in all haste great numbers of their servants, friends, and tenants and, coming to London, were received into the city. For the Londoners were right sorry for the death of the Duke of Gloucester, who had ever sought their favor; insomuch that now they would have been contented to have joined with the Dukes in seeking revenge of so noble a man's death, procured and brought to pass without law or reason, as the common bruit then walked; although peradventure he was not as yet made away.

[**490**] Here the Dukes and other fell in counsel, and many things were proponed.[14] Some would that they should by force revenge the Duke of Gloucester's death; other thought it meet that the Earls Marshal and Huntingdon, and certain others, as chief authors of all the mischief, should be pursued and punished for their demerits, having trained up the King in vice and evil customs even from his youth. But the Dukes, after their displeasure was somewhat assuaged, determined to cover the stings of their griefs for a time and, if the King would amend his manners, to forget also the injuries past.

[**491**] . . . At that self time the Archbishop of Canterbury absented himself from the parliament, in hope that the King would be his friend and stand his very good lord, for that he had promised nothing should be done against him in the parliament whilst he was absent. But, nevertheless, at the importunate suit of the said Sir John Bushy and others, the Archbishop was condemned unto perpetual exile and appointed to avoid[15] the realm within six weeks [September, 1397].

[13]Knew.
[14]Proposed.
[15]Leave.

And therewith the King sent secretly to the Pope for order that the Archbishop might be removed from his see to some other, which suit was obtained, and Roger Walden Lord Treasurer was ordained archbishop in his place, as after shall appear. . . .

[**493**] Hereupon there were sundry of the nobles that lamented these mischiefs, and specially showed their griefs unto such by whose naughty[16] counsel they understood the King to be misled; and this they did to the end that they being about him might either turn their copies[17] and give him better counsel, or else he, having knowledge what evil report went of him, might mend his manners misliked of his nobles. But all was in vain, for so it fell out that, in this parliament holden at Shrewsbury [January, 1398], Henry Duke of Hereford accused Thomas Mowbray Duke of Norfolk of certain words which he should utter in talk had betwixt them, as they rode together lately before betwixt London and Brentford, sounding highly to the King's dishonor. And, for further proof thereof, he presented a supplication to the King wherein he appealed the Duke of Norfolk in field of battle for a traitor, false and disloyal to the King and enemy unto the realm. This supplication was read before both the Dukes, in presence of the King; which done, the Duke of Norfolk took upon him to answer it, declaring that, whatsoever the Duke of Hereford had said against him other than well, he lied falsely like an untrue knight as he was. And when the King asked of the Duke of Hereford what he said to it, he, taking his hood off his head, said: "My sovereign lord, even as the supplication which I took[18] you importeth, right so I say for truth, that Thomas Mowbray Duke of Norfolk is a traitor [**1.1.39**], false and disloyal to your royal majesty, your crown, and to all the states of your realm."

Then the Duke of Norfolk, being asked what he said to this, he answered: "Right dear lord, with your favor that I make answer unto your cousin here, I say (your reverence saved) that Henry of Lancaster Duke of Hereford, like a false and disloyal traitor [**144**] as he is, doth lie in that he hath or shall say of me otherwise than well." "No more," said the King, "we have heard enough"; and herewith commanded the Duke of Surrey, for that turn Marshal of England, to arrest in his name the two Dukes. The Duke of Lancaster father to the Duke of Hereford, the Duke of York, the Duke of Aumerle Con-

[16]Evil.
[17]Change their tune.
[18]Gave.

stable of England, and the Duke of Surrey Marshal of the realm undertook as pledges, body for body, for the Duke of Hereford; but the Duke of Norfolk was not suffered to put in pledges, and so, under arrest, was led unto Windsor Castle and there guarded with keepers that were appointed to see him safely kept.

Now, after the dissolving of the parliament at Shrewsbury, there was a day appointed about six weeks after for the King to come unto Windsor, to hear and to take some order betwixt the two Dukes which had thus appealed each other. There was a great scaffold erected within the castle of Windsor for the King to sit with the lords and prelates of his realm; and so, at the day appointed, he with the said lords and prelates being come thither and set in their places, the Duke of Hereford, appellant, and the Duke of Norfolk, defendant, were sent for to come and appear before the King, sitting there in his seat of justice. And then began Sir John Bushy to speak for the King, declaring to the lords how they should understand that where the Duke of Hereford had presented a supplication to the King, who was there set to minister justice to all men that would demand the same, as appertained to his royal majesty, he therefore would now hear what the parties could say one against another; and withal,[19] the King commanded the Dukes of Aumerle and Surrey (the one being Constable and the other Marshal) to go unto the two Dukes, appellant and defendant, requiring them on his behalf to grow to some agreement; and, for his part, he would be ready to pardon all that had been said or done amiss betwixt them touching any harm or dishonor to him or his realm. But they answered both assuredly that it was not possible to have any peace or agreement made betwixt them.

[**494**] When he heard what they had answered, he commanded that they should be brought forthwith before his presence to hear what they would say. Herewith an herald in the King's name, with loud voice, commanded the Dukes to come before the King, either of them to show his reason or else to make peace together without more delay. When they were come before the King and lords, the King spoke himself to them, willing them to agree and make peace together [**152**]. "For it is," said he, "the best way ye can take." The Duke of Norfolk, with due reverence, hereunto answered it could not be so brought to pass, his honor saved. Then the King asked of the Duke of Hereford what it was that he demanded of the Duke of Norfolk, "and what is

[19]In addition.

the matter that ye cannot make peace together and become friends?"

Then stood forth a knight who, asking and obtaining license to speak for the Duke of Hereford, said: "Right dear and sovereign lord, here is Henry of Lancaster Duke of Hereford and Earl of Derby, who saith, and I for him likewise say, that Thomas Mowbray Duke of Norfolk is a false and disloyal traitor to you and your royal majesty and to your whole realm; and likewise, the Duke of Hereford saith, and I for him, that Thomas Mowbray Duke of Norfolk hath received eight thousand nobles to pay the soldiers that keep your town of Calais, which he hath not done as he ought [**88**]; and, furthermore, the said Duke of Norfolk hath been the occasion of all the treason that hath been contrived in your realm for the space of these eighteen years [**95**], and by his false suggestions and malicious counsel he hath caused to die and to be murdered your right dear uncle, the Duke of Gloucester, son to King Edward [the Third] [**100**]. Moreover, the Duke of Hereford saith, and I for him, that he will prove this with his body against the body of the said Duke of Norfolk within lists." The King herewith waxed angry and asked the Duke of Hereford if these were his words; who answered, "Right dear lord, they are my words, and hereof I require right, and the battle against him."

There was a knight also that asked license to speak for the Duke of Norfolk and, obtaining it, began to answer thus: "Right dear sovereign lord, here is Thomas Mowbray Duke of Norfolk, who answereth and saith, and I for him, that all which Henry of Lancaster hath said and declared, saving the reverence due to the King and his Council, is a lie [**125**]; and the said Henry of Lancaster hath falsely and wickedly lied as a false and disloyal knight, and both hath been and is a traitor against you, your crown, royal majesty, and realm. This will I prove and defend, as becometh a loyal knight, to do with my body against his. Right dear lord, I beseech you therefore, and your Council, that it may please you in your royal discretion to consider and mark what Henry of Lancaster Duke of Hereford, such a one as he is, hath said."

The King then demanded of the Duke of Norfolk if these were his words and whether he had any more to say. The Duke of Norfolk then answered for himself: "Right dear sir, true it is that I have received so much gold to pay your people[20] of the town of Calais, which I have done [**126**]; and I do avouch that your town of Calais is as

[20]Soldiers.

well kept at your commandment as ever it was at any time before, and that there never hath been by any of Calais any complaint made unto you of me. Right dear and my sovereign lord, for the voyage that I made into France about your marriage, I never received either gold or silver of you [**129**]; nor yet for the voyage that the Duke of Aumerle and I made into Almaine,[21] where we spent great treasure. Marry, true it is, that once I laid an ambush to have slain the Duke of Lancaster, that there sitteth; but nevertheless he hath pardoned me thereof and there was good peace made betwixt us, for the which I yield him hearty thanks [**135**]. This is that which I have to answer, and I am ready to defend myself against mine adversary. I beseech you therefore of right, and to have the battle against him in upright judgment."

After this, when the King had commoned with his Council a little, he commanded the two Dukes to stand forth, that their answers might be heard. The King then caused them once again to be asked if they would agree and make peace together [**152**], but they both flatly answered that they would not; and, withal, the Duke of Hereford cast down his gage and the Duke of Norfolk took it up [**69**]. The King, perceiving this demeanor betwixt them, swore by Saint John Baptist that he would never seek to make peace betwixt them again. And therefore Sir John Bushy, in name of the King and his Council, declared that the King and his Council had commanded and ordained that they should have a day of battle appointed them at Coventry [**198**]. Here writers disagree about the day that was appointed, for some say it was upon a Monday in August, other upon Saint Lambert's Day being the seventeenth of September, other on the eleventh of September [1398]; but true it is that the King assigned them not only the day but also appointed them lists and place for the combat, and thereupon great preparation was made as to such a matter appertained.

At the time appointed the King came to Coventry, where the two Dukes were ready according to the order prescribed therein, coming thither in great array, accompanied with the lords and gentlemen of their lineages[22] [**1.3.6 SD**]. The King caused a sumptuous scaffold or theater and royal lists there to be erected and prepared. The Sunday before they should fight, after dinner, the Duke of Hereford came to the King (being lodged about a quarter of a mile without the town

[21]Germany.
[22]Retinues.

in a tower that belonged to Sir William[b] Bagot) to take his leave of him. The morrow after, being the day appointed for the combat, about the spring of the day came the Duke of Norfolk to the court to take leave likewise of the King. The Duke of Hereford armed him in his tent, that was set up near to the lists, and the Duke of Norfolk put on his armor betwixt the gate and the barrier of the town, in a beautiful house having a fair parclose[23] of wood toward the gate, that none might see what was done within the house.

The Duke of Aumerle, that day being High Constable of England, and the Duke of Surrey, Marshal, placed themselves betwixt them, well armed and appointed; and, when they saw their time, they first entered into the lists with a great company of men appareled in silk sendal embroidered with silver both richly and curiously, every man having a tipped staff to keep the field in order. About the hour of prime[24] came to the barriers of the lists the Duke of Hereford, mounted on a white courser barded[25] with green and blue velvet embroidered sumptuously with swans and antelopes of goldsmith's work; armed at all points. The Constable and Marshal came to the barriers, demanding of him what he was. He answered: "I am Henry of Lancaster Duke of Hereford, which am come hither to do mine endeavor against Thomas Mowbray Duke of Norfolk as a traitor untrue to God, the King, his realm, and me [**35**]." Then incontinently he swore upon the holy evangelists that his quarrel was true and just, and upon that point he required to enter the lists. Then he put up his sword, which before he held naked in his hand, and, putting down his visor, made a cross on his horse and, with spear in hand, entered into the lists and descended from his horse and set him down in a chair of green velvet at the one end of the lists, and there reposed himself, abiding the coming of his adversary.

[**495**] Soon after him entered into the field with great triumph King Richard, accompanied with all the peers of the realm; and in his company was the Earl of Saint-Pol, which was come out of France in post to see this challenge performed. The King had there above ten thousand men in armor, lest some fray or tumult might rise amongst his nobles by quarreling or partaking.[26] When the King was set in

[b]John.
[23]Screen.
[24]Nine o'clock.
[25]Caparisoned.
[26]Taking sides.

his seat, which was richly hanged and adorned, a king-at-arms[27] made open proclamation prohibiting all men, in the name of the King and of the High Constable and Marshal, to enterprise or attempt to approach or touch any part of the lists upon pain of death, except such as were appointed to order or marshal the field [**42**]. The proclamation ended, another herald cried: "Behold here Henry of Lancaster Duke of Hereford, appellant, which is entered into the lists royal to do his devoir[28] against Thomas Mowbray Duke of Norfolk, defendant, upon pain to be found false and recreant!"

The Duke of Norfolk hovered on horseback at the entry of the lists, his horse being barded with crimson velvet embroidered richly with lions of silver and mulberry trees; and when he had made his oath before the Constable and Marshal that his quarrel was just and true, he entered the field manfully, saying aloud, "God aid him that hath the right!" [**25**]; and then he departed from his horse and sat him down in his chair, which was of crimson velvet curtained about with white and red damask. The Lord Marshal viewed their spears to see that they were of equal length, and delivered the one spear himself to the Duke of Hereford, and sent the other unto the Duke of Norfolk by a knight. Then the herald proclaimed that the traverses[29] and chairs of the champions should be removed, commanding them on the King's behalf to mount on horseback and address themselves to the battle and combat.

The Duke of Hereford was quickly horsed, and closed his beaver and cast his spear into the rest; and when the trumpet sounded set forward courageously toward his enemy six or seven paces. The Duke of Norfolk was not fully set forward when the King cast down his warder[30] [**118**] and the heralds cried, "Ho, ho!" Then the King caused their spears to be taken from them and commanded them to repair again to their chairs, where they remained two long hours [**121**] while the King and his Council deliberately consulted what order was best to be had in so weighty a cause. Finally, after they had devised and fully determined what should be done therein, the heralds cried silence; and Sir John Bushy, the King's secretary, read the sentence and determination of the King and his Council, in a long roll, the effect whereof was that Henry Duke of Hereford should within fifteen

[27]Chief herald.
[28]Utmost.
[29]Curtains.
[30]Baton.

days depart out of the realm, and not to return before the term of ten years were expired except by the King he should be repealed again, and this upon pain of death [**139**]; and that Thomas Mowbray Duke of Norfolk, because he had sown sedition in the realm by his words, should likewise avoid the realm, and never to return again into England nor approach the borders or confines thereof upon pain of death [**148**]; and that the King would stay the profits of his lands till he had levied thereof such sums of money as the Duke had taken up of the King's treasurer for the wages of the garrison of Calais which were still unpaid.

When these judgments were once read, the King called before him both the parties and made them to swear that the one should never come in place where the other was, willingly, nor keep any company together in any foreign region [**184**]; which oath they both received humbly and so went their ways. The Duke of Norfolk departed sorrowfully out of the realm into Almaine, and at the last came to Venice, where he for thought[31] and melancholy deceased [**4.1.97**]; for he was in hope (as writers record) that he should have been borne out in the matter by the King; which when it fell out otherwise it grieved him not a little. The Duke of Hereford took his leave of the King at Eltham, who there released four years of his banishment [**1.3.211**]; so he took his journey over into Calais and from thence went into France, where he remained. A wonder it was to see what number of people ran after him in every town and street where he came [**1.4.24**], before he took the sea, lamenting and bewailing his departure, as who would say that when he departed, the only shield, defense, and comfort of the commonwealth was vaded[32] and gone.

At his coming into France, King Charles [the Sixth], hearing the cause of his banishment (which he esteemed to be very light), received him gently[33] and him honorably entertained, insomuch that he had by favor obtained in marriage the only daughter of the Duke of Berry, uncle to the French King, if King Richard had not been alet[34] in that matter; who, being thereof certified, sent the Earl of Salisbury [March, 1399] with all speed into France both to surmise,[35] by untrue suggestion, heinous offenses against him and also to require the French King

[31]Grief.
[32]Departed.
[33]Courteously.
[34]Interposing hindrances.
[35]Allege falsely.

that in no wise he would suffer his cousin to be matched in marriage with him that was so manifest an offender [**2.1.167**].

[**496**] . . . But yet, to content the [English] King's mind, many blank charters [**1.4.48**] were devised and brought into the city [of London], which many of the substantial and wealthy citizens were fain[36] to seal, to their great charge, as in the end appeared [1398]. And the like charters were sent abroad into all shires within the realm, whereby great grudge and murmuring arose among the people; for when they were so sealed, the King's officers wrote in the same what liked them, as well for charging the parties with payment of money as otherwise.

In this meantime [John of Gaunt] the Duke of Lancaster departed out of this life [**2.1.149**] at the Bishop of Ely's place in Holborn [February, 1399], and lieth buried in the cathedral church of Saint Paul in London, on the north side of the high altar, by the Lady Blanch his first wife. The death of this Duke gave occasion of increasing more hatred in the people of this realm toward the King, for he seized into his hands all the goods that belonged to him, and also received all the rents and revenues of his lands which ought to have descended unto the Duke of Hereford by lawful inheritance [**160**]; in revoking his letters patents [**202**], which he had granted to him before, by virtue whereof he might make his attorneys general to sue livery [**2.3.129**] for him, of any manner of inheritances or possessions that might from thenceforth fall unto him; and that his homage might be respited with making reasonable fine: whereby it was evident that the King meant his utter undoing.

This hard dealing was much misliked of all the nobility, and cried out against of the meaner sort; but namely[37] the Duke of York was therewith sore moved [**2.1.163**], who, before this time, had borne things with so patient a mind as he could, though the same touched him very near, as the death of his brother the Duke of Gloucester, the banishment of his nephew the said Duke of Hereford, and other more injuries in great number; which, for the slippery youth of the King, he passed over for the time and did forget as well as he might. But now, perceiving that neither law, justice, nor equity could take place where the King's willful will was bent upon any wrongful purpose, he considered that the glory of the public wealth[38] of his country must

[36]Obliged.
[37]Particularly.
[38]Welfare.

needs decay by reason of the King his lack of wit and want of such as would (without flattery) admonish him of his duty; and therefore he thought it the part of a wise man to get him in time to a resting-place [**211**] and to leave the following of such an unadvised captain as with a leaden sword would cut his own throat.

Hereupon he, with the Duke of Aumerle his son, went to his house at Langley, rejoicing that nothing had mishappened in the commonwealth through his device or consent. The common bruit ran that the King had set to farm the realm of England [**1.4.45**] unto Sir William Scrope Earl of Wiltshire and then Treasurer of England, to Sir John Bushy, Sir John Bagot, and Sir Henry Greene, knights. About the same time, the Earl of Arundel's son, named Thomas, which was kept in the Duke of Exeter's house, escaped out of the realm by means of one William Scott, mercer, and went to his uncle Thomas Arundel late Archbishop of Canterbury, as then sojourning at Cologne. . . .

In this year [1399], in a manner throughout all the realm of England, old bay trees withered [**2.4.8**] and, afterward, contrary to all men's thinking, grew green again: a strange sight, and supposed to import some unknown event. In this meantime the King, being advertised that the wild Irish daily wasted and destroyed the towns and villages within the English Pale, and had slain many of the soldiers which lay there in garrison for defense of that country, determined to make eftsoons[39] a voyage thither [**1.4.38**], and prepared all things necessary for his passage now against the spring. A little before his setting forth, he caused a jousts to be holden at Windsor of forty knights and forty esquires, against all comers; and they to be appareled in green, with a white falcon, and the Queen [Isabella][40] to be there well accompanied with ladies and damsels. When these jousts were finished, the King departed toward Bristol, from thence to pass into Ireland, leaving the Queen with her train still at Windsor. He appointed for his Lieutenant General in his absence his uncle the Duke of York [**2.1.220**]. And so, in the month of April [1399], as divers authors write, he set forward from Windsor and finally took shipping at Milford; and from thence, with two hundred ships and a puissant power of men-of-arms and archers, he sailed into Ireland. . . .

[**497**] Now, whilst he was thus occupied in devising how to reduce them [the Irish] into subjection, and taking orders for the good stay and quiet government of the country, divers of the nobility, as well

[39] Again.

[40] Richard's second wife, aged twelve in 1399.

prelates as other, and likewise many of the magistrates and rulers of the cities, towns, and commonalty, here in England, perceiving daily how the realm drew to utter ruin, not like to be recovered to the former state of wealth whilst King Richard lived and reigned (as they took it), devised, with great deliberation and considerate advice, to send and signify by letters unto Duke Henry, whom they now called (as he was indeed) Duke of Lancaster and Hereford, requiring him with all convenient speed to convey himself into England; promising him all their aid, power, and assistance if he, expelling King Richard as a man not meet for the office he bore, would take upon him the scepter, rule, and diadem of his native land and region [**225**].

He, therefore, being thus called upon by messengers and letters from his friends, and chiefly through the earnest persuasion of Thomas Arundel late Archbishop of Canterbury, who (as before ye have heard) had been removed from his see and banished the realm by King Richard's means, got him down to Brittany, together with the said Archbishop; where he was joyfully received of the Duke and Duchess, and found such friendship at the Duke's hands that there were certain ships rigged and made ready for him, at a place in Base[41] Brittany called Le Port Blanc [**277**], as we find in the chronicles of Brittany; and when all his provision was made ready, he took the sea, together with the said Archbishop of Canterbury and his nephew Thomas Arundel, son and heir to the late Earl of Arundel, beheaded at the Tower Hill, as you have heard. There were also with him Reginald Lord Cobham, Sir Thomas Erpingham, and Sir Thomas Ramston, knights; John Norbury, Robert Waterton, and Francis Quoint, esquires [**279**]. Few else were there, for (as some write) he had not past fifteen lances, as they termed them in those days, that is to say, men-of-arms furnished and appointed as the use then was. Yet other write that the Duke of Brittany delivered unto him three thousand men-of-war to attend him, and that he had eight ships well furnished for the war, where Froissart yet speaketh but of three. Moreover, where Froissart and also the chronicles of Brittany avouch that he should land at Plymouth, by our English writers it seemeth otherwise, for it appeareth by their assured report that he, approaching to the shore, did not straight take land but lay hovering aloof, and showed himself now in this place and now in that, to see what countenance was made by the people, whether they meant enviously to resist him or friendly to receive him.

[41]Lower; *i.e.*, western.

[**498**] When the Lord Governor, Edmund Duke of York, was advertised that the Duke of Lancaster kept still the sea and was ready to arrive (but where he meant first to set foot on land there was not any that understood the certainty), he sent for the Lord Chancellor, Edmund Stafford Bishop of Exeter, and for the Lord Treasurer, William Scrope Earl of Wiltshire, and other of the King's Privy Council, as John Bushy, William Bagot, Henry Greene, and John Russell, knights [**2.2.72**]. Of these he required to know what they thought good to be done in this matter concerning the Duke of Lancaster being on the seas. Their advice was to depart from London unto Saint Albans, and there to gather an army to resist the Duke in his landing; but to how small purpose their counsel served the conclusion thereof plainly declared, for the most part that were called, when they came thither, boldly protested that they would not fight against the Duke of Lancaster, whom they knew to be evil dealt withal.

The Lord Treasurer, Bushy, Bagot, and Greene, perceiving that the commons would cleave unto and take part with the Duke, slipped away, leaving the Lord Governor of the realm and the Lord Chancellor to make what shift they could for themselves. Bagot got him to Chester and so escaped into Ireland [**140**]; the other fled to the castle of Bristol [**134**], in hope there to be in safety. The Duke of Lancaster, after that he had coasted alongst the shore a certain time and had got some intelligence how the people's minds were affected toward him, landed about the beginning of July [1399] in Yorkshire, at a place sometime called Ravenspur, betwixt Hull and Bridlington, and with him not past threescore persons (as some write); but he was so joyfully received of the lords, knights, and gentlemen of those parts that he found means (by their help) forthwith to assemble a great number of people that were willing to take his part. The first that came to him were the Lords of Lincolnshire and other countries adjoining, as the Lords Willoughby, Ross, Darcy, and Beaumont.

At his coming unto Doncaster, the Earl of Northumberland and his son Sir Henry Percy, Wardens of the Marches against Scotland, with the Earl of Westmorland, came unto him; where he swore unto those lords that he would demand no more but the lands that were to him descended by inheritance from his father and in right of his wife [**2.3.148**]. Moreover, he undertook to cause the payment of taxes and tallages[42] to be laid down, and to bring the King to good government,

[42]Feudal taxes.

and to remove from him the Cheshire men, which were envied[43] of many; for that the King esteemed of them more than of any other, haply because they were more faithful to him than other, ready in all respects to obey his commandments and pleasure. From Doncaster, having now got a mighty army about him, he marched forth with all speed through the countries, coming by Evesham unto Berkeley [**53**]. Within the space of three days all the King's castles in those parts were surrendered unto him.

The Duke of York, whom King Richard had left as Governor of the realm in his absence, hearing that his nephew the Duke of Lancaster was thus arrived and had gathered an army, he also assembled a puissant power of men-of-arms and archers (as before ye have heard); but all was in vain [**153**], for there was not a man that willingly would thrust out one arrow against the Duke of Lancaster or his partakers,[44] or in any wise offend him or his friends. The Duke of York therefore, passing forth toward Wales to meet the King at his coming forth of Ireland, was received into the castle of Berkeley, and there remained till the coming thither of the Duke of Lancaster; whom when he perceived that he was not able to resist, on the Sunday after the feast of Saint James (which as that year came about fell upon the Friday), he came forth into the church that stood without the castle and there commoned with the Duke of Lancaster. With the Duke of York were the Bishop of Norwich, the Lord Berkeley, the Lord Seymour, and other. With the Duke of Lancaster were these: Thomas Arundel Archbishop of Canterbury (that had been banished), the Abbot of Leicester, the Earls of Northumberland and Westmorland, Thomas Arundel son to Richard late Earl of Arundel, the Baron of Greystoke, the Lords Willoughby and Ross, with divers other lords, knights, and other people which daily came to him from every part of the realm. Those that came not were spoiled of all they had, so as they were never able to recover themselves again, for their goods, being then taken away, were never restored. And thus, what for love and what for fear of loss, they came flocking unto him from every part.

At the same present there was arrested and committed to safe custody the Bishop of Norwich, Sir William Elmham and Sir Walter Burley, knights, Lawrence Drew and John Golofer, esquires. On the morrow after, the foresaid Dukes, with their power, went toward Bristol, where (at their coming) they showed themselves before the

[43]Hated.
[44]Supporters.

town and castle, being an huge multitude of people. There were enclosed within the castle the Lord William Scrope Earl of Wiltshire and Treasurer of England, Sir Henry Greene and Sir John Bushy, knights, who prepared to make resistance; but when it would not prevail, they were taken and brought forth bound as prisoners into the camp before the Duke of Lancaster. On the morrow next ensuing they were arraigned before the Constable and Marshal and found guilty of treason for misgoverning the King and realm; and forthwith had their heads smit off [**3.1.29**]. Sir John Russell was also taken there, who, feigning himself to be out of his wits, escaped their hands for a time.

[**499**] In this meantime King Richard, advertised how the Duke of Lancaster was landed in England, and that the lords, gentlemen, and commons assembled themselves to take his part, he forthwith caused the Lord Henry, son to the said Duke of Lancaster, and the Lord Humphrey, son to the Duke of Gloucester, to be shut up fast in the castle of Trim; and with all speed made haste to return into England, in hope with an army to encounter the Duke before he should have time to assemble his friends together. But here you shall note that it fortuned at the same time in which the Duke of Hereford or Lancaster (whether[45] ye list to call him) arrived thus in England, the seas were so troubled by tempests and the winds blew so contrary for any passage to come over forth of England to the King, remaining still in Ireland, that for the space of six weeks he received no advertisements from thence; yet at length, when the seas became calm and the wind once turned anything favorable, there came over a ship [**2.2.122**]; whereby the King understood the manner of the Duke's arrival and all his proceedings till that day in which the ship departed from the coast of England, whereupon he meant forthwith to have returned over into England to make resistance against the Duke; but through persuasion of the Duke of Aumerle (as was thought), he stayed till he might have all his ships and other provision fully ready for his passage.

In the meantime he sent the Earl of Salisbury over into England to gather a power together by help of the King's friends in Wales and Cheshire, with all speed possible, that they might be ready to assist him against the Duke upon his arrival, for he meant himself to follow the Earl within six days after. The Earl, passing over into Wales, landed at Conway and sent forth letters to the King's friends, both in

[45]Whichever.

Wales and Cheshire, to levy their people and to come with all speed to assist the King; whose request, with great desire and very willing minds, they fulfilled, hoping to have found the King himself at Conway; insomuch that within four days' space there were to the number of forty thousand men assembled [**2.4.1, 3.2.76**], ready to march with the King against his enemies if he had been there himself in person.

But when they missed the King there was a bruit spread amongst them that the King was surely dead; which wrought such an impression and evil disposition in the minds of the Welshmen and others that, for any persuasion which the Earl of Salisbury might use, they would not go forth with him till they saw the King; only they were contented to stay fourteen days to see if he should come or not; but when he came not within that term they would no longer abide, but scaled[46] and departed away; whereas if the King had come before their breaking up, no doubt but they would have put the Duke of Hereford in adventure[47] of a field;[48] so that the King's lingering of time, before his coming over, gave opportunity to the Duke to bring things to pass as he could have wished, and took from the King all occasion to recover afterward any forces sufficient to resist him.

At length, about eighteen days after that the King had sent from him the Earl of Salisbury, he took the sea, together with the Dukes of Aumerle, Exeter, Surrey, and divers others of the nobility, with the Bishops of London, Lincoln, and Carlisle. They landed [July, 1399] near the castle of Barkloughly in Wales [**1**], about the feast of Saint James the Apostle, and stayed awhile in the same castle, being advertised of the great forces which the Duke of Lancaster had got together against him; wherewith he was marvelously amazed, knowing certainly that those which were thus in arms with the Duke of Lancaster against him would rather die than give place, as well for the hatred as fear which they had conceived at him. Nevertheless he, departing from Barkloughly, hasted with all speed toward Conway, where he understood the Earl of Salisbury to be still remaining.

He therefore taking with him such Cheshire men as he had with him at that present (in whom all his trust was reposed), he doubted not to revenge himself of his adversaries, and so at the first he passed with a good courage; but when he understood, as he went thus for-

[46]Mounted.
[47]To the risk.
[48]Battle.

ward, that all the castles, even from the borders of Scotland unto Bristol, were delivered unto the Duke of Lancaster; and that likewise the nobles and commons, as well of the south parts as the north, were fully bent to take part with the same Duke against him; and further, hearing how his trusty councillors had lost their heads at Bristol, he became so greatly discomforted that, sorrowfully lamenting his miserable state, he utterly despaired of his own safety and, calling his army together, which was not small, licensed every man to depart to his home [**217**].

The soldiers, being well bent to fight in his defense, besought him to be of good cheer, promising with an oath to stand with him against the Duke and all his partakers unto death; but this could not encourage him at all, so that in the night next ensuing he stole from his army, and with the Dukes of Exeter and Surrey, the Bishop of Carlisle, and Sir Stephen Scrope, and about half a score others, he got him to the castle of Conway, where he found the Earl of Salisbury; determining there to hold himself till he might see the world at some better stay, for what counsel to take to remedy the mischief thus pressing upon him he wist not. . . .

This surely is a very notable example, and not unworthy of all princes to be well weighed and diligently marked, that this Henry Duke of Lancaster should be thus called to the kingdom and have the help and assistance (almost) of all the whole realm, which perchance never thereof thought or yet dreamed; and that King Richard should thus be left desolate, void, and in despair of all hope and comfort, in whom if there were any offense it ought rather to be imputed to the frailty of wanton youth [**2.1.2**] than to the malice of his heart. But such is the deceivable judgment of man, which, not regarding things present with due consideration, thinketh ever that things to come shall have good success, with a pleasant and delightful end. But in this dejecting of the one and advancing of the other, the providence of God is to be respected and His secret will to be wondered at. For as in His hands standeth the donation of kingdoms, so likewise the disposing of them consisteth in His pleasure. . . .

Sir Thomas Percy Earl of Worcester, Lord Steward of the King's house, either being so commanded by the King or else upon displeasure (as some write) for that the King had proclaimed his brother the Earl of Northumberland traitor, broke his white staff (which is the representing sign and token of his office) and without delay went to Duke Henry [**2.2.59**]. When the King's servants of household saw this (for it was done before them all), they dispersed themselves, some into one country and some into another.

[**500**] . . . After this the Duke, with advice of his Council, sent the Earl of Northumberland unto the King accompanied with four hundred lances and a thousand archers; who, coming to the castle of Flint, had it delivered unto him; and from thence he hastened forth toward Conway. But before he approached near the place, he left his power behind him, hid closely in two ambushes behind a craggy mountain beside the highway that leadeth from Flint to Conway.

This done, taking not past four or five with him, he passed forth till he came before the town; and then, sending an herald to the King, requested a safe-conduct from the King that he might come and talk with him [**3.3.33**]; which the King granted. And so the Earl of Northumberland, passing the water,[49] entered the castle and, coming to the King, declared to him that, if it might please his grace to undertake that there should be a parliament assembled in the which justice might be had against such as were enemies to the commonwealth and had procured the destruction of the Duke of Gloucester and other noblemen, and herewith pardon the Duke of Hereford of all things wherein he had offended him, the Duke would be ready to come to him on his knees [**114**] to crave of him forgiveness and, as an humble subject, to obey him in all dutiful services. The King, taking advice upon these offers and other made by the Earl of Northumberland on the behalf of the Duke of Hereford, upon the Earl's oath for assurance that the same should be performed in each condition, agreed to go with the Earl to meet the Duke; and hereupon taking their horses, they rode forth. But the Earl rode before, as it were to prepare dinner for the King at Rutland; but coming to the place where he had left his people, he stayed there with them.

The King, keeping on his way, had not ridden past four miles when he came to the place where the ambushes were lodged and, being entered within danger of them[50] before he was aware, showed himself to be sore abashed. But now there was no remedy, for the Earl, being there with his men, would not suffer him to return, as he gladly would have done if he might; but being enclosed with the sea on the one side and the rocks on the other, having his adversaries so near at hand before him, he could not shift away by any means, for if he should have fled back they might easily have overtaken him ere he

[49]Moat.
[50]Into their power.

could have got out of their danger. And thus of force he was then constrained to go with the Earl, who brought him to Rutland, where they dined; and from thence they rode unto Flint to bed. . . .

But now to our purpose. King Richard being thus come unto the castle of Flint on the Monday the eighteenth of August, and the Duke of Hereford being still advertised from hour to hour by posts how the Earl of Northumberland sped, the morrow following being Tuesday and the nineteenth of August, he came thither and mustered his army before the King's presence; which undoubtedly made a passing fair show, being very well ordered by the Lord Henry Percy [**20**], that was appointed general or, rather (as we may call him), Master of the Camp, under the Duke, of the whole army. There were come already to the castle, before the approaching of the main army, the Archbishop of Canterbury, the Duke of Aumerle, the Earl of Worcester, and divers other. The Archbishop entered first, and then followed the other, coming into the first ward.[51]

[**501**] The King, that was walking aloft on the brayes[52] of the walls [**61 SD**] to behold the coming of the Duke afar off, might see that the Archbishop and the other were come, and (as he took it) to talk with him. Whereupon he forthwith came down unto them, and beholding that they did their due reverence to him on their knees, he took them up and, drawing the Archbishop aside from the residue, talked with him a good while; and, as it was reported, the Archbishop willed him to be of good comfort, for he should be assured not to have any hurt as touching his person; but he prophesied not as a prelate but as a Pilate [**4.1.239**]. For was it no hurt (think you) to his person to be spoiled of his royalty, to be deposed from his crown, to be translated from principality to prison, and to fall from honor into horror? All which befell him to his extreme heart grief (no doubt), which, to increase, means alas there were many, but, to diminish, helps (God wot) but a few. . . .

But whe'rsoever[53] this offer was made, after that the Archbishop had now here at Flint commoned with the King, he departed and, taking his horse again, rode back to meet the Duke, who began at that present to approach the castle, and compassed it round about, even down to the sea, with his people, ranged in good and seemly order at the foot of the mountains. And then the Earl of Northumber-

[51]Area between inner and outer walls.
[52]Parapet.
[53]Whether.

land, passing forth of the castle to the Duke, talked with him awhile in sight of the King, being again got up to the walls to take better view of the army, being now advanced within two bowshots of the castle, to the small rejoicing (ye may be sure) of the sorrowful King. The Earl of Northumberland, returning to the castle, appointed the King to be set to dinner (for he was fasting till then); and after he had dined, the Duke came down to the castle himself and entered the same all armed, his basinet[54] only excepted; and being within the first gate, he stayed there till the King came forth of the inner part of the castle unto him.

The King, accompanied with the Bishop of Carlisle, the Earl of Salisbury, and Sir Stephen Scrope, knight (who bore the sword before him), and a few other, came forth into the outer ward and sat down in a place prepared for him [**3.3.178**]. Forthwith, as the Duke got sight of the King he showed a reverend duty as became him in bowing his knee and, coming forward, did so likewise the second and third time, till the King took him by the hand and lift him up [**194**], saying, "Dear cousin, ye are welcome." The Duke, humbly thanking him, said: "My sovereign lord and King, the cause of my coming at this present is (your honor saved) to have again restitution of my person, my lands, and heritage, through your favorable license." The King hereunto answered: "Dear cousin, I am ready to accomplish your will, so that ye may enjoy all that is yours without exception."

Meeting thus together, they came forth of the castle and the King there called for wine; and after they had drunk they mounted on horseback and rode that night to Flint, . . . and so [by the end of August] came to London. . . .

As for the Duke, he was received with all the joy and pomp that might be of the Londoners [**5.2.12**], and was lodged in the Bishop's palace by Paul's Church. It was a wonder to see what great concourse of people and what number of horses came to him on the way as he thus passed the countries, till his coming to London, where (upon his approach to the city) the Mayor rode forth to receive him, and a great number of other citizens. Also the clergy met him with procession; and such joy appeared in the countenances of the people, uttering the same also with words, as the like [had] not lightly[55] been seen. For in every town and village where he passed, children rejoiced, women clapped their hands, and men cried out for joy. But to speak

[54]Headpiece.
[55]Commonly.

of the great numbers of people that flocked together in the fields and streets of London at his coming, I here omit; neither will I speak of the presents, welcomings, lauds, and gratifications made to him by the citizens and commonalty.

But now to the purpose. The next day after his coming to London, the King from Westminister was had to the Tower and there committed to safe custody. Many evil-disposed persons, assembling themselves together in great numbers, intended to have met with him and to have taken him from such as had the conveying [**4.1.316**] of him, that they might have slain him [**5.2.5**, **27**]. But the Mayor and aldermen gathered to them the worshipful commoners and grave citizens, by whose policy, and not without much ado, the other were revoked from their evil purpose. . . .

[**502**] After this was a parliament called [**4.1 SD**] by the Duke of Lancaster, using the name of King Richard in the writs directed forth to the lords and other states for their summons. This parliament began the thirteenth day of September [1399], in the which many heinous points of misgovernance and injurious dealings in the administration of his kingly office were laid to the charge of this noble prince King Richard.

[**503**] . . . Then forsomuch as these articles [**243**] and other heinous and detestable accusations were laid against him in open parliament, it was thought by the most part that he was worthy to be deposed from all kingly honor and princely government; and to bring the matter without slander the better to pass, divers of the King's servants, which by license had access to his person, comforted him (being with sorrow almost consumed and in manner half dead) in the best wise they could, exhorting him to regard his health and save his life.

And first they advised him willingly to suffer himself to be deposed, and to resign his right of his own accord, so that the Duke of Lancaster might without murder or battle obtain the scepter and diadem, after which (they well perceived) he gaped; by mean whereof they thought he might be in perfect assurance of his life long to continue. Whether this their persuasion proceeded by the suborning of the Duke of Lancaster and his favorers, or of a sincere affection which they bore to the King as supposing it most sure in such an extremity, it is uncertain; but yet the effect followed not, howsoever their meaning was. Notwithstanding, the King, being now in the hands of his enemies and utterly despairing of all comfort, was easily persuaded to renounce his crown and princely preeminence, so that, in hope of life only, he agreed to all things that were of him demanded [**109**]. And so (as it should seem by the copy of an instrument hereafter following) he renounced and voluntarily was deposed from his royal crown and kingly dignity, the Monday being the nine and twentieth day of September and feast of Saint Michael the Archangel in the year of our Lord 1399, and in the three and twentieth year of his reign. The copy of which instrument [touching the declaration of the commissioners sent from the states in parliament unto King Richard] here ensueth.

[**504**] . . . And although he had and might sufficiently have declared his renouncement by the reading of another, mean[56] person, yet for the more surety of the matter, and for that the said resignation should have his full force and strength, himself therefore read the scroll of resignation [**203, 222**], in manner and form as followeth. . . .

"'In the name of God, amen. I, Richard, by the grace of God King of England and of France, etc., Lord of Ireland, acquit and assoil all archbishops, bishops, and other prelates, secular or religious, of what dignity, degree, state, or condition soever they be, and also all dukes, marquises, earls, barons, lords, and all my liege men, both spiritual and secular, of what manner or degree they be, from their oath of fealty and homage, and all other deeds and privileges made unto me, and from all manner bonds of allegiance, regality, and lordship in which they were or be bounden to me, or any otherwise constrained; and them, their heirs, and successors for evermore, from the same bonds and oaths I release, deliver, and acquit, and set them for free, dissolved and acquit, and to be harmless, forasmuch as longeth[57] to my person by any manner, way, or title of right that to me might follow of the foresaid things, or any of them. And also I resign all my kingly dignity, majesty, and crown, with all the lordships, power, and privileges to the foresaid kingly dignity and crown belonging, and all other lordships and possessions to me in any manner of wise pertaining, of what name, title, quality, or condition soever they be, except the lands and possessions for me and mine obits[58] purchased and bought. And I renounce all right and all manner of title of possession which I ever had or have in the same lordships and

[56]Low-ranking.
[57]Belongs.
[58]Postmortem commemorative services.

possessions, or any of them, with any manner of rights belonging or appertaining unto any part of them. And also the rule and governance of the same kingdom and lordships, with all ministrations of the same, and all things and every each of them that to the whole empire and jurisdictions of the same belongeth of right or in any wise may belong. . . .'

"Now forthwith, in our presences and others, he subscribed the same and after delivered it unto the Archbishop of Canterbury, saying that, if it were in his power or at his assignment, he would that the Duke of Lancaster there present should be his successor and King after him. And in token hereof he took a ring of gold from his finger [**181**], being his signet, and put it upon the said Duke's finger, desiring and requiring the Archbishop of York and the Bishop of Hereford to show and make report unto the lords of the parliament of his voluntary resignation, and also of his intent and good mind that he bore toward his cousin the Duke of Lancaster to have him his successor and their King after him. . . ."

Upon the morrow after, being Tuesday and the last day of September, all the lords spiritual and temporal, with the commons of the said parliament, assembled at Westminster, where, in the presence of them, the Archbishop of York and the Bishop of Hereford, according to the King's request, showed unto them the voluntary renouncing of the King, with the favor also which he bore to his cousin of Lancaster to have him his successor; and, moreover, showed them the schedule or bill of renouncement signed with King Richard's own hand; which they caused to be read first in Latin (as it was written) and after in English. This done, the question was first asked of the lords if they would admit and allow that renouncement; the which, when it was of them granted and confirmed, the like question was asked of the commons, and of them in like manner confirmed. After this, it was then declared that nothwithstanding the foresaid renouncing, so by the lords and commons admitted and confirmed, it were necessary, in avoiding of all suspicions and surmises of evil-disposed persons, to have in writing and registered the manifold crimes and defaults before done by King Richard, to the end that they might first be openly declared to the people [**155**, **222**], and after to remain of record amongst other of the King's records forever.

[**505**] . . . Then, forsomuch as the lords of the parliament had well considered the voluntary resignation of King Richard, and that it was behooveful and, as they thought, necessary for the weal of

the realm to proceed unto the sentence of his deposing, there were appointed, by the authority of all the estates there in parliament assembled, the Bishop of Saint Asaph, the Abbot of Glastonbury, the Earl of Gloucester, the Lord Berkeley, William Thirning, justice, and Thomas Erpingham with Thomas Grey, knights, that they should give and pronounce the open sentence of the deposing of King Richard.

. . . Immediately as the sentence was in this wise passed, and that by reason thereof the realm stood void without head or Governor for the time, the Duke of Lancaster, rising from the place where before he sat, and standing where all those in the house might behold him, in reverend manner made a sign of the cross on his forehead and likewise on his breast and, after silence by an officer commanded, said unto the people there being present these words following. . . .

"In the name of the Father and of the Son and of the Holy Ghost, I, Henry of Lancaster, claim the realm of England and the crown, with all the appurtenances, as I that am descended by right line of the blood coming from that good Lord King Henry the Third, and through the right that God of His grace hath sent me, with the help of my kin and of my friends, to recover the same, which was in point to be undone for default of good governance and due justice" [**113**].

After these words thus by him uttered, he returned and sat him down in the place where before he had sitten. Then the lords, having heard and well perceived this claim thus made by this nobleman, each of them asked of other what they thought therein. At length, after a little pausing or stay made, the Archbishop of Canterbury, having notice of the minds of the lords, stood up and asked the commons if they would assent to the lords, which in their minds thought the claim of the Duke made to be rightful and necessary for the wealth of the realm and them all; whereto the commons with one voice cried, "Yea, yea, yea!" After which answer the said Archbishop, going to the Duke and kneeling down before him on his knee, addressed to him all his purpose in few words. The which when he had ended, he rose and, taking the Duke by the right hand, led him unto the King's seat (the Archbishop of York assisting him) and with great reverence set him therein, after that the Duke had first upon his knees made his prayer in devout manner unto almighty God. . . .

[**507**] Thus was King Richard deprived of all kingly honor and princely dignity, by reason he was so given to follow evil counsel,

and used such inconvenient[59] ways and means, through insolent misgovernance and youthful outrage, though otherwise a right noble and worthy prince. . . . For shortly after his resignation he was conveyed to the castle of Leeds in Kent, and from thence to Pomfret [**5.1.52**], where he departed out of this miserable life (as after you shall hear). He was seemly of shape and favor, and of nature good enough if the wickedness and naughty demeanor of such as were about him had not altered it.

His chance verily was greatly unfortunate, which fell into such calamity that he took it for the best way he could devise to renounce his kingdom, for the which mortal men are accustomed to hazard all they have to attain thereunto. But such misfortune (or the like) oftentimes falleth unto those princes which, when they are aloft, cast no doubt for perils that may follow. He was prodigal, ambitious, and much given to the pleasure of the body. He kept the greatest port,[60] and maintained the most plentiful house that ever any king in England did either before his time or since. For there resorted daily to his court above ten thousand persons [**4.1.283**] that had meat and drink there allowed them. . . .

[**508**] Moreover, such were preferred to bishoprics and other ecclesiastical livings as neither could teach nor preach, nor knew anything of the scripture of God but only to call for their tithes and duties; so that they were most unworthy the name of bishops, being lewd[61] and most vain persons disguised in bishop's apparel. Furthermore, there reigned abundantly the filthy sin of lechery and fornication, with abominable adultery, specially in the King [**3.1.11**] but most chiefly in the prelacy, whereby the whole realm by such their evil example was so infected that the wrath of God was daily provoked to vengeance for the sins of the prince and his people. . . .

Thus have ye heard what writers do report touching the state of the time and doings of this King. But if I may boldly say what I think, he was a prince the most unthankfully used of his subjects of any one of whom ye shall lightly read. . . .

[**511**] But to proceed to other doings. The solemnity of the coronation being ended, the morrow after being Tuesday, the parliament began again. . . .

Thus much ado there was in this parliament, specially about them

[59]Improper.
[60]Style of living.
[61]Ignorant.

that were thought to be guilty of the Duke of Gloucester's death, and of the condemning of the other lords that were adjudged traitors in the foresaid late parliament holden in the said one and twentieth year of King Richard's reign [**4.1.1**]. Sir John Bagot, knight, then prisoner in the Tower, disclosed many secrets unto the which he was privy; and being brought on a day to the bar, a bill was read in English which he had made containing certain evil practices of King Richard; and further, what great affection the same King bore to the Duke of Aumerle, insomuch that he heard him say that if he should renounce the government of the kingdom, he wished to leave it to the said Duke as to the most able man (for wisdom and manhood) of all other; for though he could like better of the Duke of Hereford, yet he said that he knew if he were once King he would prove an extreme enemy and cruel tyrant to the Church.

It was further contained in that bill that, as the same Bagot rode on a day behind the Duke of Norfolk in the Savoy Street toward Westminster, the Duke asked him what he knew of the manner of the Duke of Gloucester his death; and he answered that he knew nothing at all; "but the people," quoth he, "do say that you have murdered him" [**10**]. Whereunto the Duke swore great oaths that it was untrue, and that he had saved his life, contrary to the will of the King and certain other lords, by the space of three weeks and more; affirming withal that he was never in all his lifetime more afraid of death than he was at his coming home again from Calais at that time to the King's presence by reason he had not put the Duke to death. "And then," said he, "the King appointed one of his own servants, and certain other that were servants to other lords, to go with him to see the said Duke of Gloucester put to death"; swearing that, as he should answer afore God, it was never his mind that he should have died in that sort, but only for fear of the King and saving of his own life. Nevertheless, there was no man in the realm to whom King Richard was so much beholden as to the Duke of Aumerle; for he was the man that, to fulfill his mind, had set him in hand with all that was done against the said Duke and the other lords. There was also contained in that bill what secret malice King Richard had conceived against the Duke of Hereford, being in exile, whereof the same Bagot had sent intelligence unto the Duke into France by one Roger Smart, who certified it to him by Piers Buckton and others, to the intent he should the better have regard to himself. There was also contained in the said bill that Bagot had heard the Duke of Aumerle say that he had rather than twenty thousand pounds that the Duke of Hereford were dead [**19**], not for any fear he had of him but for the trouble and mischief that he was like to procure within the realm.

[**512**] After that the bill had been read and heard, the Duke of Aumerle rose up and said that, as touching the points contained in the bill concerning him, they were utterly false and untrue; which he would prove with his body, in what manner soever it should be thought requisite [**84**].

. . . On the Saturday next ensuing, Sir William Bagot and the said John Hall[c] were brought both to the bar, and Bagot was examined of certain points and sent again to prison. The Lord Fitzwater herewith rose up and said to the King that, "Where the Duke of Aumerle excuseth himself of the Duke of Gloucester's death, I say," quoth he, "that he was the very cause of his death"; and so he appealed him of treason, offering by throwing down his hood as a gage to prove it with his body [**34**]. There were twenty other lords also that threw down their hoods, as pledges to prove the like matter against the Duke of Aumerle. The Duke of Aumerle threw down his hood to try it against the Lord Fitzwater, as against him that lied falsely in that he had charged him with by that his appeal. These gages were delivered to the Constable and Marshal of England, and the parties put under arrest.

The Duke of Surrey stood up also against the Lord Fitzwater [**60**], avouching that, where he had said that the appellants were causers of the Duke of Gloucester's death, it was false, for they were constrained to sue the same appeal, in like manner as the said Lord Fitzwater was compelled to give judgment against the Duke of Gloucester and the Earl of Arundel; so that the suing of the appeal was done by constraint, and if he said contrary he lied; and therewith he threw down his hood. The Lord Fitzwater answered hereunto that he was not present in the parliament house when judgment was given against them, and all the lords bore witness thereof. Moreover, where it was alleged that the Duke of Aumerle should send two of his servants to Calais to murder the Duke of Gloucester, the said Duke of Aumerle said that if the Duke of Norfolk affirm it, he lied falsely, and that he would prove with his body; throwing down another hood which he had borrowed. The same was likewise delivered to the Constable and Marshal of England, and the King licensed the Duke of Norfolk to return, that he might arraign his appeal [**87**]. . . .

[c]A former servant of Norfolk's.

On Wednesday following, request was made by the commons that sith King Richard had resigned and was lawfully deposed from his royal dignity, he might have judgment decreed against him, so as the realm were not troubled by him, and that the causes of his deposing might be published through the realm for satisfying of the people; which demand was granted. Whereupon the Bishop of Carlisle, a man both learned, wise, and stout of stomach,[62] boldly showed forth his opinion concerning that demand; affirming that there was none amongst them worthy or meet to give judgment upon so noble a prince as King Richard was [**117**], whom they had taken for their sovereign and liege lord by the space of two and twenty years and more. "And I assure you," said he, "there is not so rank a traitor nor so arrant a thief, nor yet so cruel a murderer apprehended or detained in prison for his offense, but he shall be brought before the justice to hear his judgment; and will ye proceed to the judgment of an anointed King, hearing neither his answer nor excuse? I say that the Duke of Lancaster, whom ye call King [**134**], hath more trespassed to King Richard and his realm than King Richard hath done either to him or us; for it is manifest and well known that the Duke was banished the realm by King Richard and his Council, and by the judgment of his own father, for the space of ten years, for what cause ye know, and yet without license of King Richard he is returned again into the realm and (that is worse) hath taken upon him the name, title, and preeminence of King. And therefore I say that you have done manifest wrong to proceed in anything against King Richard without calling him openly to his answer and defense." As soon as the Bishop had ended this tale, he was attached by the Earl Marshal [**151**] and committed to ward[63] in the abbey of Saint Albans.

[**514**] . . . This year [1399] Thomas Mowbray Duke of Norfolk died in exile at Venice [**97**]; whose death might have been worthily bewailed of all the realm if he had not been consenting to the death of the Duke of Gloucester. The same year deceased the Duchess of Gloucester [**2.2.96**], through sorrow (as was thought) which she conceived for the loss of her son and heir the Lord Humphrey, who, being sent for forth of Ireland (as before ye have heard), was taken with the pestilence and died by the way.

But now to speak of the conspiracy which was contrived by the

[62]Brave of spirit.
[63]Imprisonment.

Abbot of Westminster as chief instrument thereof [**4.1.321**]. Ye shall understand that this Abbot (as it is reported) upon a time heard King Henry say, when he was but Earl of Derby and young of years, that princes had too little and religious men too much. He, therefore, doubting now lest, if the King continued long in the estate, he would remove the great beam that then grieved his eyes and pricked his conscience, became an instrument to search out the minds of the nobility and to bring them to an assembly and council where they might consult and common together how to bring that to effect which they earnestly wished and desired, that was, the destruction of King Henry and the restoring of King Richard. For there were divers lords that showed themselves outwardly to favor King Henry where they secretly wished and sought his confusion. The Abbot, after he had felt the minds of sundry of them, called to his house, on a day in the term time [December, 1399], all such lords and other persons which he either knew or thought to be, as affectioned to King Richard, so envious to the prosperity of King Henry; whose names were: John Holland Earl of Huntingdon, late Duke of Exeter; Thomas Holland Earl of Kent, late Duke of Surrey; Edward Earl of Rutland, late Duke of Aumerle, son to the Duke of York; John Montague Earl of Salisbury; Hugh[d] Lord Despenser, late Earl of Gloucester; Thomas the Bishop of Carlisle; Sir Thomas Blount; and [John] Magdalen, a priest, one of King Richard's chapel, a man as like him in stature and proportion in all lineaments of body as unlike in birth, dignity, and conditions.

The Abbot highly feasted these lords, his special friends; and when they had well dined, they withdrew into a secret chamber where they sat down in council; and after much talk and conference had about the bringing of their purpose to pass concerning the destruction of King Henry, at length by the advice of the Earl of Huntingdon it was devised that they should take upon them a solemn jousts to be enterprised between him and twenty on his part, and the Earl of Salisbury and twenty with him, at Oxford [**5.3.14**]; to the which triumph[64] King Henry should be desired, and when he should be most busily marking the martial pastime, he suddenly should be slain and destroyed [**5.2.99**]; and so by that means King Richard, who as yet lived, might be restored to liberty and have his former estate and dignity. It was further appointed who should assemble the people,

[d]Thomas.
[64]Entertainment.

the number and persons which should accomplish and put in execution their devised enterprise. Hereupon was an indenture sexpartite made, sealed with their seals and signed with their hands, in the which each stood bound to other to do their whole endeavor for the accomplishing of their purposed exploit. Moreover, they swore on the holy evangelists to be true and secret each to other, even to the hour and point of death.

When all things were thus appointed, the Earl of Huntingdon came to the King unto Windsor, earnestly requiring him that he would vouchsafe to be at Oxford on the day appointed of their jousts; both to behold the same and to be the discoverer and indifferent[65] judge (if any ambiguity should rise) of their courageous acts and doings. The King, being thus instantly required of his brother-in-law, and nothing less imagining than that which was pretended,[66] gently granted to fulfill his request. Which thing obtained, all the lords of the conspiracy departed home to their houses, as they noised it, to set armorers on work about the trimming of their armor against the jousts, and to prepare all other furniture and things ready as to such an high and solemn triumph appertained. The Earl of Huntingdon came to his house and raised men on every side, and prepared horse and harness for his compassed purpose; and when he had all things ready, he departed toward Oxford; and at his coming thither, he found all his mates and confederates there, well appointed for their purpose, except the Earl of Rutland,[67] by whose folly their practiced[68] conspiracy was brought to light and disclosed to King Henry. For this Earl of Rutland, departing before from Westminster [January, 1400] to see his father the Duke of York, as he sat at dinner, had his counterpane[69] of the indenture of the confederacy in his bosom [**56**].

[**515**] The father, espying it, would needs see what it was; and though the son humbly denied to show it, the father, being more earnest to see it, by force took it out of his bosom and, perceiving the contents thereof, in a great rage caused his horses to be saddled out of hand, and spitefully reproving his son of treason (for whom

[65]Impartial.
[66]Intended.
[67]Aumerle.
[68]Plotted.
[69]Counterpart.

he was become surety and mainpernor[70] for his good abearing[71] in open parliament [**44**], he incontinently mounted on horseback to ride toward Windsor to the King, to declare unto him the malicious intent of his complices. The Earl of Rutland, seeing in what danger he stood, took his horse and rode another way to Windsor in post so that he got thither before his father, and when he was alighted at the castle gate, he caused the gates to be shut, saying that he must needs deliver the keys to the King [**5.3.23**]. When he came before the King's presence, he kneeled down on his knees, beseeching him of mercy and forgiveness and, declaring the whole matter unto him in order as everything had passed, obtained pardon. Therewith came his father and, being let in, delivered the indenture which he had taken from his son unto the King, who, thereby perceiving the son's words to be true, changed his purpose for his going to Oxford and dispatched messengers forth to signify unto the Earl of Northumberland his High Constable, and to the Earl of Westmorland his High Marshal, and to other his assured friends, of all the doubtful danger and perilous jeopardy. . . .

[**516**] The Lord Hugh Despenser [**5.6.7**], otherwise called Earl of Gloucester, as he would have fled into Wales, was taken and carried to Bristol, where (according to the earnest desires of the commons) he was beheaded. Magdalen [who had impersonated King Richard], fleeing into Scotland, was taken by the way and brought to the Tower. Many other that were privy to this conspiracy were taken and put to death, some at Oxford, as Sir Thomas Blount, Sir Bennet Seely, knight [**14**], and Thomas Wintersel, esquire; but Sir Leonard Brokas and Sir John Shelley, knights, John Magdalen and William Ferbey, chaplains, were drawn, hanged, and beheaded at London. There were nineteen in all executed in one place and other, and the heads of the chief conspirators were set on poles over London Bridge to the terror of others. Shortly after, the Abbot of Westminster, in whose house the conspiracy was begun (as is said), going between his monastery and mansion, for thought fell into a sudden palsy and, shortly after, without speech, ended his life. The Bishop of Carlisle was impeached and condemned of the same conspiracy; but the King of his merciful clemency pardoned him of that offense, although he died shortly after, more through fear than force of sickness, as some have written. Thus

[70]Surety.
[71]Behavior.

all the associates of this unhappy conspiracy tasted the painful penance of their pleasant pastime.

. . . And immediately after, King Henry, to rid himself of any such like danger to be attempted against him thereafter, caused King Richard to die of a violent death, that no man should afterward feign himself to represent his person, though some have said he was not privy to that wicked offense. . . .

[**517**] One writer, which seemeth to have great knowledge of King Richard's doings, saith that King Henry, sitting on a day at his table, sore sighing, said [**5.4.2**]: "Have I no faithful friend which will deliver me of him whose life will be my death and whose death will be the preservation of my life?" This saying was much noted of them which were present, and especially of one called Sir Piers of Exton. This knight incontinently departed from the court, with eight strong persons in his company, and came to Pomfret [February, 1400], commanding the esquire that was accustomed to sew[72] and take the assay[73] before King Richard to do so no more, saying, "Let him eat now, for he shall not long eat." King Richard sat down to dinner and was served without courtesy or assay, whereupon, much marveling at the sudden change, he demanded of the esquire why he did not his duty [**5.5.99**]. "Sir," said he, "I am otherwise commanded by Sir Piers of Exton, which is newly come from King Henry." When King Richard heard that word, he took the carving knife in his hand and struck the esquire on the head, saying, "The devil take Henry of Lancaster and thee together!" And with that word Sir Piers entered the chamber, well armed, with eight tall[74] men, likewise armed, every of them having a bill[75] in his hand.

King Richard, perceiving this, put the table from him and, stepping to the foremost man, wrung the bill out of his hands and so valiantly defended himself that he slew four of those that thus came to assail him [**106**]. Sir Piers, being half dismayed herewith, leapt into the chair where King Richard was wont to sit, while the other four persons fought with him and chased him about the chamber. And in conclusion, as King Richard traversed his ground from one side of the chamber to another, and coming by the chair where Sir Piers stood, he was felled with a stroke of a poleaxe which Sir Piers gave him upon

[72]Serve.
[73]Perform the tasting.
[74]Doughty.
[75]Infantry weapon resembling a halberd.

the head; and therewith rid him out of life without giving him respite once to call to God for mercy of his passed offenses [**112**]. It is said that Sir Piers of Exton, after he had thus slain him, wept right bitterly, as one stricken with the prick of a guilty conscience, for murdering him whom he had so long time obeyed as King. After he was thus dead, his body was embalmed and cered[76] and covered with lead, all save the face, to the intent that all men might see him and perceive that he was departed this life; for as the corpse was conveyed from Pomfret to London, in all the towns and places where those that had the conveyance of it did stay with it all night, they caused dirge to be sung in the evening and mass of requiem in the morning; and as well after the one service as the other, his face discovered was showed to all that coveted to behold it.

Thus was the corpse first brought to the Tower and, after, through the city to the cathedral church of Saint Paul, barefaced; where it lay three days together, that all men might behold it [**5.6.30**]. There was a solemn obsequy done for him, both at Paul's and after at Westminster, at which time, both at dirge overnight and in the morning at the mass of requiem, the King and the citizens of London were present. When the same was ended, the corpse was commanded to be had unto Langley, there to be buried in the church of the Friars Preachers. . . . He was after by King Henry the Fifth removed to Westminster and there honorably entombed with Queen Anne [of Bohemia] his [first] wife.

[76]Wrapped in a winding-sheet.

1 Henry VI

[509][1] When King Richard had resigned (as before is specified) the scepter and crown, Henry Plantagenet, born at Bolingbroke in the county of Lincoln, Duke of Lancaster and Hereford, Earl of Derby, Leicester, and Lincoln, son to John of Gaunt Duke of Lancaster, with general consent both of the lords and commons, was published, proclaimed, and declared King of England and of France and Lord of Ireland the last day of September in the year of the world 5366, of our Lord 1399, of the reign of the Emperor Wenceslaus the two and twentieth, of Charles the sixth King of France the twentieth, and the tenth of Robert the third King of Scots.

[511] . . . On the same day the King's eldest son Lord Henry, by assent of all the states[2] in the parliament, was created Prince of Wales, Duke of Cornwall, and Earl of Chester, then being of the age of twelve years.

[518] . . . In the King's absence, whilst he was forth of the realm in Scotland against his enemies [1402], the Welshmen took occasion to rebel under the conduct of their captain Owen Glendower, doing what mischief they could devise unto their English neighbors. This Owen Glendower was son to an esquire of Wales named Griffith Vichan. He dwelled in the parish of Conway, within the county of Merioneth in North Wales, in a place called Glindourwie, which is as much to say in English as "the valley by the side of the water of Dee"; by occasion whereof he was surnamed Glindour Dew.

He was first set to study the laws of the realm, and became an utter barrister or an apprentice of the law (as they term him) and served King Richard at Flint Castle when he was taken by Henry Duke of Lancaster, though other have written that he served this King Henry the Fourth, before he came to attain the crown, in room[3] of an

[1]References to *1H4* outside this section may be found at pp. 62 and 109.
[2]Lords.
[3]Position.

esquire [**3.1.22**]; and, after, by reason of variance that rose betwixt him and the Lord Reginald Grey of Ruthin about the lands which he claimed to be his by right of inheritance, when he saw that he might not prevail, finding no such favor in his suit as he looked for, he first made war against the said Lord Grey, wasting his lands and possessions with fire and sword, cruelly killing his servants and tenants [1400]. The King, advertised of such rebellious exploits enterprised by the said Owen and his unruly complices, determined to chastise them as disturbers of his peace, and so with an army entered into Wales [**64**]; but the Welshmen with their captain withdrew into the mountains of Snowdon, so to escape the revenge which the King meant toward them. The King therefore did much hurt in the countries with fire and sword, slaying divers that with weapon in hand came forth to resist him; and so with a great booty of beasts and cattle he returned. . . .

[**519**] This year [1402], the eighth day of April, deceased the Lord Thomas Beauchamp Earl of Warwick. In the month of March appeared a blazing star, first between the east part of the firmament and the north, flashing forth fire and flames round about it and, lastly, shooting forth fiery beams toward the north [**14**], foreshowing (as was thought) the great effusion of blood that followed about the parts of Wales and Northumberland.

[**520**] . . . Owen Glendower, according to his accustomed manner robbing and spoiling within the English borders, caused all the forces of the shire of Hereford to assemble together against them, under the conduct of Edmund Mortimer Earl of March. But, coming to try the matter by battle, whether by treason or otherwise, so it fortuned that the English power was discomfited, the Earl taken prisoner, and above a thousand of his people slain in the place. The shameful villainy used by the Welsh women toward the dead carcasses was such as honest[4] ears would be ashamed to hear and continent tongues to speak thereof [**1.1.43**].[5] The dead bodies might not be buried without great sums of money given for liberty to convey them away.

The King was not hasty to purchase the deliverance of the Earl March because his title to the crown was well enough known, and therefore suffered him to remain in miserable prison [**1.3.141**], wishing both the said Earl and all other of his lineage out of this life, with God and his saints in heaven, so they had been out of the way; for

[4]Virtuous.
[5]Holinshed gives details at p. 528.

then all had been well enough, as he thought. . . . About mid of August [1402] the King, to chastise the presumptuous attempts of the Welshmen, went with a great power of men into Wales to pursue the captain of the Welsh rebels, Owen Glendower; but in effect he lost his labor, for Owen conveyed himself out of the way into his known lurking-places; and, as was thought through art magic [**3.1.48**], he caused such foul weather of winds, tempest, rain, snow, and hail to be raised (for the annoyance of the King's army) that the like had not been heard of; in such sort that the King was constrained to return home, having caused his people yet to spoil and burn first a great part of the country. . . .

Archibald Earl Douglas, sore displeased in his mind for this overthrow, procured a commission to invade England, and that to his cost, as ye may likewise read in the Scottish histories. For at a place called Holmedon they were so fiercely assailed by the Englishmen, under the leading of the Lord Percy, surnamed Henry Hotspur, and George Earl of March, that with violence of the English shot they were quite vanquished and put to flight on the Rood Day in harvest [1402] with a great slaughter made by the Englishmen [**1.1.52**]. . . . There were slain, of men of estimation, Sir John Swinton, Sir Adam Gordon, Sir John Leviston, Sir Alexander Ramsey of Dalhousie, and three and twenty knights, besides ten thousand of the commons; and of prisoners, among other, were these: Mordake Earl of Fife, son to the Governor [of Scotland], Archibald Earl Douglas (which in the fight lost one of his eyes), Thomas Earl of Murray, Robert Earl of Angus, and (as some writers have) the Earls of Atholl and Menteith, with five hundred other of meaner degrees.[6]

[**521**] . . . Edmund Mortimer Earl of March,[7] prisoner with Owen Glendower, whether for irksomeness of cruel captivity or fear of death or for what other cause it is uncertain, agreed to take part with Owen against the King of England, and took to wife the daughter of the said Owen [**1.3.84**].

Strange wonders happened (as men reported) at the nativity [**3.1.13**] of this man, for, the same night he was born, all his father's horses in the stable were found to stand in blood up to the bellies. . . .

Henry Earl of Northumberland, with his brother Thomas Earl of Worcester and his son the Lord Henry Percy, surnamed Hotspur, which were to King Henry in the beginning of his reign both faithful

[6]Lower ranks.
[7]Actually Sir Edmund Mortimer, his uncle.

friends and earnest aiders, began now to envy his wealth and felicity; and especially they were grieved because the King demanded of the Earl and his son such Scottish prisoners as were taken at Holmedon and Nesbit. For of all the captives which were taken in the conflicts foughten in those two places, there was delivered to the King's possession only Mordake Earl of Fife the Duke of Albany's son [**1.1.92**], though the King did divers and sundry times require deliverance of the residue, and that with great threatenings. Wherewith the Percys, being sore offended (for that they claimed them as their own proper prisoners and their peculiar preys),[8] by the counsel of the Lord Thomas Percy Earl of Worcester, whose study was ever (as some write) to procure malice and set things in a broil [**96, 1.3.15**], came to the King unto Windsor (upon a purpose to prove[9] him), and there required of him that, either by ransom or otherwise, he would cause to be delivered out of prison Edmund Mortimer Earl of March their cousin-german [**79**], whom (as they reported) Owen Glendower kept in filthy prison, shackled with irons, only for that he took his part and was to him faithful and true.

The King began not a little to muse at this request, and not without cause; for indeed it touched him somewhat near, sith this Edmund was son to Roger Earl of March, son to the Lady Philip, daughter of Lionel Duke of Clarence, the third son of King Edward the third; which Edmund,[10] at King Richard's going into Ireland, was proclaimed heir apparent to the crown and realm; whose aunt, called Eleanor,[11] the Lord Henry Percy had married; and therefore King Henry could not well bear that any man should be earnest about the advancement of that lineage. The King, when he had studied on the matter, made answer that the Earl of March was not taken prisoner for his cause, nor in his service, but willingly suffered himself to be taken because he would not withstand the attempts of Owen Glendower and his complices [**81, 114**]; and therefore he would neither ransom him nor relieve him.

The Percys with this answer and fraudulent excuse were not a little fumed, insomuch that Henry Hotspur said openly: "Behold, the heir of the realm is robbed of his right, and yet the robber with his own will not redeem him!" So in this fury the Percys departed, minding

[8]Booty.
[9]Test.
[10]Actually his father, Roger (in 1385).
[11]Elizabeth, sister to Sir Edmund Mortimer.

nothing more than to depose King Henry from the high tipe[a] of his royalty and to place in his seat their cousin Edmund Earl of March, whom they did not only deliver out of captivity but also (to the high displeasure of King Henry) entered in league with the foresaid Owen Glendower. Herewith they, by their deputies, in the house of the Archdeacon of Bangor, divided the realm amongst them, causing a tripartite indenture to be made and sealed with their seals; by the covenants whereof all England from Severn and Trent, south and eastward, was assigned to the Earl of March; all Wales and the lands beyond Severn westward were appointed to Owen Glendower; and all the remnant from Trent northward to the Lord Percy [**3.1.70**].

This was done (as some have said) through a foolish credit given to a vain prophecy, as though King Henry was the moldwarp[12] cursed of God's own mouth [**149**], and they three were the dragon, the lion, and the wolf which should divide this realm between them. Such is the deviation (saith Hall) and not divination of those blind and fantastical dreams of the Welsh prophesiers. King Henry, not knowing of this new confederacy and nothing less minding than that which after happened, gathered a great army to go again into Wales; whereof the Earl of Northumberland and his son were advertised by the Earl of Worcester, and with all diligence raised all the power they could make and sent to the Scots which before were taken prisoners at Holmedon for aid of men, promising to the Earl of Douglas the town of Berwick and a part of Northumberland and, to other Scottish lords, great lordships and seigniories if they obtained the upper hand. The Scots, in hope of gain and desirous to be revenged of their old griefs, came to the Earl with a great company well appointed.

[**522**] The Percys, to make their part seem good, devised certain articles by the advice of Richard Scrope Archbishop of York, brother to the Lord Scrope whom King Henry had caused to be beheaded at Bristol [**1.3.270**]. These articles, being showed to divers noblemen and other states of the realm, moved them to favor their purpose, insomuch that many of them did not only promise to the Percys aid and succor by words but also by their writings and seals confirmed the same. Howbeit, when the matter came to trial, the most part of the confederates abandoned them [**2.3.1**] and at the day of the conflict left them alone. Thus, after that the conspirators had discovered[13]

[a]Summit.
[12]Mole.
[13]Revealed.

themselves, the Lord Henry Percy, desirous to proceed in the enterprise upon trust to be assisted by Owen Glendower, the Earl of March, and other, assembled an army of men-of-arms and archers forth of Cheshire and Wales. Incontinently[14] his uncle, Thomas Percy Earl of Worcester, that had the government of the Prince of Wales, who as then lay at London, in secret manner conveyed himself out of the Prince's house [**2.4.392**]; and coming to Stafford (where he met his nephew), they increased their power by all ways and means they could devise. The Earl of Northumberland himself was not with them but, being sick [**4.1.16**], had promised upon his amendment to repair unto them (as some write) with all convenient speed.

. . . And to speak a truth, no marvel it was if many envied the prosperous state of King Henry, sith it was evident enough to the world that he had with wrong usurped the crown and not only violently deposed King Richard but also cruelly procured his death; for the which undoubtedly both he and his posterity tasted such troubles as put them still in danger of their states till their direct succeeding line was quite rooted out by the contrary faction, as in Henry the Sixth and Edward the Fourth it may appear.

But now to return where we left. King Henry, advertised of the proceedings of the Percys, forthwith gathered about him such power as he might make; and being earnestly called upon [**3.2.164**] by [George Dunbar] the Scot, the Earl of [the] March [of Scotland], to make haste and give battle to his enemies before their power, by delaying of time, should still too much increase, he passed forward with such speed that he was in sight of his enemies lying in camp near to Shrewsbury before they were in doubt[15] of any such thing; for the Percys thought that he would have stayed at Burton-upon-Trent till his Council had come thither to him to give their advice what he were best to do. But herein the enemy was deceived of his expectation, sith the King had great regard of expedition and making speed for the safety of his own person; whereunto the Earl of March incited him, considering that in delay is danger and loss in lingering. . . .

By reason of the King's sudden coming in this sort, they stayed from assaulting the town of Shrewsbury, which enterprise they were ready at that instant to have taken in hand; and forthwith the Lord Percy (as a captain of high courage) began to exhort the captains and soldiers to prepare themselves to battle, sith the matter was grown

[14]Immediately.
[15]Fear.

to that point that by no means it could be avoided [**4.1.112, 5.2.82**]. "So that," said he, "this day shall either bring us all to advancement and honor, or else, if it shall chance us to be overcome, shall deliver us from the King's spiteful malice and cruel disdain; for playing the men (as we ought to do), better it is to die in battle for the commonwealth's cause than through cowardlike fear to prolong life which after shall be taken from us by sentence of the enemy."

[**523**] Hereupon the whole army, being in number about fourteen thousand chosen men, promised to stand with him so long as life lasted. There were with the Percys as chieftains of this army the Earl of Douglas a Scottish man, the Baron of Kinderton, Sir Hugh Browne, and Sir Richard Vernon, knights, with divers other stout and right valiant captains. Now when the two armies were encamped, the one against the other, the Earl of Worcester and the Lord Percy with their complices sent the articles (whereof I spoke before) by Thomas Caton and Thomas[b] Salvain, esquires, to King Henry under their hands and seals. Which articles in effect charged him with manifest perjury in that (contrary to his oath received upon the evangelists at Doncaster [**4.3.60, 101, 5.1.41**] when he first entered the realm after his exile) he had taken upon him the crown and royal dignity, imprisoned King Richard, caused him to resign his title, and finally to be murdered. Divers other matters they laid to his charge, as levying of taxes and tallages[16] contrary to his promise, infringing of laws and customs of the realm, and suffering the Earl of March to remain in prison without travailing to have him delivered. All which things they, as procurers and protectors of the commonwealth, took upon them to prove against him, as they protested unto the whole world.

King Henry, after he had read their articles with the defiance which they annexed to the same, answered the esquires that he was ready with dint of sword and fierce battle to prove their quarrel[17] false and nothing else than a forged matter, not doubting but that God would aid and assist him in his righteous cause against the disloyal and false forsworn traitors. The next day, in the morning early, being the eve of Mary Magdalene [1403], they set their battles[18] in order on both sides; and now, whilst the warriors looked when the token of battle should be given, the Abbot of Shrewsbury and one of the clerks of

[b]Roger.
[16]Feudal taxes.
[17]Complaint.
[18]Armies.

the Privy Seal were sent from the King unto the Percys to offer them pardon if they would come to any reasonable agreement [**4.3.30**]. By their persuasions the Lord Henry Percy began to give ear unto the King's offers, and so sent with them his uncle the Earl of Worcester to declare unto the King the causes of those troubles and to require some effectual reformation in the same.

It was reported for a truth that now when the King had condescended unto all that was reasonable at his hands to be required and seemed to humble himself more than was meet for his estate, the Earl of Worcester (upon his return to his nephew) made relation clean contrary to that the King had said [**5.2.1**], in such sort that he set his nephew's heart more in displeasure toward the King than ever it was before, driving him by that means to fight whether he would or not. Then suddenly blew the trumpets, the King's part crying, "Saint George, upon them!"; the adversaries cried, "Esperance! Percy!"[c] [**97**]; and so the two armies furiously joined. The archers on both sides shot for the best game, laying on such load with arrows that many died and were driven down that never rose again.

The Scots (as some write), which had the foreward[19] on the Percys' side, intending to be revenged of their old displeasures done to them by the English nation, set so fiercely on the King's foreward, led by the Earl of Stafford, that they made the same draw back and had almost broken their adversaries' array. The Welshmen also, which before had lain lurking in the woods, mountains, and marshes, hearing of this battle toward, came to the aid of the Percys and refreshed the wearied people with new succors [**4.1.126**]. The King, perceiving that his men were thus put to distress, what with the violent impression of the Scots and the tempestuous storms of arrows that his adversaries discharged freely against him and his people, it was no need to will him to stir; for suddenly, with his fresh battle,[20] he approached and relieved his men so that the battle began more fierce than before. Here the Lord Henry Percy and the Earl Douglas, a right stout and hardy captain, not regarding the shot of the King's battle nor the close order of the ranks, pressing forward together, bent their whole forces toward the King's person; coming upon him with spears and swords so fiercely that the Earl of March the Scot, perceiving their purpose, withdrew the King from that side of the field (as some write) for his

[c]Battle cry of the Percys (the final *e* of "Esperance" is sounded).
[19]Vanguard.
[20]Battalion.

great benefit and safeguard (as it appeared). For they gave such a violent onset upon them that stood about the King's standard that, slaying his standard-bearer Sir Walter Blount and overthrowing the standard, they made slaughter of all those that stood about it; as the Earl of Stafford [**5.3.7**], that day made by the King Constable of the realm, and divers other.

The Prince that day holp his father like a lusty young gentleman [**5.4.2**]; for although he was hurt in the face with an arrow, so that divers noblemen that were about him would have conveyed him forth of the field, yet he would not suffer them so to do, lest his departure from amongst his men might haply have stricken some fear into their hearts. And so, without regard of his hurt, he continued with his men, and never ceased either to fight where the battle was most hot or to encourage his men where it seemed most need. This battle lasted three long hours, with indifferent fortune on both parts, till at length the King, crying, "Saint George! Victory!" broke the array of his enemies and adventured so far that (as some write) the Earl Douglas struck him down and, at that instant, slew Sir Walter Blount [**5.3.13 SD**] and three other appareled in the King's suit and clothing, saying: "I marvel to see so many kings thus suddenly arise one in the neck of another [**5.4.25**]." The King, indeed, was raised, and did that day many a noble feat of arms, for (as it is written) he slew that day with his own hands six and thirty persons of his enemies. The other, on his part, encouraged by his doings, fought valiantly and slew the Lord Percy, called Sir Henry Hotspur. To conclude, the King's enemies were vanquished and put to flight; in which flight, the Earl of Douglas, for haste falling from the crag of an high mountain, broke one of his cullions[21] and was taken; and, for his valiantness, of the King frankly[22] and freely delivered [**5.5.27**].

There was also taken the Earl of Worcester, the procurer and setter-forth of all this mischief, Sir Richard Vernon, and the Baron of Kinderton, with divers other. There were slain upon the King's part, beside the Earl of Stafford, to the number of ten knights: Sir Hugh Shoreley, Sir John Clifton, Sir John Cokayne, Sir Nicholas Gausell, Sir Walter Blount, Sir John Calverley, Sir John Massey of Podington, Sir Hugh Mortimer, and Sir Robert Gausell, all the which received the same morning the order of knighthood; Sir Thomas Wensley was wounded to death and so passed out of this life shortly after. There died in all

[21]Testicles.
[22]Generously.

upon the King's side sixteen hundred, and four thousand were grievously wounded. On the contrary side were slain, besides the Lord Percy, the most part of the knights and esquires of the county of Chester, to the number of two hundred, besides yeomen and footmen; in all there died, of those that fought on the Percys' side, about five thousand. This battle was fought on Mary Magdalene Eve [1403], being Saturday. Upon the Monday following, the Earl of Worcester, the Baron of Kinderton, and Sir Richard Vernon, knight, were condemned and beheaded [**14**]. The Earl's head was sent to London, there to be set on the bridge. . . .

[**538**] Whilst these things were adoing in France, the Lord Henry Prince of Wales, eldest son to King Henry, got knowledge that certain of his father's servants were busy to give informations against him whereby discord might arise betwixt him and his father [**3.2**]. For they put into the King's head not only what evil rule (according to the course of youth) the Prince kept, to the offense of many, but also what great resort of people came to his house; so that the court was nothing furnished with such a train as daily followed the Prince. These tales brought no small suspicion into the King's head lest his son would presume to usurp the crown, he being yet alive; through which suspicious jealousy it was perceived that he favored not his son as in times past he had done.

[**539**] The Prince (sore offended with such persons as, by slanderous reports, sought not only to spot his good name abroad in the realm but to sow discord also betwixt him and his father) wrote his letters into every part of the realm, to reprove all such slanderous devices of those that sought his discredit. And to clear himself the better (that the world might understand what wrong he had to be slandered in such wise), about the feast of Peter and Paul, to wit the nine and twentieth day of June [1412], he came to the court with such a number of noblemen and other his friends that wished him well as the like train had been seldom seen repairing to the court at any one time in those days.

. . . He himself, only accompanied with those of the King's house, was straight admitted to the presence of the King his father, who, being at that time grievously diseased, yet caused himself in his chair to be borne into his privy chamber, where, in the presence of three or four persons in whom he had most confidence, he commanded the Prince to show what he had to say concerning the cause of his coming.

The Prince, kneeling down before his father, said [**18**]: "Most redoubted and sovereign lord and father, I am at this time come to your presence as your liege man and as your natural son, in all things to be at your commandment. . . ."

Thus were the father and the son reconciled, betwixt whom the said pickthanks[23] [**25**] had sown division, insomuch that the son, upon a vehement conceit of unkindness[24] sprung in the father, was in the way to be worn out of favor; which was the more likely to come to pass by their informations that privily charged him with riot and other uncivil demeanor unseemly for a Prince. Indeed, he was youthfully given, grown to audacity, and had chosen him companions agreeable to his age; with whom he spent the time in such recreations, exercises, and delights as he fancied. But yet it should seem (by the report of some writers) that his behavior was not offensive or at least tending to the damage of anybody; sith he had a care to avoid doing of wrong and to tether his affections within the tract of virtue; whereby he opened unto himself a ready passage of good liking among the prudent sort, and was beloved of such as could discern his disposition, which was in no degree so excessive as that he deserved in such vehement manner to be suspected.

[**543**] . . . The King, after, expelled him out of his Privy Council, banished him the court, and made the Duke of Clarence (his younger brother) President of Council in his stead [**32**].

[23]Telltales.
[24]Unnaturalness.

2 Henry IV

[519][1] About the same time [1401] Owen Glendower and his Welshmen did much hurt to the King's subjects. One night as the King was going to bed, he was in danger to have been destroyed; for some naughty[2] traitorous persons had conveyed into his bed a certain iron made with smith's craft like a caltrop,[3] with three long pricks, sharp and small, standing upright in such sort that when he had laid him down and that the weight of his body should come upon the bed, he should have been thrust in with those pricks and peradventure slain; but, as God would, the King, not thinking of any such thing, chanced yet to feel and perceive the instrument before he laid him down, and so escaped the danger. Howbeit, he was not so soon delivered from fear; for he might well have his life in suspicion and provide for the preservation of the same, sith perils of death crept into his secret chamber and lay lurking in the bed of down where his body was to be reposed and to take rest. O what a suspected state therefore is that of a king holding his regiment[4] with the hatred of his people, the heart-grudgings of his courtiers, and the peremptory practices of both together! Could he confidently compose or settle himself to sleep for fear of strangling? Durst he boldly eat and drink without dread of poisoning? Might he adventure to show himself in great meetings or solemn assemblies without mistrust of mischief against his person intended? What pleasure or what felicity could he take in his princely pomp, which he knew by manifest and fearful experience to be envied and maligned to the very death? [**1H4 1.1.1, 2H4 3.1.4**] . . .

[524] The Earl of Northumberland was now [after the Battle of Shrewsbury, 1403] marching forward with great power, which he had

[1]A reference to *2H4* outside this section may be found at p. 62.
[2]Evil.
[3]Pronged device thrown on the ground to impede cavalry.
[4]Rule.

got thither either to aid his son and brother (as was thought) or at the least toward the King to procure a peace; but the Earl of Westmorland and Sir Robert Waterton, knight, had got an army on foot and meant to meet him [**1.1.133**]. The Earl of Northumberland, taking neither of them to be his friend, turned suddenly back and withdrew himself into Warkworth Castle. The King, having set a stay in things about Shrewsbury, went straight to York, from whence he wrote to the Earl of Northumberland, willing him to dismiss his companies that he had with him and to come unto him in peaceable wise. The Earl, upon receipt of the King's letters, came unto him the morrow after Saint Lawrence' Day, having but a few of his servants to attend him, and so excused himself that the King (because the Earl had Berwick in his possession and, further, had his castles of Alnwick, Warkworth, and other fortified with Scots) dissembled the matter, gave him fair words, and suffered him (as saith Hall) to depart home, although by other it should seem that he was committed for a time to safe custody. . . .

This year [1403], in the parliament holden at London (beginning the morrow after the feast of Saint Hilary and continuing twelve weeks), the Earl of Northumberland was restored unto his former dignities, lands, and goods, the Isle of Man only excepted. . . .

[**529**] But at the same time [1405], to his further disquieting, there was a conspiracy put in practice against him at home by the Earl of Northumberland, who had conspired with Richard Scrope Archbishop of York [**189**], Thomas Mowbray Earl Marshal son to Thomas Duke of Norfolk (who for the quarrel betwixt him and King Henry had been banished, as ye have heard), the Lords Hastings, Falconbridge, Bardolf, and divers others. It was appointed that they should meet all together with their whole power upon Yorkswold, at a day assigned, and that the Earl of Northumberland should be chieftain, promising to bring with him a great number of Scots. The Archbishop, accompanied with the Earl Marshal, devised certain articles of such matters as it was supposed that not only the commonalty of the realm but also the nobility found themselves grieved with [**1.3.86, 4.1.168**]; which articles they showed first unto such of their adherents as were near about them, and after sent them abroad to their friends further off, assuring them that, for redress of such oppressions, they would shed the last drop of blood in their bodies if need were.

The Archbishop, not meaning to stay after he saw himself accompanied with a great number of men that came flocking to York to take his part in this quarrel, forthwith discovered[5] his enterprise, causing the articles aforesaid to be set up in the public streets of the city of York and upon the gates of the monasteries, that each man might understand the cause that moved him to rise in arms against the King; the reforming whereof did not yet appertain unto him. Hereupon knights, esquires, gentlemen, yeomen, and other of the commons, as well of the city, towns, and countries about, being allured either for desire of change or else for desire to see a reformation in such things as were mentioned in the articles, assembled together in great numbers; and the Archbishop, coming forth amongst them clad in armor [**4.2.8**], encouraged, exhorted, and (by all means he could) pricked them forth to take the enterprise in hand and manfully to continue in their begun purpose; promising forgiveness of sins to all them whose hap it was to die in the quarrel. And thus not only all the citizens of York, but all other in the countries about that were able to bear weapon, came to the Archbishop and the Earl Marshal. Indeed, the respect that men had to the Archbishop caused them to like the better of the cause, since the gravity of his age, his integrity of life, and incomparable learning, with the reverend aspect of his amiable personage, moved all men to have him in no small estimation [**1.1.202, 4.2.17**].

The King, advertised of these matters, meaning to prevent them, left his journey into Wales and marched with all speed toward the north parts [**1.3.76**]. Also Ralph Neville Earl of Westmorland, that was not far off, together with the Lord John of Lancaster the King's son [**82**], being informed of this rebellious attempt, assembled together such power as they might make and, together with those which were appointed to attend on the said Lord John to defend the borders against the Scots (as the Lord Henry Fitzhugh, the Lord Ralph Eevers, the Lord Robert Umfraville, and others), made forward against the rebels; and, coming into a plain within the forest of Gaultree [**4.1.20**], caused their standards to be pitched down in like sort as the Archbishop had pitched his, over against them; being far stronger in number of people than the other, for (as some write) there were of the rebels at the least twenty thousand men.

When the Earl of Westmorland perceived the force of the adversaries, and that they lay still and attempted not to come forward upon him, he subtly devised how to quail[6] their purpose; and forthwith

[5]Revealed.
[6]Frustrate.

dispatched messengers [**26**] unto the Archbishop to understand the cause (as it were) of that great assembly, and for what cause (contrary to the King's peace) they came so in armor [**31**]. The Archbishop answered [**53**] that he took nothing in hand against the King's peace but that whatsoever he did tended rather to advance the peace and quiet of the commonwealth than otherwise; and where he and his company were in arms, it was for fear of the King, to whom he could have no free access [**78**] by reason of such a multitude of flatterers as were about him; and therefore he maintained that his purpose to be good and profitable, as well for the King himself as for the realm, if men were willing to understand a truth; and herewith he showed forth a scroll [**168**] in which the articles were written (whereof before ye have heard).

The messengers, returning to the Earl of Westmorland, showed[7] him what they had heard and brought from the Archbishop. When he had read the articles, he showed in word and countenance outwardly that he liked of the Archbishop's holy and virtuous intent and purpose, promising that he and his would prosecute the same in assisting the Archbishop, who, rejoicing hereat, gave credit to the Earl and persuaded the Earl Marshal (against his will as it were) to go with him to a place appointed for them to common[8] together [**179**]. Here, when they were met with like number on either part, the articles were read over, and, without any more ado, the Earl of Westmorland and those that were with him agreed to do their best to see that a reformation might be had according to the same [**4.2.54**].

[**530**] The Earl of Westmorland, using more policy[9] than the rest, "Well," said he, "then our travail is come to the wished end; and where our people have been long in armor, let them depart home to their wonted trades and occupations [**61**]; in the meantime let us drink together in sign of agreement, that the people on both sides may see it and know that it is true that we be light at a point."[10] They had no sooner shaken hands together but that a knight was sent straightways from the Archbishop to bring word to the people that there was peace concluded, commanding each man to lay aside his arms and to resort home to their houses. The people, beholding such tokens of peace as shaking of hands and drinking together of the lords in loving manner,

[7]Told.
[8]Confer.
[9]Cunning.
[10]Arrived at an agreement.

they being already wearied with the unaccustomed travail of war, broke up their field[11] and returned homeward [**105**]; but in the meantime, whilst the people of the Archbishop's side withdrew away, the number of the contrary part increased, according to order given by the Earl of Westmorland; and yet the Archbishop perceived not that he was deceived until the Earl of Westmorland arrested both him and the Earl Marshal, with divers other [**107**]. Thus saith Walsingham.

But others write somewhat otherwise of this matter, affirming that the Earl of Westmorland, indeed, and the Lord Ralph Eevers procured the Archbishop and the Earl Marshal to come to a communication with them, upon a ground just in the midway betwixt both the armies [**4.1.179, 226**]; where the Earl of Westmorland in talk declared to them how parlous[12] an enterprise they had taken in hand, so to raise the people and to move war against the King, advising them therefore to submit themselves without further delay unto the King's mercy and his son's the Lord John, who was present there in the field with banners spread, ready to try the matter by dint of sword if they refused this counsel; and therefore he willed them to remember themselves well and, if they would not yield and crave the King's pardon, he bade them do their best to defend themselves.

Hereupon as well the Archbishop as the Earl Marshal submitted themselves unto the King, and to his son the Lord John that was there present, and returned not to their army. Whereupon their troops scaled[13] and fled their ways, but being pursued, many were taken, many slain, and many spoiled[14] of that that they had about them, and so permitted to go their ways. Howsoever the matter was handled, true it is that the Archbishop and the Earl Marshal were brought to Pomfret to the King, who in this meanwhile was advanced thither with his power; and from thence he went to York, whither the prisoners were also brought and there beheaded the morrow after Whitsunday [1405], in a place without the city; that is to understand, the Archbishop himself, the Earl Marshal, Sir John Lampley, and Sir Robert Plumpton [**4.2.122, 4.4.84**]. Unto all which persons, though indemnity were promised, yet was the same to none of them at any hand performed. . . .

After the King, accordingly as seemed to him good, had ransomed

[11]Order of battle.
[12]Very bad.
[13]Mounted.
[14]Plundered.

and punished by grievous fines the citizens of York (which had borne armor on their Archbishop's side against him), he departed from York with an army of thirty and seven thousand fighting men, furnished with all provision necessary, marching northward against the Earl of Northumberland. At his coming to Durham, the Lord Hastings, the Lord Falconbridge, Sir John Coleville of the Dale [**4.3.79**], and Sir John Griffith, being convicted of the conspiracy, were there beheaded. The Earl of Northumberland, hearing that his counsel was bewrayed[15] and his confederates brought to confusion through too much haste of the Archbishop of York, with three hundred horse got him to Berwick. The King, coming forward, quickly won the castle of Warkworth, whereupon the Earl of Northumberland, not thinking himself in surety at Berwick, fled with the Lord Bardolf into Scotland [**2.3.67**], where they were received of David Lord Fleming. . . .

[**534**] The Earl of Northumberland and the Lord Bardolf, after they had been in Wales, in France, and Flanders to purchase aid against King Henry, were returned back into Scotland and had remained there now for the space of a whole year; and, as their evil fortune would, whilst the King held a council of the nobility at London, the said Earl of Northumberland and Lord Bardolf, in a dismal[16] hour, with a great power of Scots returned into England [**4.4.97**], recovering divers of the Earl's castles and seigniories, for the people in great numbers resorted unto them [1408]. Hereupon, encouraged with hope of good success, they entered into Yorkshire and there began to destroy the country. At their coming to Thirsk they published a proclamation signifying that they were come in comfort of the English nation, as to relieve the commonwealth; willing all such as loved the liberty of their country to repair unto them with their armor on their backs and in defensible wise to assist them.

The King, advertised hereof, caused a great army to be assembled and came forward with the same toward his enemies; but ere the King came to Nottingham, Sir Thomas or (as other copies have) Ralph Rokesby Sheriff of Yorkshire assembled the forces of the country to resist the Earl and his power; coming to Grimbald Bridge beside Knaresborough, there to stop them the passage; but they, returning aside, got to Wetherby and so to Tadcaster, and finally came forward unto Bramham Moor, near to Hazelwood, where they chose their ground meet to fight upon. The Sheriff was as ready to give battle as

[15]Betrayed.
[16]Unlucky.

the Earl to receive it, and so, with a standard of Saint George spread, set fiercely upon the Earl, who, under a standard of his own arms, encountered his adversaries with great manhood. There was a sore encounter and cruel conflict betwixt the parties, but in the end the victory fell to the Sheriff [**99**]. The Lord Bardolf was taken, but sore wounded, so that he shortly after died of the hurts. As for the Earl of Northumberland, he was slain outright. . . . This battle was fought the nineteenth day of February [1408].

[**536**] . . . The Welsh rebel, Owen Glendower, made an end of his wretched life in this tenth year [1409] of King Henry his reign, being driven now in his latter time (as we find recorded) to such misery that, in manner despairing of all comfort, he fled into desert places and solitary caves where, being destitute of all relief and succor, dreading to show his face to any creature, and finally lacking meat[17] to sustain nature, for mere hunger and lack of food miserably pined away and died [**3.1.103**].

[**540**] . . . In this year [1411], and upon the twelfth day of October, were three floods in the Thames, the one following upon the other and no ebbing between [**4.4.125**]; which thing no man then living could remember the like to be seen. . . .

In this fourteenth and last year of King Henry's reign [1413], a council was holden in the White Friars in London; at the which, among other things, order was taken for ships and galleys to be builded and made ready, and all other things necessary to be provided, for a voyage which he meant to make into the Holy Land [**4.5.210**], there to recover the city of Jerusalem from the infidels. For it grieved him to consider the great malice of Christian princes, that were bent upon a mischievous purpose to destroy one another, to the peril of their own souls, rather than to make war against the enemies of the Christian faith, as in conscience (it seemed to him) they were bound. He held his Christmas this year at Eltham, being sore vexed with sickness [**4.3.83**] so that it was thought sometime that he had been dead; notwithstanding it pleased God that he somewhat recovered his strength again and so passed that Christmas with as much joy as he might.

[**541**] The morrow after Candlemas Day [1413] began a parliament which he had called at London, but he departed this life before the same parliament was ended; for now that his provisions were ready

[17]Food.

and that he was furnished with sufficient treasure, soldiers, captains, victuals, munitions, tall ships, strong galleys, and all things necessary for such a royal journey as he pretended[18] to take into the Holy Land, he was eftsoons[19] taken with a sore sickness, which was not a leprosy stricken by the hand of God (saith Master Hall) as foolish friars imagined, but a very apoplexy, of the which he languished till his appointed hour and had none other grief nor malady [**4.4.111, 130**]; so that what man ordaineth God altereth at His good will and pleasure, not giving place more to the prince than to the poorest creature living when He seeth His time to dispose of him this way or that, as to His omnipotent power and divine providence seemeth expedient. During this his last sickness, he caused his crown (as some write) to be set on a pillow at his bed's head [**4.5.5**]; and suddenly his pangs so sore troubled him that he lay as though all his vital spirits had been from him departed. Such as were about him, thinking verily that he had been departed, covered his face with a linen cloth.

The Prince his son, being hereof advertised, entered into the chamber, took away the crown, and departed [**43**]. The father, being suddenly revived out of that trance, quickly perceived the lack of his crown [**58**] and, having knowledge that the Prince his son had taken it away, caused him to come before his presence, requiring of him what he meant, so to misuse himself [**93**]. The Prince, with a good audacity, answered: "Sir, to mine and all men's judgments, you seemed dead in this world; wherefore I, as your next[20] heir apparent, took that as mine own and not as yours." "Well, fair son," said the King with a great sigh, "what right I had to it God knoweth [**184**]." "Well," said the Prince, "if you die King, I will have the garland, and trust to keep it with the sword against all mine enemies, as you have done." Then said the King, "I commit all to God, and remember you to do well." With that he turned himself in his bed and shortly after departed to God, in a chamber of the Abbot's of Westminster called Jerusalem, the twentieth day of March, in the year 1413, and in the year of his age forty-six; when he had reigned thirteen years, five months, and odd days, in great perplexity and little pleasure. . . .

We find that he was taken with his last sickness while he was making his prayers at Saint Edward's shrine, there (as it were) to take his leave and so to proceed forth on his journey. He was so suddenly

[18]Intended.
[19]Again.
[20]Nearest.

and grievously taken that such as were about him feared lest he would have died presently;[21] wherefore to relieve him (if it were possible) they bore him into a chamber that was next at hand, belonging to the Abbot of Westminster, where they laid him on a pallet before the fire and used all remedies to revive him. At length he recovered his speech, and understanding and perceiving himself in a strange place which he knew not, he willed to know if the chamber had any particular name; whereunto answer was made that it was called Jerusalem. Then said the King: "Lauds be given to the Father of heaven, for now I know that I shall die here in this chamber according to the prophecy of me declared that I should depart this life in Jerusalem [**238**]."

Whether this was true that so he spoke, as one that gave too much credit to foolish prophecies and vain tales, or whether it was feigned, as in such cases it commonly happeneth, we leave it to the advised reader to judge. . . . This King was of a mean[22] stature, well proportioned, and formally compact; quick and lively, and of a stout courage.[23] In his latter days he showed himself so gentle[24] that he got more love amongst the nobles and people of this realm than he had purchased malice and evil will in the beginning.

But yet, to speak a truth, by his proceedings, after he had attained to the crown, what with such taxes, tallages,[25] subsidies, and exactions as he was constrained to charge the people with, and what by punishing such as, moved with disdain to see him usurp the crown (contrary to the oath taken at his entering into this land upon his return from exile), did at sundry times rebel against him, he won himself more hatred than in all his lifetime (if it had been longer by many years than it was) had been possible for him to have weeded out and removed. . . .

[**543**] Such great hope and good expectation was had of this man's [Prince Henry's] fortunate success to follow that within three days after his father's decease divers noblemen and honorable personages did to him homage and swore to him due obedience [**5.2.18**], which had not been seen done to any of his predecessors, kings of this realm, till they had been possessed of the crown. He was crowned the ninth of April [1413], being Passion Sunday, which was a sore, ruggy,[26]

[21]Immediately.
[22]Average.
[23]Brave disposition.
[24]Courteous.
[25]Feudal taxes.
[26]Stormy.

and tempestuous day, with wind, snow, and sleet, that men greatly marveled thereat, making divers interpretations what the same might signify. But this King, even at first appointing with himself to show that in his person princely honors should change public manners, he determined to put on him the shape of a new man. For whereas aforetime he had made himself a companion unto misruly mates of dissolute order and life, he now banished them all from his presence (but not unrewarded or else unpreferred); inhibiting them upon a great pain not once to approach, lodge, or sojourn within ten miles of his court or presence [**5.5.67**]; and in their places he chose men of gravity, wit, and high policy, by whose wise counsel he might at all times rule to his honor and dignity [**5.2.135**]; calling to mind how once, to high offense of the King his father, he had with his fist stricken the [Lord] Chief Justice for sending one of his minions (upon desert) to prison; when the Justice stoutly commanded himself also straight to ward,[27] and he (then Prince) obeyed [**70**]. . . .

[27]Imprisonment.

Henry V

[**543**] Henry Prince of Wales, son and heir to King Henry the Fourth, born in Wales at Monmouth on the river of Wye, after his father was departed took upon him the regiment[1] of this realm of England the twentieth of March, the morrow after proclaimed King by the name of Henry the Fifth, in the year of the world 5375, after the birth of our Saviour by our account 1413, the third of the Emperor Sigismund, the three and thirtieth of Charles the sixth French King, and in the seventh year of governance in Scotland under Robert.

. . . When the King had settled things much to his purpose, he caused the body of King Richard to be removed, with all funeral dignity convenient for his estate, from Langley to Westminster, where he was honorably interred with Queen Anne, his first wife, in a solemn tomb erected and set up at the charges of this King [**4.1.312**]. . . .

[**545**] Whilst in the Lent season [1414] the King lay at Kenilworth, there came to him from Charles Dauphin of France certain ambassadors that brought with them a barrel of Paris balls,[2] which from their master they presented to him for a token that was taken in very ill part, as sent in scorn, to signify that it was more meet for the King to pass the time with such childish exercise than to attempt any worthy exploit [**1.2.254**]. Wherefore the King wrote to him that, ere aught long, he would toss him some London balls that perchance should shake the walls of the best court in France [**2.4.132**]. . . .

In the second year of his reign [1414], King Henry called his high court of parliament, the last day of April, in the town of Leicester, in which parliament many profitable laws were concluded and many petitions moved were for that time deferred. Amongst which, one was that a bill [**1.1.1**] exhibited in the parliament holden at Westminster, in the eleventh year [1410] of King Henry the Fourth (which by reason the King was then troubled with civil discord came to none effect),

[1]Rule.
[2]Tennis balls.

might now with good deliberation be pondered and brought to some good conclusion. The effect of which supplication was that the temporal lands (devoutly given, and disordinately spent by religious and other spiritual persons) should be seized into the King's hands sith the same might suffice to maintain, to the honor of the King [**12**] and defense of the realm, fifteen earls, fifteen hundred knights, six thousand and two hundred esquires, and a hundred almshouses for relief only of the poor, impotent, and needy persons; and the King to have clearly[3] to his coffers twenty thousand pounds, with many other provisions and values of religious houses which I pass over.

This bill was much noted and more feared among the religious sort, whom surely it touched very near; and therefore, to find remedy against it, they determined to assay all ways to put by and overthrow this bill [**70**]; wherein they thought best to try if they might move the King's mood with some sharp invention, that he should not regard the importunate petitions of the commons. Whereupon, on a day in the parliament, Henry Chichele Archbishop of Canterbury made a pithy oration [**1.2.33**] wherein he declared how not only the duchies of Normandy and Aquitaine, with the counties of Anjou and Maine and the country of Gascony, were by undoubted title appertaining to the King, as to the lawful and only heir of the same, but also the whole realm of France, as heir to his great grandfather King Edward the Third.

Herein did he much inveigh against the surmised[4] and false feigned Law Salic, which the Frenchmen allege ever against the Kings of England in bar of their just title to the crown of France. "The very words of that supposed law are these: *In terram Salicam mulieres ne succedant,* that is to say, Into the Salic land let not women succeed [**39**]. Which the French glossers expound to be the realm of France, and that this law was made by King Pharamond; whereas yet their own authors affirm that the land Salic is in Germany, between the rivers of Elbe and Sala [**45**]; and that when Charles the Great had overcome the Saxons he placed there certain Frenchmen which, having in disdain the dishonest[5] manners of the German women, made a law that the females should not succeed to any inheritance within that land, which at this day is called Meissen [**53**]; so that, if this be true, this law was not made for the realm of France, nor the Frenchmen pos-

[3]Entirely.
[4]Falsely contrived.
[5]Unchaste.

sessed the land Salic till four hundred and one and twenty years[6] after the death of Pharamond, the supposed maker of this Salic Law; for this Pharamond deceased in the year 426, and Charles the Great subdued the Saxons and placed the Frenchmen in those parts beyond the river of Sala in the year 805 [**64**].

"Moreover, it appeareth by their own writers that King Pepin, which deposed Childeric, claimed the crown of France as heir general for that he was descended of Blithild, daughter to King Clothair the First [**67**]. Hugh Capet also (who usurped the crown upon Charles Duke of Lorraine, the sole heir male of the line and stock of Charles the Great), to make his title seem true and appear good (though indeed it was stark naught), conveyed himself as heir to the Lady Lingard, daughter to King Charlemagne,[7] son to Louis the Emperor that was son to Charles the Great [**77**]. King Louis also the Tenth[8] (otherwise called Saint Louis), being very heir to the said usurper Hugh Capet, could never be satisfied in his conscience how he might justly keep and possess the crown of France till he was persuaded and fully instructed that Queen Isabel, his grandmother, was lineally descended of the Lady Ermengarde, daughter and heir to the above-named Charles Duke of Lorraine [**83**]; by the which marriage the blood and line of Charles the Great was again united and restored to the crown and scepter of France; so that, more clear than the sun, it openly appeareth that the title of King Pepin, the claim of Hugh Capet, the possession of Louis, yea, and the French kings to this day, are derived and conveyed from the heir female [**89**]; though they would, under the color of such a feigned law, bar the kings and princes of this realm of England of their right and lawful inheritance."

[**546**] The Archbishop further alleged out of the Book of Numbers this saying [**99**]: "When a man dieth without a son, let the inheritance descend to his daughter." At length, having said sufficiently for the proof of the King's just and lawful title to the crown of France, he exhorted him to advance forth his banner [**101**], to fight for his right, to conquer his inheritance, to spare neither blood, sword, nor fire, sith his war was just, his cause good, and his claim true. And, to the intent his loving chaplains and obedient subjects of the spiritualty might show themselves willing and desirous to aid his majesty for the recovery of his ancient right and true inheritance, the Archbishop de-

[6]379 years.
[7]Charles the Bald.
[8]Ninth.

clared that, in their spiritual convocation, they had granted to his highness such a sum of money as never by no spiritual persons was to any prince before those days given or advanced [**1.1.75, 1.2.133**].

When the Archbishop had ended his prepared tale, Ralph Neville Earl of Westmorland and as then Lord Warden of the Marches against Scotland, understanding that the King, upon a courageous desire to recover his right in France, would surely take the wars in hand, thought good to move the King to begin first with Scotland; and thereupon declared how easy a matter it should be to make a conquest there, and how greatly the same should further his wished purpose for the subduing of the Frenchmen; concluding the sum of his tale with this old saying, that "Whoso will France win, must with Scotland first begin [**167**]." Many matters he touched, as well to show how necessary the conquest of Scotland should be as also to prove how just a cause the King had to attempt it, trusting to persuade the King and all other to be of his opinion.

But after he had made an end, the Duke of Exeter, uncle to the King, a man well learned and wise, who had been sent into Italy by his father (intending that he should have been a priest), replied against the Earl of Westmorland's oration, affirming rather that he which would Scotland win, he with France must first begin. . . .

To be brief, the Duke of Exeter used such earnest and pithy persuasions to induce the King and the whole assembly of the parliament to credit his words that immediately after he had made an end all the company began to cry, "War, war! France, France!" Hereby the bill for dissolving of religious houses was clearly set aside, and nothing thought on but only the recovering of France, according as the Archbishop had moved [**222**].

. . . Moreover, at this parliament John the King's brother was created Duke of Bedford, and his brother Humphrey Duke of Gloucester. Also, Thomas Beaufort Marquis Dorset was created Duke of Exeter. . . .

[**547**] The Frenchmen having knowledge hereof, the Dauphin, who had the governance of the realm because his father was fallen into his old disease of frenzy, sent for the Dukes of Berry and Alençon and all the other lords of the Council of France; by whose advice it was determined that they should not only prepare a sufficient army to resist the King of England, whensoever he arrived to invade France, but also to stuff[9] and furnish the towns on the frontiers and seacoasts

[9]Garrison.

with convenient garrisons of men [**2.4.7**]; and, further, to send to the King of England a solemn embassage, to make to him some offers according to the demands before rehearsed. . . .

These ambassadors, accompanied with three hundred fifty horses, passed the sea at Calais and landed at Dover [1415]; before whose arrival the King was departed from Windsor to Winchester, intending to have gone to Hampton, there to have surveyed his navy; but hearing of the ambassadors' approaching, he tarried still at Winchester, where the said French lords showed themselves very honorably before the King and his nobility. At time prefixed, before the King's presence, sitting in his throne imperial, the Archbishop of Bourges made an eloquent and a long oration dissuading war and praising peace; offering to the King of England a great sum of money, with divers countries, being in very deed but base and poor, as a dowry with the Lady Katherine in marriage [**3 Ch. 29**]; so[10] that he would dissolve his army and dismiss his soldiers which he had gathered and put in areadiness. . . .

[**548**] When the King had all provisions ready and ordered all things for the defense of his realm, he, leaving behind him for governor of the realm the Queen his mother-in-law,[11] departed to Southampton to take ship into France; and, first princely appointing to advertise the French king of his coming, therefore dispatched Antelope his pursuivant-at-arms[12] with letters to him for restitution of that which he wrongfully withheld contrary to the laws of God and man [**2.4.65**]. The King further declaring how sorry he was that he should be thus compelled, for repeating of his right and just title of inheritance, to make war to the destruction of Christian people; but sithence[13] he had offered peace which could not be received, now, for fault of justice, he was forced to take arms; nevertheless exhorted the French King, in the bowels of Jesus Christ [**102**], to render him that which was his own, whereby effusion of Christian blood might be avoided. These letters, chiefly to this effect and purpose, were written and dated from Hampton the fifth of August [1415]. When the same were presented to the French King and by his Council well perused, answer was made that he would take advice and provide therein as time and place

[10]Provided.
[11]Stepmother.
[12]Heraldic officer.
[13]Since.

should be convenient; so the messenger [was] licensed to depart at his pleasure.

When King Henry had fully furnished his navy with men, munition, and other provisions, [he], perceiving that his captains misliked nothing so much as delay, determined his soldiers to go ashipboard and away. But see the hap! The night before the day appointed for their departure, he was credibly informed that Richard Earl of Cambridge brother to Edward Duke of York, and Henry Lord Scrope of Masham Lord Treasurer, with Thomas Grey a knight of Northumberland, being confederate together, had conspired his death [**2 Ch. 28, 2.2.1**]; wherefore he caused them to be apprehended. The said Lord Scrope was in such favor with the King that he admitted him sometime to be his bedfellow [**8**]; in whose fidelity the King reposed such trust that, when any private or public counsel was in hand, this lord had much in the determination of it [**96**]. For he represented so great gravity in his countenance, such modesty in behavior, and so virtuous zeal to all godliness in his talk [**127**] that whatsoever he said was thought for the most part necessary to be done and followed. Also the said Sir Thomas Grey (as some write) was of the King's Privy Council.

These prisoners, upon their examination, confessed that for a great sum of money which they had received of the French King [**89**], they intended verily either to have delivered the King alive into the hands of his enemies or else to have murdered him before he should arrive in the duchy of Normandy. When King Henry had heard all things opened which he desired to know, he caused all his nobility to come before his presence; before whom he caused to be brought the offenders also, and to them said: "Having thus conspired the death and destruction of me, which am the head of the realm and Governor of the people, it may be (no doubt) but that you likewise have sworn the confusion of all that are here with me, and also the desolation of your own country. To what horror (O Lord) for any true English heart to consider, that such an execrable iniquity should ever so bewrap you: as, for pleasing of a foreign enemy, to embrew your hands in your blood and to ruin your own native soil. Revenge herein touching my person though I seek not [**174**], yet for the safeguard of you my dear friends and for due preservation of all sorts, I am by office to cause example to be showed. Get ye hence, therefore, ye poor miserable wretches, to the receiving of your just reward, wherein God's majesty give you grace of his mercy and repentance of your heinous offenses." And so immediately they were had to execution.

This done, the King, calling his lords again afore him, said in words few and with good grace [**182**]. Of his enterprises he recounted the honor and glory whereof they with him were to be partakers; the great confidence he had in their noble minds, which could not but remember them of the famous feats that their ancestors aforetime in France had achieved, whereof the due report forever recorded remained yet in register. The great mercy of God that had so graciously revealed unto him the treason at hand, whereby the true hearts of those afore him [were] made so eminent and apparent in his eye as they might be right sure he would never forget it. The doubt[14] of danger to be nothing in respect of the certainty of honor that they should acquire; wherein himself (as they saw) in person would be lord and leader, through God's grace. To whose majesty, as chiefly was known the equity of his demand, even so to His mercy, did he only recommend the success of his travails. When the King had said, all the noblemen kneeled down and promised faithfully to serve him, duly to obey him, and rather to die than to suffer him to fall into the hands of his enemies.

This done, the King thought that surely all treason and conspiracy had been utterly extinct, not suspecting the fire which was newly kindled and ceased not to increase till at length it burst out into such a flame that, catching the beams of his house and family, his line and stock was clean consumed to ashes. Divers write that Richard Earl of Cambridge did not conspire with the Lord Scrope and Thomas Grey for the murdering of King Henry to please the French King withal [**155**], but only to the intent to exalt to the crown his brother-in-law, Edmund Earl of March, as heir to Lionel Duke of Clarence; after the death of which Earl of March (for divers secret impediments not able to have issue), the Earl of Cambridge was sure that the crown should come to him by his wife, and to his children of her begotten. And therefore (as was thought) he rather confessed himself for need of money to be corrupted by the French King than he would declare his inward mind and open his very intent and secret purpose which, if it were espied, he saw plainly that the Earl of March should have tasted of the same cup that he had drunken, and what should have come to his own children he much doubted.[15] Therefore, destitute of comfort and in despair of life to save his children, he feigned that tale, desiring rather to save his succession than himself, which he did

[14]Fear.
[15]Feared.

indeed; for his son Richard Duke of York not privily but openly claimed the crown, and Edward his son both claimed it and gained it, as after it shall appear. Which thing if King Henry had at this time either doubted or foreseen, had never been like to have come to pass, as Hall saith. . . .

[**549**] But now to proceed with King Henry's doings. After this, when the wind came about prosperous to his purpose, he caused the mariners to weigh up anchors and hoise up sails, and to set forward with a thousand ships on the vigil of Our Lady Day the Assumption; and took land at Caur, commonly called Kidcaur, where the river of Seine runneth into the sea, without resistance. At his first coming on land, he caused proclamation to be made that no person should be so hearty,[16] on pain of death, either to take anything out of any church that belonged to the same; or to hurt or do any violence either to priests, women, or any such as should be found without weapon or armor and not ready to make resistance; also that no man should renew any quarrel or strife whereby any fray might arise to the disquieting of the army.

The next day after his landing he marched toward the town of Harfleur, standing on the river of Seine between two hills; he besieged it on every side. . . .

The French King, being advertised that King Henry was arrived on that coast, sent in all haste the Lord Delabreth[a] Constable of France, the Seneschal of France, the Lord Boucicault Marshal of France, the Seneschal of Hainaut, the Lord Ligny, with other; which fortified towns with men, victuals, and artillery, on all those frontiers toward the sea. . . . And daily was the town assaulted, for the Duke of Gloucester, to whom the order of the siege was committed [**3.2.69**], made three mines under the ground [**59**]; and, approaching to the walls with his engines and ordnance, would not suffer them within to take any rest.

[**550**] For although they with their countermining [**66**] somewhat disappointed the Englishmen, and came to fight with them hand to hand within the mines, so that they went no further forward with that work, yet they were so enclosed on each side, as well by water as land, that succor they saw could none come to them. . . .

The captains within the town, perceiving that they were not able long to resist the continual assaults of the Englishmen, knowing that

[16]Unrestrained.
[a]D'Albret.

their walls were undermined and like to be overthrown (as one of their bulwarks was already, where the Earls of Huntingdon and Kent had set up their banners), sent an officer-at-arms forth about midnight after the feast day of Saint Lambert [1415], which fell that year upon the Tuesday, to beseech the King of England to appoint some certain persons as commissioners from him with whom they within might treat about some agreement. The Duke of Clarence, to whom this messenger first declared his errand, advertised the King of their request who, granting thereto, appointed the Duke of Exeter, with the Lord Fitzhugh and Sir Thomas Erpingham, to understand their minds; who at the first requested a truce until Sunday next following the feast of Saint Michael, in which meantime, if no succor came to remove the siege, they would undertake to deliver the town into the King's hands, their lives and goods saved.

The King, advertised hereof, sent them word that, except they would surrender the town to him the morrow next ensuing, without any condition, they should spend no more time in talk about the matter [**3.3.2**]. But yet at length, through the earnest suit of the French lords, the King was contented to grant them truce until nine of the clock the next Sunday, being the two and twentieth of September [1415]; with condition that if in the meantime no rescue came, they should yield the town at that hour, with their bodies and goods to stand at the King's pleasure. And for assurance thereof they delivered into the King's hands thirty of their best captains and merchants within that town as pledges. . . .

The King nevertheless was after content to grant a respite upon certain conditions, that the captains within might have time to send to the French King for succor (as before ye have heard), lest he, intending greater exploits, might lose time in such small matters. When this composition[17] was agreed upon, the Lord Bacqueville was sent unto the French King to declare in what point[18] the town stood. To whom the Dauphin answered that the King's power was not yet assembled in such number as was convenient to raise so great a siege [**44**]. This answer being brought unto the captains within the town, they rendered it up to the King of England after that the third day was expired; which was on the day of Saint Maurice, being the seven and thirtieth day after the siege was first laid. The soldiers were ransomed and the town sacked, to the great gain of the Englishmen. Some writing of this

[17]Arrangement.
[18]Plight.

yielding up of Harfleur do in like sort make mention of the distress whereto the people, then expelled out of their habitations, were driven; insomuch as parents with their children, young maids, and old folk went out of the town gates with heavy hearts (God wot), as put to their present shifts to seek them a new abode [**54**]. . . .

All this done, the King ordained captain to the town his uncle the Duke of Exeter [**51**], who established his lieutenant there, one Sir John Fastolf, with fifteen hundred men or (as some have) two thousand, and thirty-six knights. . . .

King Henry, after the winning of Harfleur, determined to have proceeded further in the winning of other towns and fortresses; but because the dead time of the winter approached, it was determined by advice of his Council that he should in all convenient speed set forward and march through the country toward Calais by land, lest his return as then homeward should of slanderous tongues be named a running away. And yet that journey was adjudged perilous by reason that the number of his people was much minished by the flux[19] and other fevers [**55**], which sore vexed and brought to death above fifteen hundred persons of the army; and this was the cause that his return was the sooner appointed and concluded. . . .

[**552**] The Englishmen were brought into some distress in this journey, by reason of their victuals in manner spent and no hope to get more, for the enemies had destroyed all the corn[20] before they came. Rest could they none take, for their enemies with alarums[21] did ever so infest them; daily it rained and nightly it freezed; of fuel there was great scarcity, of fluxes plenty; money enough, but wares for their relief to bestow it on had they none. Yet in this great necessity the poor people of the country were not spoiled,[22] nor anything taken of them without payment [**3.6.116**], nor any outrage or offense done by the Englishmen except one, which was that a soldier took a pyx[23] out of a church [**42**], for which he was apprehended; and the King not once removed till the box was restored and the offender strangled. The people of the countries thereabout, hearing of such zeal in him to the maintenance of justice, ministered to his army victuals and

[19]Dysentery.
[20]Grain.
[21]Sudden attacks.
[22]Plundered.
[23]Box for preserving the Host.

other necessaries, although by open proclamation so to do they were prohibited.

The French King, being at Rouen and hearing that King Henry was passed the river of Somme, was much displeased therewith and, assembling his Council [**3.5 SD**] to the number of five and thirty, asked their advice what was to be done. There was, amongst these five and thirty, his son the Dauphin calling himself King of Sicily, the Dukes of Berry and Brittany, the Earl of Pontrieux the King's youngest son, and other high estates.[24] At length thirty of them agreed that the Englishmen should not depart unfought withal [**12**], and five were of a contrary opinion, but the greater number ruled the matter; and so Montjoy King-at-arms[25] was sent to the King of England [**3.6.120 SD**] to defy him as the enemy of France, and to tell him that he should shortly have battle. King Henry advisedly answered: "Mine intent is to do as it pleaseth God. I will not seek your master at this time [**149**], but if he or his seek me, I will meet with them, God willing. If any of your nation attempt once to stop me in my journey now toward Calais, at their jeopardy be it; and yet wish I not any of you so unadvised as to be the occasion that I dye your tawny ground with your red blood [**170**]."

When he had thus answered the herald, he gave him a princely reward [**167**] and license to depart. Upon whose return with this answer, it was incontinently[26] on the French side proclaimed that all men-of-war should resort to the Constable to fight with the King of England. Whereupon all men apt for armor and desirous of honor drew them toward the field. The Dauphin sore desired to have been at the battle, but he was prohibited by his father [**3.5.66**].

. . . Order was taken by commandment from the King, after the army was first set in battle array, that no noise or clamor should be made in the host, so that in marching forth to this village, every man kept himself quiet; but at their coming into the village, fires were made to give light on every side [**4 Ch. 23**], as there likewise were in the French host, which was encamped not past two hundred and fifty paces distant from the English [**3.7.136**]. The chief leaders of the French host were these: the Constable of France, the Marshal [Boucicault], the Admiral [Châtillon], the Lord Rambures Master of

[24]Lords.
[25]Chief herald.
[26]Immediately.

the Crossbows, and other of the French nobility [**3.7 SD**], which came and pitched down their standards and banners in the county of Saint-Pol, within the territory of Agincourt, having in their army (as some write) to the number of threescore thousand horsemen, besides footmen, wagoners, and other.

They were lodged even in the way by the which the Englishmen must needs pass toward Calais; and all that night, after their coming thither, made great cheer and were very merry, pleasant, and full of game. The Englishmen also, for their parts, were of good comfort and nothing abashed of the matter; and yet they were both hungry, weary, sore travailed, and vexed with many cold diseases [**4 Ch. 41**]. Howbeit, reconciling themselves with God by housel[27] and shrift,[28] requiring assistance at His hands that is the only giver of victory, they determined rather to die than to yield or flee. The day following was the five and twentieth of October in the year 1415, being then Friday and the feast of Crispin and Crispinian [**4.3.57, 4.7.94**]—a day fair and fortunate to the English but most sorrowful and unlucky to the French. . . .

[**553**] King Henry, by reason of his small number of people to fill up his battles,[29] placed his vanguard so on the right hand of the main battle which himself led that the distance betwixt them might scarce be perceived and so in like case was the rearward[30] joined on the left hand, that the one might the more readily succor another in time of need. When he had thus ordered his battles, he left a small company to keep his camp and carriage,[31] which remained still in the village; and then, calling his captains and soldiers about him, he made to them a right grave oration, moving them to play the men whereby to obtain a glorious victory, as there was hope certain they should, the rather if they would but remember the just cause for which they fought and whom they should encounter, such fainthearted people as their ancestors had so often overcome. To conclude, many words of courage he uttered to stir them to do manfully, assuring them that England should never be charged with his ransom nor any Frenchman triumph over him as a captive, for either by famous death or glorious victory would he (by God's grace) win honor and fame [**4.3.20**].

[27]Communion.
[28]Confession.
[29]Battalions.
[30]Rearguard.
[31]Baggage.

It is said that, as he heard one of the host utter his wish to another, thus, "I would to God there were with us now so many good soldiers as are at this hour within England [**16**]," the King answered: "I would not wish a man more here than I have; we are indeed, in comparison to the enemies, but a few, but if God of his clemency do favor us and our just cause (as I trust He will) we shall speed well enough. But let no man ascribe victory to our own strength and might, but only to God's assistance, to whom I have no doubt we shall worthily have cause to give thanks therefor. And if so be that, for our offenses' sakes, we shall be delivered into the hands of our enemies, the less number we be the less damage shall the realm of England sustain; but if we should fight in trust of multitude of men and so get the victory (our minds being prone to pride), we should thereupon peradventure ascribe the victory not so much to the gift of God as to our own puissance, and thereby provoke His high indignation and displeasure against us; and if the enemy get the upper hand, then should our realm and country suffer more damage and stand in further danger. But be you of good comfort and show yourselves valiant! God and our just quarrel[32] shall defend us, and deliver these our proud adversaries with all the multitude of them which you see (or at the least the most of them) into our hands." . . . The Frenchmen in the meanwhile, as though they had been sure of victory, made great triumph; for the captains had determined before how to divide the spoil, and the soldiers the night before had played[33] the Englishmen at dice [**3.7.93**]. The noblemen had devised a chariot wherein they might triumphantly convey the King captive to the city of Paris [**3.5.54**], crying to their soldiers, "Haste you to the spoil, glory, and honor," little weening[34] (God wot) how soon their brags should be blown away.

[**554**] Here we may not forget how the French, thus in their jollity, sent an herald to King Henry to inquire what ransom he would offer [**4.3.80**]. Whereunto he answered that within two or three hours he hoped it would so happen that the Frenchmen should be glad to common[35] rather with the Englishmen for their ransoms than the English to take thought for their deliverance, promising for his own part that his dead carcass should rather be a prize to the Frenchmen than that

[32]Cause.
[33]*I.e.*, played for.
[34]Supposing.
[35]Confer.

his living body should pay any ransom. When the messenger was come back to the French host, the men-of-war put on their helmets and caused their trumpets to blow to the battle. They thought themselves so sure of victory that divers of the noblemen made such haste toward the battle that they left many of their servants and men-of-war behind them, and some of them would not once stay for their standards; as, amongst other, the Duke of Brabant, when his standard was not come, caused a banner to be taken from a trumpet and fastened to a spear; the which he commanded to be borne before him instead of his standard [**4.2.61**]. . . .

The King that day showed himself a valiant knight, albeit almost felled by the Duke of Alençon; yet with plain strength he slew two of the Duke's company and felled the Duke himself [**4.7.161**], whom when he would have yielded the King's guard (contrary to his mind) slew out of hand. In conclusion the King, minding to make an end of that day's journey,[36] caused his horsemen to fetch a compass about and to join with him against the rearward of the Frenchmen, in the which was the greatest number of people. When the Frenchmen perceived his intent, they were suddenly amazed and ran away like sheep, without order or array [**4.5.6**]. Which when the King perceived, he encouraged his men and followed so quickly upon the enemies that they ran hither and thither, casting away their armor; many, on their knees, desired to have their lives saved [**4.4.57**].

In the mean season, while the battle thus continued and that the Englishmen had taken a great number of prisoners, certain Frenchmen on horseback, whereof were captains Robinet of Borneuil, Rifflart of Clamas, Isambert of Agincourt, and other men-of-arms, to the number of six hundred horsemen (which were the first that fled), hearing that the English tents and pavilions were a good way distant from the army, without any sufficient guard to defend the same, either upon a covetous meaning to gain by the spoil or upon a desire to be revenged, entered upon the King's camp and there spoiled the hales,[37] robbed the tents, broke up chests, and carried away caskets, and slew such servants as they found to make any resistance [**4.7.1**]. For which treason and haskardy[38] in thus leaving their camp at the very point of fight, for winning of spoil where none to defend it, very many were

[36]Battle.
[37]Pavilions.
[38]Baseness.

after committed to prison and had lost their lives if the Dauphin had longer lived.

But when the outcry of the lackeys and boys, which ran away for fear of the Frenchmen thus spoiling the camp, came to the King's ears, he (doubting lest his enemies should gather together again and begin a new field,[39] and mistrusting further that the prisoners would be an aid to his enemies or the very enemies to their takers indeed if they were suffered to live), contrary to his accustomed gentleness, commanded by sound of trumpet that every man (upon pain of death) should incontinently slay his prisoner [**4.6.37**]. When this dolorous decree and pitiful proclamation was pronounced, pity it was to see how some Frenchmen were suddenly sticked with daggers, some were brained with poleaxes, some slain with mauls,[40] other had their throats cut [**4.7.9**] and some their bellies paunched,[41] so that in effect, having respect to the great number, few prisoners were saved.

When this lamentable slaughter was ended, the Englishmen disposed themselves in order of battle, ready to abide a new field, and also to invade and newly set on their enemies; with great force they assailed the Earls of Marle and Fauquembergue, and the Lords of Lorraine and of Thines, with six hundred men-of-arms; who had all that day kept together but now [were] slain and beaten down out of hand. Some write that the King, perceiving his enemies in one part to assemble together as though they meant to give a new battle for preservation of the prisoners, sent to them an herald [**59**] commanding them either to depart out of his sight or else to come forward at once and give battle; promising herewith that if they did offer to fight again, not only those prisoners which his people already had taken but also so many of them as, in this new conflict which they thus attempted, should fall into his hands should die the death without redemption [**66**].

[**555**] The Frenchmen, fearing the sentence of so terrible a decree, without further delay parted out of the field. And so, about four of the clock in the afternoon, the King, when he saw no appearance of enemies, caused the retreat to be blown and, gathering his army together, gave thanks to almighty God for so happy a victory, causing his prelates and chaplains to sing this psalm, *In exitu Israel de Aegypto;*

[39]Battle.
[40]Maces.
[41]Stabbed.

and commanded every man to kneel down on the ground at this verse, *Non nobis, Domine, non nobis, sed nomini tuo da gloriam* [**4.8.128**]. Which done, he caused *Te Deum,* with certain anthems, to be sung, giving laud and praise to God without boasting of his own force or any human power [**111**]. That night he and his people took rest and refreshed themselves with such victuals as they found in the French camp, but lodged in the same village where he lay the night before.

In the morning Montjoy King-at-arms and four other French heralds came to the King to know the number of prisoners and to desire burial for the dead [**4.7.76**]. Before he made them answer (to understand what they would say), he demanded of them why they made to him that request, considering that he knew not whether the victory was his or theirs [**87**]. When Montjoy by true and just confession had cleared that doubt to the high praise of the King, he desired of Montjoy to understand the name of the castle near adjoining [**91**]. When they had told him that it was called Agincourt, he said, "Then shall this conflict be called the Battle of Agincourt." He feasted the French officers-of-arms that day, and granted them their request; which busily sought through the field for such as were slain. But the Englishmen suffered them not to go alone [**121**], for they searched with them and found many hurt but not in jeopardy of their lives; whom they took prisoners and brought them to their tents. When the King of England had well refreshed himself and his soldiers (that had taken the spoil of such as were slain), he with his prisoners in good order returned to his town of Calais [**4.8.130**].

. . . It was no marvel, though, this battle was lamentable to the French nation, for in it were taken and slain the flower of all the nobility of France.

There were taken prisoners Charles Duke of Orleans, nephew to the French King, John Duke of Bourbon, the Lord Boucicault one of the Marshals of France (he after died in England), with a number of other lords, knights, and esquires, at the least fifteen hundred besides the common people [**81**]. There were slain in all, of the French part, to the number of ten thousand men, whereof were princes and noblemen bearing banners one hundred twenty and six [**85**]; to these, of knights, esquires, and gentlemen, so many as made up the number of eight thousand and four hundred (of the which five hundred were dubbed knights the night before the battle); so as of the meaner[42]

[42]Lower-ranking.

sort, not past sixteen hundred. Amongst those of the nobility that were slain, these were the chieftest [**97**]: Charles Lord Delabreth High Constable of France; Jacques of Châtillon Lord of Dampier Admiral of France; the Lord Rambures Master of the Crossbows; Sir Guichard Dauphin Great Master of France; John Duke of Alençon; Anthony Duke of Brabant brother to the Duke of Burgundy; Edward Duke of Bar; the Earl of Nevers another brother to the Duke of Burgundy; with the Earls of Marle, Vaudemont, Beaumont, Grandpré, Roussy, Fauquembergue, Foix, and Lestrale; beside a great number of lords and barons of name.

Of Englishmen, there died at this battle Edward Duke [of] York, the Earl of Suffolk, Sir Richard Ketly, and Davy Gam, esquire [**108**]; and, of all other, not above five and twenty persons [**111**], as some do report; but other writers, of greater credit, affirm that there were slain above five or six hundred persons. . . .

[**556**] After that the King of England had refreshed himself and his people at Calais, and that such prisoners as he had left at Harfleur (as ye have heard) were come to Calais unto him, the sixth day of November [1415] he with all his prisoners took shipping and the same day landed at Dover, having with him the dead bodies of the Duke of York and the Earl of Suffolk; and caused the Duke to be buried at his college of Fotheringhay, and the Earl at New Elm. In this passage the seas were so rough and troublous that two ships belonging to Sir John Cornwall Lord Fanhope were driven into Zeeland; howbeit, nothing was lost nor any person perished. The Mayor of London and the aldermen, appareled in orient-grained scarlet,[43] and four hundred commoners clad in beautiful murrey[44] (well mounted and trimly horsed, with rich collars and great chains) met the King on Blackheath [**5 Ch. 16**], rejoicing at his return. And the clergy of London, with rich crosses, sumptuous copes, and massy censers, received him at Saint Thomas of Waterings with solemn procession.

The King, like a grave and sober personage, and as one remembering from whom all victories are sent, seemed little to regard such vain pomp and shows as were in triumphant sort devised for his welcoming home from so prosperous a journey; insomuch that he would not suffer his helmet to be carried with him [**17**], whereby might have appeared to the people the blows and dints that were to be seen in the same. Neither would he suffer any ditties to be made and sung by

[43]Brilliantly dyed cloth.
[44]Mulberry-colored cloth.

minstrels of his glorious victory, for that he would wholly have the praise and thanks altogether given to God. . . .

In this fourth year of King Henry's reign [1416], the Emperor Sigismund, cousin-german to King Henry, came into England [**38**] to the intent that he might make an atonement[45] between King Henry and the French King (with whom he had been before), bringing with him the Archbishop of Reims as ambassador for the French King. . . .

[**564**] The King, now [1418] determining with all speed to besiege Rouen, prepared all things necessary for his purpose. . . .

[**566**] Thus was the fair city of Rouen compassed about with enemies, both by water and land, having neither comfort nor aid of King, Dauphin, or Duke. . . .

Finally the whole number of the Frenchmen within the city were brought to such an extremity for want of victuals that they were in danger all to have starved. Whereupon, being now past hope of relief, they determined to treat with the King of England; and so, upon New Year's Eve, there came to the walls such as they had chosen amongst them for commissioners, which made a sign, to the Englishmen lying without the gate of the bridge, to speak with some gentleman or other person of authority. . . .

[**567**] Hereupon the Duke of Clarence with the other counselors resorted to the King's lodging to inform him of the matter and to know his pleasure therein; who, after good advisement and deliberation taken, willed Sir Gilbert to advertise them that he was content to hear twelve of them, which should be safely conveyed into his presence. . . .

One of them, seen[46] in the civil laws, was appointed to declare the message in all their names; who, showing himself more rash than wise, more arrogant than learned, first took upon him to show wherein the glory of victory consisted. Advising the King not to show his manhood in famishing a multitude of poor, simple, and innocent people, but rather suffer such miserable wretches as lay betwixt the walls of the city and the trenches of his siege to pass through the camp, that they might get their living in other places; and then, if he durst manfully assault the city and by force subdue it, he should win both worldly fame and merit great meed[47] at the hands of almighty God for having compassion of the poor, needy, and indigent people.

[45]Reconciliation.
[46]Versed.
[47]Reward.

When this orator had said, the King, who no request less suspected than that which was thus desired, began awhile to muse; and after he had well considered the crafty cautel[48] of his enemies, with a fierce countenance and bold spirit he reproved them, both for their subtle dealing with him and their malapert presumption in that they should seem to go about to teach him what belonged to the duty of a conqueror. And therefore, since it appeared that the same was unknown unto them, he declared that the goddess of battle, called Bellona, had three handmaidens ever of necessity attending upon her, as Blood, Fire, and Famine [**Pr. 7**]. And whereas it lay in his choice to use them all three (yea, two or one of them, at his pleasure), he had appointed only the meekest maid of those three damsels to punish them of that city, till they were brought to reason.

And whereas the gain of a captain attained by any of the said three handmaidens was both glorious, honorable, and worthy of triumph; yet of all the three, the youngest maid which he meant to use at that time was most profitable and commodious.[49] And as for the poor people lying in the ditches, if they died through famine, the fault was theirs that like cruel tyrants had put them out of the town, to the intent he should slay them; and yet had he saved their lives, so that if any lack of charity was, it rested in them and not in him. But to their cloaked request, he meant not to gratify them within so much; but they should keep them still to help to spend their victuals. And as to assault the town, he told them that he would they should know he was both able and willing thereto, as he should see occasion; but the choice was in his hand to tame them either with Blood, Fire, or Famine, or with them all; whereof he would take the choice at his pleasure and not at theirs [**3.1.7**]. . . .

The tents were again set up, and daily they met together; and on the fourth day they accorded on this wise, that the city and castle of Rouen should be delivered unto the King of England, at what time after the midst of the nineteenth day of that present month of January [1419] the said King willed the same. . . .

[**569**] Herewith intending to build upon this frail foundation, he [John Duke of Burgundy] sent letters and ambassadors to the King of England, advertising him that if he would personally come to a communication to be had between him and Charles the French King, he

[48]Device.
[49]Advantageous.

doubted not but by his only means peace should be brought in place and bloody battle clearly exiled.

. . . Whereupon the King of England agreed to come to the town of Mantes, with condition that the Duke of Burgundy and other for the French King should come to Pontoise, that either part might meet other in a convenient place betwixt those two towns. . . .

After this solemn feast ended, the place of interview and meeting was appointed to be beside Meulan on the river of Seine, where in a fair place every part was by commissioners appointed to their ground. When the day of appointment approached, which was the last day of May [1419], the King of England, accompanied with the Dukes of Clarence and Gloucester his brethren, the Duke of Exeter his uncle, and Henry Beaufort, clerk, his other uncle which after was Bishop of Winchester and Cardinal, with the Earls of March, Salisbury, and others to the number of a thousand men-of-war, entered into his ground, which was barred about [**5.2.27**] and ported,[50] wherein his tents were pitched in a princely manner.

Likewise, for the French part came Isabel the French Queen, because her husband was fallen into his old frantic disease, having in her company the Duke of Burgundy and the Earl of Saint-Pol; and she had attending upon her the fair lady Katherine [of Valois] her daughter, with six and twenty ladies and damsels; and had also for her furniture a thousand men-of-war. The said Lady Katherine was brought by her mother only to the intent that the King of England, beholding her excellent beauty, should be so enflamed and rapt in her love that he, to obtain her to his wife, should the sooner agree to a gentle peace and loving concord [**5.2**]. But though many words were spent in this treaty, and that they met at eight several times, yet no effect ensued nor any conclusion was taken by this friendly consultation, so that both parties after a princely fashion took leave each of other and departed, the Englishmen to Mantes and the Frenchmen to Pontoise.

. . . By reason whereof no conclusion sorted to effect of all this communication, save only that a certain spark of burning love was kindled in the King's heart by the sight of the Lady Katherine. . . .

[**572**] Whilst these victorious exploits were thus happily achieved by the Englishmen, and that the King lay still at Rouen in giving thanks to almighty God for the same, there came to him eftsoons[51] ambassadors from the French King and the Duke of Burgundy to

[50]Gated.
[51]Again.

move him to peace. The King, minding not to be reputed for a destroyer of the country which he coveted to preserve, or for a causer of Christian blood still to be spilt in his quarrel, began so to incline and give ear unto their suit and humble request that, at length, after often sending to and fro, and that the Bishop of Arras and other men of honor had been with him, and likewise the Earl of Warwick and the Bishop of Rochester had been with the Duke of Burgundy, they both finally agreed upon certain articles, so[52] that the French King and his commons would thereto assent.

Now was the French King and the Queen with their daughter Katherine at Troyes in Champagne governed and ordered by them which so much favored the Duke of Burgundy that they would not, for any earthly good, once hinder or pull back one jot of such articles as the same Duke should seek to prefer. And therefore what needeth many words? A truce tripartite was accorded between the two Kings and the Duke and their countries; and order taken that the King of England should send, in the company of the Duke of Burgundy, his ambassadors unto Troyes in Champagne, sufficiently authorized to treat and conclude of so great matter. The King of England, being in good hope that all his affairs should take good success as he could wish or desire, sent to the Duke of Burgundy his uncle the Duke of Exeter, the Earl of Salisbury, the Bishop of Ely, the Lord Fanhope, the Lord Fitzhugh, Sir John Robsert, and Sir Philip Hall, with divers doctors,[b] to the number of five hundred horse; which in the company of the Duke of Burgundy came to the city of Troyes the eleventh of March [1420]. The King, the Queen, and the Lady Katherine them received and heartily welcomed, showing great signs and tokens of love and amity [**12**].

After a few days they fell to council, in which at length it was concluded that King Henry of England should come to Troyes and marry the Lady Katherine; and the King her father after his death should make him heir of his realm, crown, and dignity. It was also agreed that King Henry, during his father-in-law's life, should in his stead have the whole government of the realm of France, as Regent thereof; with many other covenants and articles, as after shall appear. . . .

The Duke of Burgundy, accompanied with many noblemen, received him two leagues without the town and conveyed him to his lodging. All his army was lodged in small villages thereabout. And

[52]Provided.

[b]*I.e.*, of law and divinity.

after that he had reposed himself a little, he went to visit the French King, the Queen, and the Lady Katherine, whom he found in Saint Peter's Church, where was a very joyous meeting betwixt them (and this was on the twentieth day of May); and there the King of England and the Lady Katherine were affianced [**398**]. After this, the two Kings and their Council assembled together divers days, wherein the first concluded agreement was in divers points altered and brought to a certainty, according to the effect above-mentioned. When this great matter was finished, the Kings swore for their parts to observe all the covenants of this league and agreement. Likewise the Duke of Burgundy . . . received an oath. . . .

[**573**] The like oath a great number of the princes and nobles both spiritual and temporal which were present received at the same time. This done, the morrow after Trinity Sunday, being the third of June, the marriage was solemnized and fully consummate betwixt the King of England and the said Lady Katherine. Herewith was the King of England named and proclaimed heir and Regent of France. And as the French King sent the copy of this treaty to every town in France, so the King of England sent the same in English unto every city and market town within his realm, to be proclaimed and published. The true copy whereof, as we find it in the *Chronicles* of Master Hall, we have thought good here to set down, for the more full satisfying of those that shall desire to peruse every clause and article thereof, as followeth. . . .

"1. First [**96**], it is accorded between our father and us that, forsomuch as, by the bond of matrimony made for the good of the peace between us and our most dear beloved Katherine, daughter of our said father and of our most dear mother Isabel his wife, the same Charles and Isabel been[c] made our father and mother, therefore them as our father and mother we shall have and worship, as it fitteth and seemeth so worthy a prince and princess to be worshiped, principally before all other temporal persons of the world. . . .

"6. Also, that after the death of our said father aforesaid, and from thence forward, the crown and the realm of France, with all the rights and appurtenances, shall remain and abide to us, and been of us and of our heirs for evermore.

"7. And forsomuch as our said father is withholden with divers sickness, in such manner as he may not intend[53] in his own person for to dispose for the needs of the foresaid realm of France, therefore,

[c]Be.
[53]Apply himself.

during the life of our foresaid father, the faculties and exercise of the governance and disposition of the public and common profit of the said realm of France, with Council and nobles and wise men of the same realm of France, shall be and abide to us. . . .

[**574**] "24. Also, that during our father's life we shall not call nor write us King of France; but verily we shall abstain us from that name as long as our father liveth.

"25. Also, that our said father, during his life, shall name, call, and write us in French in this manner [**367**], *Notre très-cher fils Henri, Roi d'Angleterre, héritier de France,* and in Latin in this manner, *Praecarissimus filius noster Henricus, Rex Angliae et haeres Franciae."*

[**583**] . . . This Henry was a king of life without spot; a prince whom all men loved, and of none distained;[54] a captain against whom Fortune never frowned nor mischance once spurned; whose people him so severe a justicer both loved and obeyed (and so human withal) that he left no offense unpunished nor friendship unrewarded; a terror to rebels and suppressor of sedition; his virtues notable, his qualities most praiseworthy.

In strength and nimbleness of body, from his youth few to him comparable; for in wrestling, leaping, and running no man well able to compare. In casting of great iron bars and heavy stones he excelled commonly all men; never shrinking at cold nor slothful for heat; and when he most labored, his head commonly uncovered; no more weary of harness[55] than a light cloak; very valiantly abiding at needs both hunger and thirst; so manful of mind as never seen to quinch[56] at a wound or to smart at the pain; not to turn his nose from evil savor nor close his eyes from smoke or dust; no man more moderate in eating and drinking, with diet not delicate but rather more meet for men-of-war than for princes or tender stomachs. Every honest person was permitted to come to him, sitting at meal; where, either secretly or openly, to declare his mind. High and weighty causes, as well between men-of-war and other, he would gladly hear; and either determined them himself, or else for end committed them to others. He slept very little, but that very soundly, insomuch that when his soldiers sung at nights or minstrels played, he then slept fastest; of courage invincible, of purpose unmutable; so wisehearty always as fear was banished from him; at every alarum he first in armor and foremost in ordering. In time of war such was his providence, bounty, and hap as he had true

[54] Dishonored.
[55] Armor.
[56] Flinch.

intelligence, not only what his enemies did, but what they said and intended; of his devices and purposes, few, before the thing was at the point to be done, should be made privy.

He had such knowledge in ordering and guiding an army, with such a gift to encourage his people, that the Frenchmen had constant opinion he could never be vanquished in battle. Such wit, such prudence, and such policy[57] withal that he never enterprised anything before he had fully debated and forecast all the main chances that might happen; which done, with all diligence and courage he set his purpose forward. What policy he had in finding present remedies for sudden mischiefs, and what engines[58] in saving himself and his people in sharp distresses, were it not that by his acts they did plainly appear, hard were it by words to make them credible. Wantonness of life and thirst in avarice had he quite quenched in him; virtues indeed in such an estate of sovereignty, youth, and power, as very rare, so right commendable in the highest degree. So staid of mind and countenance, beside, that never jolly or triumphant for victory, nor sad or damped for loss or misfortune. For bountifulness and liberality, no man more free, gentle, and frank[59] in bestowing rewards to all persons according to their deserts; for his saying was that he never desired money to keep, but to give and spend.

Although that story[60] properly serves not for theme of praise or dispraise, yet what in brevity may well be remembered, in truth would not be forgotten by sloth; were it but only to remain as a spectacle for magnanimity to have always in eye, and for encouragement to nobles in honorable enterprises. Known be it, therefore, of person and form was this prince rightly representing his heroical affects;[61] of stature and proportion tall and manly, rather lean than gross, somewhat long-necked, and black-haired, of countenance amiable; eloquent and grave was his speech, and of great grace and power to persuade. For conclusion, a majesty was he that both lived and died, a pattern in princehood, a lodestar[62] [**Ep. 6**] in honor, and mirror [**2 Ch. 6**] of magnificence; the more highly exalted in his life, the more deeply lamented at his death; and famous to the world alway.

[57]Cunning.
[58]Ingenious devices.
[59]Generous.
[60]History.
[61]Disposition.
[62]Guiding star.

1 Henry VI

[**581**] This year [1421] at Windsor, on the day of Saint Nicholas in December, the Queen [Katherine] was delivered of a son named Henry, whose godfathers were John Duke of Bedford and Henry Bishop of Winchester; and Jacquette or (as the Frenchmen called her) Jacqueline of Bavière Countess of Holland was his godmother. The King, being certified hereof as he lay at siege before Meaux, gave God thanks in that it had pleased His divine providence to send him a son which might succeed in his crown and scepter. But when he heard reported the place of his nativity, were it that he [had been] warned by some prophecy or had some foreknowledge or else judged himself of his son's fortune, he said unto the Lord Fitzhugh his trusty Chamberlain these words [**3.1.194**]: "My lord, I, Henry born at Monmouth, shall small time reign and much get; and Henry born at Windsor shall long reign and all lose—but, as God will, so be it." . . .

[**582**] The Dauphin, having knowledge by espials[1] where the King of England and his power lay, came [1422] with all his puissance over the river of Loire and besieged Cosne, a town situate upon that river a six score miles distant from Paris, and appointed part of his army to waste and destroy the confines of the duchy of Burgundy, to the intent to divide the power of the King of England from the strength of the Duke of Burgundy, supposing (as it came to pass indeed) that the Duke would make haste toward Burgundy to defend his own lands. In the meantime they within Cosne were so hard handled that they promised to render their town to the Dauphin if they were not rescued by the King of England within ten days. King Henry, hearing these news, would not send any one creature but determined to go himself to the raising of that siege; and so with all diligence came to the town of Corbeil, and so to Senlis, where (whether it were with heat of the air or that he with his daily labor were feebled or weak-

[1]Scouts.

ened) he began to wax sick, yea and so sick that he was constrained to tarry and send his brother the Duke of Bedford to rescue them of Cosne, which he did to his high honor. For the Dauphin, hearing that the Duke of Bedford was coming to raise his siege, departed thence into Berry, to his great dishonor and less gain.

. . . In the mean season King Henry waxed sicker and sicker, and so in an horse-litter was conveyed to Bois de Vincennes; to whom shortly after repaired the Dukes of Bedford and Gloucester and the Earls of Salisbury and Warwick, whom the King lovingly welcomed and seemed glad of their presence.

[**583**] Now, when he saw them pensive for[2] his sickness and great danger of life wherein he presently lay, he with many grave, courteous, and pithy words, recomforted them the best he could, and therewith exhorted them to be trusty and faithful unto his son and to see that he might be well and virtuously brought up. And as concerning the rule and governance of his realms during the minority and young years of his said son, he willed them to join together in friendly love and concord, keeping continual peace and amity with the Duke of Burgundy; and never to make treaty with Charles that called himself Dauphin of Vienne [**1.1.162**], by the which any part, either of the crown of France or of the duchies of Normandy and Guienne, might be lessened or diminished; and further, that the Duke of Orleans and the other princes should still remain prisoners till his son came to lawful age, lest, returning home again, they might kindle more fire in one day than might be quenched in three.

He further advised them that, if they thought it necessary, it should be good to have his brother Humphrey Duke of Gloucester to be Protector of England during the nonage of his son; and his brother the Duke of Bedford, with the help of the Duke of Burgundy, to rule and to be Regent of France; commanding him with fire and sword to persecute the Dauphin till he had either brought him to reason and obeisance or else to drive and expel him out of the realm of France. . . .

The noblemen present promised to observe his precepts and to perform his desires, but their hearts were so pensive and replenished with sorrow that one could not for weeping behold another. Then he said the seven psalms and received the sacrament, and in saying the

[2]Anxious about.

psalms of the passion ended his days here in this world, at Bois Saint Vincent, the last of August in the year 1422.

. . . Peter Basset (a chief man in his chamber) affirmed that he deceased of a pleurisy, though the Scots and French set it down to be of Saint Fiacre's disease, that they say was a palsy with a cramp, which Enguerrand reports to be Saint Anthony's fire; but neither of them truly. *Anglorum Proelia* saith that it was a sharp fever, which happening unto him (wearied with the broils of war) in a very unseasonable time of the year, namely the dog-days, tormented him the sorer and grew to be not only dangerous but also desperate, for it left him not till life was extinguished. . . .

[**584**] His body, embalmed and closed in lead, was laid in a chariot royal, richly appareled with cloth of gold. Upon his coffin was laid a representation of his person, adorned with robes, diadem, scepter, and ball, like a king. The which chariot six horses drew, richly trapped, with several appointments.

. . . With this funeral appointment was he conveyed from Bois de Vincennes to Paris, and so to Rouen, to Abbeville, to Calais, to Dover, from thence through London to Westminster, where he was interred with such solemn ceremonies, mourning of lords, prayer of priests, and such lamenting of commons as never before then the like was seen in England. Shortly after this solemn burial his sorrowful Queen returned into England and kept her estate with the young King her son.

Thus ended this puissant prince his most noble and fortunate reign, whose life (saith Hall) though cruel Atropos abbreviated, yet neither fire, malice, nor fretting time shall appall[3] his honor or blot out the glory of him that in so small time had done so many and royal acts. In this year [1422], the one and twentieth of October, deceased the gentle and well-beloved Charles, French King the sixth of that name, who was buried at Saint Denis. So that between the death of these two Kings, namely the one of England the other of France, there was no great space of time, sith Charles departed in October and Henry in August; by the privation of whose lives which of the two realms sustained the greater loss, it is a question not to be discussed. Certain it is that they were both sovereigns tenderly loved of their subjects, as they were princes greatly favoring their people. . . .

[3]Impair.

[585] After that death had bereft the world of that noble prince King Henry the Fifth, his only son Prince Henry, being of the age of nine months or thereabouts, with the sound of trumpets was openly proclaimed King of England and France the thirtieth day of August, by the name of Henry the Sixth, in the year of the world 5389, after the birth of our Saviour 1422, about the twelfth year of the Emperor Frederick the Third, the fortieth and two (and last) of Charles the Sixth, and the third year of Mordake's regiment[4] (after his father Robert) Governor of Scotland. The custody of this young prince was appointed to Thomas Duke of Exeter [**171**] and to Henry Beaufort Bishop of Winchester [**174**]. The Duke of Bedford was deputed Regent of France, and the Duke of Gloucester was ordained Protector of England.

. . . And surely the death of this King Charles caused alterations in France. For a great many of the nobility which before, either for fear of the English puissance or for the love of this King Charles (whose authority they followed) held on the English part, did now revolt to the Dauphin with all endeavor to drive the English nation out of the French territories [**58**]. Whereto they were the more earnestly bent, and thought it a thing of greater facility, because of King Henry's young years; whom (because he was a child) they esteemed not but, with one consent, revolted from their sworn fealty. . . .

The Dauphin, which lay the same time in the city of Poitiers, after his father's decease, caused himself to be proclaimed King of France by the name of Charles the Seventh [**92**]; and, in good hope to recover his patrimony, with an haughty courage preparing war, assembled a great army. And first the war began by light skirmishes, but after it grew into main battles. . . .

[589] This year [1425] after Easter the King called a parliament at Westminster by advice of the peers; and, coming to the parliament house himself, he was conveyed through the city upon a great courser, with great triumph, the people flocking into the streets to behold the child, whom they judged to have the lively image and countenance of his father, and like to succeed him and be his heir in all princely qualities, martial policies, and moral virtues, as well as in his realms, seigniories, and dominions.

. . . During the same season Edmund Mortimer, the last Earl of March of that name (which long time had been restrained from his

[4]Rule.

liberty and finally waxed lame),[5] deceased without issue; whose inheritance descended to the Lord Richard Plantagenet, son and heir to Richard Earl of Cambridge, beheaded (as before ye have heard) at the town of Southampton [**2.5**]. . . .

[**590**] Somewhat before this season [1425] fell a great division in the realm of England which of a sparkle was like to have grown to a great flame. For whether the Bishop of Winchester, called Henry Beaufort (son to John [of Gaunt] Duke of Lancaster by his third wife), envied the authority of Humphrey Duke of Gloucester, Protector of the realm, or whether the Duke disdained at the riches and pompous estate of the Bishop, sure it is that the whole realm was troubled with them and their partakers;[6] so that the citizens of London were fain[7] to keep daily and nightly watches, and to shut up their shops, for fear of that which was doubted[8] to have ensued of their assembling of people about them [**1.3.56 SD, 3.1.85**]. The Archbishop of Canterbury and the Duke of Coimbra, called the Prince of Portugal, rode eight times in one day between the two parties, and so the matter was stayed for a time. But the Bishop of Winchester, to clear himself of blame so far as he might, and to charge his nephew the Lord Protector with all the fault, wrote a letter to the [Duke of Bedford] Regent of France the tenor whereof ensueth. . . .

[**591**] "Right high and mighty prince, and my right noble and, after one, lievest[9] lord, I recommend me unto you with all my heart. And as you desire the welfare of the King our sovereign lord, and of his realms of England and France, your own health, and ours also, so haste you hither. For by my troth, if you tarry we shall put this land in adventure with a field.[10] Such a brother you have here, God make him a good man. For your wisdom knoweth that the profit of France standeth in the welfare of England, etc. Written in great haste on All Hallow'n Eve. By your true servant to my life's end, Henry Winchester."

. . . In this parliament [1426] the Duke of Gloucester laid certain articles to the Bishop of Winchester his charge, the which with the answers hereafter do ensue as followeth [**3.1 SD**]. . . .

"1. First, whereas he, being Protector and Defender of this land,

[5]Rather his cousin Sir John Mortimer (Boswell-Stone).
[6]Supporters.
[7]Obliged.
[8]Feared.
[9]Most beloved.
[10]Battle.

desired the Tower [of London] to be opened to him and to lodge him therein, Richard Woodville, esquire (having at that time the charge of the keeping of the Tower), refused his desire and kept the same Tower against him unduly and against reason, by the commandment of my said Lord of Winchester [**1.3.15**]. . . .

"2. Item, my said Lord of Winchester, without the advice and assent of my said Lord of Gloucester or of the King's Council, purposed and disposed him to set hand on the King's person and to have removed him from Eltham [**1.1.176**], the place that he was in, to Windsor, to the intent to put him in governance as him list.

"3. Item, that where my said Lord of Gloucester (to whom of all persons that should be in the land, by the way of nature and birth, it belongeth to see the governance of the King's person), informed of the said undue purpose of my said Lord of Winchester (declared in the article next above-said) and, in letting[11] thereof, determining to have gone to Eltham unto the King to have provided as the cause required, my said Lord of Winchester, untruly and against the King's peace, to the intent to trouble my said Lord of Gloucester going to the King, purposing his death, in case that he had gone that way, set men-of-arms and archers at the end of London Bridge next Southwark [**3.1.23**]; and, in forbarring of the King's highway, let draw the chain of the stoops[12] there, and set up pipes and hurdles in manner and form of bulwarks; and set men in chambers, cellars, and windows, with bows and arrows and other weapons, to the intent to bring final destruction to my said Lord of Gloucester's person, as well as of those that then should come with him.

"4. Item, my said Lord of Gloucester saith and affirmeth that our sovereign lord his brother, that was King Henry the Fifth, told him, on a time (when our sovereign lord, being Prince, was lodged in the palace of Westminster, in the great chamber), by the noise of a spaniel there was on a night a man spied and taken behind a tapet[13] of the said chamber; the which man was delivered to the Earl of Arundel to be examined upon the cause of his being there at that time; the which, so examined, at that time confessed that he was there by the stirring and procuring of my said Lord of Winchester, ordained to have slain the said Prince there in his bed [**1.3.34**]; wherefore the said

[11]Hindering.
[12]Posts.
[13]Hanging (Holinshed).

Earl of Arundel let sack him[14] forthwith and drowned him in the Thames.

"5. Item, our sovereign lord that was, King Henry the Fifth, said unto my said lord of Gloucester that, his father King Henry the Fourth living and visited then greatly with sickness by the hand of God, my said Lord of Winchester said unto the King (Henry the Fifth, then being Prince) that the King his father so visited with sickness was not personable,[15] and therefore not disposed to come in conversation and governance of the people; and, forsomuch, counseled him to take the governance and crown of this land upon him. . . ."

[**595**] After the which words thus said (as before is declared), it was decreed also by the said lords arbitrators that the said Lord of Winchester should have these words that follow unto my said Lord of Gloucester [**3.1.134**]: "My Lord of Gloucester, I have conceived to my great heaviness that ye should have received by divers reports that I should have purposed and imagined[16] against your person, honor, and estate in divers manners; for the which ye have taken against me great displeasure. Sir, I take God to my witness, that what reports soever have been to you of me (peradventure of such as have had no great affection to me, God forgive it them), I never imagined nor purposed anything that might be hindering or prejudice to your person, honor, or estate; and therefore I pray you that ye be unto me good lord, from this time forth, for, by my will, I gave never other occasion, nor purpose not to do hereafter, by the grace of God." The which words so by him said, it was decreed by the same arbitrators that my Lord of Gloucester should answer and say [**138**]: "Fair uncle, sith ye declare you such a man as ye say, I am right glad that it is so, and for such a man I take you." And when this was done, it was decreed by the same arbitrators that every each of my Lords of Gloucester and Winchester should take either other by the hand, in the presence of the King and all the parliament, in sign and token of good love and accord; the which was done, and the parliament adjourned till after Easter.

. . . But when the great fire of this dissension between these two noble personages was thus by the arbitrators (to their knowledge and judgment) utterly quenched out and laid underboard, all other con-

[14]Had him put in a sack.
[15]Legally competent.
[16]Plotted.

troveries between other lords (taking part with the one party or the other) were appeased and brought to concord; so that, for joy, the King caused a solemn feast to be kept on Whitsunday, on which day he created Richard Plantagenet, son and heir to the Earl of Cambridge (whom his father at Southampton had put to death, as before ye have heard), Duke of York [**172**]; not foreseeing that this preferment should be his destruction, nor that his seed should of his generation be the extreme end and final conclusion [**188**]. . . .

[**596**] After that the Duke of Bedford had set all things in good order in England, he took leave of the King and, together with his wife, returned into France [1427], first landing at Calais, where the Bishop of Winchester (that also passed the seas with him) received the habit, hat, and dignity of a cardinal, with all ceremonies to it appertaining; which promotion[17] the late King (right deeply piercing into the unrestrainable ambitious mind of the man, that even from his youth was ever [wont] to check at the highest, and [having] also right well ascertained with what intolerable pride his head should soon be swollen under such a hat) did therefore all his life long keep this prelate back from that presumptuous estate [**5.1.31**]. But now, the King being young and the Regent his friend, he obtained his purpose, to his great profit and the impoverishing of the spiritualty of this realm. For by a bull legatine which he purchased from Rome, he gathered so much treasure that no man in manner had money but he, so that he was called the Rich Cardinal of Winchester [**51**]. . . .

[**597**] After this [1427], the Lord Talbot was made Governor of Anjou and Maine, and Sir John Fastolf was assigned to another place; which Lord Talbot, being both of noble birth and of haughty courage, after his coming into France obtained so many glorious victories of his enemies that his only name was and yet is dreadful to the French nation [**2.1.79, 2.3.17**]; and much renowned amongst all other people.

[**598**] . . . But the Duke of Alençon, who (as ye have heard) was lately delivered out of captivity, revived again the dulled spirits of the Dauphin and somewhat advanced, in hope of good speed,[18] the fainting hearts of his captains; so that (some occasion offered) they determined to achieve a notable feat (as they took it) against the Englishmen, which was the recovery of the city of Mans out of their hands; for so it happened that divers of the chief rulers in that city, and namely divers spiritual persons, meaning to revolt to the

[17]Preferment.
[18]Success.

Dauphin's side, advertised him by letters of their whole minds; which letters were conveyed unto him by certain friars.

The Dauphin, glad of those news, appointed the Lords Delabreth and Fayet, Marshals of France, accompanied with the Lords of Montjean, of Bueil, Dorval, Torcy, Beaumanor, the Hire, and his brother Guillaume, with five hundred other valiant captains and soldiers, to the accomplishing of this enterprise; who, coming thither at the day assigned, in the night season approached toward the walls, making a little fire on an hill in sight of the town to signify their coming; which perceived by the citizens that near to the great church were watching for the same, a burning cresset[19] was showed out of the steeple [**3.2.23**]; which suddenly was put out and quenched. What needeth many words?

The captains on horseback came to the gate; the traitors within slew the porters and watchmen and let in their friends, whereby the footmen entered first and the men-of-arms waited at the barriers, to the intent that, if need required, they might fight it out in open field. Hereby many Englishmen were slain, and a great cry and garboil[20] raised through the town, as in such surprises is wont. The cause of this mischief was not known to any but only to the conspirators; for the remnant of the citizens, being no partakers, imagined that the Englishmen had made havoc in the town and put all to the sword. The Englishmen, on the other side, judged that the citizens had begun some new rebellion against them or else had striven amongst themselves.

The Earl of Suffolk, which was Governor of the town, having perfect knowledge by such as scaped from the walls how the matter went, withdrew without any tarriance into the castle which standeth at the gate of Saint Vincent, whereof was Constable Thomas Gower, esquire; whither also fled many Englishmen; so as for urging of the enemy, press of the number, and lack of victuals, they could not have endured long; wherefore they privily sent a messenger to the Lord Talbot, which then lay at Alençon, certifying him in how hard a case they were. The Lord Talbot, hearing these news, like a careful[21] captain in all haste assembled together about seven hundred men; and in the evening departed from Alençon so as in the morning he came to a castle called Guierche, two miles from Mans, and there stayed awhile

[19]Torch.
[20]Tumult.
[21]Considerate.

till he had sent out Matthew Goffe, as an espial, to understand how the Frenchmen demeaned[22] themselves.

Matthew Goffe so well sped his business that privily in the night he came into the castle, where he learned that the Frenchmen very negligently used themselves, without taking heed to their watch, as though they had been out of all danger [**2.1.11**]. Which well understood, he returned again and within a mile of the city met the Lord Talbot and the Lord Scales, and opened unto them all things according to his credence. The lords then, to make haste in the matter (because the day approached), with all speed possible came to the postern gate; and alighting from their horses, about six of the clock in the morning they issued out of the castle, crying, "Saint George! Talbot!" [**38 SD (1)**]

The Frenchmen, being thus suddenly taken, were sore amazed, insomuch that some of them, being not out of their beds, got up in their shirts[23] and leapt over the walls [**38 SD (2)**]. Other ran naked out of the gates to save their lives, leaving all their apparel [**77 SD**], horses, armor, and riches behind them. None was hurt but such as resisted. . . .

The city of Mans being thus recovered, the Lord Talbot returned to Alençon, . . . and then [1428] was the Lord Thomas Montague Earl of Salisbury sent into France, . . . who landed at Calais with five thousand men; and so came to the Duke of Bedford, as then lying in Paris, where they fell in counsel together concerning the affairs of France; and namely[24] the Earl of Salisbury began marvelously to fancy the gaining of the city and country of Orleans.

This Earl was the man at that time by whose wit, strength, and policy[25] the English name was much fearful and terrible to the French nation [**2.2.17**]; which of himself might both appoint, command, and do all things in manner at his pleasure; in whose power (as it appeared after his death) a great part of the conquest consisted; for surely he was a man both painful,[26] diligent, and ready to withstand all dangerous chances that were at hand, prompt in counsel and of courage invincible; so that in no one man men put more trust, nor any singular person won the hearts so much of all men. . . .

[22]Employed.
[23]Nightshirts.
[24]Particularly.
[25]Cunning.
[26]Assiduous.

[**599**] After this, in the month of September [1428], the Earl came before the city of Orleans and planted his siege on the one side of the river of Loire. . . .

After the siege had continued full three weeks, the Bastard of Orleans issued out of the gate of the bridge and fought with the Englishmen; but they received him with so fierce and terrible strokes that he was with all his company compelled to retire and flee back into the city [**1.2.21 SD**]. But the Englishmen followed so fast, in killing and taking of their enemies, that they entered with them. The bulwark of the bridge, with a great tower standing at the end of the same, was taken incontinently[27] by the Englishmen, who behaved themselves right valiantly under the conduct of their courageous captain, as at this assault so in divers skirmishes against the French; partly to keep possession of that which Henry the Fifth had by his magnanimity[28] and puissance achieved, as also to enlarge the same. . . .

In this conflict many Frenchmen were taken but more were slain; and the keeping of the tower and bulwark was committed to William Glansdale, esquire [**1.4.67**]. By the taking of this bridge the passage was stopped, that neither men nor victuals could go or come by that way. . . .

The Bastard of Orleans and the Hire were appointed to see the walls and watches kept, and the Bishop saw that the inhabitants within the city were put in good order and that victuals were not vainly spent. In the tower that was taken at the bridge-end (as before you have heard), there was an high chamber, having a grate full of bars of iron by the which a man might look all the length of the bridge into the city; at which grate many of the chief captains stood many times, viewing the city and devising in what place it was best to give the assault [**10**]. They within the city well perceived this tooting-hole[29] and laid a piece of ordnance directly against the window [**15**].

It so chanced that, the nine and fiftieth day after the siege was laid, the Earl of Salisbury, Sir Thomas Gargrave, and William Glansdale, with divers other, went into the said tower [**26**] and so into the high chamber, and looked out at the grate [**60**]; and within a short space the son of the Master Gunner, perceiving men looking out at the window, took his match (as his father had taught him who was gone down to dinner) and fired the gun [**69 SD**]; the shot whereof broke

[27]Immediately.
[28]Lofty courage.
[29]Peephole.

and shivered the iron bars of the grate so that one of the same bars struck the Earl so violently on the head that it struck away one of his eyes [**83**] and the side of his cheek. Sir Thomas Gargrave was likewise stricken and died within two days [**88**].

The Earl was conveyed to Meun-on-Loire, where after eight days he likewise departed this world [**2.2.4**]. . . . The damage that the realm of England received by the loss of this nobleman manifestly appeared in that, immediately after his death, the prosperous good luck which had followed the English nation began to decline, and the glory of their victories gotten in the parties beyond the sea fell in decay.

Though all men were sorrowful for his death, yet the Duke of Bedford was most stricken with heaviness, as he that had lost his only right hand and chief aid in time of necessity. But sith that dead men cannot help the chances of men that be living, he like a prudent governor appointed the Earl of Suffolk to be his lieutenant and captain of the siege, and joined with him the Lord Scales, the Lord Talbot, Sir John Fastolf, and divers other right valiant captains. . . .

[**600**] In time of this siege at Orleans (French stories[30] say), the first week of March, 1429, unto Charles the Dauphin at Chinon, as he was in very great care and study how to wrestle against the English nation, by one Peter Baudricourt Captain of Vaucouleurs (made after Marshal of France by the Dauphin's creation), was carried a young wench of an eighteen years old, called Joan Arc, by name of her father (a sorry shepherd) James of Arc, and Isabel her mother [**1.2.51**]; brought up poorly in their trade of keeping cattle; born at Domremy (therefore reported by Bale, Joan Domremy) upon Meuse in Lorraine, within the diocese of Toul. Of favor[31] was she counted likesome, of person strongly made and manly, of courage great, hardy and stout[32] withal [**89**]; an understander of councils though she were not at them; great semblance of chastity both of body and behavior; the name of Jesus in her mouth about all her businesses; humble, obedient, and fasting divers days in the week. A person (as their books make her) raised up by power divine, only for succor to the French estate then deeply in distress; in whom, for planting a credit the rather, first the company that toward the Dauphin did conduct her, through places all dangerous as holden by the Eng-

[30]Histories.
[31]Countenance.
[32]Brave.

lish (where she never was afore), all the way and by nightertale[33] safely did she lead. Then, at the Dauphin's sending by her assignment, from Saint Katherine's Church of Fierbois in Touraine (where she never had been and knew not), in a secret place there among old iron appointed she her sword [**101**] to be sought out and brought her (that with five flower-de-luces [**99**] was graven on both sides), wherewith she fought and did many slaughters by her own hands. On warfare rode she in armor cap-a-pie[34] and mustered as a man; before her an ensign all white wherein was Jesus Christ painted with a flower-de-luce in his hand.

Unto the Dauphin into his gallery when first she was brought, and he, shadowing himself behind, setting other gay lords before him to try her cunning, from all the company, with a salutation (that indeed mars all the matter), she picked him out alone [**66**]; who thereupon had her to the end of the gallery where she held him an hour in secret and private talk [**69**], that of his privy chamber was thought very long [**118**] and therefore would have broken it off; but he made them a sign to let her say on. In which (among other), as likely it was, she set out unto him the singular feats [**64**] (forsooth) given her to understand by revelation divine [**52**] that in virtue of that sword she should achieve; which were, how with honor and victory she would raise the siege at Orleans [**53, 130**], set him in state of the crown of France, and drive the English out of the country; thereby he to enjoy the kingdom alone. Hereupon he heartened at full, appointed her a sufficient army with absolute power to lead them, and they obediently to do as she bade them. Then fell she to work and first defeated, indeed, the siege at Orleans [**1.6.2**]; by and by[35] encouraged him to crown himself King of France at Reims, that a little before from the English she had won. Thus, after, pursued she many bold enterprises, to our great displeasure a two year together; for the time she kept in state until she were taken and for heresy and witchery burned, as in particularities hereafter followeth. But in her prime time she armed at all points (like a jolly captain), rode from Poitiers to Blois, and there found men-of-war, victuals, and munition ready to be conveyed to Orleans.

Here was it known that the Englishmen kept not so diligent watch as they had been accustomed to do, and therefore this maid, with

[33]Night.
[34]From head to foot (Holinshed).
[35]Immediately.

other French captains coming forward in the dead time of the night, and in a great rain and thunder [**1.4.97 SD**], entered into the city [**1.5.14 SD**] with all their victuals, artillery, and other necessary provisions. The next day the Englishmen boldly assaulted the town, but the Frenchmen defended the walls so as no great feat worthy of memory chanced that day betwixt them, though the Frenchmen were amazed at the valiant attempt of the Englishmen. Whereupon the Bastard of Orleans gave knowledge to the Duke of Alençon in what danger the town stood without his present help; who, coming within two leagues of the city, gave knowledge to them within that they should be ready the next day to receive him.

[**601**] This accordingly was accomplished, for the Englishmen willingly suffered him and his army also to enter, supposing that it should be for their advantage to have so great a multitude to enter the city, whereby their victuals (whereof they within had great scarcity) might the sooner be consumed.

. . . Also, after this the Earl of Vendôme came to them, so that, by the daily repair of such as assembled together to strengthen the French part, they were in all to the number between twenty and three and twenty thousand men [**1.1.113**].

All which being once joined in one army, shortly after fought with the Lord Talbot (who had with him not past six thousand men) near unto a village in Beauce called Patay; at which battle the charge was given by the French so upon a sudden that the Englishmen had not leisure to put themselves in array after they had put up their stakes before their archers; so that there was no remedy but to fight at adventure.[36] This battle continued by the space of three long hours, for the Englishmen, though they were overpressed with multitude of their enemies, yet they never fled back one foot till their captain the Lord Talbot was sore wounded at the back, and so taken [**108**].

Then their hearts began to faint and they fled, in which flight were slain above twelve hundred, and forty taken, of whom the Lord Talbot, the Lord Scales, the Lord Hungerford, and Sir Thomas Rampston were chief. . . . From this battle departed, without any stroke stricken, Sir John Fastolf, the same year for his valiantness elected into the Order of the Garter [**131, 3.2.104**]. But for doubt[37] of misdealing at this brunt[38] the Duke of Bedford took from him the image

[36]Recklessly.
[37]Suspicion.
[38]Attack.

of Saint George and his garter [**4.1.15**], though afterward, by means of friends and apparent causes of good excuse, the same were to him again delivered, against the mind of the Lord Talbot.

Charles the Dauphin, that called himself French King, perceiving Fortune to smile thus upon him, assembled a great power and determined to conquer the city of Reims, that he might be there sacred,[39] crowned, and anointed according to the custom of his progenitors, that all men might judge that he was by all laws and decrees a just and lawful king. . . . When Reims was thus become French, the foresaid Charles the Dauphin, in the presence of the Dukes of Lorraine and Bar and of all the noblemen of his faction, was sacred there King of France by the name of Charles the Seventh, with all rites and ceremonies thereto belonging.

[**602**] . . . On the sixth day of November [1429], being the day of Saint Leonard, King Henry in the eighth year of his reign was at Westminster with all pomp and honor crowned King of this realm of England.

[**604**] . . . In the chase and pursuit was the Pucelle[a] taken [**5.3.30**], with divers other besides those that were slain, which were no small number [1430].

. . . Tillet telleth it thus: that she was caught at Compiègne by one of the Earl of Ligny's soldiers, from him had to Beaurevoir Castle where, kept a three months, she was after, for ten thousand pounds in money and three hundred pounds rent (all Tournois), sold into the English hands.

In which, for her pranks so uncouth and suspicious, the Lord Regent, by Peter Cauchon Bishop of Beauvais (in whose diocese she was taken), caused her life and belief, after order of law, to be inquired upon and examined. Wherein found, though a virgin, yet first, shamefully rejecting her sex abominably in acts and apparel, to have counterfeit mankind, and then, all damnably faithless, to be a pernicious instrument to hostility and bloodshed in devilish witchcraft and sorcery, sentence accordingly was pronounced against her. Howbeit, upon humble confession of her iniquities, with a counterfeit contrition pretending a careful sorrow for the same, execution [was] spared and all mollified into this, that from thenceforth she should cast off her unnatural wearing of man's habiliments and keep her to garments of her

[39]Consecrated to office.
[a]Joan of Arc (French = girl, maid).

own kind,[40] abjure her pernicious practices of sorcery and witchery, and have life and leisure in perpetual prison to bewail her misdeeds. Which to perform (according to the manner of abjuration) a solemn oath very gladly she took.

But herein (God help us!) she, fully afore possessed of the fiend, not able to hold her in any towardness of grace, falling straightway into her former abominations (and yet seeking to eke out life as long as she might), stake[41] not (though the shift were shameful) to confess herself a strumpet and (unmarried as she was) to be with child [**5.4.62**]. For trial, the Lord Regent's lenity gave her nine months' stay, at the end whereof she (found herein as false as wicked in the rest), an eight days after, upon a further definitive sentence declared against her to be relapse[42] and a renouncer of her oath and repentance, was thereupon delivered over to secular power and so executed by consumption of fire in the old marketplace at Rouen, in the selfsame stead where now Saint Michael's Church stands; her ashes afterward without the town walls shaken into the wind. Now, recounting altogether her pastoral[43] bringing up, rude, without any virtuous instruction, her campestral[44] conversation with wicked spirits [**5.3.3**], whom, in her first salutation to Charles the Dauphin, she uttered to be our Lady, Saint Katherine, and Saint Anne, that in this behalf came and gave her commandments from God her maker as she kept her father's lambs in the fields [**1.2.76**]. . . .

[**605**] These matters may very rightfully denounce unto all the world her execrable abominations, and well justify the judgment she had and the execution she was put to for the same. A thing yet (God wot) very smally shadowed, and less holpen by the very travail of the Dauphin, whose dignity abroad [was] foully spotted in this point, that, contrary to the holy degree of a right Christian prince (as he called himself), for maintenance of his quarrels in war, would not reverence to profane his sacred estate, as dealing in devilish practices with misbelievers and witches.

. . . But because the English sore mistrusted further danger, it was concluded that King Henry in his royal person with a new army should come into France, partly to visit and comfort his own subjects

[40]Sex.
[41]Sticked, scrupled.
[42]A relapsed person.
[43]As a shepherdess.
[44]In the fields.

there, and partly either by fear or favor (because a child of his age and beauty doth commonly procure them love of elder persons) to move the Frenchmen to continue their due obeisance toward him.

Wherefore, after a great host convenient for that purpose assembled, and money for maintenance of the war ready gathered, and the realm set in an order under the government of the Duke of Gloucester Protector (which during the King's absence appeased divers riots and punished the offenders), the King with a great power took shipping at Dover on Saint George's Eve [1431], within night, and landed at Calais on the morrow, being Saint George's Day and Sunday, by seven of the clock in the morning. He remained in Calais a good space, and from thence he removed to Rouen, being there received with all triumph. He tarried in that city a long time, his nobles daily consulting on their great business and weighty affairs. . . .

[**606**] But to return to the affairs of King Henry, who in the month of November removed from Rouen to Pontoise, and so to Saint Denis, to the intent to make his entry into Paris and there to be sacred King of France. There were in his company, of his own nation, his uncle the Cardinal of Winchester, the Cardinal and Archbishop of York, the Dukes of Bedford, York, and Norfolk, the Earls of Warwick, Salisbury, Oxford, Huntington, Ormonde, Mortain, and Suffolk. . . .

To speak with what honor he was received into the city of Paris, what pageants were prepared, and how richly the gates, streets, and bridges on every side were hanged with costly cloths of arras and tapestry, it would be too long a process and therefore I do here pass it over with silence. On the seventeenth day of December [1431] he was crowned King of France [**4.1.1**], in Our Lady Church of Paris, by the Cardinal of Winchester, the Bishop of Paris not being contented that the Cardinal should do such an high ceremony in his church and jurisdiction. After all the ceremonies were finished, the King returned toward the palace, having one crown on his head and another borne before him, and one scepter in his hand and the second borne before him.

. . . Amongst other of the chiefest prisoners, that valiant captain Poton de Sainte-Traille was one, who without delay was exchanged for the Lord Talbot, before taken prisoner at the Battle of Patay [**1.4.27**]. . . .

[**607**] When all things were agreed, King Henry came to Calais, from thence to Dover, and so by easy journies the one and twentieth day of February [1432] to London, where he was triumphantly re-

ceived and richly presented,[45] as in the *Chronicles* of Robert Fabyan it may at large appear. . . .

[**611**] And in the fifth year [1435] of this Basilian Council . . . , motion was made among Sigismund the Emperor and other Christian kings [**5.4.96**] . . . that sith such horror of bloodshed between the two nations continually so lamentably raged in France, some mediation might be made for accord; whereof one thing seemed to minister occasion of the more hope, because the Duke of Burgundy was willing (so that it were not of his own suit) to return and reconcile himself with the French King his mortal enemy and ancient adversary [**5.1**]. . . .

Upon the day of the first session, the Cardinal of Saint Cross[46] declared to the three parties [England, France, and Burgundy] the innumerable mischiefs that had followed to the whole state of the Christian commonwealth by their continual dissension and daily discord, exhorting them, for the honor of God and for the love which they ought to bear toward the advancement of His faith and true religion, to conform themselves to reason and to lay aside all rancor, malice, and displeasure; so that in concluding a godly peace [**5**], they might receive profit and quietness here in this world and of God an everlasting reward in heaven. . . .

The Englishmen would that King Charles should have nothing but what it pleased the King of England, and that not as duty but as a benefit[47] by him of his mere[48] liberality given and distributed [**5.4.128, 152**]. The Frenchmen, on the other part, would that King Charles should have the kingdom frankly and freely [**133**], and that the King of England should leave the name, arms, and title of the King of France, and to be content with the dukedoms of Aquitaine and Normandy, and to forsake Paris and all the towns which they possessed in France between the rivers of Somme and Loire being no parcel of the duchy of Normandy. To be brief, the demands of all parts were between them so far out of square[49] as hope of concord there was none at all. . . .

And after, the Duke of Burgundy, to set a veil before the King of England's eyes, sent Toison d'Or his chief herald to King Henry with letters [**4.1.11**]; excusing the matter by way of information that he

[45]Given gifts.
[46]Santa Croce.
[47]Fief (Boswell-Stone).
[48]Perfect.
[49]Order.

was constrained to enter in this league with King Charles by the daily outcries, complaints, and lamentations of his people [**57**], alleging against him that he was the only cause of the long continuance of the wars, to the utter impoverishing of his own people and the whole nation of France. Therefore, sith he could not otherwise do, but partly to content his own people and chiefly to satisfy the request of the whole general Council, was in manner compelled, for his part, to grow unto a peace and amity with King Charles [**3.3.18, 44**].

[**612**] . . . The superscription of this letter was thus: "To the high and mighty Prince Henry, by the grace of God King of England, his well-beloved cousin." Neither naming him King of France nor his sovereign lord, according as (ever before that time) he was accustomed to do [**4.1.51**]. This letter was much marveled at of the Council, after they had thoroughly considered all the contents thereof, and they could not but be much disquieted; so far forth that divers of them [were] offended so much with the untruth of the Duke that they could not temper their passions but openly called him traitor [**61**]. . . .

This year the fourteenth day of September [1435] died John Duke of Bedford, Regent of France [**3.2.114 SD**], a man both politic[50] in peace and hardy in war, and yet no more hardy than merciful when he had the victory; whose body was with all funeral solemnity buried in the cathedral church of our Lady in Rouen, on the north side of the high altar, under a sumptuous and costly monument. Which tomb when King Louis the Eleventh by certain indiscreet persons was counseled to deface, affirming that it was a great dishonor both to the King and to the realm to see the enemy of his father and theirs to have so solemn and rich a memorial, he answered, saying: "What honor shall it be to us or to you, to break this monument and to pull out of the ground the dead bones of him whom in his life neither my father nor your progenitors, with all their power, puissance, and friends, were once able to make fleet one foot backward; but by his strength, wit, and policy kept them all out of the principal dominions of the realm of France, and out of this noble and famous duchy of Normandy? Wherefore I say, first, Cod have his soul and let his body now lie in rest which, when he was alive, would have disquieted the proudest of us all [**4.7.49**]. And as for the tomb, I assure you it is not so decent nor convenient as his honor and acts deserved, although[51] it were much richer and more beautiful."

. . . After the death of that noble prince the Duke of Bedford, the

[50]Crafty.
[51]Even if.

bright sun in France toward Englishmen began to be cloudy and daily to darken. Then Frenchmen began not only to withdraw their obedience by oath to the King of England but also took sword in hand and openly rebelled. Howbeit, all these mishaps could not anything abash the valiant courages of the English people, for they, having no mistrust in God and good fortune, set up a new sail, began the war afresh, and appointed for Regent in France Richard Duke of York, son to Richard Earl of Cambridge [**4.1.163**].

Although the Duke of York was worthy (both for birth and courage) of this honor and preferment, yet so disdained of Edmund Duke of Somerset, being cousin to the King, that by all means possible he sought his hindrance, as one glad of his loss and sorry of his well doing; by reason whereof, ere the Duke of York could get his dispatch,[52] Paris and divers other of the chiefest places in France were gotten by the French King [**1.1.60, 5.2.2**]. The Duke of York, perceiving his evil will, openly dissembled that which he inwardly minded, either of them working things to the other's displeasure; till, through malice and division between them, at length by mortal war they were both consumed, with almost all their whole lines and offspring [**2.4**]. . . .

But here is one chief point to be noted, that either the disdain amongst the chief peers of the realm of England (as ye have heard) or the negligence of the King's Council (which did not foresee dangers to come) was the loss of the whole dominion of France between the rivers of Somme and Marne and, in especial, of the noble city of Paris [1436]. For where before there were sent over thousands for defense of the holds and fortresses, now were sent hundreds, yea, and scores; some rascals, and some not able to draw a bow or carry a bill. . . .[53]

[**613**] . . . Thus was the city of Paris brought into the possession of Charles the French King through the untrue demeanor[54] of the citizens, who, contrary to their oaths and promised allegiance, like false and inconstant people, so revolted from the English [**5.2.2**]. . . .

[**615**] About this season [1437] Queen Katherine, mother to the King of England, departed out of this life and was buried by her husband in the abbey of Westminster. This woman, after the death of King Henry the Fifth her husband, being young and lusty, following

[52]Leave to depart.
[53]Infantry weapon resembling a halberd.
[54]Behavior.

more her own wanton appetite than friendly counsel, and regarding more private affection than princelike honor, took to husband privily a gallant gentleman and a right beautiful person, endued with many goodly gifts both of body and mind, called Owen Tudor, a man descended of the noble lineage and ancient line of Cadwallader last King of the Britons. By this Owen she brought forth three goodly sons, Edmund, Jasper, and another that was a monk in Westminster and lived a small time; also a daughter which in her youth departed out of this transitory life.

King Henry, after the death of his mother, because they were his brethren of one womb, created Edmund Earl of Richmond and Jasper Earl of Pembroke; which Edmund of Margaret, daughter and sole heir to John Duke of Somerset, begat Henry who after was King of this realm, called Henry the Seventh, of whom ye shall hear more in place convenient. . . .

[**618**] After this meeting, thus prorogued,[55] Philip Duke of Burgundy, partly moved in conscience to make amends to Charles Duke of Orleans (as yet prisoner in England) for the death of Duke Louis his father, whom Duke John, father to this Duke Philip, cruelly murdered in the city of Paris, and partly intending the advancement of his niece the Lady Mary, daughter to Adolf Duke of Cleves (by the which alliance he trusted that all old rancor should cease), contrived ways to have the said Duke of Orleans set at liberty [**3.3.72**] upon promise by him made to take the said Lady Mary unto wife. This Duke had been prisoner in England ever since the battle was fought at Agincourt, upon the day of Crispin and Crispinian in the year 1415, and was set now at liberty, in the month of November in the year 1440, paying for his ransom four hundred thousand crowns, though other say but three hundred thousand.

The cause why he was detained so long in captivity was to pleasure thereby the Duke of Burgundy; for so long as the Duke of Burgundy continued faithful to the King of England, it was not thought necessary to suffer the Duke of Orleans to be ransomed lest, upon his deliverance, he would not cease to seek means to be revenged upon the Duke of Burgundy for the old grudge and displeasure betwixt their two families; and therefore such ransom was demanded for him as he was never able to pay. But after the Duke of Burgundy had broken his promise and was turned to the French part, the Council

[55]Discontinued.

of the King of England devised how to deliver the Duke of Orleans, that thereby they might displeasure the Duke of Burgundy [**73**]. Which thing the Duke of Burgundy perceiving, doubted what might follow if he were delivered without his knowledge, and therefore to his great cost practiced[56] his deliverance, paid his ransom, and joined with him [in] amity and alliance by marriage of his niece.

This Duke, being now delivered, and speaking better English than French, after his arrival in France repaired to the Duke of Burgundy and, according to his promise and convention,[57] married the Lady Mary of Cleves, in the town of Saint Omer, on whom he begat a son which after was French King and called Louis the Twelfth. . . .

[**619**] In the beginning of this twentieth year [1440 or 1443], Richard Duke of York, Regent of France [**4.1.163**] and Governor of Normandy, determined to invade the territories of his enemies both by sundry armies and in several places, and thereupon without delay of time he sent the Lord of Willoughby with a great crew of soldiers to destroy the country of Amiens; and John Lord Talbot was appointed to besiege the town of Dieppe; and the Regent himself, accompanied with Edmund Duke of Somerset [**164**], set forward into the duchy of Anjou.

. . . The Dukes of York and Somerset likewise entered into Anjou and Maine, and there destroyed towns and spoiled the people, and with great preys[58] and prisoners repaired again into Normandy.

. . . The Frenchmen a little before this season [1441] had taken the town of Évreux by treason of a fisher. Sir Francis the Arragonese, hearing of that chance, appareled six strong fellows like men of the country with sacks and baskets as carriers of corn[59] and victuals [**3.2 SD**] and sent them to the castle of Cornille, in the which divers Englishmen were kept as prisoners; and he, with an ambush of Englishmen, lay in a valley nigh to the fortress.

[**620**] The six counterfeit husbandmen entered the castle unsuspected and straight came to the chamber of the Captain; and, laying hands on him, gave knowledge to them that lay in ambush to come to their aid. The which suddenly made forth and entered the castle, slew and took all the Frenchmen, and set the Englishmen at liberty; which thing done, they set fire in the castle and departed to Rouen with their booty and prisoners. . . .

[56]Negotiated.
[57]Agreement.
[58]Booty.
[59]Grain.

But now to speak somewhat of the doings in England in the meantime [1441]. Whilst the men-of-war were thus occupied in martial feats and daily skirmishes within the realm of France, ye shall understand that, after the Cardinal of Winchester and the Duke of Gloucester were (as it seemed) reconciled either to other, yet the Cardinal and the Archbishop of York ceased not to do many things without the consent of the King or of the Duke, being (during the minority of the King) Governor and Protector of the realm, whereas the Duke (as good cause he had) greatly offended, thereupon in writing declared to the King wherein the Cardinal and the Archbishop had offended both his majesty and the laws of the realm. This complaint of the Duke of Gloucester was contained in four and twenty articles, which chiefly rested in that the Cardinal had, from time to time, through his ambitious desire to surmount all others in high degrees of honor and dignity, sought to enrich himself to the great and notorious hindrance of the King, as in defrauding him not only of his treasure but also in doing and practicing things greatly prejudicial to his affairs in France, and namely by setting at liberty the King of Scots upon so easy conditions as the King's majesty greatly lost thereby, as in particularities thus followeth. . . .

"2. First, the Cardinal, then being Bishop of Winchester, took upon him the state of cardinal, which was nayed and denied him by the King of most noble memory my lord your father (whom God assoil),[60] saying that he had as lief set his crown beside him as see him wear a cardinal's hat, he being a cardinal. For he knew full well the pride and ambition that was in his person, then being but a bishop, should have so greatly extolled[61] him into more intolerable pride when that he were a cardinal" [**5.1.31**].

[**623**] . . . About this season [1442], John the valiant Lord Talbot, for his approved prowess and wisdom as well in England as in France, both in peace and war so well tried, was created Earl of Shrewsbury [**3.4.26**] and, with a company of three thousand men, sent again into Normandy for the better defense of the same. . . .

In this year [1443] died in Guienne the Countess of Cominges, to whom the French King and also the Earl of Armagnac pretended[62] to be heir, insomuch that the Earl entered into all the lands of the said lady. And because he knew the French King would not take the matter well to have a Roland for an Oliver, he sent solemn ambassadors to

[60]Absolve.
[61]Elevated.
[62]Claimed.

the King of England, offering him his daughter in marriage [**5.1.19**], with promise to be bound (beside great sums of money which he would give with her) to deliver into the King of England's hands all such castles and towns as he or his ancestors detained from him within any part of the duchy of Aquitaine, either by conquest of his progenitors or by gift and delivery of any French King; and further, to aid the same King with money for the recovery of other cities within the same duchy from the French King or from any other person that against King Henry [had] unjustly kept and wrongfully withholden them.

[**624**] This offer seemed so profitable and also honorable to King Henry and the realm that the ambassadors were well heard, honorably received, and with rewards sent home into their country. After whom were sent for the conclusion of the marriage [**45**] into Guienne Sir Edward Hull, Sir Robert Ross, and John Grafton Dean of Saint Severinus, the which (as all the chronographers agree) both concluded[63] the marriage and by proxy affied[64] the young lady. . . .

Whilst England was unquieted (as you have heard) and France by spoil, slaughter, and burning sore defaced (a mischief in all places much lamented), therefore, to agree the two puissant kings, all the princes of Christendom [**5.4.96**] travailed so effectuously by their orators and ambassadors that a diet was appointed to be kept at the city of Tours in Touraine, where for the King of England appeared William de la Pole Earl of Suffolk.

. . . Many meetings were had, and many things moved for a final peace; but in conclusion, by reason of many doubts which rose on both parties, no full concord could be agreed upon; but in hope to come to a peace, a certain truce as well by sea as by land was concluded [1444] by the commissioners for eighteen months; which afterward again was prolonged to the year of our Lord 1449 [**2H6 1.1.40**].

In treating of this truce, the Earl of Suffolk, adventuring somewhat upon his commission, without the assent of his associates, imagined that the next[65] way to come to a perfect peace was to contrive a marriage between the French King's kinswoman the Lady Margaret, daughter to René Duke of Anjou, and his sovereign lord King Henry [**1H6 5.3.117**]. This René Duke of Anjou named himself King of Sicily, Naples, and Jerusalem [**5.5.40**], having only the name and style

[63]*I.e.,* the negotiations for.
[64]Espoused.
[65]Nearest.

of those realms, without any penny, profit, or foot of possession. This marriage was made strange to[66] the Earl at the first, and one thing seemed to be a great hindrance to it; which was because the King of England occupied a great part of the duchy of Anjou and the whole county of Maine, appertaining (as was alleged) to King René.

The Earl of Suffolk (I cannot say either corrupted with bribes or too much affectioned to this unprofitable marriage) condescended that the duchy of Anjou and the county of Maine should be delivered to the King the bride's father [**5.3.154, 2H6 1.1.57**], demanding for her marriage neither penny nor farthing, as who would say that this new affinity passed all riches and excelled both gold and precious stones [**1H6 5.3.169**]. And to the intent that of this truce might ensue a final concord, a day of interview was appointed between the two Kings in a place convenient between Chartres and Rouen. When these things were concluded, the Earl of Suffolk with his company returned into England [1444], where he forgot not to declare what an honorable truce he had taken, out of the which there was a great hope that a final peace might grow the sooner for that honorable marriage which he had concluded, omitting nothing that might extoll and set forth the personage of the lady or the nobility of her kindred [**5.5.1**].

But, although this marriage pleased the King and divers of his Council, yet Humphrey Duke of Gloucester, Protector of the realm, was much against it [**25**], alleging that it should be both contrary to the laws of God and dishonorable to the Prince if he should break that promise and contract of marriage, made by ambassadors sufficiently thereto instructed, with the daughter of the Earl of Armagnac, upon conditions both to him and his realm as much profitable as honorable. But the Duke's words could not be heard, for the Earl's doings were only liked and allowed [**88**]. . . .

[**640**] The Council, not forgetting the offer of the Gascons and that they might now have the city of Bordeaux with the country round about, by request of the inhabitants, appointed [1453] the valiant captain John Lord Talbot, Earl of Shrewsbury, to go thither with an army [**4.2.1**]. . . .

After the regaining of Bordeaux there arrived at Blay . . . Sir John Talbot (Lord Lisle by his wife) son to the said Earl of Shrewsbury [**4.3.35**]. . . .

In the meantime the French King, being advertised of all these

[66]Treated coolly by.

doings, raised an army to resist this invasion made by the Earl of Shrewsbury. And first he appointed his captains to besiege the town of Castillon, to the rescue whereof the Earl hasted forward. . . .

The Frenchmen that lay at the siege, perceiving by those good runners-away that the Earl approached, left the siege and retired in good order into the place which they had trenched, ditched, and fortified with ordnance. The Earl, advertised how the siege was removed, hasted forward toward his enemies, doubting most lest they would have been quite fled and gone before his coming. But they, fearing the displeasure of the French King (who was not far off) if they should have fled, abode the Earl's coming and so received him; who, though he first with manful courage and sore fighting won the entry of their camp, yet at length they compassed him about and, shooting him through the thigh with an handgun, slew his horse and finally killed him lying on the ground whom they durst never look in the face while he stood on his feet [**4.7.32**].

It was said that after he perceived there was no remedy but present loss of the battle, he counseled his son the Lord Lisle to save himself by flight [**4.5.10**], sith the same could not redound to any great reproach in him, this being the first journey[67] in which he had been present. Many words he used to persuade him to have saved his life; but nature so wrought in the son that neither desire of life nor fear of death could either cause him to shrink or convey himself out of the danger, and so there manfully ended his life with his said father [**4.7.15**].

[67]Battle.

2 Henry VI

[622][1] When the King had heard the accusations thus laid by the Duke of Gloucester against the Cardinal [of Winchester], he committed the examination thereof to his Council, whereof the more part were spiritual persons; so that, what for fear and what for favor, the matter was winked at and nothing said to it; only fair countenance was made to the Duke, as though no malice had been conceived against him. But venom will break out and inward grudge will soon appear, which was this year [1441] to all men apparent, for divers secret attempts were advanced forward this season against this nobleman Humphrey Duke of Gloucester, afar off, which, in conclusion, came so near that they bereft him both of life and land, as shall hereafter more plainly appear.

For, first, this year Dame Eleanor Cobham, wife to the said Duke, was accused of treason, for that she by sorcery and enchantment [**1.4.25 SD**] intended to destroy the King [**2.1.175**], to the intent to advance her husband unto the crown [**1.2.7**]. Upon this, she was examined in Saint Stephen's Chapel before the Bishop of Canterbury, and there by examination convict and judged to do open penance [**2.3.11**] in three open places within the city of London (*Polychronicon* saith she was enjoined to go through Cheapside with a taper in her hand [**2.4.16 SD**]) and after that adjudged to perpetual imprisonment in the Isle of Man, under the keeping of Sir John Stanley, knight [**2.3.13**]. At the same season were arrested [**1.4.44**], arraigned, and adjudged guilty, as aiders to the Duchess, Thomas Southwell, priest and canon of Saint Stephen's at Westminster; John Hume, priest; Roger Bolingbroke, a cunning necromancer (as it was said); and Margery Jourdain, surnamed the Witch of Eye.

[623] The matter laid against them was for that they (at the request of the said Duchess) had devised an image of wax representing the

[1]References to *2H6* outside this section may be found at pp. 60–62, 166, 167, 191, and 215.

King which by their sorcery [was] by little and little consumed, intending thereby in conclusion to waste and destroy the King's person. Margery Jourdain was burned in Smithfield [**2.3.7**], and Roger Bolingbroke was drawn to Tyburn and hanged and quartered [**8**], taking[2] upon his death that there was never any such thing by them imagined.[a] John Hume had his pardon, and Southwell died in the Tower the night before his execution, for (saith *Polychronicon*) he did prophesy of himself that he should die in his bed and not by justice. The Duke of Gloucester bore all these things patiently and said little [**2.4.26, 68**]. Edward son to the Duke of York was born this year [1441], the nine and twentieth of April, at Rouen, his father being the King's lieutenant in Normandy.

[**625**] . . . Also, the Earl of Suffolk was made Marquis of Suffolk; which Marquis, with his wife and many honorable personages of men and women, richly adorned both with apparel and jewels, having with them many costly chariots and gorgeous horse-litters, sailed into France for the conveyance of the nominated Queen [Margaret] into the realm of England. For King René her father, for all his long style, had too short a purse to send his daughter honorably to the King her spouse [**1.1.111**].

This noble company came to the city of Tours in Touraine, where they were honorably received both of the French King and of the King of Sicily. The Marquis of Suffolk, as procurator [**3**] to King Henry, espoused the said lady in the church of Saint Martin's. At the which marriage were present the father and mother of the bride, the French King himself, which was uncle to the husband, and the French Queen also, which was aunt to the wife. There were also the Dukes of Orleans, of Calabria, of Alençon, and of Brittany, seven earls, twelve barons, twenty bishops [**8**], beside knights and gentlemen. When the feast, triumph, banquets, and jousts [**1.3.54**] were ended, the lady was delivered to the Marquis, who in great estate conveyed her through Normandy unto Dieppe and so transported her into England, where she landed at Portsmouth in the month of April [1445]. This lady excelled all other as well in beauty and favor as in wit and policy, and was of stomach[3] and courage[4] more like to a man than a woman.

[2]*I.e.,* an oath.
[a]Plotted.
[3]Disposition.
[4]Spirit.

Shortly after her arrival she was conveyed to the town of Southwick in Hampshire, where she with all nuptial ceremonies was coupled in matrimony to King Henry the sixth of that name. On the eighteenth of May she came to London, all the lords of England in most sumptuous sort meeting and receiving her upon the way, and specially the Duke of Gloucester, with such honor as stood with the dignity of his person. . . . Upon the thirtieth of May next following [1445] she was crowned queen of this realm of England at Westminster, with all the solemnity thereto appertaining [**1.1.74**].

This marriage seemed to many both unfortunate and unprofitable to the realm of England [**99**], and that for many causes. First, the King had not one penny with her, and for the fetching of her the Marquis of Suffolk demanded a whole fifteenth[5] in open parliament [**133**]. And also there was delivered for her the duchy of Anjou, the city of Mans, and the whole county of Maine [**50**], which countries were the very stays and backstands to the duchy of Normandy [**114**]. And furthermore, the Earl of Armagnac took such displeasure with the King of England for this marriage that he became utter enemy to the crown of England and was the chief cause that the Englishmen were expelled out of the whole duchy of Aquitaine.

But most of all it should seem that God was displeased with this marriage, for after the confirmation thereof the King's friends fell from him, both in England and in France, the lords of his realm fell at division, and the commons rebelled in such sort that, finally, after many fields[6] foughten and many thousands of men slain, the King at length was deposed and his son killed and this Queen sent home again with as much misery and sorrow as she was received with pomp and triumph; such is the instability of worldly felicity and so wavering is false flattering Fortune.

. . . During the time of the truce [1446], Richard Duke of York and divers other captains repaired into England [**66**], both to visit their wives, children, and friends, and also to consult what should be done if the truce ended. For the which cause a parliament was called in the which it was especially concluded that by good foresight Normandy might be so furnished for defense before the end of the truce that the French King should take no advantage through want of timely provision; for it was known that, if a peace were not concluded, the French King did prepare to employ his whole puissance to make

[5]Personal property tax of one fifteenth.
[6]Battles.

open war. Hereupon money was granted, an army levied, and the Duke of Somerset appointed to be Regent of Normandy and the Duke of York thereof discharged [**1.3.209**].

I have seen in a register book belonging sometime to the abbey of Saint Albans that the Duke of York was established Regent of France after the decease of the Duke of Bedford, to continue in that office for the term of five years; which being expired, he returned home and was joyfully received of the King with thanks for his good service, as he had full well deserved in time of that his government. And further, that now, when a new Regent was to be chosen and sent over, to abide upon safeguard of the countries beyond the seas as yet subject to the English dominion, the said Duke of York was eftsoons[7] (as a man most meet to supply that room)[8] appointed to go over again, as Regent of France, with all his former allowances.

But the Duke of Somerset, still maligning the Duke of York's advancement, as he had sought to hinder his dispatch at the first when he was sent over to be Regent (as before ye have heard), he likewise now wrought so that the King revoked his grant made to the Duke of York for enjoying of that office the term of other five years, and with help of William Marquis of Suffolk obtained that grant for himself [**216**]. . . .

[**626**] By the Queen's means shortly after also was the said Marquis advanced so in authority that he ruled the King at his pleasure.

. . . In the same year also [1447] a certain armorer was appeached of treason by a servant of his own [**28, 184, 2.3.87**]. . . .

Whilst the wars between the two nations of England and France ceased (by occasion of the truce), the minds of men were not so quiet but that such as were bent to malicious revenge sought to compass their prepensed[9] purpose, not against foreign foes and enemies of their country, but against their own countrymen and those that had deserved very well of the commonwealth. And this specially for overmuch mildness in the King, who by his authority might have ruled both parts and ordered all differences betwixt them but that, indeed, he was thought too soft for Governor of a kingdom. The Queen, contrariwise, a lady of great wit and no less courage, desirous of honor and furnished with the gifts of reason, policy,[10] and wisdom, but yet

[7]Again.
[8]Office.
[9]Premeditated.
[10]Cunning.

sometime (according to her kind),[11] when she had been fully bent on a matter, suddenly like a weathercock mutable and turning.

This lady, disdaining that her husband should be ruled rather than rule, could not abide that the Duke of Gloucester should do all things concerning the order of weighty affairs, lest it might be said that she had neither wit nor stomach which would permit and suffer her husband, being of most perfect age, like a young pupil [**1.3.49**] to be governed by the direction of another man. Although this toy[12] entered first into her brain through her own imagination, yet was she pricked forward to the matter both by such of her husband's counsel as of long time had borne malice to the Duke for his plainness used in declaring their untruth (as partly ye have heard), and also by counsel from King René her father advising that she and the King should take upon them the rule of the realm, and not to be kept under [**1.1.166, 1.3.119**], as wards and mastered orphans.

What needeth many words? The Queen, persuaded by these means, first of all excluded the Duke of Gloucester from all rule and governance [**2.3.22**], not prohibiting such as she knew to be his mortal foes to invent and imagine causes and griefs against him and his, insomuch that by her procurement divers noblemen conspired against him. Of the which, divers writers affirm the Marquis of Suffolk and the Duke of Buckingham to be the chief [**1.1.168**], not unprocured by the Cardinal of Winchester and the Archbishop of York. Divers articles were laid against him in open Council, and in especial one, that he had caused men adjudged to die to be put to other execution than the law of the land assigned [**1.3.135, 3.1.58, 121**]. Surely the Duke, very well learned in the law civil, detesting malefactors and punishing offenses in severity of justice, got him hatred of such as feared condign reward [**130**] for their wicked doings. And although the Duke sufficiently answered to all things against him objected, yet because his death was determined, his wisdom and innocency nothing availed [**168**].

[**627**] But to avoid danger of tumult that might be raised if a prince so well beloved of the people should be openly executed [**236**], his enemies determined to work their feats in his destruction ere he should have any warning. For effecting whereof, a parliament was summoned to be kept at Bury [**2.4.70**]; whither resorted all the peers of the realm, and amongst them the Duke of Gloucester, which, on the second day of the session, was by the Lord Beaumont, then High

[11]Sex.
[12]Whim.

Constable of England (accompanied with the Duke of Buckingham and others), arrested [**3.1.97**], apprehended, and put in ward,[13] and all his servants sequestered from him; and thirty-two of the chief of his retinue were sent to divers prisons, to the great admiration[14] of the people. The Duke, the night after he was thus committed to prison, being the four and twentieth of February [1447], was found dead in his bed; and his body showed [**3.2.146 SD**] to the lords and commons as though he had died of a palsy or of an impostume.[b]

But all indifferent[15] persons (as saith Hall) might well understand that he died of some violent death [**123**]. Some judged him to be strangled [**170**], some affirm that an hot spit was put in at his fundament, other write that he was smouldered[16] between two featherbeds; and some have affirmed that he died of very grief, for that he might not come openly to his answer. His dead corpse was conveyed to Saint Albans and there buried. . . .

Some think that the name and title of Gloucester hath been unlucky to divers which for their honors have been erected by creation of princes to that style and dignity, as Hugh le Despenser,[17] Thomas of Woodstock son to King Edward the Third, and this Duke Humphrey, which three persons by miserable death finished their days; and after them King Richard the Third, also Duke of Gloucester, in civil war slain. . . .

Ofttimes it happeneth that a man, in quenching of smoke, burneth his fingers in the fire; so the Queen, in casting how to keep her husband in honor and herself in authority, in making away of this nobleman brought that to pass which she had most cause to have feared; which was the deposing of her husband and the decay of the House of Lancaster, which of likelihood had not chanced if this Duke had lived [**3.1.159**]; for then durst not the Duke of York have attempted to set forth his title to the crown, as he afterward did, to the great trouble of the realm and destruction of King Henry and of many other noblemen beside. This is the opinion of men, but God's judgments are unsearchable, against whose decree and ordinance prevaileth no human counsel.

[13]Prison.
[14]Wonder.
[b]Abscess.
[15]Impartial.
[16]Smothered.
[17]Thomas le Despenser, created Earl of Gloucester 1397, beheaded for treason 1400.

But to conclude of this noble Duke: he was an upright and politic governor, bending all his endeavors to the advancement of the commonwealth, very loving to the poor commons, and so beloved of them again [**1.1.158**]; learned, wise, full of courtesy; void of pride and ambition (a virtue rare in personages of such high estate but, where it is, most commendable). . . .

In this six and twentieth year [1448] of the reign of this King, but in the first of the rule of the Queen, I find nothing done worthy of rehearsal within the realm of England but that the Marquis of Suffolk, by great favor of the King and more desire of the Queen, was erected to the title and dignity of Duke of Suffolk [**1.1.64**], which he a short time enjoyed. For Richard Duke of York (being greatly allied by his wife to the chief peers and potentates of the realm, beside his own progeny),[18] perceiving the King to be no ruler but the whole burden of the realm to rest in direction of the Queen and the Duke of Suffolk, began secretly to allure his friends of the nobility; and privily declared unto them his title and right to the crown, and likewise did he to certain wise governors of divers cities and towns [**2.2**]. Which attempt was so politicly[19] handled and so secretly kept that provision to his purpose was ready before his purpose was openly published; and his friends opened themselves ere the contrary part could them espy; for in conclusion, all shortly in mischief burst out, as ye may hereafter hear.

During these doings Henry Beaufort Bishop of Winchester, and called the Rich Cardinal, departed out of this world [**3.3.29**] and [was] buried at Westminster [1447]. He was son to John [of Gaunt] Duke of Lancaster. . . .

[**629**] The King little regarding the matter, and the Queen led by evil counsel, rather furthered such mischiefs as daily began to grow by civil discord than sought to reform them; so that the Normans and Gascons, understanding in what state things stood here, turned to the French part, as hereafter it may appear. About the same time also [1448] began a new rebellion in Ireland [**3.1.282**]; but Richard Duke of York, being sent thither to appease the same [**312**], so assuaged the fury of the wild and savage people there that he won him such favor amongst them as could never be separated from him and his lineage [**1.1.194**]; which in the sequel of this history may more plainly appear.

[18]Lineage.
[19]Cunningly.

The Frenchmen, having perfect understanding of the unreadiness of the realm of England, displayed their banners and set forth their armies, and in short space got (by yielding) Constance, Gisors, Castle Gaillard, Pont Audemer, Saint-Lô, Fécamp, Newcastle,[20] Touques, Mauléon, Argenton, Lisieux, and divers other towns and places within the country of Normandy. Likewise in Guienne was the town of Maulisson rendered to the Earl of Foix. These towns were not yielded voluntarily by the English soldiers; but they were compelled thereto by the inhabitants of the towns which, having intelligence of the feeble estate of the realm of England, rose against the captains, opened the gates to the enemies, or constrained them to render upon composition.[21] By which enforcement was the rich city of Rouen delivered, for surely the Duke of Somerset and the Earl of Shrewsbury had well kept that city if they had been no more vexed with the citizens than they were with their enemies. . . .

[**630**] After this overthrow obtained [1450], the French King assembled an army royal and, coming before Caen, besieged it on all sides; and, after making his approaches, fiercely assaulted the walls. But the Duke of Somerset and the other captains within the town manfully withstood their enemies, showing both force and great policy in defending and beating back the assailants. . . .

The Duke, pitiful, moved with the sorrow of his wife and love of his children, rendered the town against the mind of Sir David Hall. . . . The conditions of the surrender were that the Duke of Somerset and his might depart in safeguard with all their goods and substance. Sir David Hall, with divers of his trusty friends, departed to Cherbourg, and from thence sailed into Ireland to the Duke of York, making relation to him of all these doings; which thing kindled so great a rancor [**3.1.296**] in the Duke's heart and stomach[22] that he never left persecuting the Duke of Somerset until he had brought him to his fatal end and confusion.

. . . Thus was Normandy lost clearly out of the Englishmen's hands [**85**] after it had continued in their possession the space of thirty years by the conquest of Henry the Fifth. . . .

For whilst the French thus triumphed in Normandy, three cruel enemies among many (as by civil war and sedition ensuing appeared) sore urged the utter ruin of this realm at home. One was presumption

[20]Neufchâtel.
[21]Arrangement.
[22]Spirit.

in governance by some that were most unmeet to rule, as the Queen with her Privy Councillors and minions; then the deadly malice and pride, with insatiable covetise,[23] in the states[24] both spiritual and temporal; and lastly the general grudge of the people for the universal smart that through misgovernment everywhere they suffered; who [were] thus forwearied with the peise[25] of burdens too heavy for them any longer to bear.

[**631**] Herewith, perceiving how (through want of provident wisdom in the Governor) all things went to wrack as well within the realm as without, they began to make exclamation against the Duke of Suffolk, charging him to be the only cause of the delivery of Anjou and Maine, the chief procurer of the Duke of Gloucester's death [**3.2.248**], the very occasion of the loss of Normandy, the swallower-up of the King's treasure [**4.1.74**], the remover of good and virtuous counselors from about the Prince, and the advancer of vicious persons and of such as by their doings showed themselves apparent adversaries to the commonwealth.

The Queen hereat, doubting[26] not only the Duke's destruction but also her own confusion, caused the parliament, before begun at the Black Friars, to be adjourned to Leicester; thinking there, by force and rigor of law, to suppress and subdue all the malice and evil will conceived against the Duke and her. At which place few of the nobility would appear; wherefore it was again adjourned to Westminster, where was a full appearance. In the which session the commons of the nether house put up to the King and the lords many articles of treason, misprision, and evil demeanor[27] against the Duke of Suffolk, the effect whereof with his answers here ensueth. . . .

4. Further, it was alleged that he, being ambassador for the King of England to Charles calling himself the French King, promised to René King of Sicily and to Charles d'Angiers his brother, enemies to the King, the release of Anjou, with the deliverance of the county of Maine and the city of Mant or Mans, without the knowledge of the other ambassadors with him accompanied. Which promise, after his return, he caused to be performed, to the King's disinheritance and loss irrecoverable, and to the strength of his enemies and feeblishment

[23]Desire of wealth.
[24]Lords.
[25]Weight.
[26]Fearing.
[27]Conduct.

of the duchy of Normandy. To this article he answered that his commission was to conclude and do all things according to his discretion for the obtaining of a peace; and because without delivery of those countries he perceived that the truce could not be obtained, he agreed to the release and deliverance of them. . . .

"9. Item, when armies have been prepared and soldiers ready waged[28] to pass over the sea to deal with the King's enemies, the said Duke, corrupted by rewards of the French King, hath restrained and stayed the said armies to pass any further [**3.1.104**]. . . ."

All these objections he utterly denied or faintly avoided, but none fully excused. . . .

[**632**] The Queen, which entirely loved the Duke, doubting some commotion and trouble to arise if he were let go unpunished, caused him for a color[29] to be committed to the Tower, where he remained not past a month but was again delivered and restored to the King's favor, as much as ever he was before. This doing so much displeased the people that, if politic provision had not been [made], great mischief had immediately ensued.

. . . When the King perceived that there was no remedy to appease the people's fury by any colorable[30] ways, shortly to pacify so long an hatred, he first sequestered the Lord Say (being Treasurer of England) and other the Duke's adherents from their offices and rooms, and after [1450] banished [**3.2.295**] the Duke of Suffolk, as the abhorred toad and common noyance of the whole realm, for term of five years, meaning by this exile to appease the malice of the people for the time and, after (when the matter should be forgotten), to revoke him home again [**349**].

But God's justice would not that so ungracious a person should so escape; for when he shipped in Suffolk, intending to transport himself over into France, he was encountered with a ship-of-war appertaining to the Duke of Exeter, Constable of the Tower of London, called *The Nicholas of the Tower*. The captain of that bark with small fight [**4.1 SD**] entered into the Duke's ship and, perceiving his person present, brought him to Dover Road and there, on the one side of a cockboat [**68**], caused his head to be stricken off and left his body with the head lying there on the sands [**142, 1.4.36**]. Which corpse, being there found by a chaplain of his, was conveyed to Wingfield College

[28]Pledged.
[29]Pretense.
[30]Plausible.

in Suffolk and there buried. This end had William de la Pole Duke of Suffolk, as men judge by God's providence for that he had procured the death of that good Duke of Gloucester, as before is partly touched.

Soon after, another disquiet befell here [1450]. Those that favored the Duke of York and wished the crown upon his head for that (as they judged) he had more right thereto than he that wore it, procured a commotion in Kent on this manner. A certain young man, of a goodly stature and right pregnant of wit, was enticed to take upon him the name of John Mortimer [**3.1.359**], cousin to the Duke of York (although his name was John Cade or, of some, John Mend-all, an Irishman, as *Polychronicon* saith), and not for a small policy, thinking by that surname that those which favored the House of the Earl of March would be assistant to him. . . .

This captain assembling a great company of tall[31] personages, assured them that the enterprise which he took in hand was both honorable to God and the King and profitable to the whole realm. For if either by force or policy they might get the King and Queen into their hands, he would cause them to be honorably used and take such order for the punishing and reforming of the misdemeanors of their bad counselors that neither fifteens [**4.7.24**] should hereafter be demanded nor once any impositions or taxes be spoken of. The Kentish people, moved at these persuasions and other fair promises of reformation, in good order of battle (though not in great number) came with their captain unto the plain of Blackheath, between Eltham and Greenwich, and there kept the field more than a month, pilling[32] the country about; to whom the city of London at that time was very favorable. . . .

And to the intent the cause of this glorious captain's coming thither might be shadowed under a cloak of good meaning (though his intent nothing so) he sent unto the King an humble supplication [**4.4 SD**] affirming that his coming was not against his grace but against such of his counselors as were lovers of themselves and oppressors of the poor commonalty, flatterers of the King and enemies to his honor, suckers of his purse and robbers of his subjects, partial to their friends and extreme to their enemies, through bribes corrupted and for indifferency doing nothing.

[**634**] . . . Then went the King again to London, and within two days after went against the Kentishmen with fifteen thousand men well

[31]Brave.
[32]Pillaging.

prepared for the war; but the said Kentishmen fled the night before his coming into the wood country near unto Sevenoaks. Whereupon the King returned again to London.

The Queen (that bore rule), being of his retreat advertised, sent Sir Humphrey Stafford, knight, and William his brother, with many other gentlemen, to follow the Kentishmen, thinking that they had fled; but they were deceived, for at the first skirmish both the Staffords were slain [**4.3 SD**] and all their company discomfited.

. . . Jack Cade, upon victory against the Staffords, appareled himself in Sir Humphrey's brigandine[33] set full of gilt nails [**12**], and so in some glory returned again toward London, divers idle and vagrant persons out of Sussex, Surrey, and other places still increasing his number. Thus this glorious captain, guarded with a multitude of rustical people, came again to the plain of Blackheath and there strongly encamped himself; to whom were sent from the King the Archbishop of Canterbury and Humphrey Duke of Buckingham, to common[34] with him of his griefs and requests.

These lords found him sober in talk, wise in reasoning, arrogant in heart, and stiff in opinion, as who that by no means would grant to dissolve his army except the King in person would come to him and assent to the things he would require. The King, upon the presumptuous answers and requests of this villainous rebel, beginning as much to doubt his own menial servants as his unknown subjects (which spared not to speak that the captain's cause was profitable for the commonwealth), departed in all haste to the castle of Kenilworth [**4.4.39**] in Warwickshire, leaving only behind him the Lord Scales to keep the Tower of London [**4.5 SD**]. The Kentish captain, being advertised of the King's absence, came first into Southwark [**4.4.27**] and there lodged at the White Hart [**4.8.25**], prohibiting to all his retinue murder, rape, and robbery, by which color of well meaning he the more allured to him the hearts of the common people.

After that, he entered into London, cut the ropes of the drawbridge [**4.4.49**], and struck his sword on London stone [**4.6 SD**], saying [**1**], "Now is Mortimer lord of this city!" And after a glozing[35] declaration made to the Mayor touching the cause of his thither coming, he departed again into Southwark; and upon the third day of July [1450]

[33]Body armor made of a tough fabric to which was riveted a lining of small overlapping plates (in this case the rivet heads having been gilded for ornament).

[34]Confer.

[35]Smoothly deceptive.

he caused Sir James Fines Lord Say and Treasurer of England to be brought to the Guildhall and there to be arraigned [**4.7.26**]; who, being before the King's justices put to answer, desired to be tried by his peers for the longer delay of his life. The captain, perceiving his dilatory plea, by force took him from the officers and brought him to the standard[36] in Cheap, and there (before his confession ended) caused his head to be stricken off [**116**], and pitched it upon an high pole which was openly borne before him through the streets.

And not content herewith, he went to Mile End and there apprehended Sir James Cromer [**118**], then Sheriff of Kent and son-in-law to the said Lord Say, causing him likewise (without confession or excuse heard) to be beheaded and his head to be fixed on a pole; and with these two heads this bloody wretch entered into the city again and, as it were in a spite, caused them in every street to kiss together [**145**], to the great detestation of all the beholders. . . . He also put to execution in Southwark divers persons, some for breaking his ordinance and other being of his old acquaintance [**4.6.9 SD**], lest they should bewray[37] his base lineage, disparaging him for his usurped surname of Mortimer [**6**].

The Mayor and other the magistrates of London, perceiving themselves neither to be sure of goods nor of life well warranted, determined to repel and keep out of their city such a mischievous caitiff[38] and his wicked company. And to be the better able so to do, they made the Lord Scales and that renowned captain Matthew Goffe privy both of their intent and enterprise, beseeching them of their help and furtherance therein. The Lord Scales promised them his aid with shooting off the artillery in the Tower, and Matthew Goffe was by him appointed to assist the Mayor and Londoners in all that he might [**4.5.11**]; and so he and other captains appointed for defense of the city took upon them in the night to keep the bridge, and would not suffer the Kentishmen once to approach. The rebels, who never soundly slept for fear of sudden assaults, hearing that the bridge was thus kept, ran with great haste to open that passage [**3**], where between both parties was a fierce and cruel fight.

[**635**] Matthew Goffe, perceiving the rebels to stand to their tackling[39] more manfully than he thought they would have done, advised

[36]Conduit.
[37]Betray.
[38]Villain.
[39]Weapons.

his company not to advance any further toward Southwark till the day appeared, that they might see where the place of jeopardy rested, and so to provide for the same; but this little availed. For the rebels with their multitude drove back the citizens from the stoops[40] at the bridge foot to the drawbridge, and began to set fire in divers houses. . . . Yet the captains, not sparing, fought on the bridge all the night valiantly; but in conclusion, the rebels got the drawbridge and drowned many; and slew John Sutton, alderman, and Robert Heisand, a hardy citizen, with many other, beside Matthew Goffe [**4.7 SD**], a man of great wit and much experience in feats of chivalry, the which in continual wars had spent his time in service of the King and his father.

This sore conflict endured in doubtful wise on the bridge till nine of the clock in the morning, for sometime the Londoners were beaten back to Saint Magnus' corner [**4.8.1**], and suddenly again the rebels were repelled to the stoops in Southwark, so that both parts, being faint and weary, agreed to leave off from fighting till the next day, upon condition that neither Londoners should pass into Southwark nor Kentishmen into London. Upon this abstinence, this rakehell captain, for making him more friends, broke up the jails of the King's Bench and Marshalsea, and so were many mates set at liberty very meet for his matters in hand [**4.3.18**].

The Archbishop of Canterbury, being Chancellor of England and as then for his surety lying within the Tower, called to him the Bishop of Winchester, who for some safeguard lay then at Holywell. These two prelates, seeing the fury of the Kentish people, by their late repulse, to be somewhat assuaged, passed by the river of Thames from the Tower into Southwark, bringing with them, under the King's Great Seal, a general pardon unto all the offenders [**4.8.9**], and caused the same to be openly published. The poor people were so glad of this pardon and so ready to receive it that, without bidding farewell to their captain, they withdrew themselves the same night every man toward his home.

But Jack Cade, despairing of succors and fearing the reward of his lewd[41] dealings, put all his pillage and goods that he had robbed into a barge and sent it to Rochester by water, and himself went by land, and would have entered into the castle of Queenborough with a few men that were left about him but he was there let[42] of his purpose;

[40]Posts.
[41]Base.
[42]Hindered.

wherefore he, disguised in strange[43] attire, privily fled into the wood country beside Lewes in Sussex, hoping so to escape. The captain and his people being thus departed, not long after proclamations were made in divers places of Kent, Sussex, and Surrey, that whosoever could take the foresaid captain alive or dead should have a thousand marks for his travail [**70**]. . . .

After which proclamation thus published, a gentleman of Kent named Alexander Iden awaited so his time that he took the said Cade in a garden [**4.10.8**] in Sussex, so that there he was slain [**63**] at Hothfield and brought to London in a cart; where he was quartered, his head [**5.1.66**] set on London Bridge, and his quarters sent to divers places to be set up in the shire of Kent. After this, the King himself came into Kent and there sat in judgment upon the offenders [**4.9.12**]; and if he had not mingled his justice with mercy, more than five hundred by rigor of law had been justly put to execution. Yet he, punishing only the stubborn heads and disordered ringleaders, pardoned [**20**] the ignorant and simple persons, to the great rejoicing of all his subjects. . . .

[**637**] The Duke of York, pretending[44] (as ye have heard) a right to the crown as heir to Lionel Duke of Clarence, came this year [1450] out of Ireland [**24, 5.1.1**] unto London, in the parliament time, there to consult with his special friends: as John Duke of Norfolk, Richard Earl of Salisbury, and the Lord Richard his son (which after was Earl of Warwick), Thomas Courtenay Earl of Devonshire, and Edward Brooke Lord Cobham. After long deliberation and advice taken, it was thought expedient [1451] to keep their chief purpose secret; and that the Duke should raise an army of men, under a pretext to remove divers counselors about the King, and to revenge the manifest injuries done to the commonwealth by the same rulers. Of the which, as principal, the Duke of Somerset [**4.9.30**] was namely[45] accused, both for that he was greatly hated of the commons for the loss of Normandy and for that it was well known that he would be altogether against the Duke of York in his challenge to be made (when time served) to the crown. . . .

Therefore, when the Duke of York had thus, by advice of his special friends, framed the foundation of his long-intended enterprise, he assembled [1452] a great host [**25**], to the number of ten thousand able men, in the marches of Wales, publishing openly that the cause

[43]Unusual.
[44]Claiming.
[45]Particularly.

of this his gathering of people was for the public wealth[46] of the realm. The King, much astonished by the matter, by advice of his Council raised a great power and marched forward toward the Duke. But he, being thereof advertised, turned out of that way which by espials[47] he understood that the King held, and made straight toward London; and having knowledge that he might not be suffered to pass through the city, he crossed over the Thames at Kingston Bridge and so kept on toward Kent, where he knew that he had both friends and well-willers. And there, on Burnt Heath, a mile from Dartford and twelve miles from London, he embattled and encamped himself very strongly, environing his field with artillery and trenches. The King, hereof advertised, brought his army with all diligence unto Blackheath and there pitched his tents.

Whilst both these armies lay thus embattled, the King sent [**36, 5.1.17**] the Bishop of Winchester and Thomas Bourchier Bishop of Ely, Richard Woodville Lord Rivers, and Richard Andrew the Keeper of his Privy Seal to the Duke, both to know the cause of so great a commotion and also to make a concord if the requests of the Duke and his company seemed consonant to reason. The Duke, hearing the message of the bishops, answered that his coming was neither to damnify[48] the King in honor nor in person, neither yet any good man; but his intent was to remove from him certain evil-disposed persons of his Council, bloodsuckers of the nobility, pollers[49] of the clergy, and oppressors of the poor people.

Amongst these he chiefly named Edmund Duke of Somerset [**36**], whom if the King would commit to ward to answer such articles as against him in open parliament should be both proponed[50] and proved, he promised not only to dissolve his army but also offered himself (like an obedient subject) to come to the King's presence and to do him true and faithful service according to his loyal and bounden duty. . . .

[**639**] After all this ado, it was so agreed upon by advice, for the avoiding of bloodshed and pacifying of the Duke and his people, that the Duke of Somerset was committed to ward [**4.9.38**], as some say,

[46]Welfare.
[47]Scouts.
[48]Injure.
[49]Plunderers.
[50]Proposed.

or else commanded to keep himself privy in his own house for a time. . . .

Howsoever the matter went, truth it is that the Duke of York, the first of March [1452], dissolved his army [**5.1.44**], broke up his camp, and came to the King's tent, where, contrary to his expectation and against promise made by the King (as other write), he found the Duke of Somerset going at large and set at liberty [**83**]; whom the Duke of York boldly accused of treason [**95**], bribery, oppression, and many other crimes. The Duke of Somerset not only made answer to the Duke's objections but also accused him of high treason [**106**], affirming that he with his fautors[51] and complices had consulted together how to come by the scepter and regal crown of this realm. By means of which words the King removed straight to London, and the Duke of York (as prisoner) rode before him; and so was kept awhile.

The King assembled together a great Council at Westminster to hear the accusations of the two Dukes. . . .

Whilst the Council treated of saving or dispatching of this Duke of York, a rumor sprang through London that Edward Earl of March, son and heir apparent to the said Duke, with a great army of Marchmen, was coming toward London; which tidings sore appalled the Queen and the whole Council. . . . These two things sore troubled the heads of the Council, which, lest inward sedition might hinder outward conquests, set the Duke of York at liberty and permitted him to go to his castle of Wigmore in the marches of Wales; by whose absence the Duke of Somerset rose in such high favor, both with the King and Queen, that his word only ruled and his voice alone was heard.

Nevertheless, the said Duke of York had first made his submission and took his oath to be true, faithful, and obedient subject to King Henry the Sixth, King of England, in Saint Paul's Church at London, there being present the King and most of his nobility. . . .

[**641**] Thus was the duchy of Aquitaine, which had continued in the English possession from the year of our Lord 1155 unto this present year [1453], which is near hand three hundred years, by the marriage of Eleanor, daughter and heir to William Duke of Aquitaine, wife to King Henry the Second, finally reduced and brought again to the French obedience and servitude. . . On the thirteenth day of

[51]Supporters.

October this year was the Queen delivered at Westminster of a fair son, who was christened and named Edward.

His mother sustained not a little slander and obloquy of the common people, who had an opinion that the King was not able to get a child and therefore sticked not to say that this was not his son, with many slanderous words greatly sounding to the Queen's dishonor [**3H6 2.2.133, 147**]; much part perchance untruly. . . .

After the wars foully ended in foreign parties, civil dissension began again at home, divided specially into two factions. As King Henry, descended of the House of Lancaster, possessed the crown from his grandfather King Henry the Fourth (first author of that title), so Richard Duke of York, as heir to Lionel Duke of Clarence, third son to King Edward the Third, enforced. By reason whereof, the nobles as well as the common people were into parts divided, to the utter destruction of many a man, and to the great ruin and decay of this region; for while the one party sought to destroy the other, all care of the commonwealth was set aside, and justice and equity clearly exiled.

The Duke of York (above all things) first sought means how to stir up the malice of the people against the Duke of Somerset, imagining that, he being made away, his purpose should the sooner take effect. He also practiced[52] to bring the King into the hatred of the people, as that he should not be a man apt to the government of a realm, wanting both wit and stomach sufficient to supply such a room. Many of the high estates, not liking the world and disallowing the doings both of the King and his Council, were fain[53] enough of some alteration. Which thing the Duke well understanding, chiefly sought the favor of the two Nevilles, both named Richard, one Earl of Salisbury the other Earl of Warwick, the first being the father and the second the son [**2H6 5.1.147**]. . . .

[**642**] When the Duke of York had fastened his chain between these two strong pillars, he with his friends wrought so effectuously and handled his business so politicly that the Duke of Somerset was arrested in the Queen's great chamber and sent to the Tower of London, where he kept his Christmas without great solemnity [1453].

. . . . But when the King was amended again and resumed to him his former government, either of his own mind or by the Queen's pro-

[52]Plotted.
[53]Glad.

curement the Duke of Somerset was set at liberty [1455]; by which doing great envy and displeasure grew. . . .

The Duke of York and his adherents, perceiving that neither exhortation nor charging him with his crimes prevailed against the Duke of Somerset, they meant to mend the matter by open war [**194, 211**]; and, soon after, he being in the marches of Wales, accompanied with his special friends the Earls of Salisbury and Warwick, the Lord Cobham, and others, assembled a power and in warlike manner marched toward London. The King, informed hereof, assembled likewise a great host [1455]. . . .

[**643**] The King, advertised of this answer, more willful than tolerable, appointed him rather to try battle than deliver the Duke of Somerset to his enemies. . . . The fight [First Battle of Saint Albans] for a time was right sharp and cruel, for the Duke of Somerset, with the other lords, coming to the succors of their companions that were put to the worse, did what they could to beat back the enemies; but the Duke of York sent ever fresh men to succor the weary and to supply the places of them that were hurt, whereby the King's army was finally brought low and all the chieftains of the field slain and beaten down [**5.2.31, 5.3.30**].

For there died [**5.2.66**], under the sign of the Castle [**67**], Edmund Duke of Somerset, who (as hath been reported) was warned long before to avoid all castles [**1.4.38**].

[**657**] . . . which Edward the Third had issue [**2.2.10**]: Edward Prince of Wales; William of Hatfield his second son; Lionel, the third, Duke of Clarence; John of Gaunt, fourth, Duke of Lancaster; Edmund of Langley, fifth, Duke of York; Thomas of Woodstock, sixth, Duke of Gloucester; and William of Windsor, seventh [**17**].

The said Edward Prince of Wales, which died in the lifetime of his father, had issue Richard, which succeeded Edward the Third his grandsire; Richard died without issue; William of Hatfield, the second son of Edward the Third, died without issue; Lionel, the third son of Edward the Third, Duke of Clarence, had issue Philip his daughter and heir, which was coupled in matrimony unto Edmund Mortimer Earl of March, and had issue Roger Mortimer Earl of March, her son and heir; which Roger had issue Edmund Earl of March, Roger Mortimer, Anne, Eleanor [**38**]; which Edmund, Roger, and Eleanor died without issue.

And the said Anne coupled in matrimony to Richard Earl of Cambridge, the son of Edmund of Langley, the fifth son of Edward the Third [**46**], and had issue Richard Plantagenet commonly called Duke of York. John of Gaunt, the fourth son of Edward and the younger brother of the said Lionel, had issue Henry Earl of Derby, who incontinently[54] after that King Richard resigned the crowns of the realms and lordship of Ireland, unrighteously entered upon the same, then being alive Edmund Mortimer Earl of March, son to Roger Mortimer Earl of March, son and heir of the said Philip, daughter and heir of the said Lionel [**50**], the third son of the said King Edward the Third, to the which Edmund the right and title of the said crowns and lordship by law and custom belonged. To the which Richard Duke of York, as son to Anne, daughter to Roger Mortimer Earl of March, son and heir of the said Philip, daughter and heir of the said Lionel, the third son of King Edward the Third, the right, title, dignity royal, and estate of the crowns of the realms of England and France, and the lordship of Ireland, pertaineth and belongeth afore any issue of the said John of Gaunt, the fourth son of the same King Edward.

[54]Immediately.

3 Henry VI

[643][1] Humphrey Duke of Buckingham [**1.1.10**], being wounded [at the First Battle of Saint Albans, 1455], and James Butler Earl of Ormonde and Wiltshire, and Thomas Thorpe Lord Chief Baron of the Exchequer, seeing Fortune thus against them, left the King alone and with a number fled away. . . .

This done, saith one historian, the Duke of York, the Earls of Warwick and Salisbury, came unto the King [**1**] where he was and besought him on their knees of grace and forgiveness for that they had done in his presence, and besought him of his highness to take them to grace and as his true liege men. . . . And upon the day next after, the King and the Duke of York, the Earls of Warwick and Salisbury, came all to London. . . .

[**644**] The Duke of York, having gotten the victory, remembered well that he had published abroad how the only cause of this war was for the advancement of the commonwealth, and therefore, using all courtesy, would not touch the King's person after any violent sort but with all honor and due reverence conveyed him to London and so to Westminster. . . .

[**652**] During this time the King called a parliament in the city of Coventry which began the twentieth of September [1460], in the which were attainted[2] of high treason Richard Duke of York, Edward Earl of March his son and heir, Richard Earl of Warwick, Edmund Earl of Rutland, Richard Earl of Salisbury, John Lord Clifford. . . .

[**653**] After the King's navy was gained and his captains (as before ye have heard) on the sea taken, the lords lying at Calais [the Earls of March, Salisbury, and Warwick], being advertised from the Lord Falconbridge (who after the taking of Montford lay still in Kent) that the people of that country and other parts were altogether

[1]References to *3H6* outside this section may be found at pp. 186 and 221 (2).
[2]Convicted.

bent in their favor (and no less addicted to do them service both with body and goods than the Irishmen seemed to be at their receiving of the said Duke of York and his younger son Edmund Earl of Rutland, whom they so highly honored that they offered to live and die in their quarrel), they conceived thereupon so great hope in their friends within the realm that they determined to pass the sea; and, therewith entering their ships, with fifteen hundred men landed all at Sandwich. . . .

Now as they passed through Kent there came to them the Lord Cobham, John Guildford, William Peche, Robert Horne, and many other gentlemen; so that before they aproached to London their number was esteemed[3] above forty thousand fighting men; for, the fame of their landing being once known, gentlemen and yeomen resorted to them out of all the south parts of the realm. . . .

[**654**] But shortly after, the Earls of March and Warwick and other of their affinity came to London and were of the Mayor and citizens joyously received, to whom resorted Thomas Archbishop of Canterbury, the Bishops of London, Lincoln, Salisbury, Ely, and Exeter, with many other prelates and religious persons, amongst whom also was the Pope's legate, to treat of peace if need so required. . . .

The King, having knowledge of all these doings, assembled a great army and, accompanied with the Duke of Somerset (lately come from Guines) and the Duke of Buckingham and divers other great lords that took his part, came to Northampton, where the Queen, perceiving her puissance to be able to match in fight with the adversaries, took upon her to encourage her friends and well-willers; for the King studied of nothing but of peace, quietness, and solitary life.

. . . The fight continued right fierce and cruel, with uncertain victory, till the hour of nine, at which time the King's army was discomfited and of the same slain and drowned in the river few less than ten thousand; and the King himself, left comfortless alone, was taken by the adversaries, as a man in great misery.

. . . The Duke of Somerset and other which narrowly escaped fled with the Queen and Prince into the bishopric of Durham. The Earls, having got the victory in this bloody battle [of Northampton], conveyed the King to London and lodged him in the Bishop's palace. . . .

[**655**] In the meantime the Duke of York, advertised of all these

[3]Estimated.

things, sailed from Dublin toward England and landed at the Red Bank near to the city of Chester with no small company; and from Chester by long journeys[4] he came to the city of London, which he entered the Friday before the feast of Saint Edward the Confessor [1460], with a sword borne naked before him, with trumpets also sounding, and accompanied with a great train of men-of-arms and other of his friends and servants. At his coming to Westminster he entered the palace [**25**] and, passing forth directly through the great hall, stayed not till he came to the chamber where the King and lords used to sit in the parliament time, commonly called the upper house or chamber of the peers. . . .

Master Edward Hall in his *Chronicle* maketh mention of an oration which the Duke of York uttered, sitting in the regal seat [**26, 50**] there in the chamber of the peers, either at this his first coming in amongst them or else at some one time after; the which we have thought good also to set down, though John Whethamstede the Abbot of Saint Albans, who lived in those days and by all likelihood was there present at the parliament, maketh no further recital of any words which the Duke should utter at that time in that his book of records where he entreateth of this matter. But for the oration (as Master Hall hath written thereof) we find as followeth. During the time (saith he) of this parliament, the Duke of York, with a bold countenance, entered into the chamber of the peers and sat down in the throne royal, under the cloth of estate (which is the King's peculiar seat), and in the presence of the nobility as well spiritual as temporal, after a pause made, he began to declare his title to the crown, in this form and order as ensueth [**2H6 2.2**]. . . .

[**657**] After long debating of the matter, and deliberate consultation amongst the peers, prelates, and commons, upon the vigil of All Saints [1460] it was condescended:[5] forsomuch as King Henry had been taken as King by the space of thirty and eight years and more, that he should enjoy the name and title of King and have possession of the realm during his natural life [**3H6 1.1.71**]. And if he either died or resigned or forfeited the same by breaking or going against any point of this concord, then the said crown and authority royal should immediately be devoluted[6] and come to the Duke of York, if he then lived, or else to the next heir of his lineage [**172**]. And that the Duke

[4]Daily travels.
[5]Agreed.
[6]Passed on.

of York from thenceforth should be Protector and Regent of the land. This was the determination of the parliament to and fro,[7] tending to peace between the King and the Duke (which was ratified accordingly), as by the articles ensuing doth appear. . . .

[**658**] "Item, the said Richard Duke of York shall promit[8] and bind him by his solemn oath [**196**] in manner and form as followeth:

" 'In the name of God, amen. I, Richard Duke of York, promise and swear, by the faith and truth that I owe to Almighty God, that I shall never consent, procure, or stir, directly or indirectly, in privy or apert,[9] neither (as much as in me is) shall suffer to be done, consented, procured, or stirred, anything that may sound to the abridgment of the natural life of King Henry the Sixth, or to the hurt or diminishing of his reign or dignity royal, by violence or any other way, against his freedom or liberty.' "

[**659**] . . . And upon the Saturday next ensuing, Richard Duke of York was by sound of trumpet solemnly proclaimed heir apparent to the crown of England and Protector of the realm [**240**]. . . .

The Duke of York, well knowing that the Queen would spurn against all this, caused both her and her son to be sent for by the King. But she, as wont rather to rule than to be ruled, and thereto counseled by the Dukes of Exeter and Somerset, not only denied to come [**211**] but also assembled a great army [**256**], intending to take the King by fine force out of the lords' hands. The Protector in London, having knowledge of all these doings, assigned the Duke of Norfolk and Earl of Warwick, his trusty friends, to be about the King, while he, with the Earls of Salisbury and Rutland and a convenient number, departed out of London the second day of December [1460] northward; and appointed the Earl of March his eldest son to follow him with all his power. The Duke came to his castle of Sandal beside Wakefield [**206**] on Christmas Eve, and there began to make muster of his tenants and friends [**1.2.36**]. The Queen, thereof ascertained, determined to cope with him ere his succor were come.

Now she, having in her company the Prince [Edward] her son, the Dukes of Exeter and Somerset, the Earl of Devonshire, the Lord Clifford, the Lord Ross, and in effect all the lords of the north parts, with eighteen thousand men or (as some write) two and twenty thou-

[7]Pro and con.
[8]Promise.
[9]Public.

sand, marched from York to Wakefield, and bade base to[10] the Duke, even before his castle gates [**49**]. He, having with him not fully five thousand persons [**66**], contrary to the minds of his faithful counselors, would needs issue forth to fight with his enemies [**70**]. . . .

But when he was in the plain field between his castle and the town of Wakefield, he was environed on every side like fish in a net; so that though he fought manfully, yet was he within half an hour slain and dead, and his whole army discomfited. With him died, of his trusty friends, his two bastard uncles Sir John and Sir Hugh Mortimer [**62, 1.4.2**], Sir Davy Hall, Sir Hugh Hastings, Sir Thomas Neville, William and Thomas Aparre, both brethren; and two thousand and eight hundred others, whereof many were young gentlemen and heirs of great parentage in the south parts; whose kin revenged their deaths within four months next, as after shall appear.

In this conflict was wounded and taken prisoner Richard Earl of Salisbury, Sir Richard Limbrick, Ralph Stanley, John Harrow, Captain Hanson, and divers others. The Lord Clifford, perceiving where the Earl of Rutland was conveyed out of the field (by one of his father's chaplains and schoolmaster to the same Earl) and overtaking him, stabbed him to the heart with a dagger as he kneeled afore him [**1.3**]. This Earl was but a child at that time of twelve years of age, whom neither his tender years nor dolorous countenance, with holding up both his hands for mercy (for his speech was gone for fear), could move the cruel heart of the Lord Clifford to take pity upon him, so that he was noted of great infamy for that his unmerciful murder upon that young gentleman.

But the same Lord Clifford, not satisfied herewith, came to the place where the dead corpse of the Duke of York lay, caused his head to be stricken off, and set on it a crown of paper; fixed it on a pole and presented it to the Queen, not lying far from the field, in great despite,[11] at which great rejoicing was showed. But they laughed then that shortly after lamented, and were glad then of other men's deaths that knew not their own to be so near at hand. Some write that the Duke was taken alive and in derision caused to stand upon a molehill [**1.4.67**]; on whose head they put a garland [**94**] instead of a crown which they had fashioned and made of sedges or bulrushes; and having so crowned him with that garland, they kneeled down afore him

[10]Challenged.
[11]Scorn.

(as the Jews did unto Christ) in scorn, saying to him: "Hail, King without rule! Hail, King without heritage! Hail, Duke and prince without people or possessions!" And at length, having thus scorned him with these and divers other the like despiteful words, they struck off his head, which (as ye have heard) they presented to the Queen [**175, 179**].

Many deemed that this miserable end chanced to the Duke of York as a due punishment for breaking his oath of allegiance unto his sovereign lord King Henry; but others held him discharged thereof because he obtained a dispensation from the Pope, by such suggestion as his procurators made unto him, whereby the same oath was adjudged void [**1.2.22**], as that which was received unadvisedly, to the prejudice of himself and disheriting of all his posterity. After this victory by the Queen [at Wakefield], the Earl of Salisbury and all the prisoners were sent to Pomfret and there beheaded; whose heads (together with the Duke of York's head) were conveyed to York and there set on poles over the gate of the city [**1.4.179**], in despite of them and their lineage [January, 1461]. The Earl of March, now after the death of his father very Duke of York, lying at Gloucester, was wonderfully amazed when the sorrowful news of these mishaps came unto him [**2.1.46**]; but after comfort given to him by his faithful lovers and assured allies, he removed to Shrewsbury, declaring to the inhabitants of that town, and to them of the other towns in those parties, the murder of his father, the jeopardy of himself, and the present ruin of the commonwealth.

[**660**] The people on the marches of Wales, for the favor which they bore to the Mortimers' lineage, more gladly offered him their aid and assistance than he could desire the same, so that he had incontinently[12] a puissant army to the number of three and twenty thousand ready to go against the Queen and the murderers of his father. But when he was setting forward, news was brought to him that Jasper Earl of Pembroke, half brother to King Henry, and James Butler Earl of Ormonde and Wiltshire had assembled a great number of Welsh and Irish people to take him. He, herewith quickened, retired back and met with his enemies in a fair plain near to Mortimer's Cross, not far from Hereford East, on Candlemas Day in the morning [February 2, 1461]. At which time the sun (as some write) appeared to the Earl of March like three suns [**25**], and suddenly joined all

[12]Immediately.

together in one. Upon which sight he took such courage that he, fiercely setting on his enemies, put them to flight; and for this cause men imagined that he gave the sun in his full brightness for his badge or cognizance [**40**]. Of his enemies were left dead on the ground three thousand and eight hundred.

. . . The Queen, nevertheless, encouraged by her late victory [at Wakefield], with a multitude of northern people marched toward London. . . . At length they approached to Saint Albans, hearing that the Duke of Norfolk and the Earl of Warwick, with other whom the Duke of York had left to govern the King in his absence [**111**], had (by the King's assent) assembled a great host and were encamped near to that town. . . .

When the day was closed, those [Yorkists] that were about the King (in number a twenty thousand), hearing how evil their fellows had sped, began utterly to despair of the victory and so fell without any long tarriance to running away [**137**]. By reason whereof the nobles that were about the King, perceiving how the game went, and withal[13] saw no comfort in the King but rather a good will and affection toward the contrary part [**122**], they withdrew also, leaving the King. . . .

Such was the success[14] of this Second Battle fought at Saint Albans, upon Shrove Tuesday the seventeenth of February [1461], in which were slain three and twenty hundred men, of whom no nobleman is remembered save Sir John Grey, which the same day was made knight, with twelve other, at the village of Colney. Now after that the noblemen and other were fled, and the King left in manner alone without any power of men to guard his person, he was counseled by an esquire called Thomas Hoo, a man well languaged and well seen[15] in the laws, to send some convenient messenger to the northern lords, advertising them that he would now gladly come unto them (whom he knew to be his very friends and had assembled themselves together for his service), to the end he might remain with them, as before he had remained under the government of the southern lords.

According to the advice and counsel of this esquire, the King thought it good to send unto them, and withal[16] appointed the same esquire to bear the message, who first went and declared the same unto the Earl of Northumberland and, returning back to the King,

[13]Besides.
[14]Outcome.
[15]Versed.
[16]Thereupon.

brought certain lords with him who conveyed the King first unto the Lord Clifford's tent, that stood next to the place where the King's people had encamped. This done, they went and brought the Queen and her son Prince Edward unto his presence [**137**], whom he joyfully received, embracing and kissing them in most loving wise and yielding hearty thanks to almighty God, whom it had pleased thus to strengthen the forces of the northern men, to restore his dearly beloved and only son again into his possession. Thus was the Queen fortunate in her two battles [Wakefield and Second Saint Albans], but unfortunate was the King in all his enterprises, for where his person was present the victory still fled from him to the contrary part. The Queen caused the King to dub her son Prince Edward knight [**2.2.61**], with thirty other persons which the day before fought on her side against his part.

[**661**] . . . All these devices were shortly altered to another form because true report came not only to the Queen but also to the city [of London] that the Earl of March, having vanquished the Earls of Pembroke and Wiltshire, had met with the Earl of Warwick (after this last battle at Saint Albans) at Chipping Norton by Cotswold [**2.1.95**], and that they with both their powers were coming toward London. The Queen, having little trust in Essex and less in Kent, but least of all in London, with her husband and son departed from Saint Albans into the north country [**2.2.1**], where the foundation of her aid and refuge only rested.

The Duchess of York, seeing her husband and son slain, and not knowing what should succeed of her eldest son's chance, sent her two younger sons George and Richard over the sea to the city of Utrecht in Almaine,[17] where they were of Philip Duke of Burgundy well received; and so remained there till their brother Edward had got the crown and government of the realm [**2.1.146**]. The Earls of March and Warwick, having perfect knowledge that the King and Queen, with their adherents, were departed from Saint Albans, rode straight to London, entering there with a great number of men-of-war the first week of Lent [1461]. Whose coming thither was no sooner known but that the people resorted out of Kent, Essex, and other the counties adjoining in great numbers, to see, aid and comfort this lusty[18] prince and flower of chivalry, in whom the hope of their joy and trust of their quietness only consisted.

[17]Germany (including the Low Countries).
[18]Vigorous.

This prudent young prince, minding to take time when time served, called a great Council both of the lords spiritual and temporal and to them repeated the title and right that he had to the crown, rehearsing also the articles concluded between King Henry and his father, by their writing signed and sealed and also confirmed by act of parliament; the breaches whereof he neither forgot nor left undeclared. After the lords had considered of this matter, they determined by authority of the said Council that because King Henry had done contrary to the ordinances in the last parliament concluded, and was insufficient of himself to rule the realm, he was therefore to be deprived of all kingly estate; and incontinently was Edward Earl of March, son and heir to Richard Duke of York, by the lords in the said Council assembled, named, elected, and admitted for King and Governor of the realm.

On which day, the people of the Earl's part being in their muster in Saint John's Field, and a great number of the substantial citizens there assembled to behold their order, the Lord Falconbridge, who took the musters, wisely anon declared to the people the offenses and breaches of the late agreement committed by King Henry the Sixth; and demanded of the people whether they would have him to rule and reign any longer over them. To whom they with whole voice answered, "Nay, nay!" Then he asked them if they would serve, love, honor, and obey the Earl of March as their only King and sovereign lord. To which question they answered, "Yea, yea!" crying "King Edward!" with many great shouts and clapping of hands in assent and gladness of the same.

The lords were shortly advertised of the loving consent which the commons frankly and freely had given. Whereupon, incontinently, they all with a convenient number of the most substantial commons, repaired to the Earl at Baynard's Castle, making just and true report of their election and admission, and the loving assent of the commons. . . .

Thus far touching the tragical state of this land under the rent regiment[19] of King Henry, who (besides the bare title of royalty and naked name of king) had little appertaining to the port[20] of a prince. For whereas the dignity of princedom standeth in sovereignty, there were of his nobles that imbeciled[21] his prerogative by sundry practices,

[19]Rule.
[20]Deportment.
[21]Weakened.

specially by main force, as seeking either to suppress or to exile or to obscure or to make him away. . . .

[**663**] After that this prince, Edward Earl of March, had taken upon him the government of this realm of England (as before ye have heard), the morrow next ensuing, being the fourth of March [1461], he rode to the church of Saint Paul and there offered;[22] and after *Te Deum* sung with great solemnity, he was conveyed to Westminster and there sat in the hall with the scepter royal in his hand; whereto people in great numbers assembled. His claim to the crown was declared to be by two manner of ways: the first, as son and heir to Duke Richard his father, right inheritor to the same; the second, by authority of parliament [**3.3.114**] and forfeiture committed by King Henry. Whereupon it was again demanded of the commons if they would admit and take the said Earl as their Prince and sovereign lord; which all with one voice cried, "Yea, yea!"

[**664**] This part thus played, he entered into Westminster Church under a canopy with solemn procession, and there as King offered; and herewith taking the homages of all the nobles there present, he returned by water to London and was lodged in the Bishop's palace; and, on the morrow after, he was proclaimed King by the name of Edward the Fourth throughout the city [**2.6.88**]. This was in the year of the world 5427, and after the birth of our Saviour 1461 after our count, beginning the year at Christmas, but after the usual account of the Church of England 1460, the twentieth of Emperor Frederick the Third, the nine and thirtieth and last of Charles the seventh French King, and first year of the reign of James the third King of Scots.

Whilst these things were adoing in the south parts, King Henry, being in the north country, assembled a great army, trusting (for all this) to subdue his enemies, namely[23] sith their chief ringleader the Duke of York was dispatched out of the way. But he was deceived, for out of the dead stock sprang a branch more mighty than the stem: this Edward the Fourth. . . .

By which means he [King Edward] gathered together a puissant army, to the intent by battle (sithence[24] none other ways would serve) at once to make an end of all. So, his army and all things prepared, he departed out of London the twelfth day of March [1461]. . . . King Henry, on the other part, having his army in readiness, com-

[22]Made an offering.
[23]Particularly.
[24]Since.

mitted the governance thereof to the Duke of Somerset, the Earl of Northumberland, and the Lord Clifford, as men desiring to revenge the death of their parents, slain at the First Battle at Saint Albans [**2.2–6**].

. . . The Lord Fitzwalter . . . was slain, and with him the Bastard of Salisbury, brother to the Earl of Warwick, a valiant young gentleman and of great audacity.

When the Earl of Warwick was informed hereof, like a man desperate he mounted on his hackney and hasted puffing and blowing to King Edward, saying: "Sir, I pray God have mercy of their souls which in the beginning of your enterprise have lost their lives! And because I see no succors of the world but in God, I remit the vengeance to Him our Creator and Redeemer." With that he alighted down and slew his horse with his sword [**2.3.24**], saying, "Let him flee that will, for surely I will tarry with him that will tarry with me"; and kissed the cross of his sword as it were for a vow to the promise. King Edward, perceiving the courage of his trusty friend the Earl of Warwick, made proclamation that all men which were afraid to fight should depart [**50**]; and to all those that tarried the battle he promised great rewards; with addition, that any soldier which voluntarily would abide and afterward, either in or before the fight, should seem to flee or turn his back, then he that could kill him should have a great reward and double wages.

After this proclamation ended, the Lord Falconbridge, Sir Walter Blount, Robert Horne, with the foreward,[25] passed the river at Castleford, three miles from Ferrybridge, intending to have environed the Lord Clifford and his company. But they, being thereof advertised, departed in great haste toward King Henry's army; yet they met with some that they looked not for, and were so trapped ere they were aware. For the Lord Clifford, either for heat or pain putting off his gorget,[26] suddenly with an arrow (as some say, without an head) was stricken into the throat and immediately rendered his spirit [**2.6.41 SD**]. . . .

[**665**] This deadly conflict [the Battle of Towton] continued ten hours in doubtful state of victory, uncertainly heaving and setting on both sides; but in the end, King Edward so courageously comforted his men that the other part was discomfited and overcome [March, 1461]. . . .

[25]Vanguard.
[26]Throat armor.

After this great victory, King Edward rode to York, where he was with all solemnity received; and first he caused the heads of his father, the Earl of Salisbury, and other his friends to be taken from the gates and to be buried with their bodies; and there he caused the Earl of Devonshire and three other to be beheaded, and set their heads in the same place [**86**]. King Henry, after he heard of the irrecoverable loss of his army, departed incontinently with his wife and son to the town of Berwick [**2.5.128**] and, leaving the Duke of Somerset there, went into Scotland and, coming to the King of Scots, required of him and his Council aid and comfort.

. . . When King Henry was somewhat settled in the realm of Scotland, he sent his wife and his son into France [**3.1.28**] to King René her father, trusting by his aid and succor to assemble an army and once again to recover his right and dignity; but he in the meantime made his abode in Scotland, to see what way his friends in England would study for his restitution.

The Queen, being in France [1462], did obtain of the young French King [**3.3.1**], then Louis the Eleventh, that all her husband's friends and those of the Lancastrial band might safely and surely have resort into any part of the realm of France, prohibiting all other of the contrary faction any access or repair into that country. Thus ye have heard how King Henry the Sixth, after he had reigned eight and thirty years and odd months, was driven out of this realm. But now, leaving him with the princes of his part consulting together in Scotland, and Queen Margaret his wife gathering of men in France, I will return where I left, to proceed with the doings of King Edward.

This young prince, having with prosperous success obtained so glorious a victory in the mortal Battle at Towton, and chased all his adversaries out of the realm or at the least ways put them to silence, returned after the manner and fashion of a triumphant conqueror [**2.6.87**], with great pomp, unto London; where, according to the old custom of the realm, he called a great assembly of persons of all degrees; and the nine and twentieth day of June [1461] was at Westminster with solemnity crowned and anointed King. . . .

In the same parliament the Earl of Oxford, far stricken in age, and his son and heir the Lord Aubrey Vere [**3.3.101**], either through malice of their enemies or for that they had offended the King, were both, with divers of their counselors, attainted and put to execution; which caused John Earl of Oxford ever after to rebel [**106**]. . . . Also, after this, he created his two younger brethren dukes; that is to say, Lord George Duke of Clarence, Lord Richard Duke of Gloucester [**2.6.103**]; and the Lord John Neville, brother to Richard Earl of Warwick, he first made Lord Montague and afterwards created him Marquis Montague.

[**667**] . . . But all the doubts[27] of trouble that might ensue by the means of King Henry's being at liberty were shortly taken away and ended, for he himself, whether he was past all fear or that he was not well established in his wits and perfect mind or for that he could not long keep himself secret, in disguised attire boldly entered [**3.1.13**] into England [1465].

He was no sooner entered but he was known and taken of one Cantlow [**97**], and brought toward the King; whom the Earl of Warwick met on the way by the King's commandment and brought him through London to the Tower, and there he was laid in sure hold [**3.2.120**]. . . .

After that King Edward had reduced the state of the public affairs unto his liking . . . , it was thought meet by him and those of his Council that a marriage were provided for him in some convenient place; and therefore was the Earl of Warwick sent over into France to demand the Lady Bona [**2.6.90**], daughter to Louis Duke of Savoy and sister to the Lady Carlot then Queen of France; which Bona was at that time in the French court [1464].

The Earl of Warwick, coming to the French King then lying at Tours, was of him honorably received and right courteously entertained [**3.3.46**]. His message was so well liked and his request thought so honorable for the advancement of the Lady Bona, that her sister Queen Carlot obtained both the good will of the King her husband and also of her sister the foresaid lady; so that the matrimony on that side was clearly assented to [**134**], and the Earl of Dammartin appointed (with others) to sail into England for the full finishing of the same. But here consider the old proverb to be true which saith that marriage goeth by destiny. For during the time that the Earl of Warwick was thus in France and (according to his instructions) brought the effect of his commission to pass, the King, being ahunting in the forest of Wichwood besides Stony Stratford, came for his recreation to the manor of Grafton where the Duchess of Bedford then sojourned, wife to Sir Richard Woodville Lord Rivers, on whom was then attendant a daughter of hers called the Lady Elizabeth Grey,

[27]Fears.

widow of Sir John Grey, knight, slain at the last Battle of Saint Albans [**3.2.2**], as before ye have heard.

[**668**] This widow, having a suit to the King for such lands as her husband had given her in jointure, so kindled the King's affection toward her that he not only favored her suit but more her person; for she was a woman of a more formal countenance than of excellent beauty, and yet both of such beauty and favor that, with her sober demeanor, sweet looks, and comely smiling (neither too wanton nor too bashful), besides her pleasant tongue and trim wit [**85**], she so allured and made subject unto her the heart of that great prince that, after she had denied him to be his paramour [**70**] (with so good manner and words so well set as better could not be devised), he finally resolved with himself to marry her [**89**]; not asking counsel of any man till they might perceive it was no booty[28] to advise him to the contrary of that his concluded purpose; sith he was so far gone that he was not revocable, and therefore had fixed his heart upon the last resolution, namely to apply an wholesome, honest, and honorable remedy to his affections fired with the flames of love, and not to permit his heart to the thralldom of unlawful lust; which purpose was both princely and profitable. . . .

But yet the Duchess of York his mother letted[29] this match as much as in her lay; and when all would not serve, she caused a precontract to be alleged, made by him with the Lady Elizabeth Lucy.[a] But, all doubts resolved, all things made clear, and all cavillations avoided, privily in a morning he married the said Lady Elizabeth Grey at Grafton beforesaid where he first began to fancy her [1464]. And in the next year after she was with great solemnity crowned queen at Westminster. Her father also was created Earl Rivers and made High Constable of England. . . . The French King was not well pleased to be thus dallied with [**3.3.178**], but he shortly (to appease the grief of his wife and her sister the Lady Bona) married the said Lady Bona to the Duke of Milan.

Now when the Earl of Warwick had knowledge, by letters sent to him out of England from his trusty friends, that King Edward had gotten him a new wife, he was not a little troubled in his mind; for that he took it his credence[30] thereby was greatly minished and his

[28]No use.
[29]Hindered.
[a]Eleanor Butler (Elizabeth Lucy was one of Edward's mistresses).
[30]Reputation.

honor much stained [**184**], namely in the court of France; for that it might be judged he came rather like an espial[31] to move a thing never minded, and to treat a marriage determined before not to take effect. Surely he thought himself evil used that, when he had brought the matter to his purposed intent and wished conclusion, then to have it quail[32] on his part, so as all men might think at the least wise that his prince made small account of him, to send him on such a sleeveless[33] errand.

All men for the most part agree that this marriage was the only cause why the Earl of Warwick conceived an hatred against King Edward, whom he so much before favored. Other affirm other causes, and one specially: for that King Edward did attempt a thing once in the Earl's house which was much against the Earl's honesty[34] (whether he would have deflowered his daughter or his niece [**188**] the certainty was not for both their honors openly revealed), for surely such a thing was attempted by King Edward, which loved well both to behold and also to feel fair damsels. . . .

In this year also [1466] the King's daughter the Lady Elizabeth, after wife to King Henry the Seventh, was born. . . .

[**670**] In this meantime the Earl of Warwick, bearing a continual grudge in his heart toward King Edward since his last return out of France, persuaded so with his two brethren the Archbishop [of York] and the Marquis [Montague] that they agreed to join with him in any attempt which he should take in hand against the said King [1468]. The Archbishop was easily allured to the Earl's purpose, but the Marquis could by no means be reduced to take any part against King Edward of a long time [**4.1.143**], till the Earl had both promised him great rewards and promotions[35] and also assured him of the aid and power of the greatest princes of the realm. And even as the Marquis was loath to consent to his unhappy conspiracy, so with a faint heart he showed himself an enemy unto King Edward; which double dissimulation was both the destruction of him and his brethren. . . .

[**671**] Beside all this, the Earl of Warwick, being a far casting[36] prince, perceived somewhat in the Duke of Clarence whereby he

[31]Spy.
[32]Fail.
[33]Profitless.
[34]Honor.
[35]Preferments.
[36]Planning.

judged that he bore no great good will toward the King his brother [**59**]; and thereupon, feeling his mind by such talk as he of purpose ministered, understood how he was bent and so won him to his purpose; and, for better assurance of his faithful friendship, he offered him his eldest daughter in marriage [**118**], with the whole half deal[37] of his wife's inheritance.

. . . The Duke of Clarence, being come to Calais with the Earl of Warwick, after he had sworn on the sacrament to keep his promise and pact made with the said Earl whole and inviolate, he married the Lady Isabel, eldest daughter to the Earl, in Our Lady's Church there [1469]. . . .

[**672**] Shortly after, the conspiracy of the evil-disposed people grew to an open rebellion, so that there assembled to the number of fifteen thousand men, even ready bent to set on the city of York. . . .

After they saw that they could not get York, because they wanted ordnance, they determined with all speed to march toward London, intending to raise such a toy[38] in the people's minds that they should think King Edward neither to be a lawful prince nor yet profitable to the commonwealth. King Edward, having perfect knowledge of all the doings of the Earl of Warwick and of his brother the Duke of Clarence, was by divers letters certified of the great army of the northern men with all speed coming toward London; and therefore in great haste he sent to William Lord Herbert, whom (as ye have heard) he had created Earl of Pembroke; requiring him without delay to raise his power and encounter with the northern men [**131**].

. . . And to assist him with archers was appointed Humphrey Lord Stafford [**130**] of Southwick, named but not created Earl of Devonshire by the King, in hope that he would serve valiantly in that journey.[39] He had with him eight hundred archers.

[**673**] . . . The King in this meantime had assembled his power and was coming toward the Earl [of Warwick], who, being advertised thereof, sent to the Duke of Clarence requiring him to come and join with him. The Duke, being not far off, with all speed repaired to the Earl [**4.2.3**]; and so they joined their powers together and, upon secret knowledge had, that the King (because they were entered into terms by way of communication to have a peace) took

[37]Share.
[38]Notion.
[39]Campaign.

small heed to himself, nothing doubting[40] any outward attempt of his enemies.

The Earl of Warwick, intending not to lose such opportunity of advantage [**13**], in the dead of the night, with an elect company of men-of-war (as secretly as was possible), set on the King's field,[41] killing them that kept the watch; and, ere the King was ware (for he thought of nothing less than of that which then happened), at a place called Wolney,[42] four miles from Warwick, he was taken prisoner [**4.3.27 SD (2)**] and brought to the castle of Warwick [1469]. And to the intent his friends should not know what was become of him, the Earl caused him by secret journeys in the night to be conveyed to Middleham Castle in Yorkshire, and there to be kept under the custody of the Archbishop of York and other his friends in those parties [**52**]. King Edward, being thus in captivity, spoke ever fair to the Archbishop and to his other keepers, so that he had leave divers days to go hunt [**4.5.8**]; which exercise he used, as it should seem, not so much for regard of his recreation as for the recovery of his liberty [**11**]. . . .

Now, on a day, upon a plain when he was thus abroad, there met [**16**] with him Sir William Stanley, Sir Thomas a Borough,[b] and divers other of his friends, with such a great band of men that neither his keepers would, nor once durst, move him to return unto prison again. Some have thought that his keepers were corrupted with money or fair promises and therefore suffered him thus to scape out of danger [**26**].

[**674**] . . . When Queen Margaret, that sojourned with Duke René her father, heard tell that the Earl of Warwick was come to the French court, with all diligence she came [1470] to Amboise to see him with her only son Prince Edward [**3.3.199**].

With her also came Jasper Earl of Pembroke and John Earl of Oxford, which, after divers imprisonments lately escaped, fled out of England into France and came by fortune to this assembly. These persons, after entreaty had of their affairs, determined by means of the French King to conclude a league and amity between them. And first to begin withal, for the sure foundation of their new entreaty, Edward Prince of Wales wedded[c] Anne, second daughter to the Earl

[40]Fearing.
[41]Camp.
[42]Honiley (?) (Boswell-Stone).
[b]Thomas Burgh.
[c]Was betrothed to.

of Warwick [**249**], which lady came with her mother into France. After which marriage, the Duke [of Clarence] and the Earls took a solemn oath that they should never leave the war till either King Henry the Sixth or his son Prince Edward were restored to the crown; and that the Queen and the Prince should depute and appoint the Duke and the Earl [of Warwick] to be governors and conservators of the commonwealth, till time the Prince were come to estate. . . .

[**675**] The French King lent both ships, men [**204**], and money unto Queen Margaret and to her partakers;[43] and appointed the Bastard of Bourbon [**252**] Admiral of France, with a great navy, to defend them against the navy of the Duke of Burgundy which he laid at the mouth of the river Seine ready to encounter them, being of greater force than both the French navy and the English fleet. And yet King René did also help his daughter with men and munition of war.

. . . When the Earl [of Warwick] had taken land [1470], he made proclamation in the name of King Henry the Sixth, upon high pains commanding and charging all men able to bear armor to prepare themselves to fight against Edward Duke of York [**4.3.30**], which contrary to right had usurped the crown. It is almost not to be believed how many thousands men-of-war at the first tidings of the Earl's landing resorted unto him [**4.2.2**].

King Edward, wakened with the news of the Earl's landing and the great repair of people that came flocking in unto him, sent forth letters into all parts of his realm to raise an army; but of them that were sent for few came, and yet of those few the more part came with no great good wills. Which when he perceived, he began to doubt the matter, and therefore, being accompanied with the Duke of Gloucester his brother, the Lord Hastings his Chamberlain (which had married the Earl's sister and yet was ever true to the King his master), and the Lord Scales brother to the Queen, he departed into Lincolnshire. And because he understood that all the realm was up against him, and some part of the Earl of Warwick's power was within half a day's journey of him, following the advice of his Council, with all haste possible he passed the Washes in great jeopardy and, coming to Lynn [**4.5.21**], found there an English ship and two hulks of Holland ready (as Fortune would) to make sail.

Whereupon he, with his brother the Duke of Gloucester, the Lord

[43]Supporters.

Scales, and divers other his trusty friends, entered into the ship. The Lord Hastings tarried awhile after, exhorting all his acquaintance that of necessity should tarry behind to show themselves openly as friends to King Henry [**4.7.28**] for their own safeguard, but heartily required them in secret to continue faithful to King Edward. This persuasion declared, he entered the ship with the other, and so they departed, being in number, in that one ship and two hulks, about seven or eight hundred persons, having no furniture of apparel or other necessary things with them saving apparel for war. . . .

As King Edward with sail and oar was thus making course toward the Duke of Burgundy's country (whither he determined at the first to go), it chanced that seven or eight gallant ships of Easterlings,[44] open enemies both to England and France, were abroad on those seas and, espying the King's vessels, began to chase him [whereupon Edward escaped]. . . .

[**677**] But to return to the Prince's affairs. When the fame was once spread abroad that King Edward was fled the realm, an innumerable number of people resorted to the Earl of Warwick to take his part [**4.2.2**]; but all King Edward's trusty friends went to divers sanctuaries; and, amongst other, his wife Queen Elizabeth took sanctuary at Westminster [**4.4.31**], and there, in great penury, forsaken of all her friends, was delivered of a fair son [**18**] called Edward, which was with small pomp like a poor man's child christened, the godfathers being the Abbot and Prior of Westminster and the godmother the Lady Scrope.

. . . When he [the Earl of Warwick] had settled all things at his pleasure, upon the twelfth day of October [1470] he rode to the Tower of London and there delivered King Henry out of the ward[45] [**4.6.16**], where he before was kept, and brought him to the King's lodging, where he was served according to his degree.

On the five and twentieth day of the said month, the Duke of Clarence, accompanied with the Earls of Warwick and Shrewsbury, the Lord Strange, and other lords and gentlemen, some for fear and some for love and some only to gaze at the wavering world, went to the Tower; and from thence brought King Henry, appareled in a long gown of blue velvet, through London to the church of Saint Paul; the people on every side the streets rejoicing and crying "God save the King!" as though each thing had succeeded as they would

[44]Hanse citizens.
[45]Prison.

have had it; and when he had offered (as kings use to do), he was conveyed to the Bishop's palace, where he kept his household like a king. . . .

When King Henry had thus readepted[46] and eftsoons[47] gotten his regal power and authority, he called his high court of parliament, to begin the six and twentieth day of November [1470] at Westminster; in the which King Edward was adjudged a traitor [**54**] to the country and an usurper of the realm. His goods were confiscate and forfeited [**55**].

[**678**] . . . Moreover, all statutes made by King Edward were clearly[48] revoked, and the crowns of the realms of England and France were by authority of the same parliament entailed to King Henry the Sixth and to his heirs male; and, for default of such heirs, to remain to George Duke of Clarence [**56**] and to his heirs male; and further, the said Duke was enabled to be next[49] heir to his father Richard Duke of York, and to take from him all his lands and dignities, as though he had been his eldest son at the time of his death. . . .

Besides this, the Earl of Warwick . . . was made Governor of the realm, with whom as fellow was associate George Duke of Clarence [**41**].

. . . When Queen Margaret understood by her husband's letters that the victory was gotten by their friends, she with her son Prince Edward and her train entered their ships to take their voyage into England [**60**]; but the winter was so sharp, the weather so stormy, and the wind so contrary that she was fain[50] to take land again and to defer her journey till another season.

About the same season [1471] Jasper Earl of Pembroke went into Wales to visit his lands in Pembrokeshire, where he found Lord Henry, son to his brother Edmund Earl of Richmond, having not full ten[51] years of age, he being kept in manner like a captive, but honorably brought up by the Lady Herbert, late wife to William Earl of Pembroke. . . .

The Earl of Pembroke took this child, being his nephew, out of the custody of the Lady Herbert and, at his return, brought the

[46]Recovered.
[47]Again.
[48]Entirely.
[49]Nearest.
[50]Obliged.
[51]Fourteen.

child with him to London to King Henry the Sixth [**65**]; whom when the King had a good while beheld, he said to such princes as were with him: "Lo, surely this is he to whom both we and our adversaries, leaving the possession of all things, shall hereafter give room and place" [**74**]. So this holy man showed, before the chance that should happen, that this Earl Henry, so ordained by God, should in time to come (as he did indeed) have and enjoy the kingdom and whole rule of this realm of England; so that it might seem probable, by the coherence of holy Henry's predictions with the issue falling out in truth with the same, that for the time he was endued with a prophetical spirit [**68**]. And surely the epithet or title of "holy" is not for naught attributed unto him, for it is to be read in writers that he was by nature given to peaceableness, abhorring blood and slaughter, detesting civil tumults, addicted to devotion, very frequent in prayer, and not esteeming so highly of courtly gallantness as stood with the dignity of a prince. In consideration whereof he procured against himself an apostasy of his people both native and foreign, who revolted and fell from fealty. . . .

But Duke Charles [of Burgundy] would not consent openly to aid King Edward; but yet secretly, underhand by others, he lent unto him fifty thousand florins of the Cross of Saint Andrew; and, further, caused four great ships to be appointed for him in the haven of De Verre, otherwise called Camphire, in Zeeland, which in those days was free for all men to come unto [**90, 4.7.6**]. And the Duke hired for him fourteen ships of the Easterlings, well appointed, and for the more surety took a bond of them to serve him truly till he were landed in England and fifteen days after.

[**679**] . . . When therefore all King Edward's furniture and provision for his journey were once ready, having now with him about two thousand able men-of-war, beside mariners, he entered into the ships with them, in the haven before Flushing in Zeeland, upon the second day of March [1471]; . . . and forward they sailed, directing their course straight over toward the coast of Norfolk.

. . . But after the King perceived . . . how things stood thereabouts, he caused his ships to make course toward the north parts.

The same night following, a great storm of winds and weather rose, sore troubling the seas, and continued till the fourteenth day of that month, being Thursday, on the which day, with great danger by reason of the tempestuous rage and torment of the troubled seas, he arrived at the head of Humber, where the other ships were scattered from him, each one severed from other; so that of necessity they were driven to land in sunder where they best might, for doubt to be cast away in that perilous tempest. The King, with the Lord Hastings his Chamberlain and other to the number of five hundred men, being in one ship, landed within Humber on Holderness side, at a place called Ravenspur [**8**], even in the same place where Henry Earl of Derby, after called King Henry the Fourth, landed when he came to deprive King Richard the Second of the crown and to usurp it to himself. . . .

Touching the folks of the country, there came few or none to him. . . . And hereupon they suffered him to pass, not seeking to annoy him, till they might understand more of his purposed meaning. The King, perceiving how the people were bent, noised abroad that he came to make none other challenge but to his inheritance of the duchy of York [**23, 46**]; and withal[52] meant to pass first into the city of York; and so forward toward London to encounter with his adversaries that were in the south parts. . . .

[**680**] When King Edward had thus gotten into the city of York, he made such means among the citizens that he got of them a certain sum of money; and leaving a garrison [**38**] within the city (contrary to his oath), for fear lest the citizens after his departure might haply move some rebellion against him, he set forward the next day toward Tadcaster, a town ten miles from thence belonging to the Earl of Northumberland. The next day he took his way toward Wakefield and Sandal, a castle and lordship belonging to the inheritance of the Dukes of York, leaving the castle of Pomfret upon his left hand where the Marquis Montague with his army lay and did not once offer to stop him.

Whether the Marquis suffered him to pass by so, with his good will or no, divers have diversly conjectured. . . .

About Wakefield and the parts there adjoining, some company of his friends came to him, whereby his power was increased; but nothing in such numbers as he looked for. From Wakefield he crossed on the left hand, so to come again into the highway, and came to Doncaster and from thence unto Nottingham. Here came to him Sir William Parr and Sir James Harrington, with six hundred men well armed and appointed. Also there came to him Sir Thomas Burgh and Sir Thomas Montgomery, with their aides; which caused

[52]Therewith.

him at their first coming to make proclamation in his own name [**70**], to wit, of King Edward the Fourth, boldly affirming to him that they would serve no man but a king [**49**]. . . .

[**681**] The King then from Nottingham came to Leicester, where three thousand able men, and well furnished for the war, came unto him. These were such as he knew would live and die in his quarrel,[53] the most part of them belonging unto the Lord Hastings, the King's Chamberlain. And thus he, being more strongly accompanied than before, departed from Leicester and came before the walls of the city of Coventry the nine and twentieth day of March [1471]. The Earl of Warwick was withdrawn into this city [**4.8.59**], keeping himself enclosed therein with his people, being in number six or seven thousand men. The King sent to him [**5.1.16**] and willed him to come forth into the field, and there to make an end of the quarrel in plain battle; but the Earl at that present refused so to do.

. . . The King therefore three days together provoked[54] him to come forth; but when he saw it would not be, he removed to Warwick an eight miles from Coventry where he was received as King; and so made his proclamations from that time forth in all places where he came under his accustomed name and title of King. . . .

In this meanwhile the Earl of Warwick still looked for the Duke of Clarence [**11**], who by the said Earl's appointment had assembled a power of men-of-war about London. . . .

When they were now within half a mile approached together, the King . . . went forth to meet his brother of Clarence; and in like sort the Duke of Clarence took with him a few of the nobility that were about him and, leaving his army in good order, departed from them to meet the King; and so they met betwixt both the hosts, with so sweet salutations, loving demeanor, and good countenances as better might not be devised betwixt brethren of so high and noble estate [**103**]. O what a heart's joy was this to the people, to see such an accord and mutual atonement[55] between these peers! . . .

[**682**] Wherefore (by the advice of his brethren and others of his Council), accordingly as it had been ordained before this his last setting forth from Warwick, he kept on his way toward London, coming to Daventry on the Saturday at night.

[**683**] . . . But now touching King Edward's proceeding forward

[53]Cause.
[54]Challenged.
[55]Reconciliation.

on his journey toward London, ye have to understand that upon the Tuesday the ninth of April [1471] he came to Saint Albans, from whence he sent comfortable advertisements to the Queen his wife remaining within the sanctuary at Westminster [**5.5.90**], and to others his faithful friends in and about London, to understand by covert means how to deal to obtain the favor of the citizens, so as he might be of them received. . . .

Thus, what through love that many bore to King Edward, and what through fear that divers stood in lest the city, being taken by force, might haply have been put to the sack, with the loss of many an innocent man's life, the Mayor, aldermen, and others the worshipful of the city fell at a point[56] among themselves to keep the city to King Edward's use, so as he might have free passage and entry into the same at his pleasure. The Archbishop of York, perceiving the affections of the people, and how the most part of them were now bent in favor of King Edward, upon the said King's approach toward the city, he sent forth secretly a messenger to him, beseeching him to receive him again into his favor, promising to be faithful to him in time to come and to acquit this good turn hereafter with some singular benefit and pleasure.

The King, upon good causes and considerations thereunto him moving, was contented to receive him again into his favor. The Archbishop, hereof assured, rejoiced greatly, well and truly acquitting him concerning his promise made to the King in that behalf. The same night following was the Tower of London recovered to King Edward's use. And on the morrow, being Thursday and the eleventh of April, King Edward quietly made his entry into the city with his power, having five hundred smoky gunners[57] marching foremost, being strangers[58] [**4.8.2**], of such as he had brought over with him. He first rode unto Paul's Church and from thence he went to the Bishop's palace, where the Archbishop of York presented himself unto him and, having King Henry by the hand, delivered him unto King Edward [**52**]; who being seized of his person and divers other his adversaries, he went from Paul's to Westminster, where he made his devout prayers, giving God most hearty thanks for his safe return thither again. . . .

The Earl of Warwick, accompanied with John Duke of Exeter,

[56]Came to an agreement.
[57]Matchlockmen, parading with slow matches alight and smoking.
[58]Foreigners.

Edmund Duke of Somerset [**5.1.72**], John Earl of Oxford [**58**], and John Neville Marquis Montague his brother [**67**], understanding that King Edward was not only received into London but also had got King Henry into his hands, perceived that the trial of the matter must needs be committed to the hazard of battle [**110**]. . . .

[**684**] Hereupon removed they toward Barnet, a town standing in the midway betwixt London and Saint Albans aloft on a hill. . . . King Edward . . . marched forth, having his said army divided into four battles.[59] He took with him King Henry and came that evening unto Barnet, ten small miles distant from London. . . .

At length, after sore fight and greater slaughter made on both sides, King Edward, having the greater number of men (as some write, though other affirm the contrary), began somewhat to prevail.

[**685**] . . . The Earl of Warwick . . . rushed into the midst of his enemies, whereas[60] he . . . was amongst the press of his enemies stricken down and slain [**5.2.1, 49**].

The Marquis Montague, thinking to succor his brother, was likewise overthrown and slain [**40**]. . . .

King Edward, having got this victory, refreshing himself and his people awhile at Barnet, returned the same day unto London like a triumphant conqueror, leading with him King Henry as a captive prisoner. . . .

On the Tuesday in Easter week [April 16, 1471] came knowledge to King Edward that Queen Margaret the wife of King Henry, with her son Prince Edward, was landed upon Easter day at Weymouth in Dorsetshire [**31, 5.3.7**]. . . .

Queen Margaret and her son Prince Edward, with the other that landed at Weymouth, went from thence to an abbey nearby called Cerne. Thither came unto them Edmund Duke of Somerset [**15**] and Thomas Courtenay Earl of Devonshire, with others, and welcomed them into England, comforting the Queen in the best manner they could and willed her not to despair of good success; for, albeit they had lost one field[61] (whereof the Queen had knowledge the same day, being Monday in Easter week the fifteenth of April, and was therefor right sorrowful), yet they doubted not but to assemble such a puissance (and that very shortly) forth of divers parts of the realm, as, being faithful and wholly bent to spend their lives and

[59]Battalions.
[60]Where.
[61]Battle.

shed the best blood in their bodies for her sake and her son's, it should be hard for King Edward to resist them with all the power he had or could make.

[**686**] . . . To be short, they wrought so that they raised the whole powers of Cornwall and Devonshire, and with a great army departing forth of Exeter, they took the right[62] way to Glastonbury, and from thence to Bath, raising the people in all parts where they came. . . .

[**687**] King Edward had ever good espials to advertise him still what his enemies did and which way they took. At length he came with all his army unto a village called Cheltenham, like a five miles distant from Tewkesbury, where he had certain knowledge that his enemies were already come to Tewkesbury [**19**] and were encamped there, purposing to abide him in that place and to deliver him battle [**5.4.82**].

[**688**] . . . The Duke of Gloucester, pursuing after them that fled with the Duke of Somerset to their camp, where the rest of their army stood, entered the trench, and after him the King, where he bore himself so knightly that thereupon the Queen's part went to wrack and was put to flight; the King and other falling in chase after them, so that many were slain. . . . This was the last fought field or pitched battle tried between the potentates of this land in King Edward the Fourth's days; which chanced on the fourth of May, being Saturday, in the eleventh year of his reign and in the year of our Lord 1471. . . .

In the winning of the camp,[63] such as stood to it were slain out of hand. Prince Edward was taken, as he fled toward the town, by Sir Richard Crofts and kept close. . . . After the field was ended, proclamation was made that whosoever could bring forth Prince Edward alive or dead should have an annuity of a hundred pounds during his life; and the Prince's life to be saved if he were brought forth alive [**5.5.9**]. Sir Richard Crofts, nothing mistrusting the King's promise, brought forth [**11**] his prisoner Prince Edward, being a fair and well-proportioned young gentleman; whom when King Edward had well advised,[64] he demanded of him how he durst so presumptuously enter into his realm with banner displayed [**14**].

Whereunto the Prince boldly answered [**17, 37**], saying: "To recover my father's kingdom and heritage, from his father and grand-

[62]Direct.
[63]Battle.
[64]Regarded.

father to him, and from him after him to me, lineally descended." At which words King Edward said nothing but with his hand thrust him from him or (as some say) struck him with his gauntlet [**38**]; whom incontinently George Duke of Clarence, Richard Duke of Gloucester, Thomas Grey Marquis Dorset, and William Lord Hastings that stood by suddenly murdered [**39**]; for the which cruel act the more part of the doers in their latter days drank of the like cup, by the righteous justice and due punishment of God. His body was homely interred with the other simple corpses in the church of the monastery of Black Monks[65] in Tewkesbury. . . .

The same Tuesday the King departed from Tewkesbury toward Worcester and by the way had knowledge that Queen Margaret was found in a poor house of religion not far from thence, into the which she was withdrawn for safeguard of herself on Saturday in the morning, being the day of the battle [**5.5 SD**]. She was after brought to London as prisoner, and so kept till her father [René Duke of Anjou] ransomed her [1475] with great sums of money which he borrowed of Louis the eleventh King of France [**5.7.38**].

[**690**] . . . Moreover, here is to be remembered that poor King Henry the Sixth, a little before deprived (as ye have heard) of his realm and imperial crown, was now in the Tower spoiled of his life by Richard Duke of Gloucester (as the constant[66] fame ran), who (to the intent that his brother King Edward might reign in more surety) murdered the said King Henry with a dagger [**5.6.57, 63**]. . . .

[**691**] He [Henry the Sixth] was of a seemly stature, of body slender, to which proportion all other members were answerable; his face beautiful, wherein continually was resident the bounty of mind with the which he was inwardly endued. Of his own natural inclination he abhorred all the vices as well of the body as of the soul. . . .

This King, having enjoyed as great prosperity as favorable Fortune could afford and as great troubles on the other side as she frowning could pour out, yet in both the states he was patient and virtuous, that he may be a pattern of most perfect virtue as he was a worthy example of Fortune's inconstancy. He was plain, upright, far from fraud, wholly given to prayer, reading of scriptures, and almsdeeds [**2H6 1.3.58**]; of such integrity of life that the Bishop which had been his confessor ten years avouched that he had not all that time committed any mortal crime; so continent as suspicion of unchaste life never touched him;

[65]Benedictines.
[66]Consistent.

and, having in Christmas a show of young women with their bare breasts laid out presented before him, he immediately departed with these words, "Fie, fie, for shame; forsooth, you be to blame."

. . . He was religiously affected (as the time then was) that at principal holidays he would wear sackcloth next his skin. Oath he used none, but in most earnest matters these words, *forsooth* and *forsooth.*

. . . Not long before his death, being demanded why he had so long held the crown of England unjustly, he replied: "My father was King of England, quietly enjoying the crown all his reign; and his father, my grandsire, was also King of England; and I even a child in my cradle was proclaimed and crowned king without any interruption [**3H6 3.1.76**]; and so held it forty years well near; all the states doing homage unto me, as to my antecessors. . . ."

[**693**] After this [1471] was the Earl [of Pembroke] besieged in the town of Pembroke by Morgan Thomas; but the siege was raised by David Thomas, brother to the said Morgan, a faithful friend to the Earl; and then the Earl by his help was conveyed to Tenby, where he got ships and, with his nephew the Lord Henry Earl of Richmond, sailed into Brittany [**4.6.97**], where of the Duke they were courteously entertained,[67] with assurance made that no creature should do them any wrong or injury within his dominions.

. . . Beside this, John Earl of Oxford, which after Barnet Field both manfully and valiantly kept Saint Michael's Mount in Cornwall, either for lack of aid or persuaded by his friends, gave up the Mount [1474] and yielded himself to King Edward (his life only saved, which to him was granted). But to be out of all doubtful[68] imaginations, King Edward also sent him over the sea to the castle of Hames [**5.5.2**], where, by the space of twelve years, he was in strong prison shut up and warily looked to.

King Edward was not a little disquieted in mind for that the Earls of Pembroke and Richmond were not only escaped out of the realm but also well received and no worse entertained of the Duke of Brittany. He sent therefore in secret wise grave and close messengers to the said Duke, the which should not stick to promise the Duke great and rich rewards so that he would deliver both the Earls into their hands and possession. The Duke, after he had heard them that were sent, made this answer, that he could not with his honor deliver them to whom he had given his faith to see them preserved from all injury; but this he

[67]Welcomed.
[68]Full of fear.

said he would do for the King of England that they should be so looked unto as he needed not to doubt of any attempt to be made against him by them or by their means.

The King, receiving this answer, wrote lovingly to the Duke of Brittany that he would consider[69] his friendship with convenient rewards if it should please him to be as good as his promise. The Duke, perceiving gain coming by the abode of the two English Earls in his country, caused them to be separated in sunder and all their servants, being Englishmen, to be sequestered from them, and in their places appointed Bretons to attend them.

[**726**] . . . And finally, after many a meeting, much wooing, and many great promises, she [the Lady Elizabeth Grey] well espied the King's affection toward her so greatly increased that she durst somewhat the more boldly say her mind, as to him whose heart she perceived more fervently set, than to fall off for a word. And in conclusion, she showed him plain that, as she wist[70] herself too simple to be his wife, so thought she herself too good to be his concubine [**3.2.97**].

. . . [Later King Edward, in defense of his decision to marry Elizabeth Grey, said:] "That she is a widow and hath already children; by God's blessed Lady, I am a bachelor and have some too [**102**]; and so each of us hath a proof that neither of us is like to be barren. . . ."

[69]Requite.
[70]Knew.

Richard III

[**690**] . . . The dead corpse [of Henry the Sixth], on the Ascension Eve [1471], was conveyed with bills[1] and glaives[2] pompously (if you will call that a funeral pomp) from the Tower to the church of Saint Paul; and there, laid on a bier or coffin, barefaced, the same in presence of the beholders did bleed [**1.2.55**]; where it rested the space of one whole day. From thence he was carried to the Black Friars and bled there likewise; and on the next day after it was conveyed in a boat, without priest or clerk, torch or taper, singing or saying, unto the monastery of Chertsey [**29**], distant from London fifteen miles, and there was it first buried. . . .

[**703**] About this season [1477], through great mishap, the spark of privy malice was newly kindled betwixt the King [Edward the Fourth] and his brother the Duke of Clarence, insomuch that where one of the Duke's servants was suddenly accused (I cannot say whether of truth or untruly suspected by the Duke's enemies) of poisoning, sorcery, or enchantment, and thereof condemned and put to execution for the same, the Duke, which might not suffer the wrongful condemnation of his man (as he in his conscience judged) nor yet forbear but to murmur and reprove the doing thereof, moved the King with his daily exclamation to take such displeasure with him that, finally, the Duke was cast into the Tower; and therewith adjudged for a traitor and privily drowned in a butt of malmsey[3] [**1.4.276**] the eleventh of March [1478], in the beginning of the seventeenth year of the King's reign.

Some have reported that the cause of this nobleman's death rose of a foolish prophecy, which was that after King Edward, one should reign whose first letter of his name should be a *G* [**1.1.39**]. Wherewith the King and Queen were sore troubled, and began to conceive a grievous grudge against this Duke and could not be in quiet till they

[1]Halberds.
[2]Swords.
[3]A sweet wine.

had brought him to his end. And as the devil is wont to encumber the minds of men which delight in such devilish fancies, they said afterward that that prophecy lost not his effect when, after King Edward, Gloucester usurped his kingdom. Other alleged that the cause of his death was for that the Duke, being destitute of a wife, by the means of his sister the Lady Margaret Duchess of Burgundy, procured to have the Lady Mary, daughter and heir to her husband Duke Charles.

Which marriage King Edward (envying the prosperity of his brother) both gainsaid and disturbed, and thereby old malice revived betwixt them which the Queen [**64, 2.2.137**] and her blood (ever mistrusting and privily barking at the King's lineage)[4] ceased not to increase. But sure it is that, although King Edward were consenting to his death, yet he much did both lament his unfortunate chance and repent his sudden execution [**2.1.86, 96**]; insomuch that when any person sued to him for the pardon of malefactors condemned to death, he would accustomably say and openly speak, "Oh unfortunate brother, for whose life not one would make suit [**106**]," openly and apparently meaning by such words that by the means of some of the nobility he was deceived and brought to confusion. . . .

[**708**] But whilst he was busy in hand to make his purveyance for wars thus against France [1483], whether it was with melancholy and anger which he took with the French King's doings and uncourteous usage or were it by any superfluous surfeit (to the which he was very much given), he suddenly fell sick and was so grievously taken that, in the end, he perceived his natural strength in such wise to decay that there was little hope of recovery in the cunning of his physicians [**1.1.137**], whom he perceived only to prolong his life for a small time. . . .

[**710**] Having thus spoken and set things in good stay, as might be supposed, he shortly after departed this life at Westminster, the ninth of April in the year 1483, after he had reigned two and twenty years, one month, and eight days. His body was with funeral pomp conveyed to Windsor and there buried. . . . For the description of his person and qualities I will refer you to that which Sir Thomas More hath written of him in that *History* which he wrote and left unfinished of his son Edward the Fifth and of his brother King Richard the Third; which we shall (God willing) hereafter make you partaker of, as we find the same recorded among his other works, word for word. . . .

[4]Family.

[**711**] King Edward . . . died at Westminster the ninth day of April, . . . leaving much fair issue, that is to wit, Edward the Prince, a thirteen years of age, Richard Duke of York, two years younger, Elizabeth, whose fortune and grace was after to be Queen, wife unto King Henry the Seventh and mother unto the Eighth, [and four other daughters]. . . .

He was a goodly personage and princely to behold, of heart courageous, politic[5] in counsel, in adversity nothing abashed, in prosperity rather joyful than proud, in peace just and merciful, in war sharp and fierce, in the field bold and hardy, and natheless no further (than wisdom would) adventurous; whose wars who so [hath] well considered he shall no less commend his wisdom where he voided[6] than his manhood where he vanquished. He was of visage lovely, of body mighty, strong, and clean made; howbeit, in his latter days, with overliberal diet [**139**], somewhat corpulent and burly, and natheless not uncomely. He was, of youth, greatly given to fleshly wantonness, from which health of body, in great prosperity and fortune, without a special grace hardly refraineth. . . .

[**712**] All three [sons of Richard Duke of York], as they were great states[7] of birth, so were they great and stately of stomach,[8] greedy and ambitious of authority, and impatient of partners. Edward, revenging his father's death, deprived King Henry and attained the crown. George Duke of Clarence was a goodly noble prince, and at all times fortunate, if either his own ambition had not set him against his brother or the envy of his enemies his brother against him. For were it by the Queen [**64**] and lords of her blood, which highly maligned the King's kindred (as women commonly, not of malice but of nature, hate them whom their husbands love), or were it a proud appetite of the Duke himself, intending to be King, at the least wise heinous treason was there laid to his charge; and, finally, were he faulty were he faultless, attainted[9] was he by parliament and judged to the death, and thereupon hastily drowned in a butt of malmsey. Whose death King Edward (albeit he commanded it), when he wist[10] it was done, piteously bewailed and sorrowfully repented.

[5]Cunning.
[6]Kept clear.
[7]Lords.
[8]Disposition.
[9]Convicted.
[10]Knew.

Richard, the third son, of whom we now entreat, was in wit and courage equal with either of them, in body and prowess[a] far under them both; little of stature, ill-featured of limbs, crookbacked, his left shoulder much higher than his right [**14**]; hard-favored of visage, and such as is in states called warly,[11] in other men otherwise; he was malicious, wrathful, envious, and from afore his birth ever froward.[12] It is for truth reported that the Duchess his mother had so much ado in her travail [**4.4.168**] that she could not be delivered of him uncut; and that he came into the world with the feet forward [**3H6 5.6.71**], as men be borne outward, and (as the fame runneth also) not untoothed [**53, R3 2.4.28**], whether men of hatred report above the truth or else that Nature changed her course in his beginning which in the course of his life many things unnaturally committed. . . .

None evil captain was he in the war, as to which his disposition was more meetly than for peace. Sundry victories had he, and sometimes overthrows; but never on default as for his own person, either of hardiness or politic order. Free was he called of dispense, and somewhat above his power liberal; with large gifts he got him unsteadfast friendship for which he was fain[13] to pill[14] and spoil in other places and got him steadfast hatred. He was close and secret, a deep dissembler, lowly of countenance, arrogant of heart, outwardly companionable where he inwardly hated, not letting[15] to kiss whom he thought to kill; despiteous and cruel, not for evil will alway, but ofter for ambition, and either for the surety or increase of his estate.

Friend and foe was much what[16] indifferent where his advantage grew; he spared no man's death whose life withstood his purpose. He slew with his own hands King Henry the Sixth, being prisoner in the Tower, as men constantly said, and that without commandment or knowledge of the King [**3H6 5.5.86**], which would undoubtedly (if he had intended that thing) have appointed that butcherly office to some other than his own born brother. Some wise men also ween[17] that his drift,[18] covertly conveyed, lacked not in helping forth his brother of

[a]Moral goodness, probity.
[11]Bellicose.
[12]Refractory.
[13]Obliged.
[14]Plunder.
[15]Scrupling.
[16]Matter.
[17]Suppose.
[18]Plot.

Clarence to his death [**R3 1.1.150**]; which he resisted openly [**1.3.139, 2.1.87**], howbeit somewhat (as men deemed) more faintly than he that were heartily minded to his wealth.[19]

And they that thus deem think that he long time in King Edward's life forethought to be king, in case that the King his brother (whose life he looked that evil diet [**1.1.139**] should shorten) should happen to decease (as indeed he did) while his children were young. And they deem that for this intent he was glad of his brother's death the Duke of Clarence, whose life must needs have hindered him so intending [**146**], whether the same Duke of Clarence had kept him true to his nephew the young King or enterprised to be King himself. But of all this point is there no certainty, and whoso divineth upon conjectures may as well shoot too far as too short. . . .

But now to return to the course of this history. Were it that the Duke of Gloucester had of old foreminded this conclusion or was now at erst[20] thereunto moved and put in hope by the occasion of the tender age of the young princes his nephews (as opportunity and likelihood of speed[21] putteth a man in courage of that he never intended), certain it is that he contrived their destruction, with the usurpation of the regal dignity upon himself. And forsomuch as he well wist and holp to maintain a long-continued grudge and heartburning between the Queen's kindred and the King's blood, either party envying other's authority, he now thought that their division should be (as it was indeed) a furtherly[b] beginning to the pursuit of his intent [**1.3**].

Nay, he was resolved that the same was a sure ground for the foundation of all his building, if he might first (under the pretext of revenging of old displeasure) abuse the anger and ignorance of the t'one party to the destruction of the t'other, and then win to his purpose as many as he could; and those that could not be won might be lost ere they looked therefor. For of one thing was he certain, that if his intent were perceived, he should soon have made peace between both the parties with his own blood. King Edward in his life, albeit that this dissension between his friends somewhat irked him, yet in his good health he somewhat the less regarded it because he thought, whatsoever business should fall between them, himself should alway be able to rule both the parties.

[19]Well-being.
[20]First.
[21]Success.
[b]Favorable.

[**713**] But in his last sickness, when he perceived his natural strength so sore enfeebled that he despaired all recovery, then he, considering the youth of his children, albeit he nothing less mistrusted than that that happened, yet well foreseeing that many harms might grow by their debate while the youth of his children should lack discretion of themselves and good counsel of their friends (of which either party should counsel for their own commodity,[22] and rather by pleasant advice to win themselves favor than by profitable advertisement[23] to do the children good), he called some of them before him that were at variance [**2.1.7, 18**], and in especial the Lord Marquis Dorset the Queen's son by her first husband.

So did he also William the Lord Hastings, a nobleman, then Lord Chamberlain, against whom the Queen specially grudged for the great favor the King bore him, and also for that she thought him secretly familiar with the King in wanton company. Her kindred also bore him sore,[c] as well for that the King had made him Captain of Calais (which office the Lord Rivers, brother to the Queen, claimed of the King's former promise) as for divers other great gifts which he received that they looked for. When these lords, with divers other of both the parties, were come in presence, the King, lifting up himself, and underset with pillows, as it is reported, on this wise said unto them. . . .

[**714**] But the lords, recomforting him with as good words as they could, and answering for the time as they thought to stand with his pleasure, there in his presence, as by their words appeared, each forgave other and joined their hands together when (as it after appeared by their deeds) their hearts were far asunder. As soon as the King was departed [**2.2.40**], the noble Prince his son drew toward London, which at the time of his decease [April 9, 1483] kept his household at Ludlow in Wales [**121**]. . . .

To the governance and ordering of this young prince, at his sending thither, was there appointed Sir Anthony Woodville Lord Rivers and brother unto the Queen; a right honorable man, as valiant of hand as politic in counsel. Adjoined were there unto him other of the same party; and in effect, everyone, as he was nearest of kin unto the Queen, so was he planted next[24] about the Prince. That drift by the Queen not unwisely devised, whereby her blood might of youth be rooted into

[22]Self-interest.
[23]Advice.
[c]Bore a grudge against him.
[24]Nearest.

the Prince's favor, the Duke of Gloucester turned unto their destruction; and upon that ground set the foundation of all his unhappy building. For whomsoever he perceived either at variance with them, or bearing himself their favor, he broke unto them, some by mouth and some by writing.

. . . With these words and writings, and such other, the Duke of Gloucester soon set on fire them that were of themselves easy to kindle, and in special twain: Edward[d] Duke of Buckingham and William Lord Hastings, then Chamberlain; both men of honor and of great power, the one by long succession from his ancestry, the other by his office and the King's favor. These two, not bearing each to other so much love as hatred both unto the Queen's part, in this point accorded together with the Duke of Gloucester that they would utterly remove from the King's [Edward the Fifth's] company all his mother's friends under the name of their enemies.

Upon this concluded, the Duke of Gloucester, understanding that the lords which at that time were about the King intended to bring him up to his coronation accompanied with such power of their friends that it should be hard for him to bring his purpose to pass without the gathering and great assembly of people and in manner of open war, whereof the end (he wist) was doubtful and in which, the King being on their side, his part should have the face and name of a rebellion, he secretly therefore by divers means caused the Queen to be persuaded and brought in the mind that it neither were need, and also should be jeopardous, the King to come up strong[25] [**124**].

For whereas now every lord loved other and none other thing studied upon but about the coronation and honor of the King, if the lords of her kindred should assemble in the King's name much people, they should give the lords, betwixt whom and them had been sometime debate, to fear and suspect lest they should gather this people not for the King's safeguard (whom no man impugned) but for their destruction; having more regard to their old variance than their new atonement.[26] For which cause they should assemble on the other party much people again for their defense (whose power she wist well far stretched), and thus should all the realm fall on aroar. And of all the hurt that thereof should ensue (which was likely not to be little, and the most harm there like to fall where she least would), all the world

[d]Henry.
[25]With strong forces.
[26]Reconciliation.

would put her and her kindred in the wite,[e] and say that they had unwisely and untruly also broken the amity and peace that the King her husband so prudently made between his kin and hers in his deathbed and which the other party faithfully observed.

[**715**] The Queen, being in this wise persuaded [**139**], such word sent unto her son and unto her brother, being about the King, and over[27] that the Duke of Gloucester himself and other lords, the chief of his band, wrote unto the King so reverently, and to the Queen's friends there so lovingly, that they, nothing earthly mistrusting, brought the King up in great haste, not in good speed, with a sober company. Now was the King in his way to London gone from Northampton, when these Dukes of Gloucester and Buckingham came thither [**147**]; where remained behind the Lord Rivers the King's uncle, intending on the morrow to follow the King and to be with him at Stony Stratford [**2.4.2**], certain miles thence, early ere he departed.

. . . And thus in a goodly array they [Gloucester and Buckingham] came to the King and, on their knees in very humble wise, saluted his grace, which received them in very joyous and amiable manner, nothing earthly knowing nor mistrusting as yet.

. . . And forthwith they arrested [**42**] the Lord Richard [Grey] and Sir Thomas Vaughan, knight, in the King's presence, and brought the King and all back unto Northampton, where they took again further counsel. And there they sent away from the King whom it pleased them and set new servants about him, such as liked[28] better them than him. At which dealing he wept and was nothing content, but it booted not.

. . . But for all this comfortable courtesy of the Duke of Gloucester, he sent the Lord Rivers and the Lord Richard, with Sir Thomas Vaughan, into the north country, into divers places to prison; and afterward all to Pomfret, where they were in conclusion beheaded [**3.3**].

In this wise the Duke of Gloucester took upon himself the order and governance of the young King, whom with much honor and humble reverence he conveyed upward[29] toward the city. But anon the tidings of this matter [**2.4.39**] came hastily to the Queen a little before

[e]At fault, in the wrong.
[27]Besides.
[28]Pleased.
[29]Toward.

the midnight following, and that in the sorest wise: that the King her son was taken, her brother, her son, and her other friends arrested and sent no man wist whither, to be done with God wot what. With which tidings the Queen, in great fright and heaviness, bewailing her child's reign, her friends' mischance, and her own infortune, damning the time that ever she dissuaded the gathering of power about the King, got herself in all the haste possible with her younger son and her daughters out of the palace of Westminster (in which she then lay) into the sanctuary [**66, 3.1.27**], lodging herself and her company there in the Abbot's place.

Now came there one in likewise [**2.4.39**] not long after midnight from the Lord Chamberlain [Hastings] to Doctor [Thomas] Rotherham the Archbishop of York, then Chancellor of England, to his place not far from Westminster. And for that he showed his servants that he had tidings of so great importance that his master gave him in charge not to forbear his rest, they letted[30] not to wake him, nor he to admit this messenger in to his bedside. Of whom he heard that these Dukes were gone back with the King's grace from Stony Stratford unto Northampton. "Notwithstanding, sir," quoth he, "my lord sendeth your lordship word that there is no fear, for he assureth you that all shall be well." "I assure him," quoth the Archbishop, "be it as well as it will, it will never be so well as we have seen it."

[**716**] And thereupon, by and by[31] after the messenger departed, he caused in all the haste all his servants to be called up, and so, with his own household about him and every man weaponed, he took the Great Seal with him and came yet before day unto the Queen. About whom he found much heaviness, rumble, haste, and business; carriage and conveyance of her stuff [**69**] into sanctuary—chests, coffers, packs, fardels, trussed all on men's backs; no man unoccupied, some loading, some going, some discharging, some coming for more, some breaking down the walls to bring in the next way; and some yet drew to them that holp to carry a wrong way—such made their lucre of others' loss, praising a booty above beauty. . . .

The Queen herself sat alone alow on the rushes all desolate and dismayed; whom the Archbishop comforted in best manner he could, showing[32] her that he trusted the matter was nothing so sore as she took it for, and that he was put in good hope and out of fear by the

[30]Omitted.
[31]Immediately.
[32]Telling.

message sent him from the Lord Chamberlain. "Ah, woe worth him!" quoth she, "for he is one of them that laboreth to destroy me and my blood." "Madam," quoth he, "be ye of good cheer, for I assure you, if they crown any other king than your son, whom they now have with them, we shall on the morrow crown his brother, whom you have here with you. And here is the Great Seal, which in like wise as that noble prince your husband delivered it unto me, so here I deliver it unto you, to the use and behoof of your son." And therewith he betook[33] her the Great Seal [**70**] and departed home again, yet in the dawning of the day. . . .

When the King approached near to the city, Edmund Shaw, goldsmith, then Mayor, with William White and John Matthew, sheriffs, and all the other aldermen, in scarlet, with five hundred horse of the citizens, in violet, received him reverently at Hornsea and, riding from thence, accompanied him into the city [**3.1.17**]; which he entered the fourth day of May [1483], the first and last year of his reign. But the Duke of Gloucester bore him in open sight so reverently to the Prince, with all semblance of lowliness, that, from the great obloquy in which he was so late before, he was suddenly fallen in so great trust that at the Council next assembled he was made the only man chosen and thought most meet to be Protector of the King and his realm [**1.3.14**]; so that (were it destiny or were it folly), the lamb was betaken to the wolf to keep.

[**717**] . . . Well did he wit that if he deposed the one brother, all the realm would fall to the other, if he either remained in sanctuary or should haply be shortly conveyed to his father's liberty. Wherefore incontinent,[34] at the next meeting of the lords at the Council, he proposed to them that it was a heinous deed of the Queen, and proceeding of great malice toward the King's councillors, that she should keep in sanctuary the King's brother from him, whose special pleasure and comfort were to have his brother with him. . . .

"Wherefore methinketh it were not worst to send unto the Queen, for the redress of this matter, some honorable trusty man such as both tendereth the King's weal and the honor of his Council, and is also in favor and credence with her. For all which considerations, none seemeth more meetly than our reverend father here present, my Lord Cardinal [Rotherham], who may in this matter do most good of any man, if it please him to take the pain [**3.1.32**]. . . .

[33]Delivered.
[34]Immediately.

"And if she be percase[35] so obstinate and so precisely set upon her own will that neither his wise and faithful advertisement cannot move her nor any man's reason content her, then shall we, by mine advice, by the King's authority, fetch him out of that prison [**35**] and bring him to his noble presence, in whose continual company he shall be so well cherished and so honorably entreated[36] that all the world shall to our honor and her reproach perceive that it was only malice, frowardness,[37] or folly, that caused her to keep him there. . . ."

When the Protector had said, all the Council affirmed that the motion was good and reasonable, and to the King and the Duke his brother honorable; and a thing that should cease great murmur in the realm if the mother might be by good means induced to deliver him. Which thing the Archbishop of York [Cardinal Rotherham], whom they all agreed also to be thereto most convenient, took upon him to move her and therein to do his uttermost devoir.[38] Howbeit, if she could be in no wise entreated with her good will to deliver him, then thought he, and such other as were of the spiritualty present, that it were not in any wise to be attempted to take him out against her will. . . .

"And therefore," quoth the Archbishop of York, "God forbid that any man should, for anything earthly, enterprise to break the immunity and liberty of the sacred sanctuary [**42**] that hath been the safeguard of so many a good man's life. . . . And if it happen that I bring it not so to pass, yet shall I toward it so far forth do my best that ye shall all well perceive that no lack of my devoir but the mother's dread and womanish fear shall be the let."[39]

"Womanish fear? Nay, womanish frowardness," quoth the Duke of Buckingham, "for I dare take it[40] upon my soul she well knoweth she needeth no such thing to fear, either for her son or for herself.

[**718**] ". . . But where a man is by lawful means in peril, there needeth he the tuition[41] of some special privilege; which is the only ground and cause of all sanctuaries [**48**].

"From which necessity this noble prince is far, whose love to his King, nature and kindred proveth; whose innocency to all the world,

[35]Perhaps.
[36]Treated.
[37]Perversity.
[38]Endeavor.
[39]Impediment.
[40]*I.e.,* an oath.
[41]Protection.

his tender youth proveth; and so sanctuary, as for him, neither none he needeth nor also none can have [**52**]. Men come not to sanctuary as they come to baptism, to require it by their godfathers; he must ask it himself that must have it. And reason, sith no man hath cause to have it but whose conscience of his own fault maketh him fain need to require it.

". . . And verily, I have often heard of sanctuary men, but I never heard erst of sanctuary children [**55**]."

. . . When the Duke had done, the temporal men whole and a good part of the spiritual also, thinking no hurt earthly meant toward the young babe, condescended in effect that, if he were not delivered, he should be fetched. Howbeit, they thought it best, in the avoiding of all manner of rumor, that the Lord Cardinal should first assay to get him with her good will.

[**719**] Whereupon all the Council came unto the Star Chamber at Westminster; and the Lord Cardinal, leaving the Protector with the Council in the Star Chamber, departed into the sanctuary to the Queen, with divers other lords with him [**58**]. . . .

"Truly, madam," quoth he, "and the fearder that you be to deliver him, the fearder been other men to suffer you to keep him, lest your causeless fear might cause you further to convey him; and many be there that think he can have no privilege in this place which neither can have will to ask it nor malice to deserve it. And therefore they reckon no privilege broken, though they fetch him out; which, if ye finally refuse to deliver him, I verily think they will. So much dread hath my lord his uncle, for the tender love he beareth him, lest your grace should hap to send him away."

[**720**] "Ah, sir," quoth the Queen, "hath the Protector so tender zeal that he feareth nothing but lest he should escape him? . . . But my son can deserve no sanctuary, and therefore he cannot have it! Forsooth, he hath found a goodly gloze,[42] by which that place that may defend a thief may not save an innocent. . . ."

The Lord Cardinal, perceiving that the Queen waxed ever the longer the farther off, and also that she began to kindle and chafe, and spoke more biting words against the Protector, and such as he neither believed and was also loath to hear, he said to her for a final conclusion that he would no longer dispute the matter; but if she were content to deliver the Duke to him and to the other lords present,

[42]Specious argument.

he durst lay his own body and soul both in pledge, not only for his surety but also for his estate. . . .

The Queen with these words stood a good while in a great study. . . . Wherefore, if she should needs go from him, she deemed it best to deliver him. . . .

[**721**] When the Lord Cardinal, and these other lords with him, had received this young Duke, they brought him into the Star Chamber [**95**], where the Protector took him in his arms and kissed him with these words, "Now welcome, my lord, even with all my very heart!" And he said in that of likelihood as he thought. Thereupon, forthwith they brought him unto the King his brother into the Bishop's palace at Paul's, and from thence through the city honorably into the Tower [**150**], out of the which after that day they never came abroad. When the Protector had both the children in his hands, he opened himself more boldly, both to certain other men and also chiefly to the Duke of Buckingham; although I know that many thought that this Duke was privy to all the Protector's counsel, even from the beginning [**163**]; and some of the Protector's friends said that the Duke was the first mover of the Protector to this matter, sending a privy messenger unto him straight after King Edward's death.

But others again, which knew better the subtle wit of the Protector, deny that he ever opened his enterprise to the Duke until he had brought to pass the things before rehearsed. But when he had imprisoned the Queen's kinfolks and gotten both her sons into his own hands, then he opened the rest of his purpose with less fear to them whom he thought meet for the matter; and specially to the Duke, who, being won to his purpose, he thought his strength more than half increased.

. . . Then it was agreed that the Protector should have the Duke's aid to make him King, and that the Protector's only lawful son[43] should marry the Duke's daughter, and that the Protector should grant him the quiet possession of the earldom of Hereford [**195**] which he claimed as his inheritance and could never obtain it in King Edward's time.

Besides these requests of the Duke, the Protector, of his own mind, promised him a great quantity of the King's treasure and of his household stuff [**195**]. And when they were thus at a point[44] between them-

[43]Prince Edward (died 1484).
[44]Agreed.

selves, they went about to prepare for the coronation of the young King, as they would have it seem. And that they might turn both the eyes and minds of men from perceiving of their drifts otherwhere, the lords, being sent for from all parts of the realm, came thick to that solemnity. But the Protector and the Duke, after that they had sent the Lord Cardinal [Thomas Bourchier Archbishop of Canterbury], the Archbishop of York (then Lord Chancellor), the Bishop of Ely, the Lord Stanley, and the Lord Hastings then Lord Chamberlain, with many other noblemen, to common[45] and devise about the coronation in one place [**173**], as fast were they in another place [**179**] contriving the contrary, and to make the Protector king.

To which Council, albeit there were adhibited[46] very few and they were secret, yet began there, here and thereabouts, some manner of muttering among the people [**2.3.38**], as though all should not long be well, though they neither wist what they feared nor wherefore; were it that before such great things, men's hearts of a secret instinct of nature misgive them, as the sea without wind swelleth of himself sometime before a tempest; or were it that some one man, haply somewhat perceiving, filled many men with suspicion, though he showed few men what he knew.

[**722**] . . . Thus many things coming together, partly by chance partly of purpose, caused at length not common people only, that wonde[47] with the wind, but wise men also, and some lords eke,[48] to mark the matter and muse thereon, so far forth that the Lord Stanley (that was after Earl of Derby) wisely mistrusted it and said unto the Lord Hastings that he much misliked these two several councils [**3.2.12**]. "For while we," quoth he, "talk of one matter in the t'one place, little wot we whereof they talk in the t'other place."

"My lord," quoth the Lord Hastings, "on my life, never doubt[49] you [**20**], for while one man is there which is never thence, never can there be thing once moved that should sound amiss toward me but it should be in mine ears ere it were well out of their mouths." This meant he by[50] [William] Catesby [**22**], which was of his near secret counsel and whom he very familiarly used, and in his most weighty

[45]Confer.
[46]Admitted.
[47]Flinch.
[48]Also.
[49]Fear.
[50]*I.e.,* by this meant he.

matters put no man in so special trust, reckoning himself to no man so lief,[51] sith he well wist there was no man so much to him beholden as was this Catesby, which was a man well learned in the laws of this land and, by the special favor of the Lord Chamberlain, in good authority; and much rule bore in all the county of Leicester, where the Lord Chamberlain's power chiefly lay.

But surely great pity was it that he had not had either more truth or less wit, for his dissimulation only kept all that mischief up. In whom if the Lord Hastings had not put so special trust, the Lord Stanley and he had departed with divers other lords and broken all the dance for many ill signs that he saw which he now construes all to the best. So surely thought he that there could be none harm toward him in that Council intended where Catesby was. And of truth the Protector and the Duke of Buckingham made very good semblance unto the Lord Hastings, and kept him much in company. And undoubtedly the Protector loved him well and loath was to have lost him, saving for fear lest his life should have quailed[52] their purpose.

For which cause he moved Catesby to prove[53] with some words cast out afar off whether he could think it possible to win the Lord Hastings unto their part [**3.1.170**]. But Catesby, whether he assayed him or assayed him not, reported unto them that he found him so fast and heard him speak so terrible words [**3.2.43**] that he durst no further break.[54] And of truth the Lord Chamberlain of very trust showed unto Catesby the distrust that others began to have in the matter. And therefore he, fearing lest their motion might with the Lord Hastings minish his credence, whereunto only all the matter leaned, procured the Protector hastily to rid him. And much the rather for that he trusted by his death to obtain much of the rule that the Lord Hastings bore in his country; the only desire whereof was the allective[55] that induced him to be partner and one special contriver of all this horrible treason.

Whereupon soon after, that is to wit on the Friday (being the thirteenth of June), many lords assembled in the Tower and there sat in Council, devising the honorable solemnity of the King's coronation [**3.4.1**]; of which the time appointed then so near approached

[51]Beloved.
[52]Spoiled.
[53]Ascertain.
[54]Reveal his purpose.
[55]Allurement.

that the pageants and subtleties were in making day and night at Westminster [**4**], and much victuals killed therefor that afterward was cast away. These lords so sitting together commoning of this matter, the Protector came in amongst them first about nine of the clock, saluting them courteously and excusing himself that he had been from them so long; saying merrily that he had been a sleeper that day [**23**].

After a little talking with them, he said unto the Bishop of Ely [**30**]: "My lord, you have very good strawberries at your garden in Holborn; I require you let us have a mess[f] of them." "Gladly, my lord," quoth he, "would God I had some better thing as ready to your pleasure as that." And therewithal in all the haste he sent his servant for a mess of strawberries. The Protector set the lords fast in commoning and, thereupon praying them to spare him for a little while, departed thence. And soon after one hour, between ten and eleven, he returned into the chamber amongst them, all changed, with a wonderful sour angry countenance, knitting the brows, frowning, and fretting and gnawing on his lips, and so sat him down in his place.

All the lords were much dismayed and sore marveled at this manner of sudden change and what thing should him ail. Then, when he had sitten still awhile, thus he began [**58**]: "What were they worthy to have that compass and imagine[g] the destruction of me, being so near of blood unto the King and Protector of his royal person and his realm?" At this question all the lords sat sore astonished, musing much by whom[56] this question should be meant, of which every man wist himself clear. Then the Lord Chamberlain (as he that for the love between them thought he might be boldest [**29**] with him) answered and said [**65**] that they were worthy to be punished as heinous traitors, whatsoever they were. And all the other affirmed the same. "That is," quoth he, "yonder sorceress my brother's wife [**69**] and other with her" (meaning the Queen).

At these words many of the other lords were greatly abashed that favored her. But the Lord Hastings was in his mind better content that it was moved by her than by any other whom he loved better; albeit his heart somewhat grudged that he was not afore made of counsel in this matter, as he was of the taking of her kindred and of their putting to death, which were by his assent before devised to be

[f]Serving.
[g]Plot.
[56]*I.e.*, whom by.

beheaded at Pomfret this selfsame day; in which he was not ware that it was by other devised that he himself should be beheaded the same day at London. Then said the Protector: "Ye shall all see in what wise that sorceress, and that other witch of her counsel Shore's Wife [**70**], with their affinity,[h] have by their sorcery and witchcraft wasted my body." And therewith he plucked up his doublet sleeve to his elbow, upon his left arm, where he showed a wearish[57] withered arm and small [**68**], as it was never other.

Hereupon every man's mind sore misgave them, well perceiving that this matter was but a quarrel.[58] For they well wist that the Queen was too wise to go about any such folly. And also, if she would, yet would she, of all folk least, make Shore's Wife of her counsel whom of all women she most hated as that concubine whom the King her husband had most loved. And also, no man was there present but well knew that his arm was ever such since his birth. Natheless, the Lord Chamberlain (which from the death of King Edward kept Shore's Wife [**3.1.185**], on whom he somewhat doted in the King's life, saving as it is said he that while forbore her of reverence toward the King or else of a certain kind of fidelity to his friend) answered and said [**3.4.65**]: "Certainly, my lord, if they have so heinously done they be worthy heinous punishment."

"What," quoth the Protector, "thou servest me, I ween, with if's and with and's [**74**]. I tell thee they have so done, and that I will make good on thy body, traitor!" And therewith, as in a great anger, he clapped his fist upon the board a great rap. At which token one cried "Treason!" without the chamber. Therewith a door clapped, and in come[i] there rushing men in harness,[59] as many as the chamber might hold. And anon the Protector said to the Lord Hastings, "I arrest thee, traitor!" "What me, my lord?" quoth he. "Yea, thee, traitor!" quoth the Protector. And another let fly at the Lord Stanley, which shrunk at the stroke and fell under the table or else his head had been cleft to the teeth, for as shortly as he shrank, yet ran the blood about his ears.

[**723**] Then were they all quickly bestowed in divers chambers, except the Lord Chamberlain, whom the Protector bade speed and

[h]Comrades.
[57]Wizened.
[58]Pretext.
[i]Came.
[59]Armor.

shrive him[60] apace. "For, by Saint Paul," quoth he [**75**], "I will not to dinner till I see thy head off!" It booted him not to ask why [**101**], but heavily [he] took a priest at adventure and made a short shrift[61] [**94**], for a longer would not be suffered, the Protector made so much haste to dinner; which he might not go to until this were done, for saving of his oath. So was he brought forth to the green beside the chapel within the Tower, and his head laid down upon a long log of timber and there stricken off [**105**]. . . .

A marvelous case is it to hear either the warnings of that he should have voided or the tokens of that he could not void. For the self night next before his death, the Lord Stanley sent a trusty messenger unto him at midnight in all the haste [**3.2 SD**], requiring him to rise and ride away with him, for he was disposed utterly no longer to bide; he had so fearful a dream, in which him thought that a boar with his tusks so razed [**11**] them both by the heads that the blood ran about both their shoulders. And forsomuch as the Protector gave the boar for his cognizance,[62] this dream made so fearful an impression in his heart that he was thoroughly determined no longer to tarry, but had his horse ready, if the Lord Hastings would go with him, to ride so far yet the same night that they should be out of danger ere day.

"Ha, good lord," quoth the Lord Hastings to this messenger, "leaneth my lord thy master so much to such trifles, and hath such faith in dreams [**26**], which either his own fear fantasieth or do rise in the night's rest by reason of his day's thought? Tell him it is plain witchcraft to believe in such dreams, which if they were tokens of things to come, why thinketh he not that we might be as likely to make them true by our going, if we were caught and brought back, as friends fail fleers; for then had the boar a cause likely to raze us with his tusks, as folk that fled for some falsehood. . . . And therefore go to thy master, man, and commend me to him, and pray him be merry and have no fear; for I ensure him I am as sure of the man that he wotteth of as I am of mine own hand." "God send grace, sir," quoth the messenger, and went his way.

Certain is it also that, in riding toward the Tower the same morning in which he was beheaded, his horse twice or thrice stumbled with him [**83**], almost to the falling. Which thing, albeit each man wot well daily happeneth to them to whom no such mischance is

[60]Make his confession.
[61]Confession.
[62]Badge.

toward, yet hath it been of an old rite and custom observed as a token oftentimes notably foregoing some great misfortune. Now this that followeth was no warning but an envious scorn. The same morning, ere he was up, came a knight unto him, as it were of courtesy, to accompany him to the Council, but of truth sent by the Protector to haste him thitherward; with whom he was of secret confederacy in that purpose; a mean[63] man at that time, and now of great authority.

This knight (I say), when it happened the Lord Chamberlain by the way to stay his horse and common awhile with a priest whom he met in the Tower Street [**108**], broke his tale and said merrily to him: "What, my lord, I pray you come on, whereto talk you so long with that priest? You have no need of a priest yet [**114**]." And therewith he laughed upon him, as though he would say, "Ye shall have soon." But so little wist the t'other what he meant, and so little mistrusted, that he was never merrier nor never so full of good hope in his life [**81**]; which self thing is oft seen a sign of change. . . .

Upon the very Tower Wharf, so near the place where his head was off soon after, there met he [**95**] with one Hastings, a pursuivant[64] of his own name. And at their meeting in that place, he was put in remembrance of another time in which it had happened them before to meet in like manner together in the same place. At which other time the Lord Chamberlain had been accused unto King Edward by the Lord Rivers, the Queen's brother, in such wise as he was for the while (but it lasted not long) far fallen into the King's indignation and stood in great fear of himself [**100**]. And forsomuch as he now met this pursuivant in the same place, that jeopardy so well passed, it gave him great pleasure to talk with him thereof; with whom he had before talked thereof in the same place, while he was therein.

And therefore he said, "Ha, Hastings, art thou remembered when I met thee here once with an heavy heart?" "Yea, my lord," quoth he, "that remember I well, and thanked be God they got no good nor you no harm thereby." "Thou would'st say so," quoth he, "if thou knewest as much as I know, which few know else as yet, and more shall shortly." That meant he by the lords of the Queen's kindred [**103**], that were taken before and should that day be beheaded at Pomfret, which he well wist but [was] nothing ware that the axe hung over his own head. "In faith, man," quoth he, "I was never so sorry, nor never stood in so great dread in my life, as I did when thou and

[63]Of low rank.
[64]Royal messenger.

I met here. And lo, how the world is turned! Now stand mine enemies in the danger (as thou mayst hap to hear more hereafter), and I never in my life so merry nor never in so great surety."

O good God, the blindness of our mortal nature [**3.4.95**]! When he most feared, he was in good surety; when he reckoned himself surest [**3.2.66, 84**], he lost his life, and that within two hours after. Thus ended this honorable man, a good knight and a gentle, of great authority with his prince, of living somewhat dissolute, plain and open to his enemy and secret to his friend, easy to beguile, as he that of good heart and courage forestudied no perils, a loving man and passing well beloved, very faithful and trusty enough, trusting too much. Now flew the fame of this lord's death swiftly through the city, and so forth further about, like a wind in every man's ear. But the Protector, immediately after dinner, intending to set some color[65] upon the matter, sent in all the haste for many substantial men out of the city into the Tower.

[**724**] Now, at their coming, himself with the Duke of Buckingham stood harnessed in old ill-faring briganders[66] [**3.5 SD**], such as no man should ween that they would vouchsafe to have put upon their backs except that some sudden necessity [**19**] had constrained them. And then the Protector showed them that the Lord Chamberlain, and other of his conspiracy, had contrived to have suddenly destroyed him and the Duke, there the same day in the Council [**39**]. And what they intended further was as yet not well known. Of which their treason he never had knowledge before ten of the clock the same forenoon; which sudden fear drove them to put on for their defense such harness as came next to hand. And so had God holpen them that the mischief turned upon them that would have done it. And this he required them to report.

Every man answered him fair [**62**], as though no man mistrusted the matter, which of truth no man believed. Yet for the further appeasing of the people's minds, he sent immediately after dinner in all the haste one herald-of-arms, with a proclamation to be made through the city in the King's name containing that the Lord Hastings, with divers other of his traitorous purpose, had before conspired the same day to have slain the Lord Protector and the Duke of Buckingham sitting in the Council. . . .

[65]Excuse.

[66]Body armor made of a tough fabric to which was riveted a lining of small overlapping plates.

The means whereby: namely, his evil company, sinister procuring, and ungracious example, as well in many other things as in the vicious living and inordinate abusion of his body, both with many other and also specially with Shore's Wife [**31**], which was one also of his most secret counsel in this most heinous treason, with whom he lay nightly and namely the night last past next before his death. . . .

Now was this proclamation made within two hours after that he was beheaded, and it was so curiously indicted and so fair written in parchment, in so well a set hand [**3.6.2**] and therewith of itself so long a process, that every child might well perceive that it was prepared before [**6**]. For all the time between his death and the proclaiming could scant have sufficed unto the bare writing alone, all[67] had it been but in paper and scribbled forth in haste at adventure. So that, upon the proclaiming thereof, one that was schoolmaster of Paul's, of chance standing by and comparing the shortness of the time with the length of the matter, said unto them that stood about him, "Here is a gay goodly cast,[68] foul cast away for haste." And a merchant answered him that it was written by prophecy. . . .

[**725**] Now was it so devised by the Protector and his Council that the self day in which the Lord Chamberlain was beheaded in the Tower of London, and about the selfsame hour, was there (not without his assent) beheaded at Pomfret the foreremembered lords and knights that were taken from the King at Northampton and Stony Stratford; which thing was done in the presence and by the order of Sir Richard Ratcliffe, knight; whose service the Protector specially used in that counsel and in the execution of such lawless enterprises, as a man that had been long secret with him, having experience of the world and a shrewd wit, short and rude in speech, rough and boisterous of behavior, bold in mischief, as far from pity as from all fear of God.

This knight, bringing them out of the prison to the scaffold [**3.3 SD**] and showing to the people about that they were traitors (not suffering them to declare and speak their innocency lest their words might have inclined men to pity them and to hate the Protector and his part), caused them hastily, without judgment, process, or manner of order, to be beheaded; and without other earthly guilt but only that they were good men, too true to the King and too nigh to the Queen. Now when the Lord Chamberlain and these other lords and knights

[67]Though.
[68]Contrivance.

were thus beheaded and rid out of the way, then thought the Protector . . . it were best hastily to pursue his purpose and put himself in possession of the crown ere men could have time to devise any way to resist.

But now was all the study by what means this matter, being of itself so heinous, might be first broken to the people in such wise that it might be well taken. To this counsel they took divers, such as they thought meetly to be trusted, likely to be induced to that part, and able to stand them in stead either by power or policy. . . . Among these had they John Shaw [**3.5.103**], clerk, brother to the Mayor, and Friar Penker [**104**], Provincial of the Augustine Friars, both doctors of divinity, both great preachers, both of more learning than virtue, of more fame than learning. For they were before greatly esteemed among the people; but after that, never. . . .

But certain it is that Doctor Shaw was of counsel in the beginning, so far forth that they determined that he should first break the matter in a sermon at Paul's Cross in which he should (by the authority of his preaching) incline the people to the Protector's ghostly[69] purpose. But now was all the labor and study in the device of some convenient pretext for which the people should be content to depose the Prince and accept the Protector for King. In which, divers things they devised. But the chief thing and the weightiest of all that invention rested in this, that they should allege bastardy, either in King Edward [the Fourth] himself or in his children or both, so that he should seem disabled to inherit the crown by the Duke of York, and the Prince by him.

To lay bastardy in King Edward [**86, 3.7.9**] sounded openly to the rebuke of the Protector's own mother, which was mother to them both, for in that point could be no other color[70] but to pretend[71] that his own mother was an adulteress; which notwithstanding, to further this purpose, he letted not. But nevertheless he would that point should be less and more favorably handled, not even fully plain and directly; but that the matter should be touched aslope,[j] craftily, as though men spared in that point to speak all the truth for fear of his displeasure [**3.5.93, 3.7.194**]. But the other point, concerning the bastardy that they devised to surmise[72] in King Edward's children,

[69]Devilish.
[70]Allegeable ground.
[71]Claim.
[j]Indirectly.
[72]Allege falsely.

that would he should be openly declared and enforced to the uttermost.

[727] . . . For he [Doctor Shaw] declared then that King Edward was never lawfully married unto the Queen but was before God husband unto Dame Elizabeth Lucy[k] [**5**], and so his children bastards [**4**]. And besides that, neither King Edward himself nor the Duke of Clarence, among those that were secret in the household, were reckoned very surely for the children of the noble Duke [of York], as those that by their favors[73] more resembled other known men than him. From whose virtuous conditions he said also that the late King Edward was far off.

But the Lord Protector, he said, the very noble prince, the special pattern of knightly prowess as well in all princely behavior as in the lineaments and favor of his visage, represented the very face of the noble Duke his father [**12**]. "This is," quoth he, "the father's own figure, this is his own countenance, the very print of his visage, the sure undoubted image, the plain express likeness of that noble Duke." . . .

[728] Then on the Tuesday following this sermon there came to the Guildhall in London the Duke of Buckingham [**3.5.72**]. . . . After silence commanded upon great pain in the Protector's name, the Duke stood up and . . . said unto the people with a clear and loud voice in this manner of wise.

". . . Whereof (I think) no man looketh that we should remember you of examples by name, as though [Thomas] Burdett were forgotten, that was for a word spoken in haste cruelly beheaded [**76**], by the misconstruing of the laws of this realm for the Prince's pleasure.

[729] ". . . And in that point which in good faith I am sorry to speak of, saving that it is in vain to keep in counsel that thing that all men know, the King's greedy appetite was insatiable [**80, 3.7.7**], and everywhere over all the realm intolerable.

"For no woman was there anywhere, young or old, rich or poor, whom he set his eye upon, in whom he anything liked, either person or favor, speech, pace, or countenance, but, without any fear of God or respect of his honor, murmur or grudge of the world, he would importunely pursue his appetite and have her, to the great destruction of many a good woman and great dolor to their husbands. . . . And

[k]Eleanor Butler (Elizabeth Lucy was one of Edward's mistresses).
[73]Countenances.

all were it that, with this and other importable[74] dealing, the realm was in every part annoyed, yet specially ye here, the citizens of this noble city, as well for that amongst you is most plenty of all such things as minister matter to such injuries, as for that you were nearest at hand, sith that near hereabouts was commonly his most abiding.

". . . For, as the worshipful man [Doctor Shaw] groundly[75] made open unto you, the children of King Edward the Fourth were never lawfully begotten, forsomuch as the King (leaving his very wife Dame Elizabeth Lucy) was never lawfully married unto the Queen their mother. . . .

"Whereby it may well seem the marriage not well made of which there is so much mischief grown. For lack of which lawful coupling, and also of other things which the said worshipful doctor rather signified[76] than fully explained, and which things shall not be spoken for me, as the thing wherein every man forbeareth to say that he knoweth in avoiding displeasure of my noble Lord Protector, bearing (as nature requireth) a filial reverence to the Duchess his mother. . . ."

[**730**] When the Duke had said and looked that the people, whom he hoped that the Mayor had framed[77] before, should, after this proposition made, have cried "King Richard, King Richard!" all was hushed and mute and not one word answered thereunto [**3, 25**].

. . . When the Mayor saw this, he with other partners of that council drew about the Duke and said that the people had not been accustomed there to be spoken unto but by the Recorder [**30**], which is the mouth of the city, and haply to him they would answer. With that, the Recorder, called Fitzwilliam, a sad man and an honest, which was so new come into that office that he never had spoken to the people before, and loath was with that matter to begin, notwithstanding, thereunto commanded by the Mayor, made rehearsal to the commons of that the Duke had twice rehearsed to them himself.

But the Recorder so tempered his tale that he showed everything as the Duke's words and no part his own [**33**]. But all this nothing no change made in the people, which alway after one[78] stood as they had been men amazed. . . .

At these words the people began to whisper among themselves

[74]Intolerable.
[75]Thoroughly.
[76]Hinted at.
[77]Shaped to the purpose.
[78]United.

secretly, that the voice was neither loud nor distinct but, as it were, the sound of a swarm of bees; till, at the last, in the nether end of the hall, an ambushment[1] of the Duke's servants [**34**] and [John] Nesfield's, and other belonging to the Protector, with some prentices and lads that thrust into the hall amongst the press, began suddenly at men's backs to cry out as loud as their throats would give "King Richard, King Richard!" and threw up their caps in token of joy. And they that stood before cast back their heads, marveling thereof, but nothing they said. Now when the Duke and the Mayor saw this manner, they wisely turned it to their purpose [**37**] and said it was a goodly cry and a joyful, to hear every man with one voice, no man saying nay.

"Wherefore, friends," quoth the Duke, "sith we perceive it is all your whole minds to have this nobleman for your king (whereof we shall make his grace so effectual report that we doubt not but it shall redound unto your great weal and commodity), we require ye that ye tomorrow go with us, and we with you, unto his noble grace to make our humble request unto him in manner before remembered." And therewith the lords came down,[79] and the company dissolved and departed. . . .

[**731**] Then, on the morrow after, the Mayor, with all the aldermen and chief commoners of the city, in their best manner appareled, assembling themselves together, resorted unto Baynard's Castle, where the Protector lay [**55**]. To which place repaired also (according to their appointment) the Duke of Buckingham, and divers noblemen with him beside many knights and other gentlemen. And thereupon the Duke sent word unto the Lord Protector of the being there of a great and honorable company, to move a great matter unto his grace. Whereupon the Protector made difficulty to come out unto them but if he first knew some part of their errand, as though he doubted and partly mistrusted the coming of such a number [**85**] unto him so suddenly, without any warning or knowledge whether they came for good or harm.

Then the Duke when he had showed this to the Mayor and other, that they might thereby see how little the Protector looked for this matter, they sent unto him by the messenger such loving message again, and therewith so humbly besought him to vouchsafe that they might resort to his presence to propose their intent, of which they

[1]Concealed group.
[79]*I.e.*, from the dais at the upper end of the hall.

would unto none other person any part disclose, that at the last he came forth of his chamber; and yet not down unto them but stood above in a gallery over them [**94 SD**], where they might see him and speak to him, as though he would not yet come too near them till he wist what they meant. And thereupon the Duke of Buckingham first made humble petition unto him, on the behalf of them all, that his grace would pardon them and license them to propose unto his grace the intent of their coming, without his displeasure; without which pardon obtained they durst not be bold to move him of that matter.

In which, albeit they meant as much honor to his grace as wealth to all the realm beside, yet were they not sure how his grace would take it; whom they would in no wise offend. Then the Protector (as he was very gentle of himself, and also longed sore to wit what they meant) gave him leave to propose what him liked; verily trusting (for the good mind that he bore them all) none of them anything would intend unto himward wherewith he ought to be grieved. When the Duke had this leave and pardon to speak, then waxed he bold to show him [**117**] their intent and purpose, with all the causes moving them thereunto (as ye before have heard), and finally to beseech his grace that it would like him, of his accustomed goodness and zeal unto the realm, now with his eye of pity to behold the long-continued distress and decay of the same, and to set his gracious hands to redress and amendment thereof.

All which he might well do by taking upon him the crown and governance of this realm [**131**] according to his right and title lawfully descended unto him; and, to the laud of God, profit of the land, and unto his noble grace so much the more honor and less pain, in that never prince reigned upon any people that were so glad to live under his obeisance as the people of this realm under his. When the Protector had heard the proposition he looked very strangely[80] thereat [**141**]; and answered that all were it that he partly knew the things by them alleged to be true, yet such entire love he bore unto King Edward and his children, and so much more regarded his honor in other realms about than the crown of any one (of which he was never desirous), that he could not find in his heart in this point to incline to their desire.

. . . Notwithstanding, he not only pardoned them the motion that they made him but also thanked them for the love and hearty favor

[80]Unfavorably.

they bore him, praying them for his sake to give and bear the same to the Prince. . . .

Upon this answer given, the Duke, by the Protector's license, a little round[81] as well with other noblemen about him as with the Mayor and Recorder of London. And after that (upon like pardon desired and obtained), he showed[82] aloud unto the Protector, for a final conclusion, that the realm was appointed[83] King Edward's line should not any longer reign upon them, both for that they had so far gone that it was now no surety to retreat as for that they thought it for the weal universal to take that way, although they had not yet begun it. Wherefore, if it would like his grace to take the crown upon him, they would humbly beseech him thereunto. If he would give them a resolute answer to the contrary (which they would be loath to hear), then must they needs seek and should not fail to find some other nobleman that would [**216**]. These words much moved the Protector, which else (as every man may wit) would never of likelihood have inclined thereunto.

But when he saw there was none other way but that either he must take it or else he and his both go from it, he said unto the lords and commons [**228**]: ". . . we be content and agree favorably to incline to your petition and request, and (according to the same) here we take upon us the royal estate, preeminence, and kingdom of the two noble realms England and France. . . ."

With this there was a great shout, crying [**240**] "King Richard, King Richard!" . . .

[**732**] For at the consecration of a bishop every man wotteth well by the paying for his bulls that he purposeth to be one, and though he pay for nothing else. And yet must he be twice asked whether he will be bishop or no, and he must twice say nay and the third time take it, as compelled thereunto by his own will. And in a stage play all the people know right well that one playing the Sultan is percase a souter;[m] yet if one should can so little good[n] to show out of season what acquaintance he hath with him and call him by his own name while he standeth in his majesty, one of his tormentors[o] might hap to break his head (and worthy) for marring of the play. And so they said that these matters be

[81]Rounded, whispered.
[82]Stated.
[83]Resolved.
[m]Shoemaker.
[n]Know so little how to behave as.
[o]Executioners.

kings' games, as it were stage plays, and for the more part played upon scaffolds;[p] in which poor men be but the lookers-on. And they that wise be will meddle no further. For they that sometime step up and play with them, when they cannot play their parts, they disorder the play and do themselves no good. . . .

[**733**] On the morrow, being the sixth day of July [1483], the King, with Queen Anne his wife[84] [**1.2**], came down out of the White Hall into the Great Hall at Westminster.

. . . Then both the King and Queen changed them into cloth of gold and ascended to their seats, where the Cardinal of Canterbury and other bishops them crowned [**4.1.33**] according to the custom of the realm, giving him the scepter in the left hand and the ball with the cross in the right hand; and the Queen had the scepter in her right hand and the rod with the dove in her left hand. . . .

[**734**] King Richard, after his coronation, taking his way to Gloucester to visit (in his new honor) the town of which he bore the name of old, devised (as he rode) to fulfill the thing which he before had intended. And forsomuch as his mind gave him that, his nephews living, men would not reckon that he could have right to the realm, he thought therefore without delay to rid them, as though the killing of his kinsmen could amend his cause and make him a kindly king. Whereupon he sent one John Greene (whom he specially trusted) unto Sir Robert Brakenbury, Constable of the Tower, with a letter and credence[85] also that the same Sir Robert should in any wise put the two children to death [**4.2.18**].

This John Greene did his errand unto Brakenbury, kneeling before[86] our Lady in the Tower, who plainly answered that he would never put them to death to die therefor [**24**]. With which answer John Greene returning, recounted the same to King Richard at Warwick, yet in his way. Wherewith he took such displeasure and thought[87] that the same night he said unto a secret page of his [**32**]: "Ah, whom shall a man trust? Those that I have brought up myself, those that I had weened would most surely serve me, even those fail me and at my commandment will do nothing for me." "Sir," quoth his page, "there lieth one on your pallet without that, I dare well say, to do your grace

[p]Stages.
[84]They had been married in 1472.
[85]Document commending the bearer to confidence.
[86]*I.e.,* praying before an image of.
[87]Vexation.

pleasure the thing were right hard that he would refuse." Meaning this by[88] Sir James Tirrel, which was a man of right goodly personage, and for nature's gifts worthy to have served a much better prince if he had well served God and by grace obtained as much truth and good will as he had strength and wit.

The man had an high heart and sore longed upward, not rising yet so fast as he had hoped [**36**], being hindered and kept under by the means of Sir Richard Ratcliffe and Sir William Catesby, which (longing for no more partners of the Prince's favor, and namely[89] not for him whose pride they wist would bear no peer) kept him by secret drifts out of all secret trust; which thing this page well had marked and known. Wherefore, this occasion offered of very special friendship, he took his time to put him forward and by such wise do him good that all the enemies he had (except the devil) could never have done him so much hurt. For upon this page's words King Richard arose (for this communication had he sitting at the draft,[90] a convenient carpet for such a counsel) and came out into the pallet chamber [**65 SD**], on which he found in bed Sir James and Sir Thomas Tirrel, of person like and brethren of blood but nothing of kin in conditions.[91]

[**735**] Then said the King merrily to them: "What, sirs, be ye in bed so soon?" And calling up Sir James broke to him secretly his mind in this mischievous matter, in which he found him nothing strange [**76**]. Wherefore on the morrow he sent him to Brakenbury with a letter by which he was commanded to deliver Sir James all the keys [**1.4.96**] of the Tower for one night, to the end he might there accomplish the King's pleasure in such things as he had given him commandment. After which letter delivered and the keys received, Sir James appointed the night next ensuing to destroy them, devising before and preparing the means. The Prince (as soon as the Protector left that name and took himself as King) had it showed unto him that he should not reign but his uncle should have the crown. At which word the Prince, sore abashed, began to sigh, and said, "Alas, I would my uncle would let me have my life yet, though I lose my kingdom."

Then he that told him the tale used him with good words and put him in the best comfort he could. But forthwith was the Prince and

[88]*I.e.,* meaning by this.
[89]Particularly.
[90]Privy.
[91]Personal qualities.

his brother both shut up and all other removed from them [**3.5.108**], only one (called Black Will or William Slaughter) excepted, set to serve them and see them sure. After which time the Prince never tied his points[92] nor aught raught[93] of himself; but, with that young babe his brother, lingered with thought[94] and heaviness until this traitorous death delivered them of that wretchedness. For Sir James Tirrel devised that they should be murdered in their beds, to the execution whereof he appointed Miles Forrest, one of the four that kept them, a fellow fleshed [**4.3.6**] in murder before time. To him he joined one John Dighton, his own horsekeeper, a big, broad, square, and strong knave.

Then, all the other being removed from them, this Miles Forrest and John Dighton, about midnight (the silly[95] children lying in their beds), came into the chamber and, suddenly lapping them up among the clothes, so to-bewrapped[96] them and entangled them, keeping down by force the featherbed and pillows hard unto their mouths that, within awhile, smothered [**17**] and stifled, their breath failing, they gave up to God their innocent souls into the joys of heaven, leaving to the tormentors[97] their bodies dead in the bed. Which after that the wretches perceived, first by the struggling with the pains of death and after long lying still, to be thoroughly dead, they laid their bodies naked out upon the bed and fetched Sir James to see them; which, upon the sight of them, caused those murderers to bury them at the stair foot, meetly deep in the ground under a great heap of stones.

Then rode Sir James in great haste to King Richard and showed him all the manner of the murder [**1**]; who gave him great thanks and (as some say) there made him knight [**33**]. But he allowed not[98] (as I have heard) the burying in so vile a corner, saying that he would have them buried in a better place because they were a King's sons. Lo the honorable courage[99] of a king! Whereupon they say that a priest of Sir Robert Brakenbury's took up the bodies again and secretly interred them in such place as, by the occasion of his death which only knew it, could never since come to light [**29**]. Very truth

[92]Laces.
[93]Recked, cared.
[94]Grief.
[95]Innocent.
[96]Completely bewrapped.
[97]Executioners.
[98]Approved not of.
[99]Spirit.

is it, and well known, that at such time as Sir James Tirrel was in the Tower, for treason committed against the most famous prince King Henry the Seventh, both Dighton and he were examined and confessed the murder in manner above written; but whither the bodies were removed they could nothing tell [1502].

. . . For I have heard by credible report of such as were secret with his Chamberlain that after this abominable deed done, he [Richard] never had a quiet mind. . . .

He never thought himself sure. Where[100] he went abroad, his eyes whirled about, his body privily fensed,[101] his hand ever upon his dagger, his countenance and manner like one always ready to strike again; he took ill rest anights [**5.3.162**], lay long waking and musing (sore wearied with care and watch),[102] rather slumbered than slept (troubled with fearful dreams [**4.1.85**]), suddenly sometime start up, leapt out of his bed, and ran about the chamber. . . . For hereupon soon after began the conspiracy or rather good confederation between the Duke of Buckingham and many other gentlemen against him.

[**736**] . . . Whereupon at Northampton the Duke met with the Protector himself with three hundred horses, and from thence still continued with him partner of all his devices, till that, after his coronation, they departed[103] (as it seemed) very great friends at Gloucester. From whence, as soon as the Duke came home, he so lightly turned from him and so highly conspired against him that a man would marvel whereof the change grew. And surely the occasion of their variance is of divers men diversly reported.

Some have I heard say that the Duke, a little before his coronation, among other things, required of the Protector the Earl of Hereford's lands, to the which he pretended himself just inheritor. And forsomuch as the title which he claimed by inheritance was somewhat interlaced with the title to the crown by the line of King Henry [the Sixth] before deprived, the Protector conceived such indignation that he rejected the Duke's request with many spiteful and minatory words [**4.2.116**]. Which so wounded his heart with hatred and mistrust that he never after could endure to look aright on King Richard, but ever feared his own life [**124**].

. . . But soon after his coming home to Brecknock [Castle] [**124**],

[100]When.
[101]Ready for defense.
[102]Remaining awake.
[103]Parted.

having there in his custody by the commandment of King Richard Doctor [John] Morton Bishop of Ely, who (as ye before heard) was taken in the Council at the Tower, [he] waxed with him familiar. . . .[q]

[**738**] So the next day the Duke sent for the Bishop and rehearsed to him in manner (for he was both witty and eloquent) all the communication had between them before; and so paused awhile and, after a little season, putting off his bonnet, he said: . . .

[**739**] "For when he [Richard] was once crowned King and in full possession of the whole realm, he cast away his old conditions as the adder doth her skin, verifying the old proverb, 'Honors change manners,' as the parish priest remembereth that he was never parish clerk. For when I myself sued unto him for my part of the Earl of Hereford's lands which his brother King Edward wrongfully detained and withheld from me [**92**], and also required to have the office of the High Constableship of England, as divers of my noble ancestors before this time have had and in long descent continued, in this my first suit showing his good mind toward me, he did not only first delay me and afterward deny me, but gave me such unkind words [**116**], with such taunts and retaunts, yea, in manner check and checkmate, to the uttermost proof of my patience; as though I had never furthered him but hindered him, as though I had put him down and not set him up.

"Yet all these ingratitudes and undeserved unkindnesses I bore closely and suffered patiently and covertly remembered, outwardly dissembling that I inwardly thought; and so, with a painted countenance, I passed the last summer in his company, not without many fair promises but without any good deeds. But when I was credibly informed of the death of the two young innocents, his own natural nephews, contrary to his faith and promise, to the which (God be my judge) I never agreed nor condescended [**24**], O Lord how my veins panted, how my body trembled, and how my heart inwardly grudged! Insomuch that I so abhorred the sight, and much more the company, of him that I could no longer abide in his court except I should be openly revenged; the end whereof was doubtful. . . ."

[**741**] The Bishop, being as witty[104] as the Duke was wily, did not tarry till the Duke's company were assembled but, secretly disguised, in a night departed (to the Duke's great displeasure) and came to his see of Ely, where he found money and friends and so sailed into Flanders, where he did the Earl of Richmond good service [**4.3.46**]. . . .

[q]More's *History* comes to an end shortly after this point.
[104]Wise.

When Reginald Bray had declared his message and privy instruction [from the Duke of Buckingham] to the Countess of Richmond his mistress, no marvel though she were joyous and glad, both of the good news and also for the obtaining of such a high friend in her son's cause as the Duke was. . . . And thereupon she, having in her family at that time (for the preservation of her health) a certain Welshman called Lewis, learned in physic, which for his gravity and experience was well known and much esteemed amongst great estates[r] of the realm, broke her mind to him. . . .

This physician did not long linger to accomplish her desire, but with good diligence repaired to the Queen, being still in the sanctuary at Westminster. And when he saw time propice[105] and convenient for his purpose, he said unto her: . . .

"And first consider what battle, what manslaughter, what mischief hath risen in this realm by the dissension between the two noble Houses of York and Lancaster. Which two families (as I have contrived)[106] if they may be joined in one, I think, yea, and doubt not but your line shall be again restored to the pristinate estate and degree, to your great joy and comfort and to the utter confusion of your mortal enemy the usurper King. You know very well, madam, that of the House of Lancaster the Earl of Richmond is next of blood, who is living and a lusty young bachelor; and to the House of York your daughters now are heirs. If you could agree and invent the mean how to couple your eldest daughter with the young Earl of Richmond in matrimony [**40**], no doubt but the usurper of the realm should be shortly deposed and your heir again to her right restored." . . .

[**742**] In the mean season the Countess of Richmond took into her service Christopher Urswick [**5.5.1**], an honest and wise priest, and (after an oath of him for to be secret taken and sworn) she uttered to him all her mind and counsel, adhibiting[107] to him the more confidence and truth that he all his life had favored and taken part with King Henry the Sixth, and as a special jewel put to her service by Sir Lewis her physician. So the mother, studious for the prosperity of her son, appointed this Christopher Urswick to sail into Brittany to the Earl of Richmond and to declare and reveal to him all pacts and agreements between her and the Queen agreed and concluded [**7**].

[r] Lords.
[105] Propitious.
[106] Conceived.
[107] Giving.

[**743**] . . . The Duke . . . immediately prepared open war against him [King Richard], and persuaded all his complices and partakers[108] that every man in his quarter, with all diligence, should raise up people and make a commotion. And by this means, almost in one moment, Thomas Marquis Dorset came out of sanctuary (where since the beginning of King Richard's days he had continued, whose life by the only help of Sir Thomas Lovell[s] was preserved from all danger and peril in this troublous world) [and] gathered together a great band of men in Yorkshire [**4.4.518**].

Sir Edward Courtenay and Peter his brother, Bishop of Exeter, raised another army in Devonshire and Cornwall [**498**]. In Kent, Richard Guildford and other gentlemen collected a great company of soldiers and openly began war [**503**]. But King Richard (who in the meantime had gotten together a great strength and puissance [**4.3.56**], thinking it not most for his part beneficial to disperse and divide his great army into small branches, and particularly to persecute anyone of the conjuration[109] by himself), determined (all other things being set aside) with his whole puissance to set on the chief head, which was the Duke of Buckingham. And so, removing from London, he took his journey toward Salisbury [**4.4.451**], to the intent that in his journey he might set on the Duke's army, if he might know him in any place encamped or in order of battle arrayed.

The King was scarce two days' journey from Salisbury when the Duke of Buckingham, accompanied with a great power of wild Welshmen [**4.3.47**], whom he (being a man of great courage and sharp speech), in manner against their wills, had rather thereto enforced and compelled by lordly and strait[110] commandment than by liberal wages and gentle demeanor; which thing was the very occasion why they left him desolate and cowardly forsook him. The Duke, with all his power, marched through the forest of Dean, intending to have passed the River Severn at Gloucester and there to have joined his army with the Courtenays and other western men of his confederacy and affinity.[t] Which if he had done, no doubt but King Richard had been in great jeopardy, either of privation of his realm or loss of his life or both.

[108]Supporters.
[s]Rowell.
[109]Conspiracy.
[110]Hard-pressing.
[t]Alliance.

But see the chance.[111] Before he could attain to Severn side, by force of continual rain and moisture the river rose so high that it overflowed all the country adjoining, insomuch that men were drowned in their beds, and houses with the extreme violence were overturned, children were carried about the fields swimming in cradles, beasts were drowned on hills [**4.4.510**]. Which rage of water lasted continually ten days, insomuch that in the country adjoining they call it to this day "the great water" or "the Duke of Buckingham's great water." By this flood the passages were so closed that neither the Duke could come over Severn to his adherents nor they to him. During the which time the Welshmen, lingering idly and without money, victuals, or wages, suddenly scattered and departed and, for all the Duke's fair promises, threatenings, and enforcements, would in no wise either go further nor abide.

The Duke (being thus left almost post alone)[112] was of necessity compelled to fly [**512**] and, in flight, was with this sudden fortune marvelously dismayed; and, being unpurveyed[113] what counsel he should take and what way he should follow, like a man in despair, not knowing what to do, of very trust and confidence, conveyed himself into the house of Humphrey[114] Banister his servant [**H8 2.1.109**], beside Shrewsbury, whom he had tenderly brought up and whom he above all men loved, favored, and trusted; now not doubting but that in his extreme necessity he should find him faithful, secret, and trusty; intending there covertly to lurk till either he might raise again a new army or else shortly to sail into Brittany to the Earl of Richmond. . . .

Now when it was known to his adherents (which were ready to give battle) that his host was scattered and had left him almost alone and was fled and could not be found, they were suddenly amazed and stricken with a sudden fear, that every man, like persons desperate, shifted for himself and fled.

[**744**] . . . Secondarily he [King Richard] made proclamation that what person could show and reveal where the Duke of Buckingham was should be highly rewarded [**R3 4.4.516**]; if he were a bondman, he should be enfranchised and set at liberty; if he were of free blood, he should have a general pardon and be rewarded with a thousand pounds. . . .

[111] Falling out of events.
[112] Entirely alone.
[113] Unprepared beforehand.
[114] Ralph.

While this busy search was diligently applied and put in execution, Humphrey Banister (were it more for fear of life and loss of goods or allured and provoked by the avaricious desire of the thousand pounds), he bewrayed[115] his guest and master to John Mitton, then Sheriff of Shropshire, which suddenly with a strong power of men in harness apprehended the Duke in a little grove adjoining to the mansion of Humphrey Banister [**531**]. . . . The Duke, being by certain of the King's Council diligently upon interrogatories examined what things he knew prejudicial unto the King's person, opened and declared frankly and freely all the conjuration[116] without dissembling or glozing;[117] trusting, because he had truly and plainly revealed and confessed all things that were of him required, that he should have license to speak to the King [**5.1.1**]; which (whether it were to sue for pardon and grace or whether he, being brought to his presence, would have sticked him with a dagger [**H8 1.2.199**], as men then judged) he sore desired and required. But when he had confessed the whole fact[118] and conspiracy, upon All Souls' Day, without arraignment or judgment, he was at Salisbury in the open marketplace, on a new scaffold, beheaded and put to death [**R3 5.1.28**]. . . .

While these things were thus handled and ordered in England, Henry Earl of Richmond prepared an army of five thousand manly Bretons, and forty well-furnished ships. When all things were prepared in areadiness and the day of departing and setting forward was appointed, which was the twelfth day of the month of October [1483], the whole army went on shipboard and hawsed[119] up their sails and with a prosperous wind took the sea [**4.4.434**]. But toward night the wind changed and the weather turned, and so huge and terrible a tempest so suddenly arose that with the very power and strength of the storm, the ships were disparkled,[120] severed, and separated asunder [**521**]; some by force were driven into Normandy, some were compelled to return again into Brittany. The ship wherein the Earl of Richmond was, associate only with one other bark, was all night tossed and turmoiled.

In the morning after (when the rage of the furious tempest was

[115]Betrayed.
[116]Conspiracy.
[117]Extenuation.
[118]Crime.
[119]Raised.
[120]Dispersed.

assuaged and the ire of blustering wind was some deal appeased), about the hour of noon the same day, the Earl approached to the south part of the realm of England, even at the mouth of the haven of Pole, in the county of Dorset, where he might plainly perceive all the seabanks and shores garnished and furnished with men-of-war and soldiers appointed and deputed there to defend[121] his arrival and landing (as before is mentioned). Wherefore he gave strait[122] charge and sore commandment that no person should once presume to take land and go to shore until such time as the whole navy were assembled and come together. And while he tarried and lingered, he sent out a shipboat toward the land side, to know whether they which stood there in such a number, and so well furnished in apparel defensive, were his foes and enemies or else his friends and comforters [**522**].

[**745**] They that were sent to inquire were instantly desired of the men-of-war keeping the coast (which thereof were before instructed and admonished) to descend and take land, affirming that they were appointed by the Duke of Buckingham [**525**] there to await and tarry for the arrival and landing of the Earl of Richmond, and to conduct him safely into the camp where the Duke, not far off, lay encamped with a mighty army and an host of great strength and power; to the intent that the Duke and the Earl, joining in puissances and forces together, might prosecute and chase King Richard, being destitute of men and in manner desperate, and so, by that means and their own labors, to obtain the end of their enterprise which they had before begun.

The Earl of Richmond, suspecting [**526**] their flattering request to be but a fraud (as it was indeed), after he perceived none of his ships to appear in sight, he weighed up his anchors, hawsed up his sails, and, having a prosperous and strainable[123] wind and a fresh gale sent even by God to deliver him from that peril and jeopardy, arrived safe and in all security in the duchy of Normandy, where he (to refresh and solace his soldiers and people) took his recreation by the space of three days and clearly determined with part of his company to pass all by land again into Brittany [**527**].

. . . When he was returned again into Brittany, he was certified by credible information that the Duke of Buckingham had lost his head, and that the Marquis Dorset [**4.1.42, 4.2.48**] and a great num-

[121]Ward off.
[122]Strict.
[123]Violent.

ber of noblemen of England had a little before inquired and searched for him there and were now returned to Vannes.

. . . When they knew that he was safely returned into Brittany, Lord how they rejoiced, for before that time they missed him and knew not in what part of the world to make inquiry or search for him. For they doubted and no less feared lest he had taken land in England and fallen into the hands of King Richard, in whose person they knew well was neither mercy nor compassion.

Wherefore in all speedy manner they galloped toward him and him reverently saluted. . . .

King Richard . . . came this year [1483] to the city [of Exeter], but in very secret manner; whom the Mayor and his brethren in the best manner they could did receive and then presented to him in a purse two hundred nobles which he thankfully accepted. And during his abode there he went about the city and viewed the seat of the same, and at length he came to the castle [**106**]; and, when he understood that it was called Rougemont, suddenly he fell into a dump and (as one astonished) said, "Well, I see my days be not long." He spoke this of a prophecy told him that, when he came once to Richmond, he should not long live after; which fell out in the end to be true, not in respect of this castle but in respect of Henry Earl of Richmond, who the next year following met him at Bosworth Field where he was slain.

[**746**] In this troublous season nothing was more marveled at than that the Lord Stanley had not been taken and reputed as an enemy to the King, considering the working of the Lady Margaret his wife [**94**], mother to the Earl of Richmond. But, forsomuch as the enterprise of a woman was of him reputed of no regard or estimation, and that the Lord Thomas her husband had purged[124] himself sufficiently to be innocent of all doings and attempts by her perpetrated and committed, it was given him in charge to keep her in some secret place at home, without having any servant or company; so that from thenceforth she should never send letter or messenger unto her son, nor any of his friends or confederates, by the which the King might be molested or troubled or any hurt or prejudice might be attempted against his realm and commonalty. Which commandment was awhile put in execution and accomplished, according to his dreadful commandment.

[124]Cleared himself of guilt.

Yet the wild worm[125] of vengeance wavering in his head could not be content with the death of divers gentlemen suspected of treason; but also he must extend his bloody fury against a poor gentleman called [William] Collingbourne for making a small rhyme of three of his unfortunate councillors, which were the Lord Lovell, Sir Richard Ratcliffe his mischievous minion, and Sir William Catesby his secret seducer; which meter or rhyme was thus framed:

The Cat, the Rat, and Lovell our dog
Rule all England under an hog.

Meaning by the hog [**1.3.228**] the dreadful wild boar, which was the King's cognizance. But because the first line ended in *dog* the metrician could not (observing the regiments[126] of meter) end the second verse in *boar* but called the boar an *hog*. This poetical schoolmaster, corrector of briefs[127] and longs, caused Collingbourne to be abbreviated shorter by the head and to be divided into four quarters. . . .

[**749**] While the Earl [of Richmond] was thus attendant in the French court, John Vere Earl of Oxford [**4.5.14**], which (as you have heard before) was by King Edward kept in prison within the castle of Hammes, so persuaded James Blount [**14**], Captain of the same fortress, and Sir John Fortescue, Porter[128] of the town of Calais, that he himself was not only dismissed and set at liberty but they also, abandoning and leaving their fruitful offices, did condescend to go with him into France to the Earl of Richmond and to take his part [1484]. . . .

[**750**] In the mean season King Richard was credibly advertised what promises and oaths the Earl and his confederates had made and sworn together at Rennes, and how by the Earl's means all the Englishmen were passed out of Brittany into France. Wherefore, being sore dismayed and in a manner desperate, because his crafty chevisance[u] took none effect in Brittany, he imagined and devised how to infringe and disturb the Earl's purpose by another mean; so that by the marriage of Lady Elizabeth his niece, he should pretend no claim nor title to the crown [**4.3.40**].

[125]Mad streak.
[126]Rules.
[127]Short syllables.
[128]Gatekeeper.
[u]Device.

. . . [He therefore] determined to reconcile to his favor his brother's wife Queen Elizabeth, either by fair words or liberal promises; firmly believing, her favor once obtained, that she would not stick to commit (and lovingly credit) to him the rule and governance both of her and her daughters; and so by that means the Earl of Richmond of the affinity of his niece should be utterly defrauded and beguiled.

And if no ingenious remedy could be otherwise invented to save the innumerable mischiefs which were even at hand and like to fall if it should happen Queen Anne his wife to depart out of this present life, then he himself would rather take to wife his cousin and niece the Lady Elizabeth than for lack of that affinity the whole realm should run to ruin [**4.2.60, 4.4.409**], as who said that, if he once fell from his estate and dignity, the ruin of the realm must needs shortly ensue and follow. Wherefore he sent to the Queen (being in sanctuary) divers and often messengers, which first should excuse and purge him of all things before against her attempted or procured, and after should so largely promise promotions[129] innumerable and benefits, not only to her but also to her son Lord Thomas Marquis Dorset [**311**], that they should bring her (if it were possible) into some wanhope[130] or (as men say) into a fool's paradise.

The messengers, being men both of wit and gravity, so persuaded the Queen with great and pregnant reasons, and with fair and large promises, that she began somewhat to relent and to give to them no deaf ear, insomuch that she faithfully promised to submit and yield herself fully and frankly to the King's will and pleasure [**4.4.428**]. And so she, putting in oblivion the murder of her innocent children, the infamy and dishonor spoken by[131] the King her husband, the living in adultery laid to her charge, the bastarding of her daughters, forgetting also the faithful promise and open oath made to the Countess of Richmond mother to the Earl Henry, blinded by avaricious affection and seduced by flattering words, first delivered into King Richard's hands her five daughters, as lambs once again committed to the custody of the ravenous wolf.

After, she sent letters to the Marquis her son (being then at Paris with the Earl of Richmond) willing him in any wise to leave the Earl and without delay to repair into England, where for him were

[129] Preferments.
[130] Vain hope.
[131] About.

provided great honors and honorable promotions, ascertaining[132] him further that all offenses on both parts were forgotten and forgiven, and both he and she highly incorporated in the King's heart. Surely the inconstancy of this woman were much to be marveled at [**431**], if all women had been found constant; but let men speak, yet women of the very bond of nature will follow their own sex.

[**751**] . . . After this he [Richard] procured a common[133] rumor (but he would not have the author known) to be published and spread abroad among the common people that the Queen was dead [**4.2.50**]; to the intent that she, taking some conceit of this strange fame, should fall into some sudden sickness or grievous malady; and to prove,[134] if afterward she should fortune by that or any other ways to lose her life, whether the people would impute her death to the thought of sickness or thereof would lay the blame to him.

. . . But howsoever that it fortuned, either by inward thought and pensiveness of heart or by infection of poison (which is affirmed to be most likely), within few days after, the Queen departed out of this transitory life [**4.3.39**] and was with due solemnity buried in the church of Saint Peter at Westminster [1485]. This is the same Anne [Neville], one of the daughters of the Earl of Warwick, which (as you have heard before) at the request of Louis the French King was married[v] to Prince Edward son to King Henry the Sixth [**1.2.10**]. The King, thus (according to his long desire) loosed out of the bounds of matrimony, began to cast a foolish fancy to Lady Elizabeth his niece, making much suit to have her joined with him in lawful matrimony [**43**]. . . .

Amongst the noblemen whom he most mistrusted these were the principal: Thomas Lord Stanley, Sir William Stanley his brother, Gilbert Talbot, and six hundred other; of whose purposes although King Richard were ignorant, yet he gave neither confidence nor credence to any one of them, and least of all to the Lord Stanley [**4.4.490**] because he was joined in matrimony with the Lady Margaret, mother to the Earl of Richmond [**4.2.89**], as afterward apparently ye may perceive. For when the said Lord Stanley would have departed into his country, to visit his family and to recreate and refresh his spirits (as he openly said, but the truth was, to the

[132] Assuring.
[133] Public.
[134] Ascertain.
[v] Betrothed.

intent to be in a perfect readiness to receive the Earl of Richmond at his first arrival in England), the King in no wise would suffer him to depart before he had left as an hostage in the court George Stanley Lord Strange, his first begotten son and heir [**4.4.495**]. . . .

[**752**] The Earl of Richmond . . . determined no longer to protract and defer the time but with all diligence and celerity attempted his begun enterprise. And so, obtaining of King Charles a small crew of men and borrowing certain sums of money of him and of divers other his private friends, for the which he left as debtor (or, more likely, as a pledge or hostage) Lord Thomas Marquis Dorset (whom he half mistrusted) and Sir John Bourchier, he departed from the French court and came to the city of Rouen.

While he tarried there, making provision at Harfleur in the mouth of the river of Seine for all things necessary for his navy, tidings were brought to him that King Richard (being without children and now a widower) intended shortly to marry the Lady Elizabeth his brother's daughter [**4.2.60**], and to prefer[135] the Lady Cecily her sister to a man found in a cloud, and of an unknown lineage and family. He took these news as a matter of no small moment; and so (all things considered) it was of no less importance than he took it for. For this thing only took away from him and all his companions their hope and courage that they had to obtain an happy enterprise. And therefore no marvel though it nipped him at the very stomach,[136] when he thought that by no possibility he might attain the marriage of any of King Edward's daughters, which was the strongest foundation of his building; by reason whereof he judged that all his friends in England would abandon and shrink from him.

[**753**] . . . The Earl of Richmond, because he would no longer linger and weary his friends, living continually between hope and fear, determined in all convenient haste to set forward, and carried to his ships armor, weapons, victuals, and all other ordnances[137] expedient for war.

After that all things were in readiness, the Earl, being accompanied only with two thousand men and a small number of ships, weighed up his anchors and hawsed up his sails in the month of August [1485], and sailed from Harfleur with so prosperous a wind that, the seventh day after his departure, he arrived in Wales in the

[135]Offer.
[136]Spirit.
[137]Military supplies.

evening at a place called Milford Haven and incontinent took land [**4.4.533**].

. . . For Arnold Butler . . . declared to him that the Pembrokians were ready to serve and give their attendance on their natural and immediate lord, Jasper Earl of Pembroke [**4.5.14**]. . . .

Then the Earl [of Richmond] advanced forward in good haste, making no repose or abode in any one place. . . . And suddenly he was by his espials[138] ascertained that Sir Walter Herbert [**12**] and Rice ap Thomas were in harness before him ready to encounter with his army and to stop their passage. Wherefore, like a valiant captain, he first determined to set on them and either to destroy or to take them into his favor; and after, with all his power and puissance, to give battle to his mortal enemy King Richard. But to the intent his friends should know in what readiness he was, and how he proceeded forward, he sent of his most secret and faithful servants with letters and instructions to the Lady Margaret his mother, to the Lord Stanley and his brother [Sir William Stanley], to Sir Gilbert Talbot, and to other his trusty friends; declaring to them that he, being succored and holpen with the aid and relief of his friends, intended to pass over the river of Severn at Shrewsbury and so to pass directly to the city of London.

Wherefore he required them (as his special trust and confidence was fixed in the hope of their fidelity) that they would meet him by the way with all diligent preparation, to the intent that he and they, at time and place convenient, might communicate together the deepness of all his doubtful and weighty business. When the messengers were dispatched with these commandments and admonitions, he marched forward toward Shrewsbury; and in his passing, there met and saluted him Rice ap Thomas with a goodly band of Welshmen; which, making an oath and promise to the Earl, submitted himself wholly to his order and commandment [**15**].

. . . In the evening the same day came to him Sir Gilbert Talbot [**13**], with the whole power of the young Earl of Shrewsbury, then being in ward;[139] which were accounted to the number of two thousand men. And thus, his power increasing, he arrived at the town of Stafford and there paused.

There also came Sir William Stanley [**13**] accompanied with a few persons. And after that the Earl and he had commoned no long time

[138]Scouts.
[139]A minor under control of a guardian.

together, he reverted to his soldiers, whom he had assembled together, to serve the Earl; which from thence departed to Lichfield and lay without the walls in his camp all the night. The next morning he entered into the town and was with all honor like a prince received. A day or two before, the Lord Stanley, having in his band almost five thousand men, lodged in the same town but, hearing that the Earl of Richmond was marching thitherward, gave to him place, dislodging him and his, and repaired to a town called Aderston,[w] there abiding the coming of the Earl. And this wily fox did this act to avoid all suspicion on King Richard's part.

[**754**] For the Lord Stanley was afraid lest, if he should seem openly to be a fautor[140] or aider to the Earl his son-in-law before the day of the battle, that King Richard (which yet utterly did not put in him diffidence[141] and mistrust) would put to some cruel death his son and heir apparent George Lord Strange [**4**], whom King Richard (as you have heard before) kept with him as a pledge or hostage to the intent that the Lord Stanley his father should attempt nothing prejudicial to him. . . .

Wherefore he [Richard] sent to John Duke of Norfolk, Henry Earl of Northumberland, Thomas Earl of Surrey, and to other of his especial and trusty friends of the nobility, which he judged more to prefer and esteem his wealth[142] and honor than their own riches and private commodity,[x] willing them to muster and view all their servants and tenants, and to elect and choose the most courageous and active persons of the whole number, and with them to repair to his presence with all speed and diligence.

. . . Then he (environed with his guard), with a frowning countenance and cruel visage, mounted on a great white courser [**5.3.64**], . . . he with great pomp entered the town of Leicester [**5.2.12**] after the sun set. . . .

The Earl of Richmond raised his camp and departed from Lichfield to the town of Tamworth [**13**].

. . . Yet he was not a little afeard because he could in no wise be assured of his father-in-law Thomas Lord Stanley, which, for fear of the destruction of the Lord Strange his son (as you have heard)

[w]Admaston (?).
[140]Partisan.
[141]Distrust.
[142]Well-being.
[x]Advantage.

as yet inclined to neither party. For if he had gone to the Earl, and that notified to King Richard, his son had been shortly executed [**4.5.4**].

[**755**]. . . This excuse made, he [Richmond] privily departed again from his host to the town of Aderston, where the Lord Stanley and Sir William his brother [**13**] with their bands were abiding. There the Earl came first to his father-in-law [**5.3.82**] in a little close,[143] where he saluted him and Sir William his brother; and, after divers and friendly embracings [**99**], each rejoiced of the state of other and suddenly were surprised[144] with great joy, comfort, and hope of fortunate success in all their affairs and doings. Afterward they consulted together how to give battle to King Richard if he would abide, whom they knew not to be[145] far off with an huge host.

. . . In the mean season King Richard, which was appointed now to finish his last labor by the very divine justice and providence of God (which called him to condign punishment for his mischievous deserts), marched to a place meet for two battles[146] to encounter by a village called Bosworth, not far from Leicester; and there he pitched his field[147] [**1**] on a hill called Anne Beame,[148] refreshed his soldiers, and took his rest [**79**].

The fame went that he had the same night a dreadful and terrible dream [**119**], for it seemed to him, being asleep, that he did see divers images like terrible devils, which pulled and haled him, not suffering him to take any quiet or rest. The which strange vision [had] not so suddenly struck his heart with a sudden fear but it stuffed his head and troubled his mind with many busy and dreadful imaginations [**180**]. For incontinent after, his heart being almost damped, he prognosticated before the doubtful chance of the battle to come, not using the alacrity and mirth of mind and countenance [**73**] as he was accustomed to do before he came toward the battle. And lest that it might be suspected that he was abashed for fear of his enemies, and for that cause looked so piteously, he recited and declared to his familiar friends in the morning his wonderful vision and fearful dream [**213**].

[143]Courtyard.
[144]Overcome.
[145]*I.e.,* to be not.
[146]Armies.
[147]Camp.
[148]Anne of Bohemia (Richard II's first wife).

But I think this was no dream but a punction[149] and prick of his sinful conscience [**180**]; for the conscience is so much more charged and aggrieved as the offense is greater and more heinous in degree. . . .

Now to return again to our purpose. The next day after, King Richard, being furnished with men and all habiliments of war, bringing all his men out of their camp into the plain, ordered his foreward[150] in a marvelous length [**294**], in which he appointed both horsemen and footmen, to the intent to imprint in the hearts of them that looked afar off a sudden terror and deadly fear for the great multitude of the armed soldiers; and in the forefront he placed the archers [**296**] like a strong fortified trench or bulwark. Over this battle[151] was Captain John Duke of Norfolk, with whom was Thomas Earl of Surrey his son [**297**]. After this long vanguard followed King Richard himself, with a strong company of chosen and approved men-of-war, having horsemen for wings on both sides of his battle [**300**].

After that the Earl of Richmond was departed from the communication of his friends (as you have heard before), he began to be of a better stomach and of a more valiant courage, and with all diligence pitched his field just by the camp of his enemies; and there he lodged that night [**118**]. In the morning betimes,[152] he caused his men to put on their armor and apparel themselves ready to fight and give battle [**237**].

. . . The Earl of Richmond himself, with aid of the Lord Stanley, governed the battle, accompanied with the Earl of Pembroke, having a good company of horsemen and a small number of footmen. For all his whole number exceeded not five thousand men, beside the power of the Stanleys, whereof three thousand were in the field under the standard of Sir William Stanley. The King's number was double so much and more [**11**]. When both these armies were thus ordered and all men ready to set forward, King Richard called his chieftains together and to them said as followeth. . . .

[**756**] "And although in the adeption[153] and obtaining of the garland I, being seduced and provoked by sinister counsel and diabolical temptation, did commit a wicked and detestable act, yet I have with

[149]Puncture.
[150]Vanguard.
[151]Battalion.
[152]Early.
[153]Attainment.

strait penance and salt tears (as I trust) expiated and clearly purged the same offense; which abominable crime I require you of friendship as clearly[154] to forget as I daily remember to deplore and lament the same.

". . . I doubt not but you know how the devil (continual enemy to human nature, disturber of concord, and sower of sedition) hath entered into the heart of an unknown Welshman (whose father I never knew nor him personally saw), exciting him to aspire and covet our realm, crown, and dignity, and thereof clearly to deprive and spoil us and our posterity. Ye see further how a company of traitors, thieves, outlaws, and runagates[155] of our own nation be aiders and partakers of his feat and enterprise, ready at hand to overcome and oppress us.

"You see also what a number of beggarly Bretons and faint-hearted Frenchmen be with him arrived to destroy us, our wives [**322**], and children. . . .

"And to begin with the Earl of Richmond, captain of this rebellion, he is a Welsh milksop [**326**], a man of small courage and of less experience in martial acts and feats of war [**272**]; brought up by my brother's[156] means [**325**] and mine, like a captive in a close cage, in the court of Francis Duke of Brittany. . . .

"And as for the Frenchmen and Bretons, their valiantness is such that our noble progenitors and your valiant parents have them oftener vanquished and overcome in one month than they in the beginning imagined possible to compass and finish in a whole year. . . ."

[**757**] This exhortation encouraged all such as favored him, but such as were present (more for dread than love) kissed them openly whom they inwardly hated. Other swore outwardly to take part with such whose death they secretly compassed and inwardly imagined. Other promised to invade the King's enemies; which fled and fought with fierce courage against the King [**5.2.20**]. Other stood still and looked on, intending to take part with the victors and overcomers. . . .

When the Earl of Richmond knew by his foreriders that the King was so near embattled, he rode about his army from rank to rank and from wing to wing, giving comfortable words to all men; and,

[154]Completely.

[155]Fugitives.

[156]Edward IV's (see pp. 216–17 above); Shakespeare followed the erroneous reading *moothers* (here emended).

that finished (being armed at all pieces, saving his helmet), mounted on a little hill so that all his people might see and behold him perfectly, to their great rejoicing. For he was a man of no great stature but so formed and decorated with all gifts and lineaments of nature that he seemed more an angelical creature than a terrestrial personage. His countenance and aspect was cheerful and courageous, his hair yellow like the burnished gold, his eyes gray, shining, and quick; prompt and ready in answering, but of such sobriety that it could never be judged whether he were more dull than quick in speaking (such was his temperance). Now when he had overlooked his army over every side, he paused awhile and, after, with a loud voice and bold spirit, spoke to his companions these or the like words following.

". . . In the which [quarrel] I doubt not but God will rather aid us (yea and fight [**5.3.241**] for us) than see us vanquished and overthrown by such as neither fear him nor his laws, nor yet regard justice or honesty.

"Our cause is so just that no enterprise can be of more virtue, both by the laws divine and civil. For what can be a more honest, goodly, or godly quarrel than to fight against a captain being an homicide [**247**] and murderer of his own blood or progeny, an extreme destroyer of his nobility, and, to his and our country and the poor subjects of the same, a deadly mallet, a fiery brand, and a burden intolerable?

". . . Beside this, I assure you that there be yonder, in the great battle, men brought thither for fear and not for love, soldiers by force compelled and not with good will assembled, persons which desire rather the destruction than salvation of their master and captain, and, finally, a multitude whereof the most part will be our friends and the least part our enemies.

[**758**] ". . . What virtue is in him which was the confusion of his brother and murderer of his nephews? What mercy is in him that slayeth his trusty friends as well as his extreme enemies?

". . . Therefore labor for your gain and sweat for your right. While we were in Brittany we had small livings and little plenty of wealth or welfare; now is the time come to get abundance of riches and copy[157] of profit, which is the reward of your service and merit of your pains.

[157]Copiousness.

". . . And this one thing I assure you, that in so just and good a cause and so notable a quarrel, you shall find me this day rather a dead carrion upon the cold ground [**267**] than a free prisoner on a carpet in a lady's chamber.

". . . And therefore, in the name of God and Saint George [**271**], let every man courageously advance forth [**265**] his standard!"

. . . Between both armies there was a great marsh then (but at this present, by reason of ditches cast, it is grown to be firm ground), which the Earl of Richmond left on his right hand for this intent that it should be on that side a defense for his part; and in so doing he had the sun at his back and in the faces of his enemies. When King Richard saw the Earl's company was passed the marsh [**346**], he did command with all haste to set upon them. Then the trumpets sounded and the soldiers shouted, and the King's archers courageously let fly their arrows. The Earl's bowmen stood not still but paid them home again.

[**759**] . . . While the two forewards thus mortally fought, each intending to vanquish and convince[158] the other, King Richard was admonished by his explorators and espials that the Earl of Richmond (accompanied with a small number of men-of-arms) was not far off. And as he approached and marched toward him, he perfectly knew his personage by certain demonstrations and tokens which he had learned and known of others that were able to give him full information. Now, being inflamed with ire and vexed with outrageous malice, he put his spurs to his horse and rode out of the side of the range of his battle, leaving the vanguard fighting; and like a hungry lion ran with spear in rest toward him. The Earl of Richmond perceived well the King furiously coming toward him, and because the whole hope of his wealth and purpose was to be determined by battle, he gladly proffered to encounter with him body to body and man to man.

King Richard set on so sharply at the first brunt[159] that he overthrew the Earl's standard and slew Sir William Brandon [**27**] his standard-bearer (which was father to Sir Charles Brandon, by King Henry the Eighth created Duke of Suffolk), and matched hand to hand with Sir John Cheyney, a man of great force and strength which would have resisted him but the said John was by him manfully overthrown. And so, he making open passage by dint of sword

[158]Conquer.
[159]Attack.

as he went forward, the Earl of Richmond withstood his violence and kept him at the sword's point, without advantage, longer than his companions either thought or judged; which, being almost in despair of victory, were suddenly recomforted by Sir William Stanley, which came to his succors with three thousand tall[160] men. At which very instant, King Richard's men were driven back and fled, and he himself, manfully fighting in the middle of his enemies, was slain [**5.5 SD**]; and (as he worthily had deserved) came to a bloody death as he had led a bloody life.

. . . In this battle died few above the number of a thousand persons; and of the nobility were slain John Duke of Norfolk [**13**], which was warned by divers to refrain from the field, insomuch that, the night before he should set forward toward the King, one wrote this rhyme upon his gate [**5.3.304**]:

> Jack of Norfolk, be not too bold,
> For Diccon thy master is bought and sold.

Yet all this notwithstanding, he regarded more his oath, his honor, and promise made to King Richard, like a gentleman; and, as a faithful subject to his prince, absented not himself from his master, but as he faithfully lived under him, so he manfully died with him, to his great fame and laud [**5.4.1**]. . . .

There were slain, beside him, Walter Lord Ferrers of Chartley [**5.5.13**], Sir Richard Ratcliffe, and Robert Brakenbury [**14**] Lieutenant of the Tower; and not many gentlemen more. Sir William Catesby, learned in the laws of the realm and one of the chief counselors to the late King, with divers other were two days after beheaded at Leicester. . . . Of captives and prisoners there were a great number. For after the death of King Richard was known and published, every man, in manner unarming himself and casting away his habiliments of war, meekly submitted themselves to the obeisance and rule of the Earl of Richmond [**17**]; of the which the more part had gladly so done in the beginning if they might have conveniently escaped from King Richard's espials, which, having as clear eyes as Lynx[y] and open ears as Midas, ranged and searched in every quarter [**5.3.222**].

Amongst these was Henry the fourth Earl of Northumberland [**68**], which (whether it was by the commandment of King Richard putting

[160]Brave.
[y]Lynceus the Argonaut.

diffidence in him or he did it for the love and favor that he bore unto the Earl) stood still with a great company and intermitted not in the battle; which was incontinently received into favor and made of the Council. . . . On the Earl of Richmond's part were slain scarce one hundred persons, among whom the principal was Sir William Brandon his standard-bearer. This battle was fought at Bosworth in Leicestershire, the two and twentieth day of August in the year of our Redemption 1485. The whole conflict endured little above two hours.

King Richard (as the fame went) might have escaped and gotten safeguard by fleeing. For when they which were next[161] about his person saw and perceived at the first joining of the battle the soldiers faintly and nothing courageously to set on their enemies, and not only that but also that some withdrew themselves privily out of the press and departed, they began to suspect fraud and to smell treason; and not only exhorted but determinately advised him to save himself by flight. And when the loss of the battle was imminent and apparent, they brought to him a swift and a light horse to convey him away [**5.4.8**]. He, which was not ignorant of the grudge and ill will that the common people bore toward him, casting away all hope of fortunate success and happy chance to come, answered (as men say) that on that day he would make an end of all battles or else there finish his life [**9**]. Such a great audacity and such a stomach reigned in his body. . . .

[**760**] When the Earl had thus obtained victory and slain his mortal enemy, he kneeled down and rendered to almighty God his hearty thanks with devout and godly orisons, beseeching His goodness to send him grace to advance and defend the Catholic faith and to maintain justice and concord amongst his subjects and people, by God now to his governance committed and assigned. Which prayer finished, he, replenished with incomparable gladness, ascended up to the top of a little mountain where he not only praised and lauded his valiant soldiers but also gave unto them his hearty thanks, with promise of condign recompense for their fidelity and valiant facts;[162] willing and commanding all the hurt and wounded persons to be cured, and the dead carcasses to be delivered to the sepulture [**5.5.15**]. Then the people rejoiced and clapped their hands, crying up to heaven, "King Henry, King Henry!"

When the Lord Stanley saw the good will and gladness of the

[161]Nearest.
[162]Deeds.

people, he took the crown of King Richard (which was found amongst the spoil in the field) and set it on the Earl's head [**6**], as though he had been elected King by the voice of the people, as in ancient times past in divers realms it hath been accustomed; and this was the first sign and token of his good luck and felicity. I must put you here in remembrance how that King Richard (putting some diffidence in the Lord Stanley) had with him as an hostage the Lord Strange his eldest son; which Lord Stanley (as ye have heard before) joined not at the first with his son-in-law's army for fear the King would have slain the Lord Strange his heir.

When King Richard was come to Bosworth, he sent a pursuivant[163] to the Lord Stanley commanding him to advance forward with his company and to come to his presence [**5.3.343**]; which thing if he refused to do, he swore by Christ's passion that he would strike off his son's head before he dined. The Lord Stanley answered the pursuivant that if the King did so, he had more sons alive; and as to come to him, he was not then so determined. When King Richard heard this answer he commanded the Lord Strange incontinent to be beheaded, which was at that very same season when both the armies had sight each of other. But the counselors of King Richard pondered the time and cause (knowing also the Lord Strange to be innocent of his father's offense), and persuaded the King that it was now time to fight and no time to execute.

Besides that, they advised him to keep the Lord Strange as prisoner till the battle were ended, and then at leisure his pleasure might be accomplished [**347**]. So (as God would) King Richard broke his holy oath and the lord was delivered to the keepers of the King's tents to be kept as prisoner. Which when the field was done and their master slain, and proclamation made to know where the child was, they submitted themselves as prisoners to the Lord Strange; and he gently[164] received them and brought them to the new-proclaimed King where, of him and of his father, he was received with great joy [**5.5.11**]. After this the whole camp removed with bag and baggage.

The same night, in the evening, King Henry with great pomp came to the town of Leicester, where, as well for the refreshing of his people and soldiers as for preparing all things necessary for his journey toward London, he rested and reposed himself two days. In the mean season the dead corpse of King Richard was as shamefully

[163]Royal messenger.
[164]Courteously.

carried to the town of Leicester as he gorgeously (the day before) with pomp and pride departed out of the same town. For his body was naked and despoiled to the skin, and nothing left about him, not so much as a clout to cover his privy members, and was trussed behind a pursuivant-of-arms,[165] one Blanch Senglier or White Boar, like a hog or calf, his head and arms hanging on the one side of the horse and his legs on the other side; and all besprinkled with mire and blood, he was brought to the Gray Friars' Church within the town and there lay like a miserable spectacle.

But surely, considering his mischievous acts and ungracious doings, men made wonder at such a caitiff[166] who, although he deserved no burial place either in church or churchyard, chapel or chancel, but otherwise to have been bestowed, yet in the said church he was with no less funeral pomp and solemnity interred than he would to be done at the burial of his innocent nephews whom he caused cruelly to be murdered and unnaturally killed. . . . He reigned two years, two months, and one day–too long by six and twenty months and four and twenty hours in most men's opinions to whom his name and presence was as sweet and delectable as his doings princely and his person amiable.

As he was small and little of statue, so was he of body greatly deformed, the one shoulder higher than the other. His face was small, but his countenance cruel and such that at the first aspect a man would judge it to savor and smell of malice, fraud, and deceit. When he stood musing he would bite and chew busily his nether lip [**4.2.27**], as who said that his fierce nature in his cruel body always chafed, stirred, and was ever unquiet. Beside that, the dagger which he wore he would (when he studied) with his hand pluck up and down in the sheath to the midst, never drawing it fully out. He was of a ready, pregnant, and quick wit, wily to feign and apt to dissemble. He had a proud mind and an arrogant stomach, the which accompanied him even to his death, rather choosing to suffer the same by dint of sword than, being forsaken and left helpless of his unfaithful companions, to preserve by cowardly flight such a frail and uncertain life which, by malice, sickness, or condign punishment, was like shortly to come to confusion. . . .

[**762**] King Henry, having thus got the victory at Bosworth and slain his mortal enemy there in the field, did send before his depar-

[165] Heraldic officer.
[166] Villain.

ture from Leicester Sir Robert Willoughby, knight, to the manor of Sheriff Hutton in the county of York for Edward Plantagenet Earl of Warwick, son and heir to George Duke of Clarence, then being of the age of fifteen years; whom King Richard had kept there as prisoner [**4.3.36**] during the time of his usurped reign. Sir Robert Willoughby, receiving the young Earl of the Constable of that castle, conveyed him to London, where he was shut up in the Tower for doubt lest some unquiet and evil-disposed persons might invent some occasion of new trouble by this young gentleman; and therefore King Henry thought good to have him sure. . . .

[**763**] Now although by this means all things seemed to be brought in good and perfect order, yet there lacked a wrest[167] to the harp to set all the strings in a monochord and perfect tune, which was the matrimony to be finished between the King and the Lady Elizabeth, daughter to King Edward. Which, like a good prince, according to his oath and promise, he did both solemnize and consummate shortly after, that is to say on the eighteenth day of January [1486]. By reason of which marriage peace was thought to descend out of heaven into England, considering that the lines of Lancaster and York were now brought into one knot and connexed together, of whose two bodies one heir might succeed to rule and enjoy the whole monarchy and realm of England [**5.5.27**].

[**787**] . . . Which Earl of Warwick had been kept in prison [**4.3.36**] within the Tower almost from his tender years, that is to say from the first year of the King to this fifteenth year, out of all company of men and sight of beasts, insomuch that he could not discern a goose from a capon.

. . . [Accused of supporting Perkin Warbeck], Edward Plantagenet, the forenamed Earl of Warwick, . . . submitted himself to the King's mercy; and, upon his confession, had his judgment and, according thereunto, the eight and twentieth day of November in the year 1499, was brought to the scaffold on the Tower Hill and there beheaded.

[167]Tuning-key.

Henry VIII

[796][1] This year [1509] was Thomas Ruthall made Bishop of Durham by Henry the Seventh.

. . . To whom . . . the King gave in charge to write a book of the whole estate of the kingdom.

Afterward, the King commanded Cardinal Wolsey to go to this Bishop and to bring the book away with him to deliver to his majesty. But see the mishap! . . . For this Bishop, having written two books (the one to answer the King's command and the other entreating of his own private affairs) did bind them both after one sort, in vellum, just of one length, breadth, and thickness. . . .

Now when the Cardinal came to demand the book due to the King, the Bishop unadvisedly commanded his servant to bring him the book bound in white vellum lying in his study in such a place. The servant, doing accordingly, brought forth one of those books so bound, being the book entreating of the state of the Bishop, and delivered the same unto his master, who, receiving it (without further consideration or looking on), gave it to the Cardinal to bear unto the King [**3.2.121**]. The Cardinal, having the book, went from the Bishop, and after (in his study by himself), understanding the contents thereof, he greatly rejoiced, having now occasion (which he long sought for) offered unto him to bring the Bishop into the King's disgrace.

Wherefore he went forthwith to the King, delivered the book into his hands, and briefly informed the King of the contents thereof; putting further into the King's head that, if at any time he were destitute of a mass of money, he should not need to seek further therefor than to the coffers of the Bishop, who by the tenor of his own book had accounted his proper riches and substance to the value of a hundred thousand pounds [**211**]. . . .

[1]References to *H8* outside this section may be found at pp. 252 and 253.

[**799**] After the death of the noble prince Henry the Seventh, his son Henry the Eighth began his reign the two and twentieth day of April in the year of the world 5475, after the birth of our Saviour 1509, and in the eighteenth year of his age, in the sixteenth year of Maximilian then being Emperor, in the eleventh year of Louis the Twelfth that then reigned in France, and in the twentieth year of King James the Fourth as then ruling over the Scots. . . .

[**800**] After that the funerals of the said late King were once ended, great preparation was made for the coronation of the new King, which was appointed on Midsummer Day next ensuing. During the time of which preparation the King was advised by some of his counsel to take to wife the Lady Katherine [of Aragon], late wife to his brother Prince Arthur, lest she, having so great a dowry as was appointed to her, might marry out of the realm; which should be to his hindrance. The King, being hereto persuaded, espoused the said Lady Katherine the third day of June [1509], the which marriage was dispensed with[2] by Pope Julius [the Second] at the suit of her father King Ferdinand. . . .

[**850**] During this time [1519] remained in the French court divers young gentlemen of England; and they with the French King rode daily disguised through Paris, throwing eggs, stones, and other foolish trifles at the people; which light demeanor of a King was much discommended and jested at [**1.3.1**]. And when these young gentlemen came again into England, they were all French in eating, drinking, and apparel, yea and in French vices and brags, so that all the estates[3] of England were by them laughed at, the ladies and gentlewomen were dispraised, so that nothing by them was praised but if it were after the French turn; which after turned them to displeasure, as you shall hear. . . .

[**852**] After this feast ended, the King came to Richmond and so to Greenwich, and there lay all May. In which month the King's Council secretly commoned[4] together of the King's gentleness[5] and liberality to all persons; by the which they perceived that certain young men in his Privy Chamber, not regarding his estate or degree, were so familiar and homely[6] with him that they forgot themselves. . . .

[2]Condoned by dispensation.
[3]Lords.
[4]Talked.
[5]Courtesy.
[6]Intimate.

To whom the King answered that he had chosen them of his Council, both for the maintenance of his honor and for the defense of all things that might blemish the same; wherefore, if they saw any about him misuse themselves, he committed it unto their reformation [**19**]. Then the King's Council caused the Lord Chamberlain to call before them divers of the privy chamber (which had been in the French court), and banished them the court for divers considerations, laying nothing particularly to their charges; and they that had offices were commanded to go to their offices. Which discharge out of court grieved sore the hearts of these young men, which were called the King's minions.

[**853**] The French King [Francis the First], desirous to continue the friendship lately begun betwixt him and the King of England, made means unto the Cardinal [Wolsey] that they might in some convenient place come to an interview together, that he might have further knowledge of King Henry and likewise King Henry of him [1520]. But the fame went that the Cardinal desired greatly of himself that the two Kings might meet; who, measuring by his will what was convenient, thought it should make much with his glory if, in France also, at some high assembly of noblemen, he should be seen in his vain pomp and show of dignity [**1.1.163**]. He therefore breaketh with the King of that matter [**164**], declaring how honorable, necessary, and convenient it should be for him to gratify his friend therein; and thus with his persuasions the King began to conceive an earnest desire to see the French King, and thereupon appointed to go over to Calais and so in the marches of Guines to meet with him.

. . . Also it was appointed that the King of England and the French King, in a camp between Ardres and Guines [**7**], with eighteen aides, should in June next ensuing abide all comers, being gentlemen, at the tilt, at tourney, and at barriers; whereof proclamation was made [**34**] by Orleans King-of-Arms[7] of France here in the court of England, and by Clarenceaux King-of-Arms of England in the court of France, and in the court of Burgundy, and in divers other courts and places in Almaine[8] and Italy. . . .

Moreover, now that it was concluded that the Kings of England and France should meet (as ye have heard), then both the Kings committed the order and manner of their meeting, and how many days the same should continue and what preeminence each should give to other,

[7]Chief herald.
[8]Germany (including the Low Countries).

unto the Cardinal of York [**51**], which, to set all things in a certainty, made an instrument [**169**] containing an order and direction concerning the premises by him devised and appointed. . . .

[**855**] The peers of the realm (receiving letters to prepare themselves to attend the King in this journey, and no apparent necessary cause expressed why nor wherefore) seemed to grudge that such a costly journey should be taken in hand, to their importunate charges and expenses, without consent of the whole board of the Council [**74**]. But namely[9] [Edward Stafford] the Duke of Buckingham (being a man of a lofty courage[10] but not most liberal) sore repined that he should be at so great charges for his furniture forth at this time, saying that he knew not for what cause so much money should be spent about the sight of a vain talk to be had, and communication to be ministered of things of no importance [**85**]. Wherefore he sticked not to say that it was an intolerable matter to obey such a vile and importunate person.

The Duke indeed could not abide the Cardinal [**52**], and specially he had of late conceived an inward malice against him for Sir William Bulmer's cause whose trouble was only procured by the Cardinal, who first caused him to be cast in prison. Now such grievous words as the Duke thus uttered against him came to the Cardinal's ear, whereupon he cast before hand all ways possible to have him in a trip, that he might cause him to leap headless. But because he doubted[11] his friends, kinsmen, and allies, and chiefly the Earl of Surrey Lord Admiral (which had married the Duke's daughter), he thought good first to send him somewhither out of the way lest he might cast a trump in his way [**2.1.44**]. There was great enmity betwixt the Cardinal and the Earl for that, on a time, when the Cardinal took upon him to check[12] the Earl, he had like to have thrust his dagger into the Cardinal.

At length there was occasion offered him to compass his purpose by occasion of the Earl of Kildare his coming out of Ireland. For the Cardinal, knowing he was well provided of money, sought occasion to fleece him of part thereof. The Earl of Kildare, being unmarried, was desirous to have an Englishwoman to wife; and for that he was a suitor to a widow, contrary to the Cardinal's mind, he accused him to the King of that he had not borne himself uprightly in his office in Ireland, where he was the King's lieutenant. Such accusations were framed

[9]Particularly.
[10]Disposition.
[11]Feared.
[12]Rebuke.

against him, when no bribes would come, that he was committed to prison [**41**]; and then, by the Cardinal's good preferment, the Earl of Surrey was sent into Ireland [**43, 3.2.260**] as the King's deputy in lieu of the said Earl of Kildare, there to remain rather as an exile than as lieutenant to the King, even at the Cardinal's pleasure, as he himself well perceived. . . .

Now in this meanwhile the Cardinal ceased not to bring the Duke out of the King's favor by such forged tales and contrived surmises[13] as he daily put into the King's head, insomuch that (through the infelicity of his fate) divers accidents fell out to the advantage of the Cardinal; which he not omitting, achieved the thing whereat he so studiously (for the satisfying of his cankered and malicious stomach)[14] laid full aim. Now it chanced that the Duke, coming to London with his train of men to attend the King into France, went before into Kent unto a manor place which he had there. And whilst he stayed in that country till the King set forward, grievous complaints were exhibited to him by his farmers and tenants against Charles Knyvet, his surveyor,[15] for such bribing as he had used there amongst them. Whereupon the Duke took such displeasure against him that he deprived him of his office [**1.2.172**], not knowing how that in so doing he procured his own destruction, as after appeared. . . .

[**856**] Thus landed the Emperor Charles the Fifth at Dover, under his cloth of estate of the Black Eagle, all spread on rich cloth of gold [1520]. He had with him many noblemen and many fair ladies of his blood. When he was come on land, the Lord Cardinal conducted him to the castle of Dover, which was prepared for him in most royal manner. In the morning the King rode with all haste to the castle of Dover to welcome the Emperor and, entering into the castle, alighted. . . . On Whitsunday, early in the morning, they took their horses and rode to the city of Canterbury, the more to keep solemn the feast of Pentecost; but specially to see the Queen of England his aunt [Queen Katherine] was the Emperor his intent [**1.1.177**]; of whom ye may be sure he was most joyfully received and welcomed.

. . . The chief cause that moved the Emperor to come thus on land at this time was to persuade that by word of mouth which he had before done most earnestly by letters; which was that the King should not meet with the French King at any interview, for he doubted lest,

[13]False allegations.
[14]Disposition.
[15]Overseer.

if the King of England and the French King should grow into some great friendship and faithful bond of amity, it might turn him to displeasure[16] [**182**].

But now that he perceived how the King was forward on his journey, he did what he could to procure that no trust should be committed to the fair words of the Frenchmen; and that if it were possible, the great friendship that was now in breeding betwixt the two Kings might be dissolved. And forsomuch as he knew the Lord Cardinal to be won with rewards, as a fish with a bait, he bestowed on him great gifts and promised him much more [**186**], so[17] that he would be his friend and help to bring his purpose to pass. The Cardinal (not able to sustain the least assault by force of such rewards as he presently received and of such large promises as on the Emperor's behalf were made to him) promised to the Emperor that he would so use the matter as his purpose should be sped; only he required him not to disallow the King's intent for interview to be had, which he desired in any wise to go forward, that he might show his high magnificence in France according to his first intention.

The Emperor remained in Canterbury till the Thursday being the last of May [1520] and then, taking leave of the King and of his aunt the Queen, departed to Sandwich, where he took his ships and sailed into Flanders. The same day the King made sail from the port of Dover and landed at Calais about eleven of the clock, and with him the Queen and ladies and many nobles of the realm. His grace was received into the checker[18] and there rested. The fourth of June, the King and Queen, with all their train, removed from Calais to his princely lodging, newly erected beside the town of Guines, the most noble and royal lodging that ever before was seen.

[**858**] . . . The day of the meeting was appointed to be on the Thursday the seventh of June, upon which day the two Kings met in the vale of Andren [**7**], accompanied with such a number of the nobility of both realms, so richly appointed in apparel and costly jewels, as chains, collars of *S*'s, and other the like ornaments to set forth their degrees and estates, that a wonder it was to behold and view them in their order and rooms,[19] which every man kept according to his appointment.

[16]Cause him annoyance.
[17]Provided.
[18]Room for accounts.
[19]Places.

The two Kings meeting in the field, either saluted other in most loving wise, first on horseback and, after alighting, on foot eftsoons[20] embraced with courteous words, to the great rejoicing of the beholders [**8**]; and after they had thus saluted each other, they went both together into a rich tent of cloth of gold, there set up for the purpose, in the which they passed the time in pleasant talk, banqueting, and loving devices [**26**] till it drew toward the evening; and then departed for that night, the one to Guines the other to Ardres. At this meeting of the two Kings in open sight, I then well perceived (saith Hall) the habiliments royal of the French King. . . .

[**859**] Thus with honor and noble courage these two noble Kings with their companies entered into the field and them presented unto the Queens. After reverence done, they rode round about the tilt, and so took their places appointed, abiding the answers.

. . . Thus course after course each with other his counterparty did right valiantly; but the two Kings surmounted all the rest in prowess and valiantness [**35**].

[**860**] . . . [On June 17] the Lord Cardinal, in stately attire, accompanied with the Duke of Buckingham [**13**] and other great lords, conducted forward the French King; and in their way they encountered and met the King of England and his company right in the valley of Andren, appareled in their masquing apparel; which gladded the French King. . . .

On Monday the eighteenth of June was such an hideous storm [**90**] of wind and weather that many conjectured it did prognosticate trouble and hatred shortly after to follow between princes. . . .

[**862**] After that this matter for enclosures was thus dispatched, the Cardinal, boiling in hatred against the Duke of Buckingham and thirsting for his blood, devised to make Charles Knyvet, that had been the Duke's surveyor and put from him (as ye have heard), an instrument to bring the Duke to destruction. This Knyvet, being had in examination before the Cardinal, disclosed all the Duke's life [**222**]. And first he uttered that the Duke was accustomed by way of talk to say how he meant so to use the matter that he would attain to the crown if King Henry chanced to die without issue [**1.2.134**]; and that he had talk and conference of that matter on a time with George Neville Lord of Abergavenny [**137**], unto whom he had given his daughter in marriage; and also that he threatened to punish the Cardinal [**138**] for his manifold misdoings, being without cause his mortal enemy.

[20]Again.

The Cardinal, having gotten that which he sought for, encouraged, comforted, and procured Knyvet, with many comfortable words and great promises, that he should with a bold spirit and countenance object and lay these things to the Duke's charge, with more if he knew it, when time required. Then Knyvet, partly provoked with desire to be revenged and partly moved with hope of reward, openly confessed that the Duke had once fully determined to devise means how to make the King away, being brought into a full hope that he should be King by a vain prophecy [**147**] which one Nicholas Hopkins, a monk of an house of the Chartreux Order beside Bristol called Henton, sometime his confessor, had opened unto him.

[**863**] The Cardinal, having thus taken the examination of Knyvet, went unto the King and declared unto him that his person was in danger by such traitorous purpose as the Duke of Buckingham had conceived in his heart, and showed[21] how that now there was manifest tokens of his wicked pretense;[22] wherefore he exhorted the King to provide for his own surety with speed. The King, hearing the accusation enforced to the uttermost by the Cardinal, made this answer: "If the Duke have deserved to be punished, let him have according to his deserts." The Duke hereupon was sent for up to London and, at his coming thither, was straightways attached[23] and brought to the Tower [**1.1.201**] by Sir Henry Marney, Captain of the Guard, the sixteenth of April [1521]. There was also attached the foresaid Chartreux monk [**221**], Master John de la Car [**218**] alias de la Court the Duke's confessor, and Sir Gilbert Perke [**219**], priest, the Duke's chancellor.

After the apprehension of the Duke, inquisitions were taken in divers shires of England of him, so that by the knights and gentlemen he was indicted of high treason for certain words spoken (as before ye have heard) by the same Duke, at Blechingley, to the Lord of Abergavenny; and therewith was the same lord [**213**] attached for concealment,[24] and so likewise was the Lord Montague [**217**]; and both led to the Tower. . . . Moreover, in the Guildhall within the city of London, . . . the said Duke was indicted of divers points of high treason, as by the same indictment it appeareth.

"Namely that the said Duke, intending to exalt himself and to usurp the crown, the royal power, and dignity of the realm of England, and

[21]Explained.
[22]Intention.
[23]Arrested.
[24]Suppression of the truth.

to deprive the King's majesty thereof, that he the said Duke might take upon him the same, against his allegiance had, the tenth day of March, in the second year [1511] of the King's majesty's reign, and at divers other times before and after, imagined[25] and compassed the King's death and destruction at London and at Thornbury in the county of Gloucester. . . .

[**864**] "And furthermore the same Duke, on the fourth of November, in the eleventh year of the King's reign [1519], at East Greenwich [**1.2.188**] in the county of Kent, said unto one Charles Knyvet, esquire (after that the King had reproved the Duke for retaining William Bulmer [**190**], knight, into his service), that if he had perceived that he should have been committed [**193**] to the Tower (as he doubted he should have been), he would have so wrought that the principal doers therein should not have had cause of great rejoicing; for he would have played the part [**194**] which his father intended to have put in practice against King Richard the Third at Salisbury; who made earnest suit to have come unto the presence of the same King Richard [**197, R3 5.1.1**]; which suit if he might have obtained, he, having a knife secretly about him, would have thrust it into the body of King Richard [**H8 1.2.199**] as he had made semblance to kneel down before him. And in speaking these words, he maliciously laid his hand upon his dagger [**204**] and said that, if he were so evil used, he would do his best to accomplish his pretensed[26] purpose; swearing to confirm his word by the blood of our Lord.

"Beside all this, the same Duke, the tenth of May, in the twelfth year of the King's reign [1520], at London in a place called the Rose, within the parish of Saint Lawrence Poultney in Canwick Street Ward, demanded of the said Charles Knyvet, esquire, what was the talk amongst the Londoners concerning the King's journey beyond the seas [**152**]. And the said Charles told him that many stood in doubt[27] of that journey, lest the Frenchmen meant some deceit toward the King [**156**]. Whereto the Duke answered that it was to be feared lest it would come to pass according to the words of a certain holy monk. 'For there is,' saith he, 'a Chartreux monk that divers times hath sent to me, willing me to send unto him my chancellor; and I did send unto him John de la Court my chaplain [**162**], unto whom he would not declare anything till De la Court had sworn unto him to keep all things secret and to tell

[25]Plotted.
[26]Intended.
[27]Fear.

no creature living what he should hear of him except it were to me.

" 'And then the said monk told De la Court that neither the King nor his heirs should prosper [**168**], and that I should endeavor myself to purchase the good wills of the commonalty of England; for I the same Duke and my blood should prosper and have the rule of the realm of England.' Then said Charles Knyvet, 'The monk may be deceived through the devil's illusion [**178**],' and that it was evil to meddle with such matters. 'Well,' said the Duke, 'it cannot hurt me'; and so (saith the indictment) the Duke seemed to rejoice in the monk's words. And further, at the same time, the Duke told the said Charles that, if the King had miscarried now in his last sickness, he would have chopped off the heads of the Cardinal, of Sir Thomas Lovell, knight, and of others [**184**]; and also said that he had rather die for it than to be used as he had been."

. . . These were the special articles and points comprised in the indictment and laid to his charge; but how truly, or in what sort proved, I have not further to say, either in accusing or excusing him, other than as I find in Hall and Polydore [Vergil], whose words in effect I have thought to impart to the reader, and without any partial wresting of the same either to or fro.

Saving that (I trust) I may without offense say that (as the rumor then went) the Cardinal chiefly procured the death of this nobleman [**2.1.40**], no less favored and beloved of the people of this realm in that season than the Cardinal himself was hated and envied [**50**]. Which thing caused the Duke's fall the more to be pitied and lamented, sith he was the man of all other that chiefly went about to cross the Cardinal in his lordly demeanor and heady proceedings. But to the purpose. Shortly after that the Duke had been indicted (as before ye have heard) he was arraigned in Westminster Hall before the Duke of Norfolk.

[**865**] . . . There was made within the hall at Westminster a scaffold for these lords and a presence[28] for a judge, railed and counter-railed about and barred with degrees. When the lords had taken their place, the Duke was brought to the bar and, upon his arraignment, pleaded not guilty and put himself upon his peers [**11**]. Then was his indictment read, which the Duke denied to be true, and (as he was an eloquent man [**1.2.111**]) alleged reasons to falsify[29] the indictment, pleading the matter for his own justification very pithily and earnestly.

[28]Ceremonial place.
[29]Prove false.

The King's attorney, against the Duke's reasons, alleged the examinations, confessions, and proofs of witnesses [**2.1.16**].

The Duke desired that the witnesses might be brought forth. And then came before him Charles Knyvet, Perke, De la Court, and Hopkins the monk of the priory of the Charterhouse beside Bath which like a false hypocrite had induced the Duke to the treason with his false forged prophecies [**19**]. Divers presumptions and accusations were laid unto him by Charles Knyvet which he would fain[30] have covered.[31] The depositions were read and the deponents delivered as prisoners to the officers of the Tower. Then spoke the Duke of Norfolk and said: "My lord, the King our sovereign lord hath commanded that you shall have his laws ministered with favor and right to you. Wherefore, if you have any other thing to say for yourself, you shall be heard." Then he was commanded to withdraw him, and so was led into Paradise, a house so named. The lords went to council a great while, and after took their places.

Then said the Duke of Norfolk to the Duke of Suffolk, "What say you of Sir Edward, Duke of Buckingham, touching the high treasons?" The Duke of Suffolk answered, "He is guilty"; and so said the Marquis [of Dorset] and all the other earls and lords. Thus was this prince, Duke of Buckingham, found guilty of high treason [**27**] by a duke, a marquis, seven earls, and twelve barons [**119**]. The Duke was brought to the bar, sore chafing, and sweat marvelously [**33**]; and after he had made his reverence he paused awhile. The Duke of Norfolk, as judge, said: "Sir Edward, you have heard how you be indicted of high treason. You pleaded thereto not guilty, putting yourself to the peers of the realm which have found you guilty." Then the Duke of Norfolk wept and said: "You shall be led to the King's prison and there laid on a hurdle[32] and so drawn to the place of execution, and there be hanged, cut down alive, your members cut off and cast into the fire, your bowels burned before you, your head smitten off, and your body quartered and divided at the King's will; and God have mercy on your soul. Amen."

The Duke of Buckingham said: "My Lord of Norfolk, you have said as a traitor should be said unto, but I was never any. But, my lords, I nothing malign for that you have done to me, but the eternal God forgive you my death, and I do [**65**]. I shall never sue to the King

[30]Gladly.
[31]Concealed.
[32]Frame for dragging a traitor to execution.

for life, howbeit he is a gracious prince and more grace may come from him than I desire [**70**]. I desire you, my lords and all my fellows, to pray for me." Then was the edge of the axe turned toward him [**53 SD**], and he led into a barge [**98**]. Sir Thomas Lovell desired him to sit on the cushions and carpet ordained for him. He said: "Nay, for when I went to Westminster I was Duke of Buckingham; now I am but Edward Bohun[33] [**103**], the most caitiff[34] of the world." Thus they landed at the Temple, where received him Sir Nicholas Vaux and Sir William Sandys, baronets, and led him through the city; who desired ever the people to pray for him [**77**]. . . .

On Friday the seventeenth day of May [1521], about eleven of the clock, this Duke of Buckingham, Earl of Hereford, Stafford, and Northampton, with a great power was delivered to John Keime and John Skevington, sheriffs, who led him to the scaffold on Tower Hill, where he said he had offended the King's grace through negligence and lack of grace, and desired all noblemen to beware by him and all men to pray for him [**132**], and that he trusted to die the King's true man. Thus meekly with an axe he took his death. Then the Augustine Friars took his body and head and buried them. . . .

[**870**] Edward Stafford, son to Henry Duke of Buckingham, being also Duke of Buckingham after the death of his father, was Constable of England, Earl of Hereford, Stafford, and Northampton, being in the first year of Henry the Seventh, in the year of our Redemption 1485, restored to his father's dignities and possessions. He is termed in the books of the law in the said thirteenth year of Henry the Eighth (where his arraignment is liberally set down) to be the flower and mirror of all courtesy [**53**]. This man (as before is touched) was by Henry the Seventh restored to his father's inheritance [**114**], in recompense of the loss of his father's life, taken away (as before is said) by the usurping King Richard the Third. . . .

[**872**] On the second day of February [1521] the King, as then being at Greenwich, received a bull from the Pope [Leo the Tenth] whereby he was declared Defender of the Christian Faith, and likewise his successors forever. The Cardinal of York sang the high mass that day with all the pompous solemnity that might be, and gave clean remission of sins to all that heard it. This title was ascribed unto the King because he had written a book against Luther in Germany; whereunto the said Luther answered very sharply, nothing sparing his authority nor

[33]One of Buckingham's family names.
[34]Wretched.

majesty. Of which book published by the King I will not (for reverence of his royalty), though I durst, report what I have read, because we are to judge honorably of our rulers and to speak nothing but good of the princes of the people. Only this brief clause or fragment I will add (lest I might seem to tell a tale of the man in the moon), that King Henry in his said book is reported to rage against the devil and Antichrist, to cast out his foam against Luther, to raze out the name of the Pope and yet to allow his law, etc. I suppress the rest for shame and return to our history.

In this meantime grudges and displeasures still grew and increased betwixt the King of England and the French King. . . .

The King understanding how his subjects were handled at Bordeaux by the French King's commandment [1522], in breach of the league [**1.1.95**], the French ambassador was called before the Council and the Cardinal laid sore to his charge that contrary to his promise at all times on the French King his master's behalf, affirming that he meant nothing but peace and amity to be observed in all points with the King of England, yet now the English merchants had not only their goods stayed at Bordeaux [**96**] but also they and their factors[35] were laid in prison, in full breach of all peace and amity aforetime concluded. . . .

[**891**] The King, being determined thus to make wars in France [**1.2.60**] and to pass the sea[a] himself in person, his Council considered that above all things great treasure and plenty of money must needs be provided. Wherefore by the Cardinal there was devised strange[36] commissions and sent in the end of March [1525] into every shire, and commissioners appointed and privy instructions sent to them how they should proceed in their sittings and order the people to bring them to their purpose, which was that the sixth part of every man's substance [**58**] should be paid in money or plate to the King without delay, for the furniture of his war. Hereof followed such cursing, weeping, and exclamation [**23**] against both King and Cardinal that pity it was to hear.

. . . The Cardinal travailed earnestly with the Mayor and aldermen of London about the aid of money to be granted, and likewise the commissioners appointed in the shires of the realm sat upon the same; but the burden was so grievous that it was generally denied and the

[35]Agents.
[a]The English Channel.
[36]Unheard-of.

commons in every place so moved that it was like to grow to rebellion [**29**].

. . . The Duke of Suffolk, sitting in commission about this subsidy in Suffolk, persuaded by courteous means the rich clothiers to assent thereto; but when they came home and went about to discharge and put from them their spinners, carders, fullers, weavers [**33**], and other artificers (which they kept in work aforetime), the people began to assemble in companies. . . . And herewith there assembled together, after the manner of rebels, four thousand men of Lavenham, Sudberry, Hadley, and other towns thereabouts; which put themselves in harness and rang the bells (alarm), and began still to assemble in great number.

. . . The Duke of Norfolk, being thereof advertised, gathered a great power in Norfolk and came toward the commons; and, sending to them to know their intent, received answer that they would live and die in the King's causes and be to him obedient. Hereupon he came himself to talk with them, and willing to know who was their captain, that he might answer for them all, it was told him by one John Greene, a man of fifty years of age, that Poverty was their captain, the which, with his cousin Necessity, had brought them to that doing.

. . . After this the Duke of Norfolk and the Duke of Suffolk came to Bury, and thither resorted much people of the country in their shirts, with halters about their necks, meekly desiring pardon for their offenses. The Dukes so wisely demeaned[37] themselves that the commons were appeased, and the demand of money ceased in all the realm, for well it was perceived that the commons would pay none. Then went the two Dukes to London and brought with them the chief captains of the rebellion, which were put in the Fleet. The King then came to Westminster to the Cardinal's palace and assembled there a great Council in the which he openly protested [**68**] that his mind was never to ask anything of his commons which might sound to the breach of his laws; wherefore he willed to know by whose means the commissions were so straitly[38] given forth, to demand the sixth part of every man's goods.

The Cardinal excused himself and said that, when it was moved in Council how to levy money to the King's use, the King's Council, and namely the judges [**71**], said that he might lawfully demand any sum by commission, and that by the consent of the whole Council it was

[37]Comported.
[38]Severely.

done; and took God to witness that he never desired the hindrance of the commons but like a true councillor devised how to enrich the King. The King indeed was much offended that his commons were thus entreated, and thought it touched his honor that his Council should attempt such a doubtful matter in his name, and to be denied both of the spiritualty and temporalty. Therefore he would no more of that trouble but caused letters to be sent into all shires [**98**] that the matter should no further be talked of; and he pardoned all them that had denied the demand openly or secretly [**100**]. The Cardinal, to deliver himself of the evil will of the commons purchased by procuring and advancing of this demand, affirmed and caused it to be bruited abroad that through his intercession [**106**] the King had pardoned and released all things.

[**897**] . . . There rose a secret bruit in London [1527] that the King's confessor Doctor [John] Longland, and divers other great clerks, had told the King that the marriage between him and the Lady Katherine, late wife to his brother Prince Arthur, was not lawful [**2.1.148**]; whereupon the King should sue a divorce and marry the Duchess of Alençon, sister to the French King [**2.2.42**], at the town of Calais this summer; and that the Viscount Rochford had brought with him the picture of the said lady. The King was offended with those tales and sent for Sir Thomas Seymour Mayor of the city of London, secretly charging him to see that the people ceased from such talk [**2.1.151**].

[**906**] . . . The truth is that, whether this doubt was first moved by the Cardinal [**156**] or by the said Longland, being the King's confessor, the King was not only brought in doubt whether it was a lawful marriage or no but also determined to have the case examined, cleared, and adjudged by learning, law, and sufficient authority. The Cardinal verily was put in most blame for this scruple, now cast into the King's conscience [**2.2.18**], for the hate he bore to the Emperor because he would not grant to him the archbishopric of Toledo, for the which he was a suitor [**2.1.162**]. And therefore he did not only procure the King of England to join in friendship with the French King but also sought a divorce betwixt the King and the Queen, that the King might have had in marriage the Duchess of Alençon, sister unto the French King; and (as some have thought) he travailed in that matter with the French King at Amiens; but the Duchess would not give ear thereunto.

But howsoever it came about that the King was thus troubled in conscience concerning his marriage, this followed, that, like a wise and sage prince, to have the doubt clearly removed, he called together the best learned of the realm, which were of several opinions. Wherefore he thought to know the truth by indifferent[39] judges, lest peradventure the Spaniards and other also in favor of the Queen would say that his own subjects were not indifferent judges in this behalf [**2.2.90**]. And therefore he wrote his cause to Rome, and also sent to all the universities in Italy and France, and to the great clerks of all Christendom [**92**], to know their opinions; and desired the court of Rome to send into his realm a legate which should be indifferent and of a great and profound judgment, to hear the cause debated. At whose request the whole consistory of the College of Rome sent thither Lawrence Campcius [**2.1.160**], a priest cardinal, a man of great wit and experience . . . ; and with him was joined in commission the Cardinal of York and Legate of England [**2.2.106**].

This Cardinal came to London in October [1528] and did intimate both to the King and Queen the cause of his coming; which being known great talk was had thereof. The Archbishop of Canterbury sent for the famous doctors of both the Universities to Lambeth, and there were every day disputations and commonings[40] of this matter. And because the King meant nothing but uprightly therein, and knew well that the Queen was somewhat wedded to her own opinion and wished that she should do nothing without counsel, he bade her choose the best clerks of his realm to be of her counsel, and licensed them to do the best on her part that they could, according to the truth [**113**]. Then she elected William Warham Archbishop of Canterbury and Nicholas West Bishop of Ely, doctors of the laws, and John Fisher Bishop of Rochester and Henry Standish Bishop of Saint Asaph [**2.4 SD**], doctors of divinity, and many other doctors and well-learned men, which for surety, like men of great learning, defended her cause as far as learning might maintain and hold it up.

[**907**] . . . About this time [1529] the King received into favor Doctor Stephen Gardiner [**2.2.116**], whose service he used in matters of great secrecy and weight, admitting him in the room of Doctor [Richard] Pace, the which, being continually abroad in embassages, and the same oftentimes not much necessary by the Cardinal's appointment, at length he took such grief therewith that he fell out of his right wits [**130**]. The place where the Cardinals should sit to hear

[39]Impartial.
[40]Discussions.

the cause of matrimony betwixt the King and the Queen was ordained to be at the Black Friars in London [**139**], where in the Great Hall was preparation made of seats, tables, and other furniture according to such a solemn session and royal appearance. The court was plotted[41] in tables and benches in manner of a consistory, one seat raised higher for the judges to sit in. Then, as it were in the midst of the said judges, aloft above them three degrees[42] high, was a cloth of estate hanged with a chair royal under the same wherein sat the King; and besides him, some distance from him, sat the Queen; and under the judges' feet sat the scribes and other officers [**2.4 SD**]. The chief scribe was Doctor Stephens,[43] and the Caller of the Court was one Cook of Winchester.

Then before the King and the judges, within the court, sat the Archbishop of Canterbury Warham and all the other bishops. Then stood at both ends, within, the counselors learned in the spiritual laws, as well the King's as the Queen's. The doctors of law for the King (whose names ye have heard before) had their convenient rooms. Thus was the court furnished. The judges commanded silence whilst their commission was read [**1**], both to the court and to the people assembled. That done, the scribes commanded the Crier to call the King [**6**], by the name of "King Henry of England, come into the court," etc. With that the King answered and said, "Here!" Then called he the Queen [**10**], by the name of "Katherine Queen of England, come into the court," etc. Who made no answer but rose out of her chair [**12 SD**].

And because she could not come to the King directly, for the distance severed between them, she went about by the court and came to the King, kneeling down at his feet [**12 SD**], to whom she said in effect as followeth. "Sir," quoth she, "I desire you to do me justice and right [**13**], and take some pity upon me, for I am a poor woman and a stranger,[44] born out of your dominion [**16**]; having here no indifferent counsel and less assurance of friendship [**17**]. Alas, sir, what[45] have I offended you [**19**] or what occasion of displeasure have I showed you, intending thus to put me from you after this sort? I take God to my judge I have been to you a true and humble wife

[41]Laid out.
[42]Steps.
[43]Stephen Gardiner.
[44]Foreigner.
[45]How.

[**23**], ever conformable to your will and pleasure, that never contraried or gainsaid anything thereof, and being always contented with all things wherein you had any delight, whether little or much, without grudge or displeasure. I loved for your sake all them whom you loved, whether they were my friends or enemies.

"I have been your wife these twenty years and more, and you have had by me divers children [**35**]. If there be any just cause that you can allege against me, either of dishonesty[46] or matter lawful to put me from you, I am content to depart, to my shame and rebuke; and if there be none, then I pray you to let me have justice at your hand. The King your father was, in his time, of excellent wit [**45**], and the King of Spain my father, Ferdinand, was reckoned one of the wisest princes that reigned in Spain many years before [**47**]. It is not to be doubted but that they had gathered as wise counselors unto them of every realm as to their wisdoms they thought meet; who deemed the marriage between you and me good and lawful [**50**], etc. Wherefore I humbly desire you to spare me until I may know what counsel my friends in Spain will advertise me to take [**53**]; and, if you will not, then your pleasure be fulfilled [**57**]." With that she arose up, making a low curtsy to the King, and departed from thence [**121 SD**].

The King, being advertised that she was ready to go out of the house, commanded the Crier to call her again who called her by these words [**126**]: "Katherine Queen of England, come into the court!" With that quoth Master Griffith [**127**], "Madam, you be called again." "On, on," quoth she, "it maketh no matter, I will not tarry [**131**]; go on your ways." And thus she departed, without any further answer at that time or any other, and never would appear after in any court. The King, perceiving she was departed, said these words in effect: "Forasmuch," quoth he, "as the Queen is gone, I will in her absence declare to you all that she hath been to me as true, as obedient, and as conformable a wife as I would wish or desire. [**137**] She hath all the virtuous qualities that ought to be in a woman of her dignity or in any other of a baser estate; she is also surely a noblewoman born [**141**]; her conditions[47] will well declare the same."

With that quoth Wolsey the Cardinal [**144**]: "Sir, I most humbly require your highness to declare before all this audience whether

[46]Unchastity.
[47]Personal qualities.

I have been the chief and first mover of this matter unto your majesty or no, for I am greatly suspected herein." "My Lord Cardinal," quoth the King [**156**], "I can well excuse you in this matter. Marry," quoth he, "you have been rather against me in the tempting hereof than a setter-forward or mover of the same. The special cause that moved me unto this matter was a certain scrupulosity that pricked my conscience upon certain words spoken at a time when it was by the Bishop of Bayonne the French ambassador [**172**], who had been hither sent upon the debating of a marriage to be concluded between our daughter the Lady Mary and the Duke of Orleans, second son to the King of France.

"Upon the resolution and determination whereof, he desired respite to advertise the King his master thereof whether our daughter Mary should be legitimate [**179**] in respect of this my marriage with this woman, being sometimes[b] my brother's wife. Which words, once conceived within the secret bottom of my conscience, engendered such a scrupulous doubt that my conscience was incontinently accumbered,[c] vexed, and disquieted; whereby I thought myself to be greatly in danger of God's indignation. Which appeared to be (as meseemed) the rather for that he sent us no issue male, and all such issues male [**191**] as my said wife had by me died incontinent[d] after they came into the world; so that I doubted the great displeasure of God in that behalf.

"Thus, my conscience being tossed in the waves of a scrupulous mind, and partly in despair to have any other issue than I had already by this lady now my wife, it behooved me further to consider the state of this realm and the danger it stood in for lack of a prince to succeed me [**197**]. I thought it good, in release of the weighty burden of my weak conscience, and also the quiet estate of this worthy realm, to attempt the law therein whether I may lawfully take another wife more lawfully; by whom God may send me more issue, in case this my first copulation was not good; without any carnal concupiscence and not for any displeasure or misliking of the Queen's person and age; with whom I would be as well contented to continue, if our marriage may stand with the laws of God, as with any woman alive [**226**].

[**908**] "In this point consisteth all this doubt that we go about

[b]Formerly.
[c]Encumbered.
[d]Immediately.

now to try by the learning, wisdom, and judgment of you our prelates and pastors of all this our realm and dominions, now here assembled for that purpose; to whose conscience and learning I have committed the charge and judgment, according to the which I will (God willing) be right well content to submit myself and, for my part, obey the same. Wherein, after that I perceived my conscience so doubtful, I moved it in confession to you my Lord of Lincoln [**207**], then ghostly father.[48] And, forsomuch as then you yourself were in some doubt, you moved me to ask the counsel of all these my lords; whereupon I moved you, my Lord of Canterbury [**218**], first to have your license, inasmuch as you were Metropolitan,[49] to put this matter in question; and so I did of all you my lords; to which you granted,[e] under your seals [**222**], here to be showed." "That is truth," quoth the Archbishop of Canterbury. After that the King rose up and the court was adjourned until another day [**232**].

Here is to be noted that the Queen, in presence of the whole court, most grievously accused the Cardinal of untruth, deceit, wickedness, and malice; which had sown dissension betwixt her and the King her husband; and therefore openly protested that she did utterly abhor, refuse, and forsake such a judge as was not only a most malicious enemy to her [**81**] but also a manifest adversary to all right and justice; and therewith did she appeal unto the Pope, committing her whole cause to be judged of him [**119**]. But notwithstanding this appeal, the legates sat weekly, and every day were arguments brought in on both parts, and proofs alleged for the understanding of the case; and still they assayed if they could by any means procure the Queen to call back her appeal [**234**], which she utterly refused to do. The King would gladly have had an end in the matter, but when the legates drove time[50] and determined upon no certain point, he conceived a suspicion [**235**] that this was done of purpose, that their doings might draw to none effect or conclusion.

The next court day the Cardinals sat again, at which time the counsel on both sides were there ready to answer. The King's counsel alleged the matrimony not to be lawful at the beginning because of the carnal copulation had between Prince Arthur and the Queen. This matter was very vehemently touched on that side, and to prove

[48]Confessor.
[49]Archbishop.
[e]Assented.
[50]Caused time to pass.

it they alleged many reasons and similitudes of truth; and being answered negatively again on the other side, it seemed that all their former allegations were doubtful to be tried and that no man knew the truth. And thus this court passed from sessions to sessions, and day to day, till at certain of their sessions the King sent the two Cardinals to the Queen (who was then in Bridewell)[51] to persuade with her by their wisdoms and to advise her to surrender the whole matter into the King's hands by her own consent and will; which should be much better to her honor than to stand to the trial of law and thereby to be condemned [**3.1.95**]; which should seem much to her dishonor.

The Cardinals being in the Queen's chamber of presence, the gentleman usher advertised the Queen that the Cardinals were come to speak with her [**16**]. With that she rose up and, with a skein of white thread about her neck, came into her chamber of presence, where the Cardinals were attending. At whose coming quoth she [**26**], "What is your pleasure with me?" "If it please your grace," quoth Cardinal Wolsey [**27**], "to go into your privy chamber, we will show you the cause of our coming." "My lord," quoth she, "if ye have anything to say, speak it openly before all these folk, for I fear nothing that ye can say against me but that I would all the world should hear and see it; and therefore speak your mind." Then began the Cardinal to speak to her in Latin. "Nay, good my lord," quoth she [**43**], "speak to me in English."

"Forsooth," quoth the Cardinal, "good madam, if it please you, we come both to know your mind how you are disposed to do in this matter between the King and you [**59**], and also to declare secretly our opinions and counsel unto you; which we do only for very zeal and obedience we bear unto your grace." "My lord," quoth she, "I thank you for your good will; but to make you answer in your request I cannot so suddenly, for I was set among my maids at work [**74**], thinking full little of any such matter, wherein there needeth a longer deliberation and a better head than mine to make answer; for I need counsel in this case, which toucheth me so near, and for any counsel or friendship that I can find in England they are not for my profit [**83**]. What think you, my lords, will any Englishman counsel me [**84**] or be friend to me against the King's pleasure that is his subject? Nay, forsooth. And as for my counsel in whom I will put my trust, they be not here, they be in Spain in my own country [**91**].

[51]A house belonging to the King.

"And, my lords, I am a poor woman, lacking wit to answer to any such noble persons of wisdom as you be in so weighty a matter; therefore I pray you be good to me, poor woman, destitute of friends here in a foreign region; and your counsel also I will be glad to hear [**182**]." And therewith she took the Cardinal by the hand and led him into her privy chamber with the other Cardinal; where they tarried a season talking with the Queen. Which communication ended, they departed to the King, making to him relation of her talk. Thus this case went forward from court to court till it came to judgment, so that every man expected that judgment would be given the next day. At which day the King came thither and sat him down in a chair within a door, in the end of the gallery (which opened directly against the judgment seat), to hear the judgment given; at which time all their proceedings were read in Latin.

That done, the King's counsel at the bar called for judgment. With that quoth Cardinal Campeius: "I will not give judgment till I have made relation to the Pope of all our proceedings; whose counsel and commandment in this case I will observe. The case is very doubtful, and also the party defendant will make no answer here but doth rather appeal from us, supposing that we be not indifferent. Wherefore I will adjourn this court for this time, according to the order of the court of Rome." And with that the court was dissolved and no more done. This protracting of the conclusion of the matter, King Henry took very displeasantly. Then Cardinal Campeius took his leave of the King and nobility, and returned toward Rome [**3.2.57**].

Whilst these things were thus in hand, the Cardinal of York was advised that the King had set his affection upon a young gentlewoman named Anne [**36**], the daughter of Sir Thomas Boleyn Viscount Rochford, which did wait upon the Queen. This was a great grief unto the Cardinal [**91**], as that he perceived aforehand that the King would marry the said gentlewoman if the divorce took place. Wherefore he began with all diligence to disappoint[52] that match, which, by reason of the misliking that he had to the woman, he judged ought to be avoided more than present death. While the matter stood in this state, and that the cause of the Queen was to be heard and judged at Rome, by reason of the appeal which by her was put in, the Cardinal required the Pope by letters and secret messengers that in any wise he should defer the judgment of the divorce [**26**] till he might frame the King's mind to his purpose.

[52]Frustrate.

[**909**] Howbeit, he went about nothing so secretly but that the same came to the King's knowledge [**30**]; who took so high displeasure with such his cloaked dissimulation that he determined to abase his degree, sith as an unthankful person he forgot himself and his duty toward him that had so highly advanced him to all honor and dignity. When the nobles of the realm perceived the Cardinal to be in displeasure[53] [**23**], they began to accuse him of such offenses as they knew might be proved against him [**1**], and thereof they made a book containing certain articles, to which divers of the King's Council set their hands. The King, understanding more plainly by those articles the great pride, presumption, and covetousness of the Cardinal, was sore moved against him; but yet kept his purpose secret for a while. . . .

In the meantime the King, being informed that all those things that the Cardinal had done by his power legatine within this realm were in the case of the praemunire [**340**] and provision, caused his attorney Christopher Hales to sue out a writ of praemunire against him in the which he licensed him to make his attorney. And further, the seventeenth of November [1529], the King sent the two Dukes of Norfolk and Suffolk to the Cardinal's place at Westminster [**227 SD**]; who went as they were commanded; and finding the Cardinal there, they declared that the King's pleasure was that he should surrender up the Great Seal into their hands and to depart simply unto Asher, which was an house situate nigh unto Hampton Court belonging to the bishopric of Winchester [**229**]. The Cardinal demanded of them their commission that gave them such authority; who answered again that they were sufficient commissioners and had authority to do no less by the King's mouth [**235**]. Notwithstanding, he would in no wise agree in that behalf without further knowledge of their authority, saying that the Great Seal was delivered him by the King's person to enjoy the ministration thereof, with the room[54] of the Chancellor for the term of his life; whereof for his surety he had the King's letters patents [**250**].

This matter was greatly debated between them, with many great words, insomuch that the Dukes were fain[55] to depart again without their purpose, and rode to Windsor to the King and made report accordingly [**348**]; but the next day they returned again, bringing

[53]Trouble.
[54]Position.
[55]Obliged.

with them the King's letters. Then the Cardinal delivered unto them the Great Seal and was content to depart simply, taking with him nothing but only certain provision for his house; and, after long talk between him and the Dukes, they departed with the Great Seal of England and brought the same to the King. Then the Cardinal called all his officers before him and took account [**451**] of them for all such stuff whereof they had charge. And in his gallery were set divers tables whereupon lay a great number of goodly rich stuff, as whole pieces of silk of all colors, velvet, satin, damask, taffeta, grosgrain, and other things. Also, there lay a thousand pieces of fine holland cloth.

There was laid on every table books reporting the contents of the same, and so was there inventories of all things in order against the King's coming. . . .

After this, in the King's Bench, his matter for the praemunire being called upon, two attorneys, which he had authorized by his warrant signed with his own hand, confessed the action; and so had judgment to forfeit all his lands, tenements, goods, and cattles, and to be out of the King's protection [**342**]; but the King of his clemency sent to him a sufficient protection, and left to him the bishoprics of York and Winchester, with plate and stuff convenient for his degree. . . . Also the bishopric of London, being now void, was bestowed on Doctor [John] Stokesley [**4.1.101**], then ambassador to the universities beyond the sea for the King's marriage.

[**910**] . . . On the four and twentieth of November [1529] was Sir Thomas More made Lord Chancellor [**3.2.393**], and the next day led to the Chancery by the Dukes of Norfolk and Suffolk and there sworn.

[**912**] . . . During this parliament was brought down to the commons the book of articles [**293**] which the lords had put to the King against the Cardinal; the chief whereof were these.

"1. First, that he without the King's assent had procured to be a legate, by reason whereof he took away the right of all bishops and spiritual persons [**310**].

"2. Item, in all writings which he wrote to Rome or any other foreign prince he wrote *Ego et Rex meus,* I and my King, as who would say that the King were his servant [**313**].

"3. Item, that he hath slandered the Church of England in the court of Rome. For his suggestion to be legate was to reform the Church of England. . . .

"4. Item, he without the King's assent carried the King's Great Seal with him into Flanders when he was sent ambassador to the Emperor [**316**].

"5. Item, he without the King's assent sent a commission to Sir Gregory de Cassado, knight, to conclude a league between the King and the Duke of Ferrara without the King's knowledge [**320**].

"6. Item, that he having the French pox presumed to come and breathe on the King.

"7. Item, that he caused the Cardinal's hat to be put on the King's coin [**324**].

"8. Item, that he would not suffer the King's Clerk of the Market to sit at Saint Albans.

"9. Item, that he had sent innumerable substance to Rome for the obtaining of his dignities, to the great impoverishment of the realm [**326**]."

These articles, with many more [**330**], read in the Common House[56] and signed with the Cardinal's hand, was confessed by him. And also there was showed a writing sealed with his seal by the which he gave to the King all his movables and unmovables.

[**913**] . . . In this Lent season [1530] the King, by the advice of his Council, licensed him to go into his diocese of York and gave him commandment to keep him in his diocese and not to return southward without the King's special license in writing. . . . But at this time divers of his servants departed from him to the King's service, and in especial Thomas Cromwell [**425**], one of his chief counsel and chief doer for him in the suppression of abbeys. . . .

[**915**] Then the Cardinal [at his manor of Cawood] took the Earl [of Northumberland] by the hand and had him up into the chamber, whom followed all the number of the Earl's servants. From thence he led him into his bedchamber, and, they being there all alone, the Earl said unto the Cardinal with a soft voice, laying his hand upon his arm: "My lord, I arrest you of high treason [**4.2.13**]. . . ."

[**916**] When night came the Cardinal [at Sheffield Park] waxed very sick with the lask,[57] the which caused him continually to go to the stool all that night, insomuch that he had that night fifty stools. Therefore, in consideration of his infirmity, they caused him to tarry all that day; and the next day he took his journey, with Master Kingston and them of the guard, till he came to an house of the Earl of

[56]House of Commons.
[57]Dysentery.

Shrewsbury's called Hardwick Hall, where he lay all night very evil at ease. The next day he rode to Nottingham and there lodged that night, more sick; and the next day he rode to Leicester Abbey and by the way waxed so sick that he was almost fallen from his mule [**15**]; so that it was night before he came to the abbey of Leicester, where at his coming in at the gates the Abbot with all his convent met him with divers torches light, whom they honorably received and welcomed [**17**].

[**917**] To whom the Cardinal said, "Father Abbot, I am come hither to lay my bones among you [**22**]," riding so still until he came to the stairs of the chamber where he alighted from his mule; and Master Kingston led him up the stairs, and as soon as he was in his chamber he went to bed [**24**]. This was on the Saturday at night; and then increased he sicker and sicker until Monday, that all men thought he would have died; so on Tuesday, Saint Andrew's Eve, Master Kingston came to him and bade him good morrow (for it was about six of the clock) and asked him how he did. "Sir," quoth he, "I tarry but the pleasure of God to render up my poor soul into his hands."

. . . "Sir," quoth Master Kingston, "you be in much pensiveness, doubting that thing that in good faith ye need not." "Well, well, Master Kingston," quoth the Cardinal, "I see the matter how it is framed. But if I had served God as diligently as I have done the King, he would not have given me over in my gray hairs [**3.2.455**]; but it is the just reward that I must receive for the diligent pains and study that I have had to do him service, not regarding my service to God but only to satisfy his pleasure."

. . . Then they did put him in remembrance of Christ His passion, and caused the Yeomen of the Guard to stand by to see him die and to witness of his words at his departure. And incontinent the clock struck eight, and then he gave up the ghost and departed this present life [**4.2.30**]; which caused some to call to remembrance how he said the day before that at eight of the clock they should lose their master [**26**].

Here is the end and fall of pride and arrogancy of men exalted by Fortune to dignity; for in his time he was the haughtiest man in all his proceedings alive, having more respect to the honor of his person than he had to his spiritual profession, wherein should be showed all meekness, humility, and charity. . . .

This Cardinal (as Edmund Campion in his *History of Ireland* describeth him) was a man undoubtedly born to honor [**48**]. "I think," saith he, "some prince's bastard, no butcher's son, exceeding wise, fair-spoken [**52**], high-minded, full of revenge, vicious of his body, lofty to his enemies were they never so big; to those that accepted and sought his friendship wonderful courteous; a ripe schoolman; thrall to affections;[58] brought abed with flattery; insatiable to get and more princely in bestowing [**56**], as appeareth by his two colleges at Ipswich and Oxford [**59**], the one overthrown with his fall, the other unfinished and yet, as it lyeth for an house of students, considering all the appurtenances, incomparable through Christendom; whereof Henry the Eighth is now called founder because he let it stand.[59] He held and enjoyed at once the bishoprics of York, Durham, and Winchester, the dignities of Lord Cardinal, Legate, and Chancellor, the abbey of Saint Albans, divers priories, sundry fat benefices *in commendam.*[60] A great preferrer of his servants and advancer of learning, stout in every quarrel, never happy till this his overthrow [**64**]. Wherein he showed such moderation and ended so perfectly that the hour of his death did him more honor than all the pomp of his life passed." Thus far Campion. Here it is necessary to add that notable discourse which I find in John Stow concerning the state of the Cardinal both in the years of his youth and in his settled age. . . .

This Thomas Wolsey was a poor man's son [**49**], of Ipswich in the county of Suffolk, and there born; and, being but a child, very apt to be learned [**51**], by the means of his parents he was conveyed to the University of Oxford, where he shortly prospered so in learning as he was made bachelor of art when he passed not fifteen years of age and was called most commonly through the university the Boy Bachelor. Thus, prospering in learning, he was made fellow of Magdalen College and afterward appointed to be schoolmaster of Magdalen School. . . .

[**920**] And to the advancing further of his legatine jurisdiction and honor he had masters of his faculties, masters *ceremoniarum*, and such other, to the glorying of his dignity. Then had he his two great crosses of silver, the one of his archbishopric the other of his legacy,[61] borne before him whithersoever he went or rode by two of the tallest priests that he could get within the realm [**2.4 SD**]. . . .

[58]Passions.

[59]Cardinal College (1525), refounded first as King Henry VIII's College (1532), then as Christ Church (1546).

[60]In trust (thus avoiding the prohibition against holding a plurality of benefices).

[61]Legateship.

[**921**] Now of his order in going to Westminster Hall daily in the term. . . .

Before him was borne first the Broad Seal of England and his cardinal's hat by a lord or some gentleman of worship, right solemnly; and as soon as he was once entered into his chamber of presence, his two great crosses were there attending to be borne before him. Then cried the gentlemen ushers, going before him bareheaded, and said: "On before, my lords and masters, on before; make way for my lord's grace!" Thus went he down through the hall with a sergeant-of-arms before him, bearing a great mace of silver, and two gentlemen carrying two great pillars of silver [**2.4 SD**]. . . .

Thus in great honor, triumph, and glory he reigned a long season, ruling all things within the realm appertaining unto the King. His house was resorted to with noblemen and gentlemen, feasting and banqueting ambassadors divers times, and all other right nobly. And when it pleased the King for his recreation to repair to the Cardinal's house (as he did divers times in the year) there wanted no preparations or furniture.[62] Banquets were set forth with masques and mummeries in so gorgeous a sort and costly manner that it was an heaven to behold. There wanted no dames or damsels meet or apt to dance with the masquers or to garnish the place for the time; then was there all kind of music and harmony, with fine voices both of men and children.

On a time [1527] the King came suddenly thither in a masque with a dozen masquers, all in garments like shepherds [**1.4.63 SD**] made of fine cloth of gold and crimson satin paned, and caps of the same, with visors of good physiognomy, their hairs[63] and beards either of fine goldwire silk or black silk; having sixteen torchbearers, besides their drums[64] and other persons with visors all clothed in satin of the same color. And before his entering into the hall, he came by water to the watergate without any noise; where were laid divers chambers[65] and guns charged with shot; and at his landing they were shot off [**49 SD**]; which made such a rumble in the air that it was like thunder. It made all the noblemen, gentlemen, ladies, and gentlewomen to muse what it should mean [**49**], coming so suddenly, they sitting quiet at a solemn banquet, after this sort.

[62]Necessaries.
[63]Wigs.
[64]Drummers.
[65]Breechblocks of cannon used without the barrel for the firing of salutes.

[922] First, ye shall understand that the tables were set in the chamber of presence just[f] covered, and the Lord Cardinal [Wolsey] sitting under the cloth of estate [**1.4 SD**], there having all his service alone; and then was there set a lady with a nobleman, or a gentleman and a gentlewoman [**24**], throughout all the tables in the chamber on the one side; which were made and joined as it were but one table; all which order and device was done by the Lord Sandys, then Lord Chamberlain [**7 SD**] to the King, and by Sir Henry Guildford, Comptroller [**1.3.66**] of the King's Majesty's House. Then, immediately after, the Great Chamberlain and the said Comptroller sent to look what it should mean (as though they knew nothing of the matter); who, looking out of the windows into the Thames, returned again and showed[66] him that it seemed they were noblemen and strangers that arrived at his bridge,[67] coming as ambassadors from some foreign prince [**1.4.54**].

With that quoth the Cardinal: "I desire you, because you can speak French [**57**], to take the pains to go into the hall, there to receive them according to their estates and to conduct them [**58**] into this chamber, where they shall see us and all these noble personages being merry at our banquet; desiring them to sit down with us and to take part of our fare." Then went he incontinent down into the hall, whereas[68] they received them with twenty new torches and conveyed them up into the chamber with such a noise of drums and flutes as seldom had been heard the like. At their entering into the chamber, two and two together, they went directly before the Cardinal [**63 SD**] where he sat and saluted him reverently.

To whom the Lord Chamberlain for them said: "Sir, forasmuch as they be strangers and cannot speak English [**65**], they have desired me to declare unto you that they, having understanding of this your triumphant banquet where was assembled such a number of excellent dames, they could do no less [**68**], under support of your grace, but to repair hither to view as well their incomparable beauty as for to accompany them at mumchance,[69] and then to dance with them; and, sir, they require of your grace license to accomplish this said cause of their coming." To whom the Cardinal said he was very well content

[f]Appropriately.
[66]Told.
[67]Landing stage.
[68]Where.
[69]Dice.

they should so do. Then went the masquers and first saluted all the dames and returned to the most worthy, and there opened their great cup of gold filled with crowns and other pieces of gold; to whom they set certain pieces of gold to cast at.

Thus, perusing all the ladies and gentlewomen, to some they lost and of some they won; and, marking after this manner all the ladies, they returned to the Cardinal with great reverence, pouring down all their gold so left in their cup, which was above two hundred crowns. "At all!" quoth the Cardinal, and so cast the dice and won them; whereat was made a great noise and joy. Then quoth the Cardinal to the Lord Chamberlain: "I pray you," quoth he, "that you would show them that meseemeth there should be a nobleman amongst them who is more meet to occupy this seat and place than I am [**78**]; to whom I would most gladly surrender the same according to my duty, if I knew him."

Then spoke the Lord Chamberlain to them in French, and, they rounding[70] him in the ear [**81 SD**], the Lord Chamberlain said to my Lord Cardinal: "Sir," quoth he, "they confess [**82**] that among them there is such a noble personage whom, if your grace can appoint him out from the rest, he is content to disclose himself and to accept your place." With that the Cardinal, taking good advisement[71] among them, at the last quoth he, "Meseemeth the gentleman with the black beard should be even he." And with that he arose out of his chair and offered the same to the gentleman in the black beard, with his cap in his hand. The person to whom he offered the chair was Sir Edward Neville, a comely knight, that much more resembled the King's person in that masque than any other [**86**].

The King, perceiving the Cardinal so deceived, could not forbear laughing but pulled down his visor and Master Neville's also, and dashed out such a pleasant countenance and cheer that all the noble estates there assembled, perceiving the King to be there among them, rejoiced very much. The Cardinal eftsoons[72] desired his highness to take the place of estate. To whom the King answered that he would go first and shift his apparel, and so departed into my Lord Cardinal's chamber and there new appareled him; in which time the dishes of the banquet were clean taken up and the tables spread again with new clean perfumed cloths; every man and woman sitting still until

[70]Whispering to.
[71]Scrutiny.
[72]Almost immediately afterward.

the King with all his masquers came among them again all new appareled.

Then the King took his seat under the cloth of estate, commanding every person to sit still as they did before. In came a new banquet [**98**] before the King, and to all the rest throughout all the tables, wherein were served two hundred divers dishes of costly devices and subtleties. Thus passed they forth the night with banqueting, dancing, and other triumphs, to the great comfort of the King and pleasant regard of the nobility there assembled. And thus spent this Cardinal his time from day to day and year to year, in such wealth, joy, triumph, and glory, having always on his side the King's especial favor, until Fortune envied his prosperity and overthrew all the foundations of his glory which, as they were laid upon sand, so they shrunk and slipped away; whereby ensued the ruin of his estate, even to the very loss of his life. . . .

This Cardinal (as you may perceive in this story)[73] was of a great stomach,[74] for he counted himself equal with princes [**4.2.34**] and by crafty suggestion got into his hands innumerable treasure. He forced little on[75] simony [**36**], and was not pitiful and stood affectionate[76] in his own opinion. In open presence he would lie and say untruth, and was double both in speech and meaning [**37**]. He would promise much and perform little. He was vicious of his body and gave the clergy evil example [**43**]. . . .

[**923**] After the Cardinal was dead the King removed from Hampton Court to Greenwich, where he with Queen Katherine kept a solemn[77] Christmas [1530]; and on the Twelfth Night he sat in the hall in his estate whereas were divers interludes, rich masques and disports, and after that a great banquet. Now after Christmas he came to his manor of Westminster, which before was called York Place; for after that the Cardinal was attainted[78] in the praemunire and was gone northward, he made a feoffment[79] of the same place to the King (and the chapter of the cathedral church of York, by their writing, confirmed the same feoffment), and then the King changed the name

[73]History.
[74]Pride.
[75]Had few scruples about.
[76]Obstinate.
[77]Properly ceremonial.
[78]Convicted.
[79]Investiture.

and called it the King's Manor of Westminster[80] and no more York Place [**4.1.95**].

. . . In this submission [1530] the clergy called the King Supreme Head of the Church of England, which thing they never confessed before; whereupon many things followed after, as you shall hear. . . .

While the parliament sat, on the thirtieth day of March [1531] at afternoon, there came into the Common House the Lord Chancellor [Sir Thomas More] and divers lords of the spiritualty and temporalty to the number of twelve; and there the Lord Chancellor said: "You of this worshipful house (I am sure) be not so ignorant but you know well that the King our sovereign lord hath married his brother's wife, for she was both wedded and bedded with his brother Prince Arthur; and therefore you may surely say that he hath married his brother's wife. If this marriage be good or no, many clerks do doubt. Wherefore the King, like a virtuous prince, willing to be satisfied in his conscience, and also for the surety of his realm, hath with great deliberation consulted with profound clerks and hath sent my Lord [Bishop] of London, here present, to the chief universities of all Christendom [**3.2.66**] to know their opinion and judgment in that behalf. And although that the universities of Cambridge and Oxford had been sufficient to discuss the cause, yet because they be in his realm, and to avoid all suspicion of partiality, he hath sent into the realm of France, Italy, the Pope's dominions, and Venetians, to know their judgment in that behalf; which have concluded, written, and sealed their determinations according as you shall hear read." Then Sir Brian Tuke took out of a box certain writings sealed, and read them word by word, as after ensueth, translated out of Latin into the English tongue. . . .

[**928**] On the first of September [1532], being Sunday, the King, being come to Windsor, created the Lady Anne Boleyn Marchioness of Pembroke and gave to her one thousand pounds land by the year [**2.3.63**].

[**929**] . . . There rose about the same season such sore weather, storms, and rigorous winds, continuing for the more part at north and northwest, that the King stayed at Calais for a convenient wind till Tuesday the thirteenth of November [1532] at midnight and, then taking his ship, landed at Dover the next day about five of the clock

[80]Later Whitehall Palace.

in the morning. And herewith, upon his return, he married privily the Lady Anne Boleyn [**3.2.41**] the same day, being the fourteenth day of November and the feast day of Saint Erkenwald; which marriage was kept so secret that very few knew it till Easter next ensuing when it was perceived that she was with child.

. . . In this parliament [January, 1533] was an act made that no person should appeal for any cause out of this realm to the court of Rome, but from the Commissary to the Bishop, and from the Bishop to the Archbishop, and from the Archbishop to the King; and all causes of the King to be tried in the upper house of the convocation. It was also enacted, the same time, that Queen Katherine should no more be called Queen but Princess Dowager, as the widow of Prince Arthur [**70**]. In the season of the last summer died William Warham Archbishop of Canterbury, and then was named to that see Thomas Cranmer the King's Chaplain [**74, 401**], a man of good learning and of a virtuous life which lately before had been ambassador from the King to the Pope.

After that the King perceived his new wife to be with child, he caused all officers necessary to be appointed to her, and so on Easter Eve she went to her closet openly as Queen [**404**]; and then the King appointed the day of her coronation to be kept on Whitsunday next following [**69, 406**]. And writings were sent to all sheriffs to certify the names of men of forty pounds to receive the order of knighthood or else to make fine. The assessment of the fine was appointed to Thomas Cromwell, Master of the King's Jewel House [**4.1.110**] and councillor to the King, a man newly received into high favor. He so used the matter that a great sum of money was raised to the King's use by those fines. The matter of the Queen's appeal, whereunto she still sticked and by no means could be removed from it, was commoned of both in the parliament house and also in the convocation house, where it was so handled that many were of opinion that not only her appeal but also all other appeals made to Rome were void and of none effect; for that in ancient councils it had been determined that a cause rising in one province should be determined in the same.

This matter was opened with all the circumstances to the Lady Katherine Dowager (for so was she then called), the which persisted still in her former opinion and would revoke by no means her appeal to the court of Rome. Whereupon the Archbishop of Canterbury, accompanied with the Bishops of London, Winchester, Bath, Lincoln, and divers other learned men in great number, rode to

Dunstable, which is six miles from Ampthill where the Princess Dowager lay [**24**]. And there by one Doctor Lee she was cited to appear before the said Archbishop in cause of matrimony in the said town of Dunstable; and at the day of appearance, she appeared not [**29**] but made default; and so she was called peremptory every day fifteen days together; and at the last, for lack of appearance, by the assent of all the learned men there present, she was divorced from the King and the marriage declared to be void and of none effect [**33**]. . . .

[**930**] In the beginning of May [1533] the King caused open proclamations to be made that all men that claimed to do any service or execute any office at the solemn feast of the coronation, by the way of tenure, grant, or prescription, should put their grant three weeks after Easter in the Star Chamber before Charles Duke of Suffolk, for that time High Steward of England [**17**], and the Lord Chancellor and other commissioners. The Duke of Norfolk claimed to be Earl Marshall [**18**] and to exercise his office at that feast. . . .

[**933**] First went gentlemen, then esquires, then knights, then the aldermen of the city in their cloaks of scarlet; after them the judges in their mantles of scarlet and coifs [**36 SD**]. Then followed the Knights of the Bath, being no lords, every man having a white lace on his left sleeve; then followed barons and viscounts in their parliament robes of scarlet. After them came earls, marquises, and dukes, in their robes of estate of crimson velvet furred with ermine, powdered according to their degrees. After them came the Lord Chancellor in a robe of scarlet open before, bordered with lettice.[81] After him came the King's Chapel, and the monks solemnly singing with procession; then came abbots and bishops mitered, then sergeants- and officers-of-arms; then after them went the Mayor of London with his mace, and Garter[82] in his coat-of-arms. Then went the Marquis Dorset in a robe of estate which bore the scepter of gold; and the Earl of Arundel, which bore the rod of ivory with the dove; both together.

Then went alone the Earl of Oxford, High Chamberlain of England, which bore the crown; after him went the Duke of Suffolk in his robe of estate also, for that day being High Steward of England, having a long white rod in his hand; and the Lord William Howard with the rod of the marshalship; and every Knight of the Garter had

[81]Whitish gray fur.

[82]Garter King-of-Arms (chief herald).

on his collar of the order. Then proceeded forth the Queen in a surcoat and robe of purple velvet furred with ermine, in her hair, coif, and circlet as she had the Saturday; and over her was borne the canopy by four of the Five Ports,[83] all crimson with points[84] of blue and red hanging on their sleeves; and the Bishops of London and Winchester bore up the laps[85] of the Queen's robe. The Queen's train, which was very long, was borne by the old Duchess of Norfolk; after her followed ladies, being lords' wives. . . .

When she was thus brought to the high place made in the midst of the church, between the choir and the high altar, she was set in a rich chair [**67**]. And after that she had rested awhile she descended down to the high altar and there prostrate herself while the Archbishop of Canterbury said certain collects.[86] Then she rose and the Bishop anointed her on the head and on the breast; and then she was led up again where, after divers orisons said, the Archbishop set the crown of Saint Edward [**88**] on her head and then delivered her the scepter of gold in her right hand and the rod of ivory with the dove in the left hand; and then all the choir sung *Te Deum*, etc. Which done, the Bishop took off the crown of Saint Edward, being heavy, and set on the crown made for her. Then went she to Saint Edward's Shrine and there offered, after which offering[87] done she withdrew her into a little place made for the nonce on the one side of the choir [**64**].

. . . When the Queen had a little reposed her, the company returned in the same order that they set forth [**93**]; and the Queen went crowned, and so did the ladies aforesaid. . . . Now when she was out of the sanctuary and appeared within the palace, the trumpets played marvelous freshly; then she was brought to Westminster Hall, and so to her withdrawing chamber.

[**934**] . . . The seventh of September [1533], being Sunday, between three and four of the clock in the afternoon the Queen was delivered of a fair young lady [**5.1.165**]. On which day the Duke of Norfolk came home to the christening, which was appointed on the Wednesday next following and was accordingly accomplished on the same day with all such solemn ceremonies as were thought con-

[83]Barons of the Cinque Ports.
[84]Laces.
[85]Folds or flaps hanging down on either side.
[86]Short prayers.
[87]The coronation offering of an altar cloth and a gold ingot.

venient. The godfather at the font was the Lord Archbishop of Canterbury [**5.3.162**], the godmothers the old Duchess of Norfolk [**167**] and the old Marchioness Dorset, widows; and at the confirmation the Lady Marchioness of Exeter was godmother. The child was named Elizabeth [**5.5.10**].

Upon the day of the christening, the Mayor Sir Stephen Peacock, in a gown of crimson velvet with his collar of *S*'s and all the aldermen, in scarlet with collars and chains, and all the Council of the city with them, took their barge after dinner, at one of the clock, and the citizens had another barge; and so rowed to Greenwich where were many lords, knights, and gentlemen assembled. All the walls between the King's palace and the [Franciscan] Friars were hanged with arras, and all the way strewed with green rushes. The Friars' Church was also hanged with arras.

The font was of silver and stood in the midst of the church, three steps high; which was covered with a fine cloth, and divers gentlemen with aprons and towels about their necks gave attendance about it, that no filth should come in the font. Over it hung a square canopy of crimson satin fringed with gold. About it was a rail covered with red say.[88] Between the choir and the body of the church was a close place with a pan of fire to make the child ready in. When all these things were ordered, the child was brought to the hall, and then every man set forward. . . .

Behind him the Lady Mary of Norfolk, bearing the chrisom,[89] which was very rich of pearl and stone. The old Duchess of Norfolk bore the child in a mantle of purple velvet with a long train furred with ermine [**5.5 SD**]. The Duke of Norfolk with his marshal rod went on the right hand of the said Duchess, and the Duke of Suffolk on the left hand; and before them went the officers-of-arms. The Countess of Kent bore the long train of the child's mantle, and between the Countess of Kent and the child went the Earl of Wiltshire on the right hand and the Earl of Derby on the left hand, supporting the said train. In the midst, over the said child, was borne a canopy by the Lord Rochford, the Lord Hussey, the Lord William Howard, and by the Lord Thomas Howard the Elder. After the child followed many ladies and gentlewomen. When the child was come to the

[88]Silk.
[89]White robe put on a child at baptism as a token of innocence.

church door, the Bishop of London met it with divers bishops and abbots mitered.

When the ceremonies and christening were ended, Garter Chief King-of-Arms cried aloud, "God of his infinite goodness send prosperous life and long to the high and mighty Princess of England Elizabeth!" [**1**]; and then the trumpets blew. Then the Archbishop of Canterbury gave to the Princess a standing cup of gold, the Duchess of Norfolk gave to her a standing cup of gold fretted with pearl, the Marchioness of Dorset gave three gilt bowls, pounced,[90] with a cover, and the Marchioness of Exeter gave three standing bowls, graven, all gilt, with a cover. Then was brought in wafers, comfits, and hippocras[91] in such plenty that every man had as much as he would desire. Then they set forward, the trumpets going before in the same order, toward the King's palace, as they did when they came thitherward, saving that the gifts that the godfather and the godmothers gave were borne before the child by four persons, that is to say: first, Sir John Dudley bore the gift of the Lady of Exeter, the Lord Thomas Howard the Younger bore the gift of the Lady of Dorset, the Lord Fitzwater bore the gift of the Lady of Norfolk, and the Earl of Worcester bore the gift of the Archbishop of Canterbury; and all the one side as they went was full of staff torches to the number of five hundred, borne by the guard and other of the King's servants; and about the child were borne many other proper torches by gentlemen.

In this order they brought the Princess to the Queen's chamber, and tarried there awhile with the Mayor and his brethren the aldermen. And at the last the Dukes of Norfolk and Suffolk came out from the King, thanking them heartily [**14**]; who commanded them to give thanks in his name; which being done, with other courtesies, they departed and so went to their barges. From that time forward (God himself undertaking the tuition[92] of this young princess, having predestinated her to the accomplishment of His divine purpose), she prospered under the Lord's hand as a chosen plant of His watering; and, after the revolution of certain years, with great felicity and joy of all English hearts, attained to the crown of this realm and now reigneth over the same; whose heart the Lord direct in His ways and

[90]Embossed.
[91]A sweet wine.
[92]Guardianship.

long preserve her in life, to His godly will and pleasure and the comfort of all true and faithful subjects [**18**]. . . .

[**936**] At the suit of the Lady Katherine Dowager a curse was sent from the Pope, which cursed both the King and the realm. This curse was set up in the town of Dunkirk in Flanders (for the bringer thereof durst no nearer approach), where it was taken down by one William Locke, a mercer of London. Because it was known that the Lady Katherine Dowager had procured this curse of the Pope, all the order of the court was broken; for, the Duke of Suffolk being sent to her as then lying at Buckton beside Huntington, according to that he had in commandment, discharged a great sort[g] of her household servants, and yet left a convenient number to serve her like a princess; which were sworn to serve her not as Queen but as Princess Dowager. Such as took that oath she utterly refused and would none of their service, so that she remained with the less number of servants about her [**4.2.107**].

[**938**] . . . The one and twentieth of September [1534], Doctor Taylor, Master of the Rolls, was discharged of that office and Thomas Cromwell sworn in his place the nineteenth of October [**5.1.34**]. . . .

On the nineteenth of June [1535] were three monks of the Charterhouse hanged, drawn, and quartered at Tyburn, and their heads and quarters set up about London, for denying the King to be Supreme Head of the Church. Their names were Exmew, Middlemoor, and Newdigate. Also, the one and twentieth of the same month, and for the same cause, Doctor John Fisher Bishop of Rochester was beheaded for denying of the Supremacy, and his head set upon London Bridge but his body buried within Barking Churchyard. This Bishop was of many sore lamented, for he was reported to be a man of great learning and of a very good life. The Pope had elected him a cardinal and sent his hat as far as Calais; but his head was off before his hat was on, so that they met not. On the sixth of July was Sir Thomas More beheaded for the like crime, that is to wit, for denying the King to be Supreme Head. And then the body of Doctor Fisher was taken up and buried with Sir Thomas More's in the Tower. This man was both learned and wise, and given much to a certain pleasure in merry taunts and jesting in most of his communication, which manner he forgot not at the very hour of his death.

I cannot tell (saith Master Hall) whether I should call him a foolish

[g]Number.

wise man or a wise foolish man, for undoubtedly he, beside his learning, had a great wit; but it was so mingled with taunting and mocking that it seemed to them that best knew him that he thought nothing to be well spoken except he had ministered some mock in the communication. Insomuch as, at his coming to the Tower, one of the officers demanded his upper garment for his fee, meaning his gown; and he answered he should have it, and took[93] him his cap, saying it was the uppermost garment that he had. . . .

Also, when he went up the stairs on the scaffold, he desired one of the Sheriff's officers to give him his hand to help him up, and said, "When I come down again, let me shift for myself as well as I can." Also, the hangman[94] kneeled down to him, asking him forgiveness of his death (as the manner is); to whom he said, "I forgive thee, but I promise thee thou shalt never have honesty[95] by striking off my head, my neck is so short." Also, even when he should lay down his head on the block, he, having a great gray beard, stroked out his beard and said to the hangman, "I pray you, let me lay my beard over the block, lest you should cut it." Thus with a mock he ended his life.

God had in most bountiful sort poured his blessings upon this man, enduing him with eloquence, wisdom, and knowledge; but, the grace of God withdrawn from him, he had the right use of none, no, not of reason as it should be rightly used. . . .

[**939**] The Princess Dowager, lying at Kimbolton, fell into her last sickness [**4.1.35**], whereof the King being advertised appointed the Emperor's ambassador that was ledger[96] here with him, named Eustachius Capucius, to go to visit her and to do his commendations to her, and will her to be of good comfort [**4.2.109**]. The ambassador with all diligence did his duty therein, comforting her the best he might; but she, within six days after, perceiving herself to wax very weak and feeble, and to feel death approaching at hand, caused one of her gentlewomen [**127**] to write a letter to the King commending to him her daughter and his [**132**], beseeching him to stand good father unto her; and further desired him to have some consideration of her gentlewomen that had served her, and to see them bestowed in marriage [**140**]. Further, that it would please him to appoint that her servants might have their due wages, and a year's wages beside

[93]Gave.
[94]Executioner.
[95]Honor.
[96]Permanent representative.

[**151**]. This in effect was all that she requested; and so, immediately hereupon, she departed this life the eighth of January [1536] at Kimbolton aforesaid, and was buried at Peterborough. The nine and twentieth of January Queen Anne was delivered of a child before her time which was born dead.

Appendix 1

AN OUTLINE OF ENGLISH HISTORY 1154–1603

This outline attempts to list the chief events in English history from 1154 to 1603 and the more important Elizabethan plays dealing with English history. Dates given for the plays are the assumed dates of composition.

The House of Anjou or Plantagenet (1154–1399)

Henry II (born 1133, reigned 1154–89). "Henry Curtmantle." Son of Geoffrey Plantagenet Count of Anjou and Matilda daughter of Henry I; hence great-grandson of William the Conqueror. Count of Anjou; Duke of Normandy. Married (1152) to Eleanor of Aquitaine (or Guienne), divorced wife of Louis VII of France. Father of (1) Henry; (2) Richard (later–in 1189–Richard I); (3) Geoffrey; and (4) John (later–in 1199 –King John). Conflict between Crown and Church culminating in the murder (1170) of Thomas a Becket Archbishop of Canterbury.

Richard I (born 1157, reigned 1189–99). "Richard Coeur-de-lion" or "the Lion's-heart." Second son of Henry II. Count of Anjou; Duke of Normandy. Married to Berengaria of Navarre. Father of Philip (a bastard). Joined Third Crusade (1189–92), in alliance (1190) with Philip II of France. Upon return from Palestine (1192), captured by Leopold Archduke of Austria and held prisoner by Henry VI Emperor of Germany. Liberated in 1194 upon payment of ransom of 100,000 marks. Mortally wounded while besieging a castle near Limoges (1199).

John (born 1166, reigned 1199–1216). "John Lackland." Brother of Richard I; fourth son of Henry II. Married to: (1) Hadwisa of Gloucester; (2) Isabella of Angoulême. Father of Henry (later Henry III) and Richard. Imprisonment and murder of Arthur Duke of Brittany (1203), son of Geoffrey Duke of Brittany (third son of Henry II) and Constance of Brittany. Lost to France (by 1205) inherited duchies of Normandy, Anjou, Maine, and Touraine. Conflict with Pope Innocent III over election of Archbishop of Canterbury (1205–13). England interdicted (1208). John excommunicated (1209) and deposed by the Pope (1212), who commissioned Philip II of France to carry out deposition. John, under threat of invasion by Philip, made peace by doing homage to the Pope for England (1213). French victory at Battle of Bouvines (1214). Conflict with English Barons (1213–16). Magna Carta (1215). Barons, after John had repudiated Magna Carta (1215), offered throne to Louis, son of Philip II of France (1216). French invaded England, occupying London and most of the southeast. John died (1216) before war came to an issue.

Compare John Bale's *King John* (c. 1535), the anonymous *Troublesome Reign of King John* (c. 1591), and Robert Davenport's *King John and Matilda* (c. 1628–34). Shakespeare's *King John* (c. 1591) deals with the events of 1199–1216.

HENRY III (born 1207, reigned 1216–72). Son of King John. Married to Eleanor of Provence (1236). Father of Edward (later Edward I) and Edmund "Crouchback" Earl of Lancaster. Succeeded to throne (1216) at age of nine. Regency of William Marshall Earl of Pembroke. War with France (1242); English defeat at Taillebourg and Saintes. Rebellion of Barons (1258); Provisions of Oxford. Barons' War (1264); capture of Henry by Simon de Montfort at Battle of Lewes. First House of Commons (1265). Montfort defeated by Prince Edward at Battle of Evesham (1265). Henry restored to full authority (1266). In 1270 Prince Edward joined Seventh Crusade.

EDWARD I (born 1239, reigned 1272–1307). "Edward Longshanks." Son of Henry III. Duke of Gascony; Earl of Chester. Proclaimed King although absent from England on Crusade. Married to: (1) Eleanor of Castile; (2) Margaret of France. Father of: (1) Edward (later Edward II); (2) Thomas Earl of Norfolk; and (3) Edmund Earl of Kent. War against Welsh (from 1277); conquest of Wales (1284). War with Scotland (1291–1307). First complete parliament (1295).

Compare George Peele's *Edward I* (c. 1593).

EDWARD II (born 1284, reigned 1307–27). "Edward of Carnarvon." Son of Edward I. Created Prince of Wales (1301), first heir apparent to bear this title. Married (1308) to Isabella of France, daughter of Philip IV. Father of Edward (later Edward III). Edward II's Gascon favorite, Piers Gaveston, who had been banished by Edward I, recalled and created Earl of Cornwall (1307). Barons, led by King's cousin Thomas Earl of Lancaster, demanded dismissal of Gaveston, whom, however, Edward made Deputy of Ireland (1308). Gaveston, again recalled, captured by Earl of

Warwick and executed (1312). War with Scotland resumed; Edward decisively defeated by Robert Bruce at Battle of Bannockburn (1314). Hugh Despenser and his son became Edward's favorites (1320). Barons, again rebelling, defeated at Battle of Boroughbridge; Lancaster executed (1322). Queen Isabella, in France, joined with exiled Roger Mortimer first Earl of March (1326). Together, they invaded England, captured King Edward, executed the Despensers, and assumed the royal power. Prince Edward declared King by act of parliament and King Edward deposed (1327). Edward murdered at Berkeley Castle (1327).

Compare Christopher Marlowe's *Edward II* (c. 1592).

EDWARD III (born 1312, reigned 1327–77). "Edward of Windsor." Son of Edward II. Duke of Aquitaine; Earl of Chester. Married to Philippa of Hainaut. Father of: (1) Edward of Woodstock Prince of Wales, "the Black Prince" (died 1376); (2) William of Hatfield (died in infancy); (3) Lionel Duke of Clarence; (4) John of Gaunt Duke of Lancaster; (5) Edmund of Langley Duke of York; (6) Thomas of Woodstock Duke of Gloucester; and (7) William of Windsor (died in infancy). Succeeded to throne (1327) at age of fourteen; regency of his mother Queen Isabella and Roger Mortimer Earl of March. Edward assumed the royal power in 1330; Mortimer executed and Queen confined. War with Scotland (1333). In 1337 Edward claimed French crown through his mother Isabella, daughter of Philip IV of France; thus began Hundred Years War (1337–1453). English victory at Battle of Crécy (1346); capture of Calais (1347). Renewal of Scottish War (1346). In 1349 the bubonic plague ("the Black Death") broke out in England, killing more than a third of population. In 1356 the Black Prince, stationed at Bordeaux as Governor of Gascony, took King John II of France prisoner at Poitiers. Peace of Bretigny (1360). According to terms of treaty, Edward gave up claim to French crown but retained Calais, Poitou, Aquitaine, Gascony, and other French provinces; King John was to be liberated upon payment of ransom of 3,000,000 gold crowns. (Unable to raise the money, John returned voluntarily to captivity in England, where he died in 1364.) The war went increasingly in favor of French until, by 1374, the English had lost all their continental holdings but Bordeaux, Bayonne, and Calais. Upon death of the Black Prince in 1376, his son Richard became heir apparent.

Compare the anonymous *Edward III* (1595).

RICHARD II (born 1367, reigned 1377–99, died 1400). "Richard of Bordeaux." Son of Edward the Black Prince (died 1376); grandson of Edward III. Married to: (1) Anne of Bohemia; (2) Isabella of France. Died without issue. Succeeded to throne (1377) at age of ten. Regency of his uncles John of Gaunt Duke of Lancaster and Thomas of Woodstock Duke of Gloucester. The Peasants' Rebellion or Great Revolt (1381); Jack Straw the leader in Essex, Wat Tyler in Kent. In so-called Merciless Parliament (1388), the Lords Appellant impeached King's favorites, several of whom were executed. In 1389 Richard dismissed his guardians and assumed control of government. In 1397 he retaliated against Lords Appellant, Gloucester being imprisoned at Calais and murdered, Earl of Arundel executed, Earl of Warwick imprisoned; and in 1398 he banished Earl of Nottingham (by then Duke of Norfolk) and Earl of Derby (by then Duke of Hereford). Banishment of Thomas Arundel Archbishop of Canterbury (1397). Upon death of John of Gaunt (1399), Richard confiscated Lancastrian properties. Hereford, while Richard was engaged in putting down rebellion in Ireland, returned to England to claim his Lancastrian inheritance (July, 1399); he was supported by Percys, York, and other powerful nobles. Richard captured in Wales upon his return from Ireland (August), forced by parliament to abdicate, and deposed (September). Hereford, now Duke of Lancaster, named King. Richard imprisoned (1399) and subsequently murdered (1400). "The Lancastrian Revolution."

Compare the anonymous *Jack Straw* (c. 1593), which deals with the Peasants' Rebellion, and the anonymous *Woodstock* (1592–5), which deals with the murder of Thomas of Woodstock Duke of Gloucester. Shakespeare's *Richard II* (1595) deals with the events of 1398–1400.

The House of Lancaster (1399–1461)

Henry IV (born 1367, reigned 1399–1413). Henry Bolingbroke; "Henry of Lancaster." Son of John of Gaunt Duke of Lancaster; grandson of Edward III. Earl of Derby; Duke of Hereford; Duke of Lancaster. Married to: (1) Mary Bohun; (2) Joanna of Navarre. Father of: (1) Henry Prince of Wales (later Henry V); (2) Thomas Duke of Clarence; (3) John of Lancaster Duke of Bedford; and (4) Humphrey Duke of Gloucester. Rebellion of 1400 led by Kent, Huntingdon, Salisbury, and Rutland (Aumerle); betrayed by Rutland and quickly put down; Kent, Huntingdon, and Salisbury executed. Persecution of Lollards (1401). War with Scotland (1402); English victory by Percys at Battle of Holmedon. Rebellion of 1403 led by Northumberland, his brother Worcester, and his son Henry Percy surnamed "Hotspur," in alliance with Welsh leader Owen Glendower, his son-in-law Sir Edmund Mortimer, and Scottish Earl Douglas. Defeat of rebels at Shrewsbury; Hotspur killed, Worcester executed, Northumberland (not present at Shrewsbury) pardoned with fine. Rebellion of 1405 led by Northumberland, Richard Scrope Archbishop of York, and Thomas Mowbray (son of exiled Duke of Norfolk). Aim of rebellion was to dethrone Henry in favor of Edmund Mortimer fifth Earl of March (to be distinguished from his uncle Sir Edmund Mortimer), whose title, from the point of view of hereditary right, since he was descended from Lionel Duke of Clarence (third son of Edward III), was superior to that of Henry, descended from John of Gaunt Duke of Lancaster (fourth son of Edward III). The rebellion suppressed; Mowbray and Archbishop of York executed. Northumberland fled to Scotland. Rebellion of 1408 led by Northumberland, who was defeated and killed at Battle of Bramham Moor.

Shakespeare's *1 Henry IV* (1597) deals with the events of 1402–3; his *2 Henry IV* (1598), with those of 1403–13.

HENRY V (born 1387, reigned 1413–22). "Henry of Monmouth." Son of Henry IV. Prince of Wales. Married to Katherine of Valois. Father of Henry (later Henry VI). Further persecution of Lollards (1413); arrest and escape into Wales of Sir John Oldcastle Lord Cobham. Conspiracy to enthrone Edmund Mortimer Earl of March discovered and quashed (1415); chief conspirators–Richard Earl of Cambridge, Henry Lord Scrope, and Sir Thomas Grey–executed. Henry, reviving Edward III's claim to French crown, invaded France, thus resuming Hundred Years War (1415). Capture of Harfleur (September); overwhelming English victory at Battle of Agincourt (October). Capture and execution of Sir John Oldcastle (1417). Resumption of war with France (1417); capture of Rouen by the English (1419). Treaty of Troyes (1420); provided that Henry should marry Princess Katherine of Valois (daughter of Charles VI), that he should be Regent of France during life of Charles VI, and that he or his heir should be King of France after death of Charles VI. In further fighting, Duke of Clarence was killed and Henry conquered rest of France north of the Loire (1421). Death of Henry at Vincennes (1422).

Compare the anonymous *Famous Victories of Henry V* (c. 1588) and *Sir John Oldcastle* (1599) by Michael Drayton and others. Shakespeare's *Henry V* (1599) deals with the events of 1413–22.

HENRY VI (born 1421, reigned 1422–61, 1470–1). Son of Henry V. Married to Margaret of Anjou. Father of Edward Prince of Wales (1453–71). Succeeded to throne (1422) at age of nine months. Protectorship of his uncles John Duke of Bedford and Humphrey Duke of Gloucester. Bedford, as Regent of France, continued the French war, allying himself with Philip the Good Duke of Burgundy by marriage to Philip's sister Anne (1423). The English, attempting to extend their dominion south of the Loire, besieged Orleans (1428). Siege raised by Joan of Arc (1429), who then conducted Charles the Dauphin to Reims, where he was crowned King of France. Capture of Joan at Compiègne by Burgundians, who turned her over to English (1430); her conviction of witchcraft and execution at Rouen (1431). Death of Bedford (1435). Failure of Burgundian alliance and growing political factionalism in England (Gloucester supporting the war while Cardinal Beaufort opposed it) caused war to go increasingly against English until, by 1453, they had lost all of France but Calais. Marriage of Henry to Margaret of Anjou (1445), negotiated by William de la Pole Earl (later Duke) of Suffolk. Marriage unpopular in England because its terms required that Anjou and Maine be given up to Margaret's father René Duke of Anjou. Gloucester, who had opposed the marriage, arrested for treason and shortly afterward found dead in his bed (1447). It was rumored that he had been murdered by Suffolk, the Queen's favorite, who now became Henry's chief counselor. Suffolk impeached and banished but captured at sea and summarily executed (1450). Revolt (1450) of men of Kent under leadership of Jack Cade ("Cade's Rebellion"); Complaint of the Commons of Kent. Rebels defeated, after some initial successes; Cade killed by Sheriff of Kent. John Talbot Earl of Shrewsbury killed in France (1453); end of Hundred Years War.

Richard Duke of York named Protector of the realm (1454) upon Henry's becoming imbecilic, hence incapable of rule. John Beaufort Duke of Somerset, the Queen's favorite, named Protector in place of York (1455). York accordingly took up arms, beginning Wars of the Roses (Red of Lancaster, White of York). First Battle of Saint Albans (1455), a Yorkist victory; Somerset killed. Ludlow Field (1459), a Lancastrian victory; flight of York to Ireland and of York's son Edward Earl of March to Calais. Return to England of Edward, supported by Richard Neville Earl of Warwick and his father the Earl of Salisbury (1460); return of York. Battle of Northampton (July, 1460), a Yorkist victory. York resumed protectorship, it being agreed that Henry should remain King while he lived but that York or his heir should become King after Henry's death. (Although Henry's claim to throne was stronger than York's by virtue of long possession and assent of parliament, York's claim, from the point of view of hereditary right, was stronger than Henry's by virtue of his descent from Lionel Duke of Clarence, third son of Edward III, as compared with Henry's descent from John of Gaunt Duke of Lancaster, fourth son of that King.) This arrangement, which barred Prince Edward (born 1453) from the succession, moved Queen Margaret to resume wars. Battle of Wakefield (December, 1460), a Lancastrian victory; York, together with his second son the Earl of Rutland and the Earl of Salisbury, captured and executed. Battle of Mortimer's Cross (January, 1461), a victory for Yorkists led by Edward Earl of March, now Duke of York. Second Battle of Saint Albans (February), a Lancastrian victory. The Lancastrians, however, failed to capitalize on their advantage, and Edward, as York's heir, entered London in triumph and was proclaimed King by Warwick "the Kingmaker." Towton Field (March), the largest and bloodiest battle of Wars of the Roses, an overwhelming Yorkist victory. Flight of Henry and Queen Margaret to Scotland; deposition of Henry. Coronation of Edward.

Shakespeare's *1 Henry VI* (c. 1590) deals with the events of 1422–53; his *2 Henry VI* (c. 1591), with those of 1445–55; and his *3 Henry VI* (c. 1592), with those of 1455–71.

The House of York (1461–85)

Edward IV (born 1442, reigned 1461–70, 1471–83). Son of Richard Plantagenet Duke of York; great-grandson both of Lionel Duke of Clarence (third son of Edward III) and of Edmund of Langley Duke of York (fifth son of Edward III). Earl of March; Duke of York. Married to Elizabeth Woodville (Grey). Father of: (1) Edward Prince of Wales (later Edward V); (2) Richard Duke of York; and (3) Princess Elizabeth (later wife of Henry VII). Succeeded to throne (1461) at age of nineteen. Battle of Hexham (1464), a Yorkist victory; capture and imprisonment of Henry. Marriage (1464) to Lady Elizabeth Grey (Elizabeth Woodville), widow of Sir John Grey, a Lancastrian killed at the Second Battle of Saint Albans (1461). Consequent alienation of Warwick, who had been negotiating a French marriage. Rebellion in Yorkshire instigated by Warwick (1469); capture and brief imprisonment of Edward. Rebellion in Lincolnshire (1470); Battle of Empingham, a victory for Edward. Warwick, in alliance with Edward's brother George Duke of Clarence, fled to France, where they joined exiled Queen Margaret and her son Prince Edward; betrothal of Prince Edward to Warwick's daughter Anne Neville. Landing of Warwick in south; flight of Edward to Flanders. Restoration of Henry to throne by Warwick. Edward, aided by Duke of Burgundy, landed at Ravenspur and advanced by stages on London (March, 1471); his reconciliation with Clarence. Battle of Barnet (April), a victory for Edward; Warwick killed. Landing of Margaret and Prince Edward at Weymouth. Battle of Tewkesbury (April), a Yorkist victory; Prince Edward (aged seventeen) killed, Queen Margaret captured. Murder of Henry in Tower of London (May). Quarrel (1472) between Clarence (married to Isabella Neville) and Gloucester (married to Anne Neville) over inheritance of Earl of Warwick. War with France briefly renewed (1475). Ransom of Queen Margaret (1476). Clarence convicted of treason and secretly executed (1478).

Compare Thomas Heywood's *1* and *2 Edward IV* (1599). Shakespeare's *Richard III* (c. 1593) deals with (among others) the events of 1471–83.

Edward V (born 1470, reigned April-June, 1483, died during latter part of 1483). Son of Edward IV. Earl of Pembroke; Prince of Wales.

Succeeded to throne (1483) at age of twelve. Immediately after death of his father, the young King was separated by his uncle Richard Duke of Gloucester from his maternal uncle Earl Rivers, Lord Richard Grey, and others of the Queen's party and lodged in Tower of London. Gloucester named Protector of the realm. The Queen and her second son Richard Duke of York took sanctuary at Westminster. Execution of Lord Hastings, Rivers, and Grey. The Queen compelled to allow young York to join Edward in Tower. Propagation by Dr. Ralph Shaw (Richard's chaplain) and Duke of Buckingham of charge that Edward and young York were illegitimate, Edward IV allegedly having been betrothed or married to Lady Eleanor Butler at time of his marriage to Elizabeth Woodville. Deposition of Edward V. Late in June Gloucester accepted an offer of the crown made by deputation of lords and London citizens.

Shakespeare's *Richard III* (c. 1593) deals with (among others) the events of 1483.

RICHARD III (born 1452, reigned June, 1483-August, 1485). "Richard Crookback." Brother of Edward IV; son of Richard Plantagenet Duke of York. Duke of Gloucester. Married (1472) to Anne Neville, daughter of Warwick the Kingmaker, earlier betrothed to Prince Edward (son of Henry VI). Father of Edward Prince of Wales (died 1484). Murder of Edward V and his brother Richard Duke of York in Tower of London (latter part of 1483). It is not clear whether murder was instigated by Richard, Henry Tudor Earl of Richmond, or Duke of Buckingham, each of whom, being in line of succession to crown, had a motive for eliminating direct heirs of Edward IV; most modern scholars, though conceding that Richard was not the villain depicted in such Tudor propaganda as the history by Sir Thomas More, believe he was probably responsible for the murder. Conspiracy against Richard by Richmond, Buckingham, and John Morton Bishop of Ely (1483). Rebellion in Wales led by Buckingham (October); his defeat, capture, and execution; abortive attempt at invasion from France by Richmond. Death of Richard's son Prince Edward (April, 1484). Death of Queen Anne (March, 1485). Landing by Richmond with French support at Milford Haven (August, 1485). Bosworth Field; defection of Lord Stanley to side of Richmond; death of Richard in battle. Richmond proclaimed King as Henry VII.

Compare Thomas Legge's *Richardus Tertius* (1573) and the anonymous *True Tragedy of Richard III* (1594). Shakespeare's *Richard III* (c. 1593) deals with (among others) the events of 1483–5.

THE HOUSE OF TUDOR (1485–1603)

HENRY VII (born 1457, reigned 1485–1509). Henry Tudor. Son of Edmund Tudor (son of Henry V's widow Queen Katherine by her second husband Owen Tudor) and Margaret Beaufort (great-granddaughter of John of Gaunt, fourth son of Edward III). (But the latter line had been illegitimated and hence excluded from the succession.) Earl of Richmond. Married to Elizabeth of York. Father of: (1) Arthur Prince of Wales (died 1502); (2) Prince Henry (later Henry VIII); (3) Princess Margaret (later married to James IV of Scotland, thus becoming maternal ancestor of Stuart line); and (4) Princess Mary (later married to Louis XII of France; through her second husband Charles Brandon Duke of Suffolk she became ultimately grandmother of Lady Jane Grey). Lived in exile, chiefly in Brittany, during period of Yorkist supremacy following Battle of Tewkesbury (1471–85). Upon death of Edward IV conspired with Duke of Buckingham and John Morton Bishop of Ely to seize throne; almost invaded England (1483). Landed at Milford Haven (1485); defeat and death of Richard III at Bosworth Field. Henry immediately proclaimed King by right of conquest. Marriage to Elizabeth of York (January, 1486), daughter of Edward IV, uniting rival claims of Lancaster and York; but Elizabeth's coronation delayed till November, 1487, through Henry's reluctance to recognize her claim to throne. Put down series of Yorkist rebellions: by Lord Lovel and Staffords (1486); by Lambert Simnel, who posed as Earl of Warwick (confined by Henry in Tower of London), son of Duke of Clarence, brother of Edward IV (1487); and by Perkin Warbeck, who posed as Richard Duke of York, second son of Edward IV (1492–9). War with France (1491); Peace of Étaples (1492). Suppression of Cornish insurrection and capture of Warbeck (1497); execution of Warbeck and the Earl of Warwick (1499). Marriage of Prince Arthur to Katherine of Aragon, daughter of Ferdinand King of Aragon and Isabella Queen of Castile (1501). Death of Prince Arthur, aged fifteen (1502). Papal dispensation secured to permit marriage of Katherine to Prince Henry (aged eleven in 1502). (The marriage was delayed by diplomatic maneuvering till after Henry VII's death.) Peace with Scotland (1502); marriage of Princess Margaret to James IV of Scotland. Henry instituted Court of Star Chamber, greatly increased the royal power, and amassed enormous personal wealth.

Compare John Ford's *Perkin Warbeck* (1634).

HENRY VIII (born 1491, reigned 1509–47). Second son of Henry VII. Succeeded to throne (1509) at age of seventeen. Married to: (1) Katherine of Aragon; (2) Anne Boleyn; (3) Jane Seymour; (4) Anne of Cleves; (5) Katherine Howard; and (6) Katherine Parr. Father of: (1) Mary (later–in 1553–Mary I); (2) Elizabeth (later–in 1558–Elizabeth I); and (3) Edward (later–in 1547–Edward VI). Marriage (1) to Katherine of Aragon (1509), widow of his older brother Prince Arthur (died 1502). War with France (1511); Battle of the Spurs (1513), an English victory under Henry's personal command. War with Scotland (1513) culminating in Flodden Field, an overwhelming English victory in which James IV of Scotland was killed. Peace with Scotland and France (1514). Thomas Wolsey made Archbishop of York and Lord Chancellor (1515); then Cardinal and Papal Legate (1516). Birth of Princess Mary (1516). Meeting with Francis I of France at the Field of the Cloth of Gold near Calais (1520). Awarded title of *Fidei Defensor* (Defender of the Faith) by Pope Leo X for writing treatise defending seven sacraments in controversy with Martin Luther (1521). The Divorce Question (1527–33). Wolsey's failure to secure annulment of papal dispensation permitting Henry's marriage to his brother's widow Katherine led to his being removed from office (1529) and charged with treason (1530); he died while under arrest, on his way to imprisonment in Tower of London. Sir Thomas More made Lord Chancellor (1529). Thomas Cromwell became Henry's chief adviser (1530). Henry first named Supreme Head of the Church of England (1531). Secret marriage (2) to Anne Boleyn (January, 1533). Divorce granted Henry by an ecclesiastical court under the jurisdiction of Thomas Cranmer Archbishop of Canterbury (1533). Birth of Princess Elizabeth (September, 1533). First Act of Supremacy (1534), separating the Church of England from the Roman Catholic Church and requiring that the King be accepted as "the only Supreme Head on earth of the Church of England." The Act of Succession (1534); this, in settling the crown on children of Anne Boleyn, had the effect of illegitimating Princess Mary. Execution of Sir Thomas More and John Fisher Bishop of Rochester for refusing to acknowledge royal supremacy (1535). Dissolution of the smaller monasteries (1536), carried out by Cromwell as Vicar-General of the Church. Rebellion in Yorkshire (the Pilgrimage of Grace) put down (1536); Robert Aske and other leaders executed. Execution of Queen Anne on charge of adultery (1536). Marriage (3) to Jane Seymour (1536); birth of Prince Edward and death of Queen Jane (1537). Dissolution of the larger monasteries (1539). Bill of Six Articles (1539), asserting against the attacks of the Reformers the chief points of the Old Religion, among them transubstantiation, private masses, auricular confession, and a celibate clergy. Marriage (4) to Anne of Cleves (1540); fall and execution of Cromwell; annulment of marriage to Anne. Marriage (5) to Katherine Howard (1540); her execution on charge of adultery (1542). War resumed with Scotland (1542–3); Battle of Solway Moss (1542), an English victory. Marriage (6) to Katherine Parr (1543), who outlived Henry. War resumed with France (1544–6); Boulogne captured by the English.

Compare *Sir Thomas More* (c. 1596) by Anthony Munday and others, the anonymous *Thomas Lord Cromwell* (1602), and Samuel Rowley's *When You See Me You Know Me* (1603–5). Shakespeare's *Henry VIII* (1613) deals with the events of 1520–44.

EDWARD VI (born 1537, reigned 1547–53). Son of Henry VIII by his third wife Jane Seymour. Prince of Wales. Succeeded to throne at age of nine. Protectorship of Edward's maternal uncle Edward Seymour Earl of Hertford, now Duke of Somerset. War with Scotland resumed (1547); Battle of Pinkie, an English victory. Strong Protestant reaction led by Somerset and Archbishop Cranmer led to repeal (1547) of Six Articles (1539) and to other reforms, such as iconoclasm in churches, elimination of altars, authorized use of English Bible, use of a Book of Homilies, and passage of First Act of Uniformity (1549), which forbade the Roman Catholic mass and required use of Cranmer's First Prayer Book. Rebellions in Norfolk (led by Robert Ket) and in Devonshire and Cornwall put down (1549). Somerset forced to resign the Protectorship (1549), which passed to John Dudley Earl (later Duke) of Northumberland. Somerset executed on charges of treason (1552). Further ecclesiastical reforms codified in Forty-two Articles (1553), the work largely of Archbishop Cranmer and Nicholas Ridley Bishop of London. Northumberland, upon a failure of King's health in 1553, persuaded Edward to sign a will excluding his half sisters Mary and Elizabeth from the succession and devising the succession to Lady Jane Grey, to whom Northumberland promptly married his son Guildford Dudley; and on Edward's death he proclaimed Jane Queen. However, popular sentiment was strongly in favor of Mary, and after a reign of nine days Jane was deposed and the crown transferred to Mary. Conviction of treason of Northumberland, Lady Jane Grey, and Guildford Dudley; execution of Northumberland (1553).

MARY I (born 1516, reigned 1553–8). Mary Tudor; "Bloody Mary." Half sister of Edward VI; daughter of Henry VIII by his first wife Katherine of Aragon. Married to Philip II of Spain. Succeeded to throne after a nine-day usurpation by Lady Jane Grey perpetrated by Jane's father-in-law the Duke of Northumberland. Legitimated by act of parliament (1553). Opposition to a projected Spanish marriage (with its implication of a Catholic succession) led to a rebellion in Kent (January, 1554) under leadership of Sir Thomas Wyatt (son of the poet); rebellion put down and Wyatt executed. Execution of Lady Jane Grey and her husband Guildford Dudley (February, 1554). Papal authority restored in England with the return as Papal Legate of Cardinal Reginald Pole (1554), who had been in exile since 1536 for his opposition to Henry VIII's divorce from Katherine of Aragon. Marriage to Philip II of Spain, son of Emperor Charles V (1554). Repeal of laws establishing Protestantism in England and reestablishment of Roman Catholicism (1555). (It was, however, impossible to recover properties of dissolved monasteries.) Persecution (from 1555) of the Protestants, of whom about 300 were executed during Mary's reign. Revival of French war (1557), which at first went well but which ended with loss of Calais, last English foothold on Continent (January, 1558).

Compare *Sir Thomas Wyatt* (1602) by Thomas Dekker and John Webster, Thomas Drue's *Duchess of Suffolk* (1623–4), and Thomas Heywood's *1 If You Know Not Me You Know Nobody* (1603–5).

ELIZABETH I (born 1533, reigned 1558–1603). Half sister of Mary I and Edward VI; daughter of Henry VIII by his second wife Anne Boleyn. Supported Mary's claim to the throne against that of Lady Jane Grey (1553). Took no part in Wyatt's Rebellion (1554), though suspected of complicity therein and briefly imprisoned. Named successor by Mary on her deathbed (1558). Restoration of Protestantism and royal supremacy; Elizabethan Settlement. Rebellion of Scottish lords against Mary Stuart Queen of Scots (1567); her flight to England and imprisonment by Elizabeth (1568). (Mary, as a granddaughter of Margaret Tudor daughter of Henry VII, was next in line of succession after line of Henry VIII, but according to Catholic opinion, Mary rather than the allegedly illegitimate Elizabeth should have succeeded to throne in 1558.) Unsuccessful rebellion in North in favor of Mary led by the Earls of Northumberland and Westmorland (1569). Excommunication of Elizabeth by Pope Pius V (1570). Ridolfi Conspiracy (1571). Saint Bartholomew's Day Massacre in France (1572). Persecution of the English Catholics. Support of the Netherlands against Spanish occupation. Babington Conspiracy (1586). Mary Queen of Scots convicted of complicity in Babington Conspiracy and executed (1587). Invincible Armada (1588). Rebellion in Ireland (1599). Essex's Rebellion (1601); his execution. Peaceful succession of James VI of Scotland (son of Mary Queen of Scots) as James I of England (1603).

Compare Thomas Heywood's *2 If You Know Not Me You Know Nobody* (1603–5).

Appendix 2

GENEALOGICAL TABLES

(a) THE HOUSE OF ANJOU OR PLANTAGENET

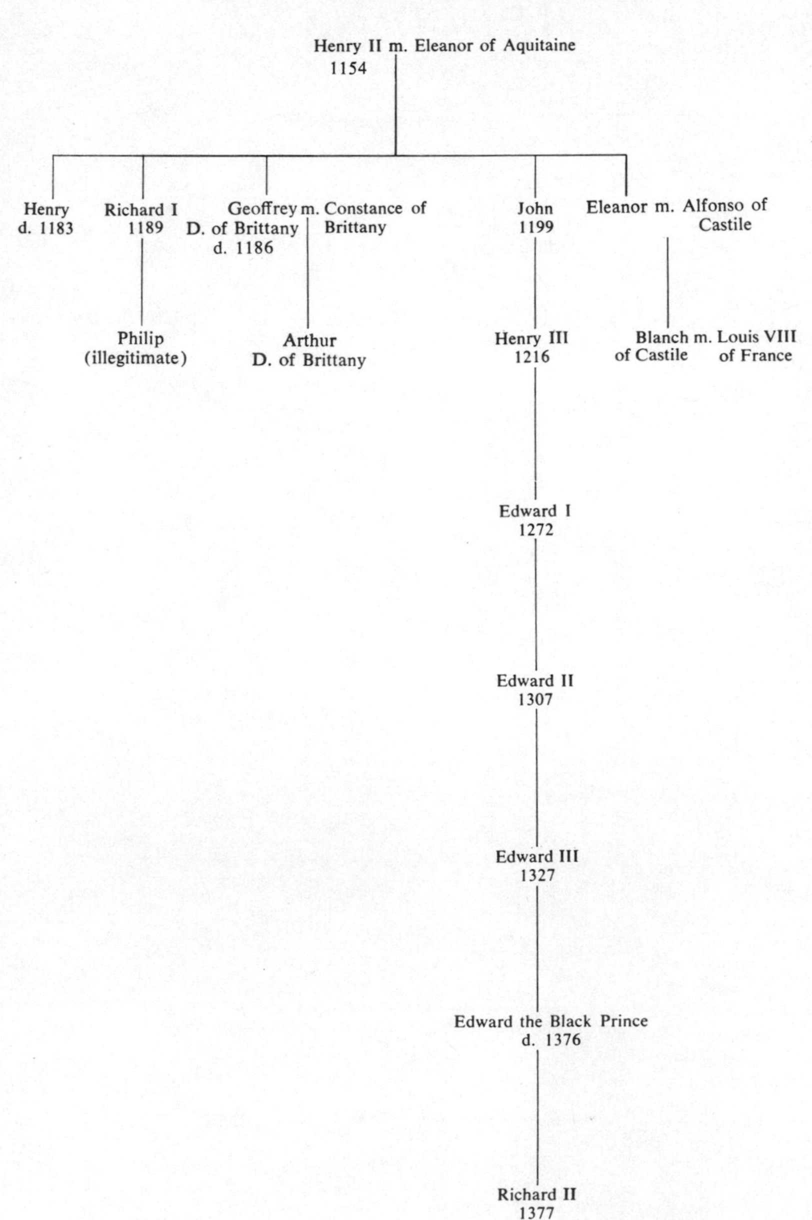

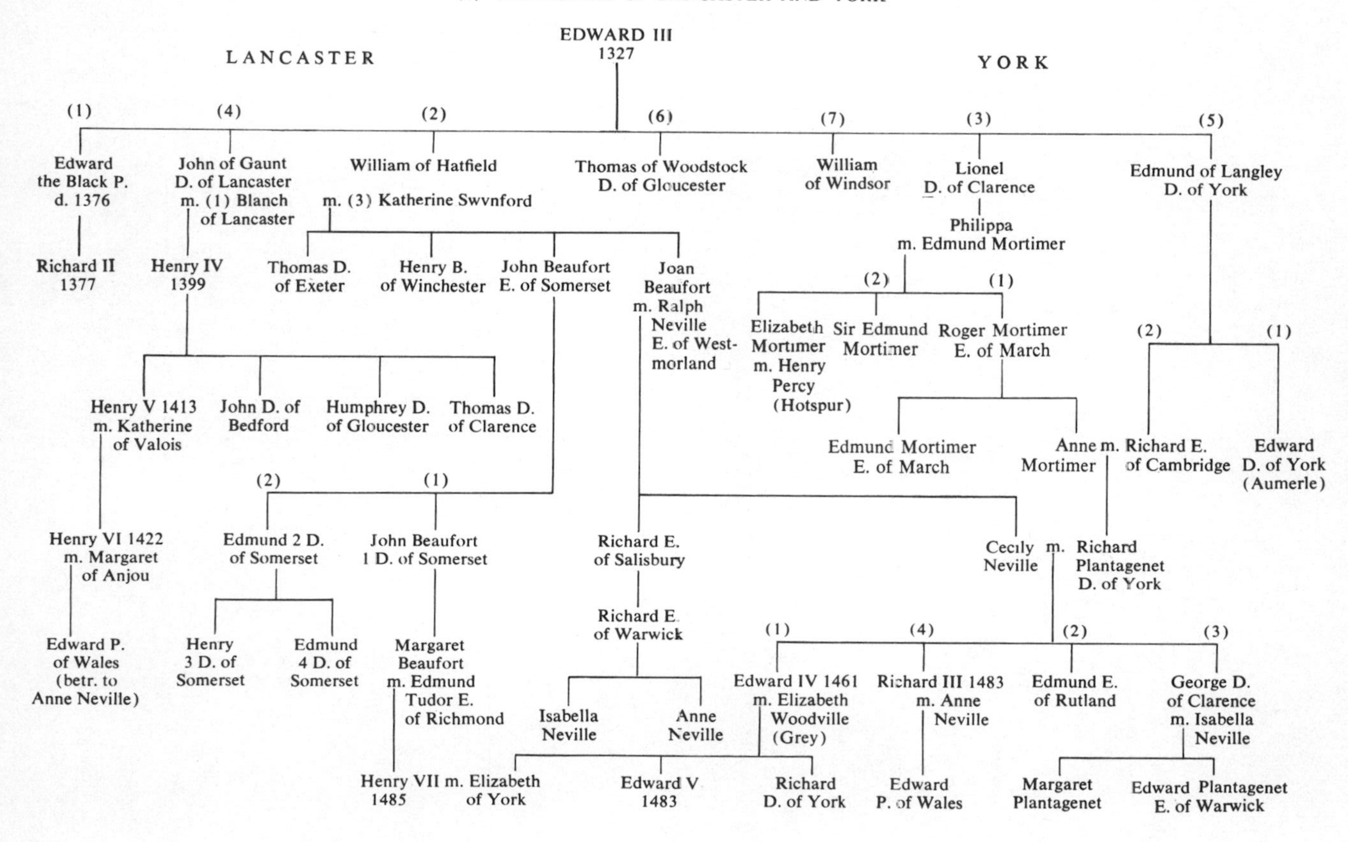
(b) THE HOUSES OF LANCASTER AND YORK
EDWARD III
1327
LANCASTER
YORK
(1)
(4)
(2)
(6)
(7)
(3)
(5)
Edward
the Black P.
d. 1376
John of Gaunt
D. of Lancaster
m. (1) Blanch
of Lancaster
William of Hatfield
m. (3) Katherine Swynford
Thomas of Woodstock
D. of Gloucester
William
of Windsor
Lionel
D. of Clarence
Edmund of Langley
D. of York
Philippa
m. Edmund Mortimer
Richard II
1377
Henry IV
1399
Thomas D.
of Exeter
Henry B.
of Winchester
John Beaufort
E. of Somerset
Joan
Beaufort
m. Ralph
Neville
E. of West-
morland
(2)
(1)
Elizabeth
Mortimer
m. Henry
Percy
(Hotspur)
Sir Edmund
Mortimer
Roger Mortimer
E. of March
(2)
(1)
Henry V 1413
m. Katherine
of Valois
John D. of
Bedford
Humphrey D.
of Gloucester
Thomas D.
of Clarence
Edmund Mortimer
E. of March
Anne m. Richard E.
Mortimer
of Cambridge
Edward
D. of York
(Aumerle)
(2)
(1)
Henry VI 1422
m. Margaret
of Anjou
Edmund 2 D.
of Somerset
John Beaufort
1 D. of Somerset
Richard E.
of Salisbury
Cecily m. Richard
Neville
Plantagenet
D. of York
Richard E.
of Warwick
(1)
(4)
(2)
(3)
Edward P.
of Wales
(betr. to
Anne Neville)
Henry
3 D. of
Somerset
Edmund
4 D. of
Somerset
Margaret
Beaufort
m. Edmund
Tudor E.
of Richmond
Isabella
Neville
Anne
Neville
Edward IV 1461
m. Elizabeth
Woodville
(Grey)
Richard III 1483
m. Anne
Neville
Edmund E.
of Rutland
George D.
of Clarence
m. Isabella
Neville
Henry VII m. Elizabeth
1485
of York
Edward V
1483
Richard
D. of York
Edward
P. of Wales
Margaret
Plantagenet
Edward Plantagenet
E. of Warwick

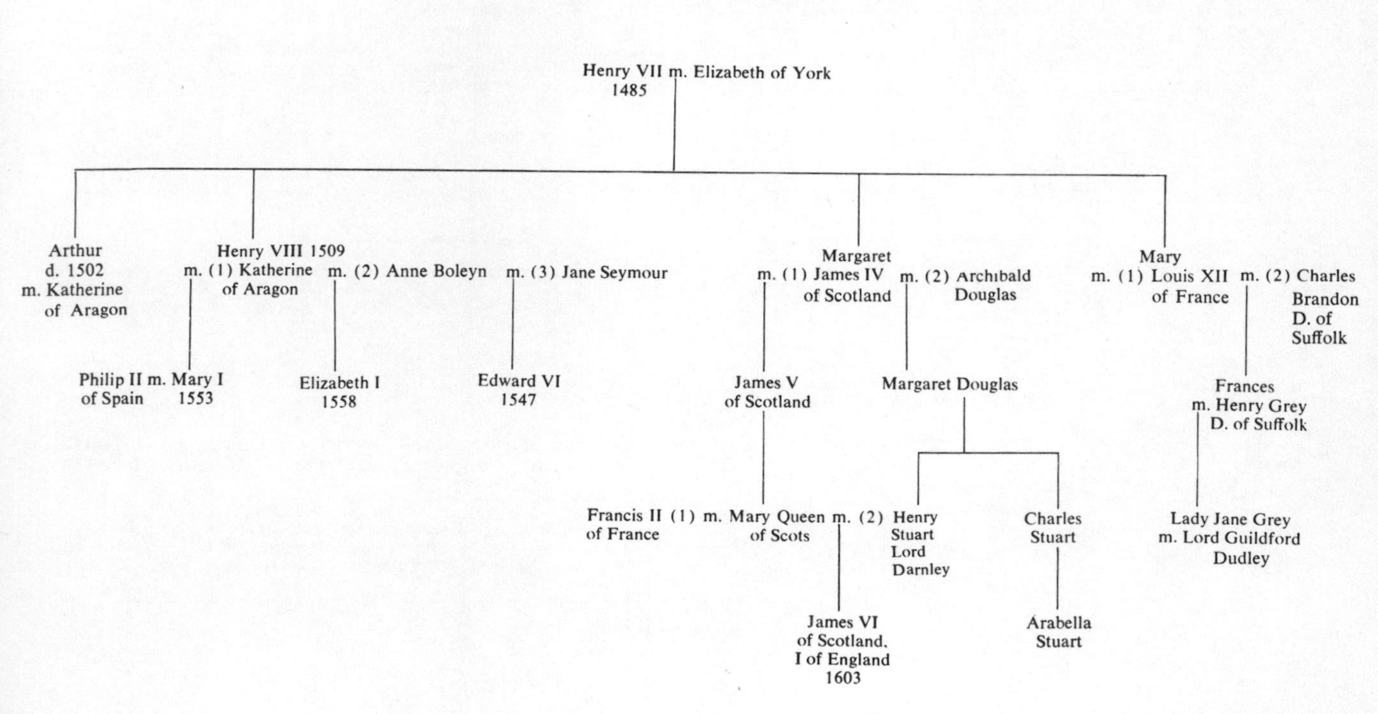
(c) THE HOUSE OF TUDOR
Henry VII m. Elizabeth of York
1485
Arthur
d. 1502
m. Katherine
of Aragon
Henry VIII 1509
m. (1) Katherine
of Aragon
m. (2) Anne Boleyn
m. (3) Jane Seymour
Philip II m. Mary I
of Spain 1553
Elizabeth I
1558
Edward VI
1547
Margaret
m. (1) James IV
of Scotland
m. (2) Archibald
Douglas
James V
of Scotland
Margaret Douglas
Francis II (1) m. Mary Queen m. (2) Henry
of France of Scots
Stuart
Lord
Darnley
Charles
Stuart
James VI
of Scotland.
I of England
1603
Arabella
Stuart
Mary
m. (1) Louis XII
of France
m. (2) Charles
Brandon
D. of
Suffolk
Frances
m. Henry Grey
D. of Suffolk
Lady Jane Grey
m. Lord Guildford
Dudley

Appendix 3

A MAP OF ENGLAND AND WESTERN FRANCE

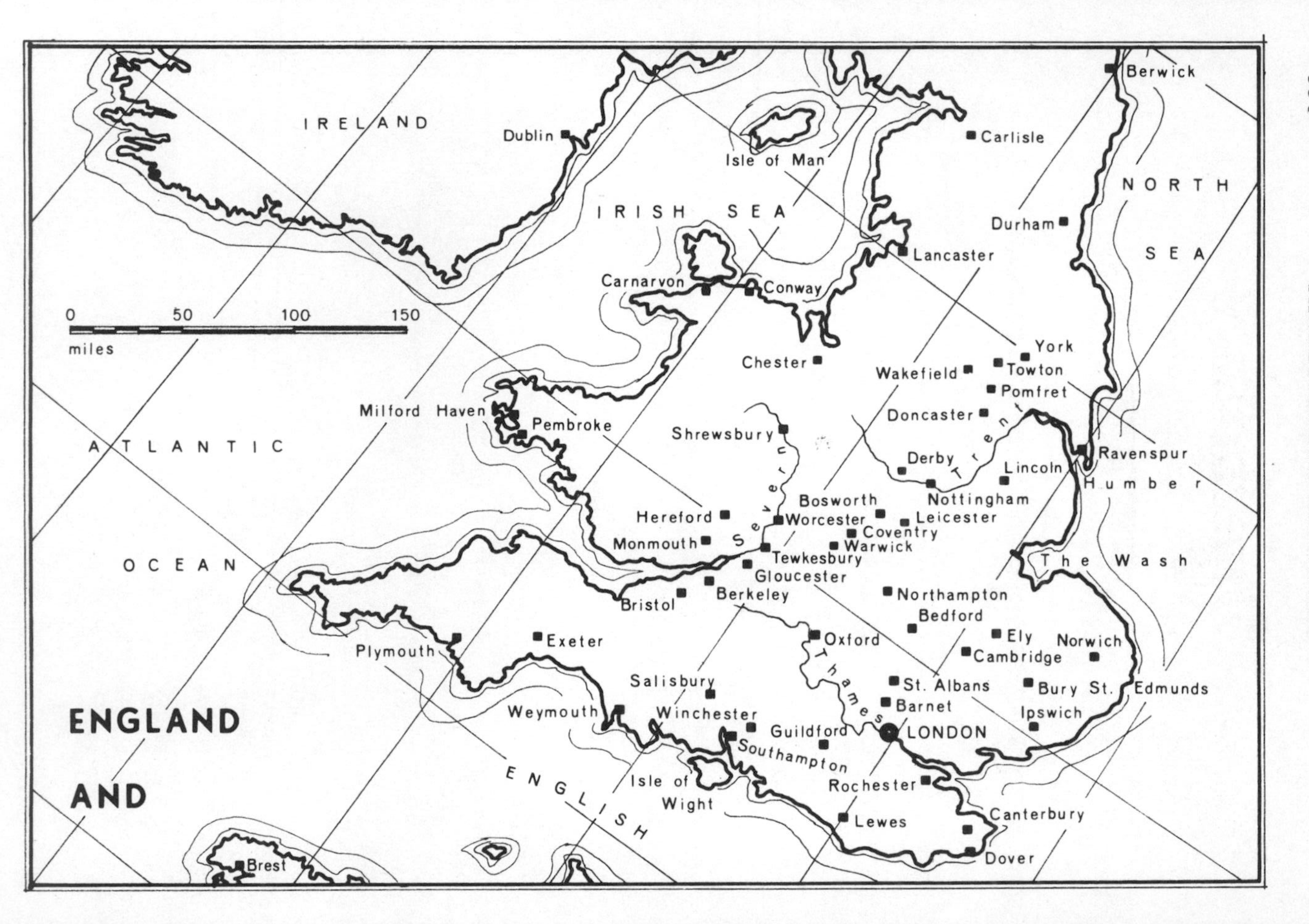
ENGLAND
AND
IRELAND
IRISH SEA
NORTH
SEA
ATLANTIC
OCEAN
ENGLISH
0
50
100
150
miles
Berwick
Dublin
Carlisle
Isle of Man
Durham
Lancaster
Carnarvon
Conway
Chester
York
Wakefield
Towton
Pomfret
Doncaster
Milford Haven
Pembroke
Shrewsbury
Derby
Trent
Lincoln
Ravenspur
Humber
Nottingham
Bosworth
Hereford
Worcester
Leicester
Coventry
Severn
Monmouth
Warwick
Tewkesbury
The Wash
Gloucester
Berkeley
Bristol
Northampton
Bedford
Ely
Norwich
Exeter
Oxford
Plymouth
Cambridge
Thames
Salisbury
St. Albans
Bury St. Edmunds
Barnet
Ipswich
Weymouth
Winchester
Guildford
LONDON
Southampton
Isle of Wight
Rochester
Lewes
Canterbury
Dover
Brest

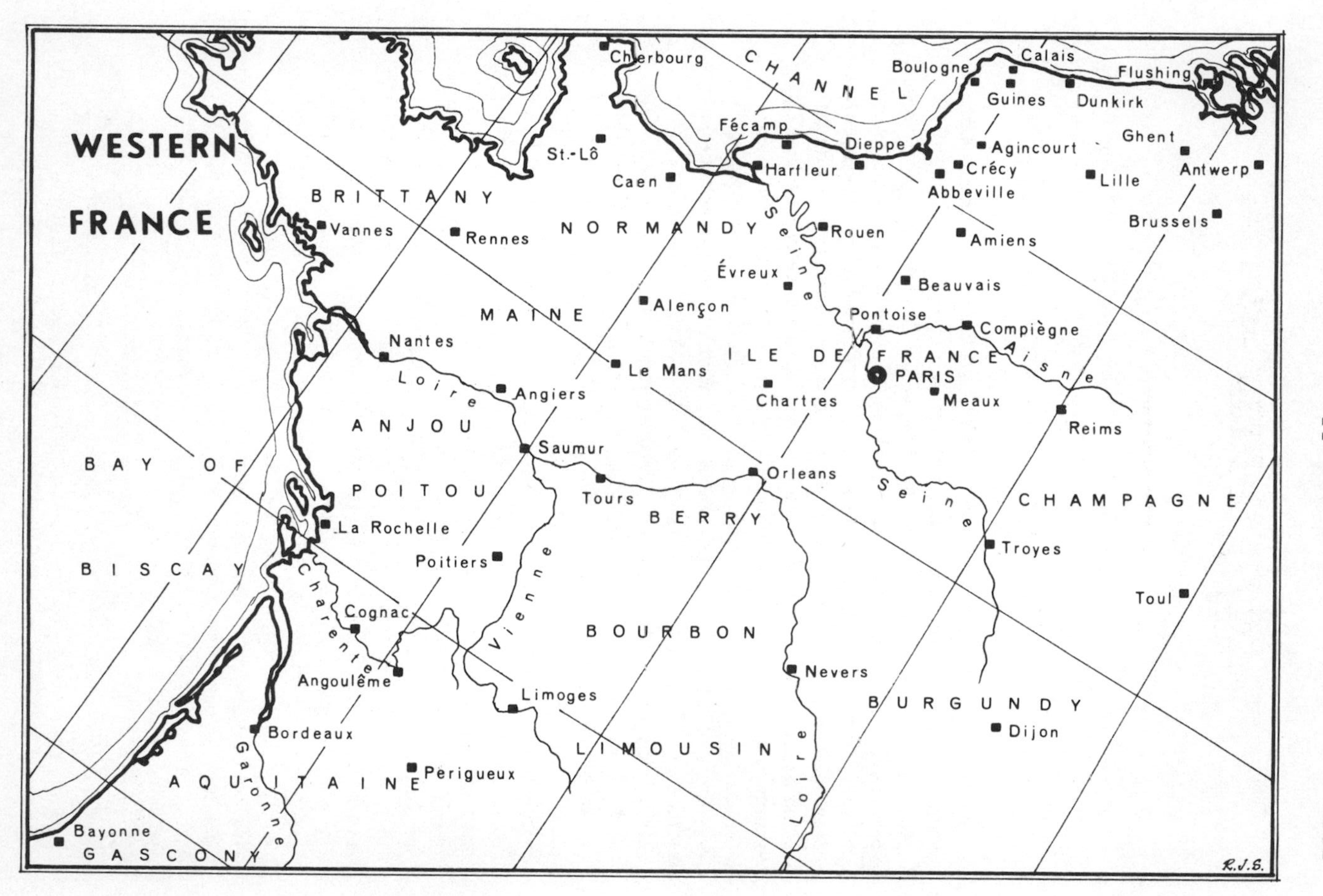
WESTERN
FRANCE
CHANNEL
BAY OF
BISCAY
BRITTANY
NORMANDY
MAINE
ILE DE FRANCE
CHAMPAGNE
ANJOU
POITOU
BERRY
BOURBON
BURGUNDY
LIMOUSIN
AQUITAINE
GASCONY
Cherbourg
Boulogne
Calais
Flushing
Guines
Dunkirk
Fécamp
Dieppe
Agincourt
Ghent
St.-Lô
Harfleur
Crécy
Lille
Antwerp
Caen
Abbeville
Brussels
Vannes
Rennes
Rouen
Amiens
Seine
Évreux
Beauvais
Alençon
Pontoise
Compiègne
Nantes
Le Mans
PARIS
Aisne
Loire
Angiers
Chartres
Meaux
Reims
Saumur
Orleans
Tours
La Rochelle
Troyes
Poitiers
Vienne
Toul
Cognac
Charente
Nevers
Angoulême
Limoges
Dijon
Bordeaux
Garonne
Perigueux
Bayonne
R.J.S.

Appendix 4

THE TEXT OF THIS EDITION

The copy-text for this edition is the 1587 edition of Holinshed's *Chronicles,* that edition which was used by Shakespeare. (Printer's copy was prepared from the exemplar in the Princeton University Library, and proofs have been read against the exemplar in the University of Arizona Library; no "substantive" press-variants were noted.) Archaic spellings have been modernized except where modernization would have obscured meaning, and the more familiar modern English forms of place-names have generally been preferred (for example, *Portugal* to *Portingale, Burgundy* to *Bourgogne, Brittany* to *Britaine, Sicily* to *Sicil, Kenilworth* to *Killingworth,* etc.). Punctuation has also been modernized, the only noteworthy peculiarity of style being that names and titles appearing together have normally been printed without appositional commas (for example, *John Duke of Bedford, Thomas Mowbray Duke of Norfolk, Thomas of Woodstock Duke of Gloucester,* etc.). Bracketed references have been supplied to the 1587 edition of Holinshed and to Shakespeare's plays; these references are explained in the Preface. Words whose precise meaning might not be clear to an undergraduate student of English literature have been glossed at the foot of the page, and an occasional historical explanation has been supplied. No attempt has been made, however, to correct Holinshed's errors of chronology, nomenclature, or fact, although attention has been called in the notes to some of the more confusing of such errors. Occasional dates, names, and brief interpolations for the sake of clarity have been supplied in square brackets. Errors in the copy-text presumably caused by scribe or compositor have been corrected, silently in the case of "accidental" errors, with listing in this appendix in the case of "substantive" errors. The following list of substantive emendations gives, first, the reading of the present edition together with a reference to the page and line-number in question; then, in parentheses, the reading of the copy-text together with the page-reference in question.

King Lear (Vol. 1, *History of England*): 1.1 Bladud (12 Baldud).

Macbeth (Vol. 2, *History of Scotland*): 11.18 entered (150 enter). 11.23 conveyed (150 conuay). 11.26 buried (150 burie). 18.35 Bothgowanan

[Boswell-Stone] (171 Botgosuane). 20.17 chanced (172 chanced yet). 20.18 yet the son (172 the sonne yet).

King John (Vol. 3, *History of England*): 32.33 castles (157 castell). 38.7 speeded (164 speedeth). 40.8 hearts (165 heart). 47.17 whilst that (177 that whilest). 49.20 into (184 unto). 51.36 Stonar (191 Stanchorre). 51.36 Thanet (191 Tenet). 56.11–17 [Holinshed's text of the *Persa* has been corrected by reference to the edition by Leo, 1958].

Richard II: 60.26 monuments (430 minuments). 63.34 Dukes (488 duke). 78.23 Bishop (498 bishops). 90.30 that sort (511 the fort). 93.21 Thomas (514 Iohn). 95.13 the son's (515 his sonnes).

1 Henry IV: 100.4 rebels (520 rebell). 101.26 bear (521 heare). 107.8 knight (523 knights).

2 Henry IV: 113.16 son's (530 sonne).

Henry V: 135.9 Lestrale (555 Lestrake). 141.11 *Praecarissimus* (574 *Praeclarissimus*).

1 Henry VI: 144.21 might (583 may). 144.26 it (583 that it). 149.29 Lords (595 lord). 154.24,25 Arc (600 Are). 154.27 Domremy (600 Domprin). 158.14 was (604 was she). 158.21 Anne (604 Annes). 166.15 Grafton (624 Gralton).

2 Henry VI: 173.24 especial (627 especiallie). 176.4 Pont Audemer (629 Ponteau de Mere). 176.4 Fécamp (629 Festampe). 176.4 Touques (629 Tonque). 180.2 Sevenoaks (634 Senocke). 183.4 Surrey (635 Southerie). 183.8 Iden (635 Eden). 187.36 Edmund (657 of Edmund). 188.1 Edward (657 Henrie).

3 Henry VI: 193.9 Mortimer (659 Mortimers). 217.12 espied (726 espieng).

Richard III: 224.8 special (714 speciallie). 225.36 a (715 a a). 226.4 fright (715 flight). 229.12 best (719 all best). 233.16 them, all (722 them all,). 235.19 so far yet (723 yet so farre). 241.25 would (730 will). 243.28 that (731 that, that). 243.33 and (731 that). 244.6 for (731 that for). 245.17 old (734 his old). 246.19 Tirrel (735 Tirrels). 248.27 Earl [Hall] (736 duke). 249.25 company (739 last companie). 252.17 unpurveyed (743 vnpurneid). 255.15 there (745 here). 256.28 Rennes (750 Reimes). 256.30 chevisance [Hall] (750 chieuance). 257.23 with (750 what with). 258.14 of (751 or). 258.30 were (751 were not). 264.20 brother's [Hall] (756 moothers). 264.23 parents (756 parts). 264.25 possible (756 possiblie).

Henry VIII: 279.15 was (863 is). 284.2 royalty (872 roiallie). 285.11 bells (alarm) [Hall "belles *Alarme*"] (891 bels alarme). 293.30 as that he (909 as he that). 301.23 even he (922 euen be). 307.3 widows (934 widow).

Appendix 5

BIBLIOGRAPHY

The bibliography is divided into four sections:

(a) Primary Sources (Chiefly Historical and Biographical). This includes such works as Hall's *Union of the Two Noble and Illustrious Families of Lancaster and York* and Cavendish's *Life and Death of Cardinal Wolsey.*

(b) Primary Sources (Chiefly Dramatic). This includes such works as Shakespeare's *Richard II* and Marlowe's *Edward II.* Play-titles have been normalized.

(c) Secondary Sources (Chiefly Historical and Biographical). This includes such works as E. F. Jacob's *The Fifteenth Century* and Paul Murray Kendall's *Richard the Third.*

(d) Secondary Sources (Chiefly Literary). This includes such works as E. M. W. Tillyard's *Shakespeare's History Plays.*

The following abbreviations have been used:

EETS: Early English Text Society.
ELH: English Literary History.
ES: English Studies.
HLQ: Huntington Library Quarterly.
JEGP: Journal of English and Germanic Philology.
JHI: Journal of the History of Ideas.
MLQ: Modern Language Quarterly.
MLR: Modern Language Review.
MSR: Malone Society Reprints.
N&Q: Notes and Queries.
PMLA: Publications of the Modern Language Association of America.
PQ: Philological Quarterly.
RES: Review of English Studies.
RN: Renaissance News.

SJ: Shakespeare Jahrbuch.
SP: Studies in Philology.
SQ: Shakespeare Quarterly.
TLS: Times Literary Supplement.

(a) Primary Sources (Chiefly Historical and Biographical)

BACON, SIR FRANCIS, *The History of the Reign of King Henry the Seventh,* 1629; ed. J. Spedding *et al., Works,* vol. 6, 1858.

BALDWIN, WILLIAM, *et al., A Mirror for Magistrates,* 1559; ed. L. B. Campbell, 1938.

The Brut, or The Chronicles of England, ed. F. W. D. Brie, 2 vols., EETS, 131, 136, 1906–8.

CAVENDISH, GEORGE, *The Life and Death of Cardinal Wolsey,* 1641; in *Two Early Tudor Lives,* ed. R. S. Sylvester and D. P. Harding, 1962.

Chronicles of London, ed. C. L. Kingsford, 1905.

Chronique de la Trahison et Mort de Richard Deux, Roi d'Angleterre, ed. B. Williams, English Historical Society Publications, 1846.

DANIEL, SAMUEL, *The Civil Wars Between the Two Houses of Lancaster and York,* 1595; ed. L. Michel, 1958.

An English Chronicle of the Reigns of Richard II, Henry IV, Henry V, and Henry VI Written Before the Year 1471, ed. J. S. Davies, Camden Society, 1856.

FABYAN, ROBERT, *The New Chronicles of England and France,* 1516, 1533; ed. H. Ellis, 1811.

FOXE, JOHN, *Acts and Monuments of These Latter and Perilous Days,* 1563, 1570; ed. J. Pratt and J. Stoughton, 8 vols., 1877.

FROISSART, JEAN, *The Chronicles,* tr. Lord Berners, 1523–5; ed. W. P. Ker, 6 vols., 1901–3.

GEOFFREY OF MONMOUTH, *Historia Regum Britanniae,* 1508; tr. J. A. Giles, 1842.

GRAFTON, RICHARD, *A Chronicle at Large and Mere History of the Affairs of England,* 1569; ed. H. Ellis, 2 vols., 1809.

HALL, EDWARD, *The Union of the Two Noble and Illustrious Families of Lancaster and York,* 1548; ed. H. Ellis, 1809, 1965.

HARDYNG, JOHN, *The Chronicle of John Hardyng . . . with the Continuation . . .* [*by Richard Grafton*], 1543; ed. H. Ellis, 1812.

HAYWARD, SIR JOHN, *The First Part of the Life and Reign of King Henry the IV,* 1599.

HIGDEN, RANULF, *Polychronicon,* tr. J. Trevisa, 1482; ed. C. Babington and J. R. Lumby, 9 vols., 1865–86.

HIGGINS, JOHN, and THOMAS BLENERHASSET, *Parts Added to the Mirror for Magistrates,* ed. L. B. Campbell, 1946.

Historical Poems of the XIVth and XVth Centuries, ed. R. H. Robbins, 1959.

History of the Arrival of Edward IV in England, ed. J. Bruce, Camden Society, 1838.

HOLINSHED, RAPHAEL, WILLIAM HARRISON, EDMUND CAMPION, and RICHARD STANYHURST, *The Chronicles of England, Scotland, and Ireland,* 2 vols., 1577. [Contains numerous woodcuts.]

HOLINSHED, RAPHAEL, JOHN HOOKER, FRANCIS THYNNE, ABRAHAM FLEMING, and JOHN STOW, *The Chronicles of England, Scotland, and Ireland,* 3 vols. in 2, 1587; ed. H. Ellis, 6 vols., 1807–8. [The 1587 edition, that which was used by Shakespeare, is greatly enlarged over that of 1577 (though it lacks the woodcuts); the reprint of 1807–8, while generally accurate, is not reliable for individual readings.]

HOLINSHED, RAPHAEL, *et al., Holinshed's Chronicle as Used in Shakespeare's Plays,* ed. A. and J. Nicoll, Everyman's Library, 1927. [Selections arranged in chronological order of Shakespeare's plays.]

———, *Holinshed's Chronicles: Richard II 1398–1400, Henry IV, and Henry V,* ed. R. S. Wallace and A. Hansen, 1923. [Complete selections, as indicated.]

———, *Shakspere's Holinshed: The Chronicle and the Historical Plays Compared,* ed. W. G. Boswell-Stone, 1896. [Selections, with corresponding Shakespearian texts, arranged in chronological order of Shakespeare's plays.]

INGULF, *Ingulphus's Chronicle of the Abbey of Croyland with the Continuations by Peter of Blois and Anonymous Writers,* tr. H. T. Riley, 1854.

JEWKES, W. T., and B. J. LANDFIELD, eds., *Joan of Arc: Fact, Legend, and Literature,* 1964. [A collection of various sources.]

LANDER, J. R., *The Wars of the Roses,* 1966. [A collection of various sources.]

LITTLETON, T., and R. R. REA, eds., *To Prove a Villain: The Case of King Richard III,* 1964. [A collection of various sources.]

MANCINI, DOMINIC, *The Usurpation of Richard III,* ed. C. A. J. Armstrong, 1936.

MONSTRELET, ENGUERRAND DE, *The Chronicles,* tr. T. Johnes, 5 vols., 1809.

MORE, SIR THOMAS, *The History of King Richard III,* 1557; ed. J. R. Lumby, 1883; R. S. Sylvester, *Works,* vol. 2 (1963).

The Paston Letters A.D. 1422–1509, ed. J. Gairdner, 6 vols., 1904.

ROPER, WILLIAM, *The Life of Sir Thomas More,* 1628; in *Two Early Tudor Lives,* ed. R. S. Sylvester and D. P. Harding, 1962.

The St. Albans Chronicle 1406–1420, ed. V. H. Galbraith, 1937.

SPEED, JOHN, *The History of Great Britain,* 1611.

STOW, JOHN, *The Chronicles of England,* 1580. [Entitled *The Annals of England* in the edition of 1592.]

———, *A Summary of English Chronicles,* 1565.
———, *A Survey of London,* 1598; ed. C. L. Kingsford, 1908.
Three Fifteenth-Century Chronicles with Historical Memoranda by John Stow, ed. J. Gairdner, Camden Society, 1880.
THE "TRANSLATOR OF LIVIUS," *The First English Life of King Henry the Fifth,* 1513; ed. C. L. Kingsford, 1911.
VERGIL, POLYDORE, *An Abridgement of the Notable Work of Polydore Vergil,* tr. T. Langley, 1546.
———, *Anglica Historia,* 1534; *Three Books of Polydore Vergil's English History, Comprising the Reigns of Henry VI, Edward IV, and Richard III,* ed. H. Ellis, Camden Society, 1844.
———, *The Anglica Historia of Polydore Vergil A.D. 1485–1537,* ed. and tr. D. Hay, Camden Society, 1950.
WALSINGHAM, THOMAS, *Historia Anglicana,* ed. H. T. Riley, 2 vols., Rolls Series, 1862–4.
WHETHAMSTEDE, JOHN, *Registrum Abbatiae Johannis Whethamstede,* ed. H. T. Riley, 2 vols., Rolls Series, 1872–3.

(b) Primary Sources (Chiefly Dramatic)

ADAMS, J. Q., ed., *Chief Pre-Shakespearean Dramas,* 1924. [Includes *Gorboduc, Cambyses, The Famous Victories of Henry V.*]
An Alarum for London, ed. W. W. Greg, MSR, 1913.
ARMSTRONG, WILLIAM A., ed., *Elizabethan History Plays,* Oxford World's Classics, 1965. [Includes Bale's *King John, Edward III, Woodstock, Perkin Warbeck, King John and Matilda.*]
BALE, JOHN, *King John,* ed. J. H. P. Pafford, MSR, 1931; Armstrong, 1965 (*q.v.*).
BARNES, BARNABE, *The Devil's Charter,* ed. R. B. McKerrow, *Materialien zur Kunde des älteren Englischen Dramas,* 1904.
BROOKE, C. F. TUCKER, ed., *The Shakespeare Apocrypha,* 1908. [Includes *Locrine, Edward III, Sir John Oldcastle, Sir Thomas More, Thomas Lord Cromwell.*]
BULLOUGH, GEOFFREY, ed., *Narrative and Dramatic Sources of Shakespeare,* 7 vols., 1957–. [Vol. 3 treats *R2, 1H6, 2H6, 3H6, R3;* vol. 4, *KJ, 1H4, 2H4, H5, H8;* vol. 7 will treat *KL, C, M.*]
CHAPMAN, GEORGE, *Caesar and Pompey,* in *Tragedies,* ed. T. M. Parrott, 1910.
———, *1* and *2 Charles Duke of Byron,* in *Tragedies,* ed. T. M. Parrott, 1910.
The Contention Betwixt the Two Famous Houses of York and Lancaster. [See Shakespeare's *2 Henry VI.*]
CUNLIFFE, JOHN W., ed., *Early English Classical Tragedies,* 1912. [Includes *Gorboduc, The Misfortunes of Arthur.*]
DAVENPORT, ROBERT, *King John and Matilda,* ed. Armstrong 1965 (*q.v.*).

DEKKER, THOMAS, and JOHN WEBSTER, *Sir Thomas Wyatt,* in *Works,* ed. F. Bowers, 1953.

DRAYTON, MICHAEL, *et al., Sir John Oldcastle,* ed. P. Simpson, MSR, 1908; Brooke, 1908 (*q.v.*).

DRUE, THOMAS, *The Duchess of Suffolk,* 1631.

Edward III, ed. Brooke, 1908 (*q.v.*); Armstrong, 1965 (*q.v.*); Everitt, 1965 (*q.v.*).

EVERITT, E. B., ed., *Six Early Plays Related to the Shakespeare Canon,* 1965. [Includes *King Leir, The Troublesome Reign of King John, Edward III, Woodstock.*]

The Famous Victories of Henry V, ed. Adams, 1924 (*q.v.*).

FLETCHER, JOHN, and PHILIP MASSINGER, *Sir John van Olden Barnavelt,* ed. W. P. Frijlinck, 1922.

FORD, JOHN, *Perkin Warbeck,* ed. D. K. Anderson, 1965; Armstrong, 1965 (*q.v.*).

HAZLITT, W. C., ed., *Shakespeare's Library,* 2d ed., 6 vols., 1875. [A collection of sources.]

HEYWOOD, THOMAS, *1* and *2 Edward IV,* ed. S. De Ricci, 1922.

———, *1* and *2 If You Know Not Me You Know Nobody,* ed. M. Doran, MSR, 1934.

HUGHES, THOMAS, *The Misfortunes of Arthur,* ed. Cunliffe, 1912 (*q.v.*).

JACK STRAW, ed. K. Muir and F. P. Wilson, MSR, 1957.

JONSON, BEN, *Catiline,* in *Ben Jonson,* ed. C. H. Herford *et al.,* vol. 5, 1937.

———, *Sejanus,* ed. J. A. Barish, Yale Ben Jonson, 1965.

KING LEIR, ed. W. W. Greg, MSR, 1908; Everitt, 1965 (*q.v.*).

LEGGE, THOMAS, *Richardus Tertius,* ed. B. Field, Shakespeare Society, 1844.

Locrine, ed. R. B. McKerrow, MSR, 1908; Brooke, 1908 (*q.v.*).

LODGE, THOMAS, *The Wounds of Civil War,* ed. J. D. Wilson, MSR, 1910.

MARLOWE, CHRISTOPHER, *Edward II,* ed. W. D. Briggs, 1914.

———, *The Massacre at Paris,* ed. H. S. Bennett, 1931.

———, *1* and *2 Tamburlaine,* ed. U. Ellis-Fermor, 1930.

MAY, THOMAS, *Cleopatra Queen of Egypt,* 1626.

MUNDAY, ANTHONY, *et al., Sir Thomas More,* ed. Brooke, 1908 (*q.v.*); W. W. Greg, MSR, 1911.

NORTON, THOMAS, and THOMAS SACKVILLE, *Gorboduc,* ed. Cunliffe, 1912 (*q.v.*); Adams, 1924 (*q.v.*).

PEELE, GEORGE, *The Battle of Alcazar,* ed. J. Yoklavich, in *Works,* gen. ed. C. T. Prouty, vol. 2, 1961.

———, *Edward I,* ed. F. S. Hook, in *Works,* gen. ed. C. T. Prouty, vol. 2, 1961.

PRESTON, THOMAS, *Cambyses,* ed. Adams, 1924 (*q.v.*).

ROWLEY, SAMUEL, *When You See Me You Know Me,* ed. F. P. Wilson, MSR, 1952.

SHAKESPEARE, WILLIAM, *Antony and Cleopatra,* ed. M. R. Ridley, Arden Shakespeare, 1954.

———, *Coriolanus,* ed. J. D. Wilson, New Cambridge Shakespeare, 1960.

———, *Cymbeline,* ed. J. M. Nosworthy, Arden Shakespeare, 1955.

———, *1 Henry IV,* ed. A. R. Humphreys, Arden Shakespeare, 1960.

———, *2 Henry IV,* ed. A. R. Humphreys, Arden Shakespeare, 1966.

———, *Henry V,* ed. J. H. Walter, Arden Shakespeare, 1954.

———, *1 Henry VI,* ed. A. S. Cairncross, Arden Shakespeare, 1962.

———, *2 Henry VI,* ed. A. S. Cairncross, Arden Shakespeare, 1957. [*The Contention Betwixt the Two Famous Houses of York and Lancaster,* pr. 1594, is a memorial reconstruction of *2H6.*]

———, *3 Henry VI,* ed. A. S. Cairncross, Arden Shakespeare, 1964. [*The True Tragedy of Richard Duke of York,* pr. 1595, is a memorial reconstruction of *3H6.*]

———, *Henry VIII,* ed. R. A. Foakes, Arden Shakespeare, 1957.

———, *Julius Caesar,* ed. T. S. Dorsch, Arden Shakespeare, 1955.

———, *King John,* ed. E. A. J. Honigmann, Arden Shakespeare, 1954.

———, *King Lear,* ed. K. Muir, Arden Shakespeare, 1952.

———, *Macbeth,* ed. K. Muir, Arden Shakespeare, 1951.

———, *Richard II,* ed. P. Ure, Arden Shakespeare, 1956.

———, *Richard III,* ed. J. D. Wilson, New Cambridge Shakespeare, 1954.

SPENCER, CHRISTOPHER, ed., *Five Restoration Adaptations of Shakespeare,* 1965. [Includes Davenant's *Macbeth,* Tate's *King Lear,* Cibber's *Richard III.*]

Thomas Lord Cromwell, ed. Brooke, 1908 (*q.v.*).

The Troublesome Reign of King John, Praetorius Facsimiles, 1888; ed. Everitt, 1965 (*q.v.*).

The True Tragedy of Richard Duke of York. [See Shakespeare's *3 Henry VI.*]

The True Tragedy of Richard III, ed. W. W. Greg, MSR, 1929.

Woodstock, ed. A. P. Rossiter, 1946; Armstrong, 1965 (*q.v.*); Everitt, 1965 (*q.v.*).

(c) Secondary Sources (Chiefly Historical and Biographical)

ANGLO, SYDNEY, "The *British History* in Early Tudor Propaganda," *Bulletin of the John Rylands Library,* 44 (1961), pp. 17–48.

ASTON, MARGARET, *Thomas Arundel: A Study of Church Life in the Reign of Richard II,* 1967.

BAGLEY, J. J., *Margaret of Anjou Queen of England,* 1948.

BENBOW, R. MARK, "The Providential Theory of Historical Causation in Holinshed's *Chronicles:* 1577 and 1587," *Texas Studies in Literature and Language,* 1 (1959–60), pp. 264–76.

BINDOFF, S. T., *Tudor England,* Pelican History of England, 1950.

BLACK, J. B., *The Reign of Elizabeth 1558–1603,* Oxford History of England, 1936; 2d ed., 1959.

BOWLE, JOHN, *Henry VIII: A Biography,* 1964.

BROWNFIELD, CLARENCE, "Holinshed and His Editors," *TLS,* August 7, 1937, p. 576.

———, "The Holinshed Family," *TLS,* September 19, 1936, p. 748.

BURNE, A. H., *The Agincourt War: A Military History of the Latter Part of the Hundred Years War from 1369 to 1453,* 1956.

———, *The Battlefields of England,* 1950.

———, *The Crécy War: A Military History of the Hundred Years War from 1337 to the Peace of Bretigny 1360,* 1955.

CHAMBERS, R. W., *Thomas More,* 1935.

CHRIMES, S. B., *Lancastrians, Yorkists, and Henry VII,* 1964.

CHRISTIE, MABEL E., *Henry VI,* 1922.

DAVIES, GODFREY, *The Early Stuarts 1603–1660,* Oxford History of England, 1937.

DEAN, LEONARD F., "Tudor Theories of History Writing," *University of Michigan Contributions in Modern Philology,* 1 (1941), pp. 1–24.

DICK, HUGH G., "Thomas Blundeville's *The true order and Methode of wryting and reading Hystories* (1574)," *HLQ,* 3 (1939–40), pp. 149–70.

DICKENS, A. G., *The English Reformation,* 1964.

DODSON, SARAH C., "Abraham Fleming, Writer and Editor," *University of Texas Studies in English,* 34 (1955), pp. 51–66.

ELTON, G. R., *England Under the Tudors,* 1962.

FELLHEIMER, JEANNETTE, "Geoffrey Fenton's *Historie of Guicciardin* and Holinshed's *Chronicles* of 1587," *MLQ,* 6 (1945), pp. 285–98.

FERGUSON, ARTHUR B., *The Indian Summer of English Chivalry,* 1960.

GAIRDNER, JAMES, *Henry the Seventh,* 1889.

———, *History of the Life and Reign of Richard the Third to Which is Added the Story of Perkin Warbeck,* rev. ed., 1898.

HALLER, WILLIAM, *Foxe's Book of Martyrs and the Elect Nation,* 1963.

HAY, DENYS, *Polydore Vergil: Renaissance Historian and Man of Letters,* 1952.

HOLMES, MARTIN, "Some Woodcuts in Holinshed's *Chronicle* [1577]," *Journal of the British Archaeological Association,* 15 (1952), pp. 30–4.

HUTCHINSON, F. E., *Cranmer and the English Reformation,* 1951.

HUTCHISON, HAROLD F., *The Hollow Crown: A Life of Richard II,* 1961.

JACOB, E. F., *The Fifteenth Century 1399–1485*, Oxford History of England, 1961.

———, *Henry V and the Invasion of France*, 1947.

JOHNSTONE, HILDA, *Edward of Carnarvon 1284–1307*, 1946. [Edward II.]

KANTOROWICZ, ERNST, *The King's Two Bodies: A Study in Mediaeval Political Theology*, 1957.

KELLY, AMY RUTH, *Eleanor of Aquitaine and the Four Kings*, 1950.

KENDALL, PAUL MURRAY, *Richard the Third*, 1956.

———, *Warwick the Kingmaker*, 1957.

———, *The Yorkist Age: Daily Life During the Wars of the Roses*, 1962.

KINGSFORD, CHARLES LETHBRIDGE, *English Historical Literature in the Fifteenth Century*, 1913.

———, *Henry V: The Typical Mediaeval Hero*, 1901.

LEVINE, MORTIMER, "Richard III: Usurper or Lawful King?" *Speculum*, 34 (1959), pp. 391–401.

LEVY, F. J., *Tudor Historical Thought*, 1967.

MAC GIBBON, DAVID, *Elisabeth Woodville*, 1938.

MACKIE, J. D., *The Earlier Tudors 1485–1558*, Oxford History of England, 1952.

MC KISACK, M., *The Fourteenth Century 1307–1399*, Oxford History of England, 1959.

MATTINGLY, GARRETT, *The Armada*, 1959.

———, *Catherine of Aragon*, 1941.

MILLER, WILLIAM E., "Abraham Fleming: Editor of Shakespeare's Holinshed," *Texas Studies in Literature and Language*, 1 (1959–60), pp. 89–100.

MYERS, A. R., "The Character of Richard III," *History Today*, 4 (1954), pp. 511–21.

———, *England in the Late Middle Ages 1307–1536*, Pelican History of England, 1956.

NEALE, J. E., *Queen Elizabeth*, 1934.

NORGATE, KATE, *John Lackland*, 1902.

———, *Richard the Lion Heart*, 1924.

PAINTER, SIDNEY, *The Reign of King John*, 1949.

PALLISER, MRS. BURY, *Historic Devices, Badges, and War-Cries*, 1870.

PERROY, ÉDOUARD, *The Hundred Years War*, 1951.

POLLARD, A. F., *Henry VIII*, 1902.

———, "The Making of Sir Thomas More's *Richard III*," in *Historical Essays in Honour of James Tait*, ed. J. G. Edward 1933, pp. 223–38.

———, *Wolsey*, 1929.

POOLE, AUSTIN LANE, *From Domesday Book to Magna Carta 1087–1216*, Oxford History of England, 1951.

POWICKE, F. M., *King Henry III and the Lord Edward*, 2 vols., 1947.

———, *The Thirteenth Century 1216–1307,* Oxford History of England, 1953.

PRESCOTT, H. F. M., *Mary Tudor,* 1940; rev. ed., 1952.

ROSKELL, J. S., "William Catesby, Counsellor to Richard III," *Bulletin of the John Rylands Library,* 42 (1959), pp. 145–74.

ROWSE, A. L., *Bosworth Field: From Medieval to Tudor England,* 1966.

———, *The England of Elizabeth,* 1951.

———, *The Expansion of Elizabethan England,* 1955.

SCOFIELD, CORA L., *The Life and Reign of Edward the Fourth,* 2 vols., 1923.

SOMERVILLE, ROBERT, *History of the Duchy of Lancaster,* 1953.

THORNLEY, ISABEL D., "The Destruction of Sanctuary," in *Tudor Studies Presented to A. F. Pollard,* 1924, pp. 182–207.

TRIMBLE, WILLIAM RALEIGH, "Early Tudor Historiography: 1485–1548," *JHI,* 11 (1950), pp. 30–41.

VICKERS, K. H., *Humphrey Duke of Gloucester,* 1907.

WARREN, W. L., *King John,* 1961.

WHEELER, THOMAS, "The New Style of the Tudor Chroniclers," *Tennessee Studies in Literature,* 7 (1962), pp. 71–7.

WILLIAMS, C. H., "England: The Yorkist Kings, 1461–1485," in *The Cambridge Medieval History,* 8 (1936), pp. 418–49.

WILLIAMS, E. CARLETON, *My Lord of Bedford 1389–1435: Being a Life of John of Lancaster,* 1963.

WOODHOUSE, R. I., *The Life of John Morton,* 1895.

WRIGHT, LOUIS B., *Middle-Class Culture in Elizabethan England,* 1935.

(d) Secondary Sources (Chiefly Literary)

ADKINS, MARY G. M., "A Theory About *The Life and Death of Jack Straw," University of Texas Studies in English,* 28 (1949), pp. 57–82.

———, "Sixteenth-Century Religious and Political Implications in *Sir John Oldcastle," University of Texas Studies in English,* 22 (1942), pp. 86–104.

ALEXANDER, PETER, "Conjectural History, or Shakespeare's *Henry VIII," Essays and Studies,* 16 (1931), pp. 85–120.

ANDERSON, DONALD K., *"Richard II* and *Perkin Warbeck," SQ,* 13 (1962), pp. 260–3.

ARMSTRONG, WILLIAM A., "The Authorship and Political Meaning of *Cambises," ES,* 36 (1955), pp. 289–99.

———, "The Topicality of *The Misfortunes of Arthur," N&Q,* 200 (1955), pp. 371–3.

BATTENHOUSE, ROY W., *"Henry V* as Heroic Comedy," in *Essays on Shakespeare and Elizabethan Drama in Honor of Hardin Craig,* ed. R. Hosley, 1962, pp. 163–82.

BEGG, EDLEEN, "Shakespeare's Debt to Hall and to Holinshed in *Richard III*," *SP*, 32 (1935), pp. 189–96.

BENTLEY, GERALD EADES, *The Jacobean and Caroline Stage*, 7 vols., 1939–68.

BLACK, MATTHEW W., "The Sources of Shakespeare's *Richard II*," in *J. Q. Adams Memorial Studies*, ed. J. G. McManaway *et al.*, 1948, pp. 199–216.

BONJOUR, ADRIEN, "The Road to Swinstead Abbey," *ELH*, 18 (1951), pp. 253–74.

BOWLING, W. G., "The Wild Prince Hal in Legend and Literature," *Washington University Studies*, 13 (1926), pp. 305–34.

BRADDY, HALDEEN, "Shakespeare's *Henry V* and the French Nobility," *Texas Studies in Literature and Language*, 3 (1961–2), pp. 189–96.

BRERETON, J. LE GAY, "The Sources of Ford's *Perkin Warbeck*," *Anglia*, 34 (1911), pp. 194–234.

BROCKBANK, J. P., "The Frame of Disorder: *Henry VI*," in *Early Shakespeare*, ed. J. R. Brown and B. Harris, 1961, pp. 72–99.

CAMPBELL, LILY B., *Shakespeare's "Histories": Mirrors of Elizabethan Policy*, 1947.

CHAMBERS, E. K., *The Elizabethan Stage*, 4 vols., 1923.

———, *William Shakespeare: A Study of Facts and Problems*, 2 vols., 1930.

CHAPMAN, RAYMOND, "The Wheel of Fortune in Shakespeare's Historical Plays," *RES*, 1 (1950), pp. 1–7.

CHURCHILL, GEORGE B., *Richard the Third up to Shakespeare*, 1900.

CRAIG, HARDIN, "Shakespeare and the History Play," in *J. Q. Adams Memorial Studies*, ed. J. G. McManaway *et al.*, 1948, pp. 55–64.

DE LUNA, B. N., *Jonson's Romish Plot*, 1967. [*Catiline*.]

DODSON, SARAH, "The Northumberland of Shakespeare and Holinshed," *University of Texas Studies in English*, 19 (1939), pp. 74–85.

DORIUS, R. J., "A Little More Than a Little," *SQ*, 11 (1960), pp. 13–26.

———, ed., *Discussions of Shakespeare's Histories: Richard II to Henry V*, 1964.

EDWARDS, PHILIP, "Shakespeare's Romances: 1900–1957," *Shakespeare Survey*, 11 (1958), pp. 1–18.

ELLIOTT, JOHN R., "Shakespeare and the Double Image of King John," *Shakespeare Studies*, 1 (1965), pp. 64–84.

ELSON, JOHN JAMES, "The Non-Shakespearian *Richard II* [*Woodstock*] and Shakespeare's *Henry IV, Part 1*," *SP*, 32 (1935), pp. 177–88.

———, "Studies in the King John Plays," in *J. Q. Adams Memorial Studies*, ed. J. G. McManaway *et al.*, 1948, pp. 183–97.

EVANS, G. BLAKEMORE, "The 'Dering MS.' of Shakespeare's *Henry IV* and Sir Edward Dering," *JEGP*, 54 (1955), pp. 498–503.

FISH, CHARLES, "Henry IV: Shakespeare and Holinshed," *SP*, 61 (1964), pp. 205–18.

GREG, W. W., *The Shakespeare First Folio,* 1955.

HEFFNER, RAY, "Shakespeare, Hayward, and Essex," *PMLA*, 45 (1930), pp. 754–80. [John Hayward's *Henry IV,* 1600.]

HOBDAY, C. H., "Why the Sweets Melted: A Study in Shakespeare's Imagery," *SQ,* 16 (1965), pp. 3–17. [*Edward III.*]

HOLZKNECHT, KARL J., "Shakespeare's History Plays," in *The Backgrounds of Shakespeare's Plays,* 1950, pp. 293–321.

HUMPHREYS, ARTHUR R., "Shakespeare and the Tudor Perception of History," in *Shakespeare Celebrated,* ed. L. B. Wright, 1966, pp. 89–112.

HUNTER, G. K., "*Henry IV* and the Elizabethan Two-part Play," *RES,* 5 (1954), pp. 236–48.

———, "*Macbeth* in the Twentieth Century," *Shakespeare Survey,* 19 (1966), pp. 1–11.

JACKSON, SIR BARRY, "On Producing *Henry VI,*" *Shakespeare Survey,* 6 (1953), pp. 49–52.

JENKINS, HAROLD, "Shakespeare's History Plays: 1900–1951," *Shakespeare Survey,* 6 (1953), pp. 1–15.

———, *The Structural Problem in Shakespeare's Henry the Fourth,* 1956.

JONES, WILLIAM M., "The Turning of Trent in *1 Henry IV,*" *RN,* 17 (1964), pp. 304–7.

KING, LUCILLE, "The Use of Hall's *Chronicles* in the Folio and Quarto Texts of *Henry VI,*" *PQ,* 13 (1934), pp. 321–32.

KINGSFORD, CHARLES LETHBRIDGE, "Fifteenth-century History in Shakespeare's Plays," in *Prejudice and Promise in Fifteenth-century England,* 1925, pp. 1–21.

KIRSCHBAUM, LEO, "The Authorship of *1 Henry VI,*" *PMLA,* 67 (1952), pp. 809–22.

LARSEN, THORLEIF, "The Historical and Legendary Background of Peele's *Battle of Alcazar,*" *Transactions of the Royal Society of Canada,* ser. 3, 33 (1939), pp. 185–97.

LAW, ROBERT ADGER, "The Chronicles and the Three Parts of *Henry VI,*" *University of Texas Studies in English,* 33 (1954), pp. 13–32.

———, "The Composition of *Macbeth* with Reference to Holinshed," *University of Texas Studies in English,* 31 (1952), pp. 35–41.

———, "Deviations from Holinshed in *Richard II,*" *University of Texas Studies in English,* 29 (1950), pp. 91-101.

———, "Holinshed's Leir Story and Shakespeare's," *SP,* 47 (1950), pp. 42–50.

———, "*King Leir* and *King Lear:* An Examination of the Two Plays," in *Studies in Honor of T. W. Baldwin,* ed. D. C. Allen, 1958, pp. 112–24.

———, "Links Between Shakespeare's History Plays," *SP,* 50 (1953), pp. 168–87.

———, "*Richard the Third:* A Study in Shakespeare's Composition," *PMLA,* 60 (1945), pp. 689–96.

LORDI, ROBERT J., "The Relationship of *Richardus Tertius* to the Main Richard III Plays," *Boston University Studies in English,* 5 (1961), pp. 139–53.

MARTIN, MARY FORSTER, "Stow's *Annals* and *The Famous Historie of Sir Thomas Wyat,*" *MLR,* 53 (1958), pp. 75-7.

MATCHETT, WILLIAM H., "The Sources of *The Life and Death of King John,*" in *King John,* Signet Classic Shakespeare, 1966, pp. 153–63.

MICHEL, LAURENCE, and CECIL C. SERONSY, "Shakespeare's History Plays and Daniel: An Assessment," *SP,* 52 (1955), pp. 549–77.

MOORMAN, F. W., "Shakespeare's History Plays and Daniel's *Civil Wars,*" *SJ,* 40 (1904), pp. 69–83.

MUIR, KENNETH, "A Reconsideration of *Edward III,*" *Shakespeare Survey,* 6 (1953), pp. 39–48.

———, *Shakespeare's Sources: I, Comedies and Tragedies,* 1957.

OLIVER, LESLIE M., "Thomas Drue's *Duchess of Suffolk:* A Protestant Drama," *Studies in Bibliography,* 3 (1950–1), pp. 241–6.

PALMER, JOHN, *Political Characters of Shakespeare,* 1945.

PAUL, H. N., *The Royal Play of Macbeth,* 1950.

PERRETT, WILFRID, *The Story of King Lear from Geoffrey of Monmouth to Shakespeare,* 1904.

PHIALAS, PETER G., "Shakespeare's Henry V and the Second Tetralogy," *SP,* 62 (1965), pp. 155–75.

PRATT, SAMUEL M., "Shakespeare and Humphrey Duke of Gloucester: A Study in Myth," *SQ,* 16 (1965), pp. 201–16.

QUINN, MICHAEL, "Providence in Shakespeare's Yorkist Plays," *SQ,* 10 (1959), pp. 45–52.

REESE, GERTRUDE, "Political Import of *The Misfortunes of Arthur,*" *RES,* 21 (1945), pp. 81–9.

REESE, M. M., *The Cease of Majesty: A Study of Shakespeare's History Plays,* 1961.

RIBNER, IRVING, *The English History Play in the Age of Shakespeare,* 1957; rev. ed., 1965.

———, "Morality Roots of the Tudor History Play," *Tulane Studies in English,* 4 (1954), pp. 21–43.

———, "The Political Problem in Shakespeare's Lancastrian Tetralogy," *SP,* 49 (1952), pp. 171–84.

———, "Shakespeare and Legendary History: *Lear* and *Cymbeline,*" *SQ,* 7 (1956), pp. 47–52.

———, "The Tudor History Play: An Essay in Definition," *PMLA,* 69 (1954), pp. 591–609.

RICHMOND, H. M., *Shakespeare's Political Plays,* 1967.

ROSSITER, A. P., "Ambivalence: The Dialectic of the Histories," in *Angel with Horns,* 1961, pp. 40–64.

SCHELLING, FELIX E., *The English Chronicle Play,* 1902.

SEN GUPTA, S. C., *Shakespeare's Historical Plays,* 1964.

SHAABER, M. A., "The Unity of *Henry IV,*" in *J. Q. Adams Memorial Studies,* ed. J. G. McManaway *et al.,* 1948, pp. 217–27.

SIMPSON, RICHARD, "The Politics of Shakspere's Historical Plays," *New Shakespeare Society's Transactions,* 1 (1874), pp. 396–441.

SMALL, S. A., "The Political Import of the Norton Half of *Gorboduc,*" *PMLA,* 46 (1931), pp. 641–6.

SMITH, ROBERT METCALF, *Froissart and the English Chronicle Play,* 1915.

STRIBRNY, ZDENEK, *Shakespearovy Historické Hry,* 1959. ["Shakespeare's History Plays (A Summary)," pp. 249–69.]

TILLYARD, E. M. W., *The Elizabethan World Picture,* 1944.

———, "Shakespeare's Historical Cycle: Organism or Compilation?" *SP,* 51 (1954), pp. 34–9.

———, *Shakespeare's History Plays,* 1946.

TRAVERSI, DEREK, *Shakespeare: From Richard II to Henry V,* 1957.

URE, PETER, "Shakespeare's Play and the French Sources of Holinshed's and Stow's Account of Richard II," *N&Q,* 198 (1953), pp. 426–9.

WAITH, EUGENE M., ed., *Shakespeare The Histories: A Collection of Critical Essays,* 1965.

WALLERSTEIN, RUTH, *King John in Fact and Fiction,* 1917.

WEDGWOOD, C. V., "Shakespeare Between Two Civil Wars," in *Shakespeare Celebrated,* ed. L. B. Wright, 1966, pp. 1–30.

WILSON, F. P., *Marlowe and the Early Shakespeare,* 1953.

WILSON, J. DOVER, *The Fortunes of Falstaff,* 1944.

———, "Shakespeare's *Richard III* and *The True Tragedy of Richard the Third,* 1594," *SQ,* 3 (1952), pp. 299–306.

ZEEFELD, W. GORDON, "The Influence of Hall on Shakespeare's English Historical Plays," *ELH,* 3 (1936), pp. 317-53.